CADOGANguides

take the kids
London
JOSEPH FULLMAN

Cadogan Guides is an imprint of New Holland Publishers (UK) Ltd
London • Cape Town • Sydney • Auckland

New Holland Publishers (UK) Ltd
Garfield House
86–88 Edgware Road
London W2 2EA

80 McKenzie Street
Cape Town 8001
South Africa

Unit 1, 66 Gibbes Street
Chatswood, NSW 2067
Australia

218 Lake Road
Northcote
Auckland
New Zealand

cadogan@nhpub.co.uk
www.cadoganguides.com
t 44 (0)20 7724 7773
Distributed in the United States by Globe Pequot, Connecticut

Copyright © Joseph Fullman 2000, 2002, 2004, 2006, 2008
© 2008 New Holland Publishers (UK) Ltd
Maps © Cadogan Guides, drawn by Kingston Presentation Graphics
Original Photography: Travel Pictures, www.travelpictures.co.uk
Cover Photos: © LUKE MACGREGOR/Reuters/Corbis; © Rune Hellestad/Corbis; © Walter Bibikow/Corbis; © Bill Varie/Corbis; © Tim Graham/Corbis; © Sandro Vannini/Corbis
Additional Picture Credits: p.34 © Arcaid/Corbis; p.131 © Museum of London; p.40, p.44, p.58, p.63, p.71, p.76, p.109, p.133 © Kicca Tommasi; p.42–3 © Zoological Society of London; p.46 © Alex Robinson; p.47 © The Wallace Collection, London; p.48, p.52, p.53, p.65, p.72, p.76, p.83, p.88, p.100, p.107, p.136, p.138, p.139, p.141 © Visit London; p.51, p.59 © Nicholas Kane 2000; p.52 © The British Museum; p.54 © Nigel Young; pp.56, p.57, p.75, p.60 © The British Museum Shop; p.64 © Linda McQueen; p.65 © London Tourist Board, © National Portrait Gallery; p.66 © Stephen Finn/Fotolia; p.68 © National Gallery; p.73 © Rainforest Café; p.78 © London Transport Museum; p.79 © Jacqueline Chnéour; p.83 © Peter Durant/arcblue.com; p.88 © Dariusz Urbanczyk/Fotolia; p.96 © Stephen Finn/Fotolia; p.100, p.111, p.113 © Imperial War Museum; p.102 © margie/Fotolia; p.103, p.107 © Dalí Universe; p.106 © Evgeniya Sharp/Fotolia; p.107 © London IMAX; p.108 © Richard Bryant/Arcaid/Corbis; p.111 © Construction Photography/Corbis; p.114, p.116 © London Dungeon; p.114, p.122 © Hay's Galleria, © Shakespeare's Globe Theatre; p.128 © Stu/Fotolia; p.132 © Barbican Centre/J.P. Stankowski; pp.135–6, p.139 © Science Museum; p.138 © The Natural History Museum; p.141 © Victoria & Albert Museum; p.142 © HRP 2001; p.143 © Royal Albert Hall.

Art direction: Sarah Gardner
Editor: Nicola Jessop
Proofreading: Elspeth Anderson
Indexing: Isobel McLean
Printed and bound in Italy by Legoprint
A catalogue record for this book is available from the British Library
ISBN 978-1-86011-398-7

About the series

take the kids guides are written specifically for parents, grandparents and carers. Each guide not only draws on what is of particular interest to kids, but also takes into account the realities of child-care – from tired legs to low boredom thresholds – enabling both grown-ups and their charges to have a great day out or a fabulous holiday.

About the authors

Joseph Fullman

Joseph Fullman is a professional travel writer who has lived in London all his life and cherishes happy childhood memories of traipsing around the country with his determinedly enthusiastic mum and dad. He is the author of Cadogan's *Take the Kids England* and *Costa Rica* and co-author of *Belize* and *Take the kids* Paris & Disneyland® Resort Paris. He has also contributed to the Rough Guides to Central America, Costa Rica, Italy and Turkey.

Series consultant

Helen Truszkowski is series consultant of Cadogan's *take the kids* series, author of *take the kids* Travelling and author of *take the kids* Paris & Disneyland® Resort Paris. Helen is an established travel writer and photographer. Over the past decade her journeys have taken her around the globe, including six months working in South Africa. She contributes to a range of magazines worldwide, and is a former travel editor of *Executive Woman* magazine. Helen's son, George, has accompanied her on her travels since he was a few weeks old.

Contents

There's more for kids to do in London than you probably think.

You may know that the Science Museum is one of the best interactive museums in the country, but do you also know that it organizes sleepovers for children wanting to explore and experiment in the dead of night? And were you aware that you can catch a canal boat to London Zoo where you can stroke a snake, watch flying displays by birds of prey and get up close and personal with monkeys and gorillas? Or that at the Victoria & Albert Museum you can have a go at reconstructing the Crystal Palace built for the Great Exhibition of 1851? Or spend the night pretending to be pirates aboard the *Golden Hinde,* a replica 17th-century sailing ship? And did you realize that not only are most of London's major museums and galleries now free, but they offer a huge range of facilities for families ranging from backpack trails and activity sheets to workshops and story-tellings? Or that kids can ride horses in Hyde Park or explore the cosmos and the ocean depths at the IMAX 3D cinema in Waterloo? Well, you do now.

London is one of the most accommodating cities on earth for young visitors. Almost every month some new attraction opens. The 'Gorilla Kingdom' enclosure at London Zoo, the Unicorn Theatre in Southwark, the BFI Southbank and Benjamin Franklin House are among the most recent additions to the thriving London scene.

This guide aims to spring more than a few surprises of its own, bringing to your attention London's lesser-known sights and some tales of life in the capital, as well as giving you the low-down on all the main attractions – the parks, palaces, museums, cinemas, arcades and experiences that make London perfect for discerning families and fun-hungry kids.

Guide to the Guide

Finding your way around this guide is easy. It is divided into four manageable sections as follows:

Travel provides information on every aspect of getting to and around London.

Ideas, Ideas is full of helpful hints and tips to help you get to know the city: what you can do for free, a London calendar, some days out organized along themes and some stress-free tours.

See it, Do it is the main sightseeing section – the heart of the book, divided into 15 child-size areas. In each we've identified the primary sights, and secondary sights nearby; the best local shopping and places to eat; and other worthwhile attractions around and about. For every attraction there is up-to-date information on how to get there, access, opening times and admission prices, as well as workshops and activities specifically organized for kids. Some indication of appropriate age ranges is also given, as well as how long you should allow for each attraction. Throughout, the text is sprinkled with questions and challenges designed to help you and your children get the most from your stay, plus stories to keep them occupied as you travel from A to B. 'Kids in' details the capital's best indoor attractions and entertainment, including everything from theatre shows and cinema clubs to music workshops and back-stage tours. 'Kids out' identifies the best outdoor ones from parks to farm trips. There's even a section on the best places to watch and participate in a number of sports and activities. Should you fancy a change of scenery, we've also provided details of day trips – to historic Windsor and the university towns of Cambridge and Oxford, or to Chessington and Thorpe Park for some roller-coaster thrills – all within around an hour's journey of the city.

Need to know makes up the final section of the guide with chapters covering all the practical information you need for living and travelling in London: essential details on medical care, post offices, supermarkets, banks, policemen, nappies and so on, as well as a selection of the best child-friendly hotels, restaurants and shops.

Get ready – the adventure begins here.

TRAVEL

London is one of the busiest gateway cities in the world, welcoming thousands of flights every day. Competition between airlines on the major routes is fierce and, wherever you're flying from, you should be able to pick up a cheap deal. Of course, when travelling with children, you may decide to forgo potential savings in return for extra comfort and some in-flight care and entertainment.

> **Flight times to London**
> New York 6–7 hours
> Miami 4–5 hours
> Los Angeles 9–10 hours
> Hawaii 18 hours
> Montreal 6 hours
> Toronto 7 hours

Flights

Many of the larger airlines, including British Airways, Air Canada and American Airlines, provide on-board services for families. These can include such life-savers as designated flight attendants, play packs, seat-back computer games and children's TV channels. Charter flights may be cheap but they can be particularly hellish for children. International air tickets for children aged 2 or under are often free, or at least heavily discounted, sometimes costing just 10 per cent of the adult fare. (One reduced fare is allowed per adult.) Between the ages of 3 and 11, your child will be charged anything between 50 and 85 per cent of the full adult fare but once over 12 your child is, in the eyes of the airline, officially an adult and no longer entitled to any form of discount.

Pushchairs are usually carried free on airlines and can often be taken right up to the point of boarding. Carrycots, however, are not supposed to be brought on board, although some airlines allow the collapsible kind. It can make more sense to pre-book a sky cot. Most airlines also allow the use of car seats, so long as they have been certified as safe for use on planes.

Transatlantic flights

Transatlantic flights touch down at London's two major airports: Heathrow, **t** 0870 000 0123, **www**.heathrowairport.com, situated 15 miles west of central London, one of the world's largest airports with four terminals (work on a controversial fifth terminal will start in the near future), and Gatwick, **t** 0870 000 2468, **www**.gatwickairport.com, some 25 miles to the south, with two terminals.

Of London's other three airports, Stansted, **t** 0870 000 0303, **www**.stanstedairport.com, is the furthest from central London – some 35 miles to the northeast. Of these three, it's also the largest, the busiest (specializing in budget flights and cut-price deals) and has a pleasant, open-plan terminal designed by architect Sir Norman Foster. London City, **t** (020) 7646 0088, **www**.londoncityairport.com, is the closest, 9 miles east – it welcomes just a handful of flights each day from Britain and Europe – while Luton, **t** (01582) 405 100, **www**.londonluton.co.uk, which like Stansted mainly handles budget flights from Europe, is 31 miles to the north.

From North America

The best way to get a cheap deal is to either book well in advance – preferably months – or to try and pick up some sort of last-minute deal. Needless to say, the latter method is not recommended if you're looking for a stress-free holiday. In addition to the major airlines, you should also check out the internet's plethora of cheap flight websites and consolidators – companies which buy blocks of unsold tickets to sell on at a discount – although do note that these tickets are usually non-refundable and tend to incur high penalties for any alteration. Because of the restrictions on flight times, high cancellation fees and the potential for delays, charter flights are not recommended when travelling with children.

Major airlines
Air Canada
t US/Canada 1 888 247 2262
www.aircanada.com
American Airlines
t US 1 800 433 7300
www.aa.com
British Airways
t US 1 800 AIRWAYS
www.britishairways.com
Continental Airlines
t US/Canada 800 231 0856
www.continental.com
Delta Airlines
t US/Canada 1 800 221 1212

www.delta.com
United Airlines
t US 1 800 538 2929
www.united.com
Virgin Atlantic Airways
t US 1 800 821 5438
www.virgin-atlantic.com

Consolidators in North America
Air Brokers Travel
t US 1 800 883 3273
www.airbrokers.com
Airline Consolidator
t US 1 888 468 5385
www.airlineconsolidator.com

Australia and New Zealand
Air New Zealand
t Australia 1 800 809 298
t New Zealand 0800 737 000
www.airnz.co.nz
British Airways
t Australia (1 300) 767 177
t New Zealand (09) 966 9777
www.britishairways.com
Cathay Pacific
t Australia (13) 1747
t New Zealand 0800 800 454
www.cathaypacific.com
Qantas
t Australia (13) 1313
t New Zealand 0800 808 767
www.qantas.com.au

Arriving by plane

Arriving at an airport after a long-haul flight can be a fraught experience. Thankfully, Heathrow and Gatwick have good facilities to help ease the strain.

Heathrow

Train – the Heathrow Express
t 0845 600 1515
www.heathrowexpress.com
Every 15mins from 5.10am–11.25pm
Fares Adult single First Class £24.50, Express Class £15.50; under-16 single First Class £12.20, Express Class £7.70

The Heathrow Express, a direct train link between the airport and Paddington mainline

---

> ### Cheap flight websites
> www.cheapair.com
> www.cheapflights.com
> www.cheap-flight-finder.com
> www.cheaptickets.com
> www.flights.com
> www.lastminute.com
> www.moments-notice.com
> www.travelocity.com

station, is the quickest route into town. It costs from £15.50 (or £29 return) but takes just 15 minutes – tickets can be bought at Heathrow, on the train or in advance online which entitles you to a £1 discount (allow at least three days for delivery within the UK, five days for abroad). Paddington is connected to London's underground network with stations on the Bakerloo, Hammersmith and City, Circle and District lines. There is a black cab rank outside.

Train – Heathrow Connect
t 0845 678 6975
www.heathrowconnect.com
Every 30mins from 4.42am–11.03pm
Fares Single to Paddington £6.90

The slower, cheaper alternative to the Heathrow Express, Heathrow Connect is a stopping service linking the airport with Paddington mainline station. There are seven or eight stops in all (depending on which terminal you arrive at). The journey takes 25–30mins. Unlike the Heathrow Express, travelcards are valid on this service.

Underground
www.tfl.gov.uk/tube
5.30am–12 midnight daily
Fares Adult single £4, child £2

One-day travelcards, which allow you unlimited travel on London's buses, trains and underground, are available from 9.30am on weekdays and at any time on weekends. Alternatively, if your stay is going to be a long one, you may consider getting an Oyster card. See **Getting Around**, p.14.

Heathrow is the first stop on the eastbound Piccadilly Line, which means you should be able to get a seat and find somewhere to put your luggage. On the downside, it can take up to an hour to reach central London and, unless your eventual destination is on the Piccadilly Line (Knightsbridge, Green Park, Piccadilly Circus, Leicester Square, etc.), you will have to negotiate corridors and escalators whilst laden with luggage and children as you change to another line. Alternatively, you may prefer to get off at ⊖ Earl's Court or South Kensington and take a taxi the rest of the way.

National Express Bus
t 08705 80 80 80
www.nationalexpress.com
Every 15–30mins from 5.30am– 9.35pm
Fares Adult single £4, child £2, under-3s **free**
Equipped for disabled passengers

There are over 40 National Express Airbus departures a day from Heathrow bound for London Victoria by way of Notting Hill, Marble Arch and Russell Square. The journey takes 1hr 40mins.

Taxi
This is the most expensive option. Make sure you take a licensed black cab from the official rank. The cab fare from Heathrow to central London should be around £40–50 (over £60 if travelling after 8pm when a higher tariff applies).

Gatwick

Train – the Gatwick Express
t 0845 850 1530 for timetable information
www.gatwickexpress.co.uk
4.35am, 5.20am, every 15mins from
5.50am–12.35am, then 12.50am, 1.35am
Fares Adult single First Class £22.50, Express Class £14.90; under-16s First Class £11.25, Express Class £7.45, under-5s **free**

By far the most practical way to get into town. The trains are not quite as speedy as their Heathrow counterparts but make good time – 30mins platform to platform from Gatwick to Victoria. There is also a stopping service during the day for passengers requiring East Croydon (20mins) or Clapham Junction (35mins), which takes 50mins to reach Victoria. Tickets can be bought at Gatwick, on the train (Express service only) or pre-booked on the phone or online (which entitles you to a discount, although allow at least three days for delivery within the UK, five days for abroad).

National Express Bus
t 08705 80 80 80
www.nationalexpress.com
Hourly from 6.20am–11.20pm
Fares Adult £6.60, under-16s £3.30

The bus is cheaper than the train, but is very slow and can take over two hours to reach Victoria, calling at Coulsdon, Wallington, Mitcham, Streatham and Pimlico on the way.

Taxi
Only an option for the seriously wealthy or the seriously tired out. The journey will take over an hour and cost upwards of £80. There is a black cab rank outside the arrivals hall.

London City Airport
t (020) 7646 0088
www.londoncityairport.com
Train – Docklands Light Railway
Trains run to central London on Mon–Sat
5.29am–12.30am, Sun 6.58am–11.30pm
Fares (*See* Top tips p.18 for DLR savings.)
City Airport is now served by its own DLR station, connecting it to central London via Bank Station.
Adult £4, child £2.

Taxi
A taxi from the airport should take around 30mins to the city centre and cost around £15–20.

Luton
t (01582) 405 100
www.london-luton.co.uk
Train – Luton Airport Express
A free shuttle bus connects the airport to Luton Parkway station in about 5mins.
Mon–Fri 7am–10pm, Sat & Sun 9am–8pm. Journey time is 25–35mins
Fare Adult single £10, child £5

Midland Mainline trains run from Luton Parkway to Kings Cross/St Pancras every 15–20 minutes from 5.08am till 1.16am. The journey takes 21 minutes. First Capital Connect operates a 25-minute service to Kings Cross Thameslink Station.

Airbus
t 08705 80 80 80
www.nationalexpress.com
t 0870 608 7261
www.greenline.co.uk
www.easybus.co.uk
Between them, National Express, Greenline and Easybus ensure that a bus leaves the airport for Central London every half hour 24hrs a day. The bus takes 1hr 15mins (an extra 15mins during peak times) to reach its destination of Victoria Coach Station.

Fares Adult single £11/£10/£8, child £4.50/£8/£4, under-3s (not occupying a seat) **free**. Easybus sometimes offer tickets for as little as £2 on their website

Stansted

Train –The Stansted Express
t 0845 850 0150
www.stanstedexpress.co.uk
The first train is at 6am; trains run every 30mins until 8am, then every 15mins till 6pm, every 30mins until 12 midnight
Fares Adult single First Class £22.50, Express Class £14.50; under-16s First Class £11, Express Class £7.25
The train links Stansted aiport with Tottenham Hale on the Underground's Victoria Line and Liverpool Street Station (east of the city centre). The journey takes 42mins.

National Express Bus
t 08705 80 80 80
www.nationalexpress.com
Approximately every 30mins, 24hrs a day
Fares Adult single £10, child single £5
A bit cheaper than the train, the bus takes over an hour more (journey time 2hrs), stopping en route at Finchley Road and Marble Arch before reaching Victoria Station. This could be an advantage with luggage, as long as you have plenty of time.

Terravision
www.terravision.it
Times vary. To Victoria: every 30mins–1 hour, 24 hrs a day. To Liverpool Street: every 30mins from 6am–1am
Fares Adult single £8, child (5–12) single £4
Nonstop services to Victoria (75mins) and Liverpool Street (55mins).

Arriving by rail, road or ferry

By rail

Eurostar
t 08705 186 186
www.eurostar.com

Over twenty times a day from Paris and Brussels
Fares Vary. A non-flexible, non-exchangeable, non-refundable ticket booked 21 days in advance, can be bought for as little as adult £59, child £50, under-4s **free**. The closer you leave booking to departure and the less flexible you are with your travel times, the more expensive the fare.
Check-in time 30mins
No baggage weight limit
Wheelchair users need to inform Eurostar staff of their requirements when booking
Following the opening of the new high-speed terminal at St Pancras in November 2007, it now takes just 2 hours 15 minutes to reach London from Paris, and an even more impressive 1 hour 50 minutes to get there from Brussels, aboard a Eurostar train. Time under the sea is 25 minutes. The high-speed terminal is adjacent to the mainline station of the same name, which is connected to the Underground network. This means that, once through Customs, you're only a few minutes from central London. Trains run from St Pancras and King's Cross stations to other mainline stations such as Victoria and Charing Cross, while the Underground station is on the Northern and Victoria lines. A taxi to the centre should cost about £10–£15 (more after 8pm when a higher tariff applies). There's a black cab rank outside the station.

By ferry
The completion of the Channel Tunnel in the early 1990s was supposed to sound the death knell for the ferry industry. The advantages of ferry travel – restaurants, bars, fabulously bad cabaret et al – would, it was believed, pale in comparison to a seasick-free, 25-minute jaunt under the Channel. That didn't really prove to be the case. As successful as Eurostar has been, its sister car-carrying Eurotunnel service has proved much less popular. It seems that people like the chance to stretch their legs and have a meal during the crossing. The ferry companies' aggressive pricing policy has kept them (literally) afloat and forced Eurotunnel into financial difficulties. Ten years after the tunnel opened, the Anglo-French consortium in charge of Eurotunnel were running at a staggering loss of some £2.8 billion a year, although this has been reduced to a more 'manageable' £200 milllion in the past couple of years.

The main ferry links land you at Dover, Newhaven or Portsmouth, from where you can continue your journey to one of London's eight mainline stations: Charing Cross, Euston, King's Cross, Liverpool Street, Paddington, St Pancras, Victoria or Waterloo. All have connections to the Underground network.

Prices are highly competitive. Under-4s usually travel free , there are discounts for under-14s, and most lines can boast good family facilities – restaurants, baby-changing rooms, children's play areas and video rooms.

Calais–Dover is the quickest and most popular ferry route. P&O Ferrries, **t** 0870 598 0333, (**www**.poferries.com) operate 25 sailings a day during the high season; the journey takes 1 hour 15 minutes. Fares vary hugely and it's best to shop around for the best current deal. A family of four travelling in a medium-sized car should expect to pay anything between £120 and £180 for a flexible return, depending on the time of year.

Driving via the Channel Tunnel

Eurotunnel – Calais to Folkestone

t 0870 535 3535
www.eurotunnel.com
Four departures an hour during peak times
Fares Thanks to ongoing competition from ferry companies, Eurotunnel have brought down their fares markedly of late. One-way tickets start at £49. The fare is for car space only regardless of the number of passengers.
Check-in time At least 25mins but no more than 2hrs before departure.
No baggage weight limit. Wheelchair users need to inform staff of their requirements when booking

Eurotunnel transports cars on purpose-built carriers through the Channel Tunnel between Calais and Folkestone. The French terminal is situated off junction 13 of the A16 motorway, while the British equivalent can be reached via junction 11a of the M20. The journey time is a mere 35mins. Most people choose to stay in their car, although you can get out and wander down the corridor to stretch your legs. Toilets and a buffet service are provided. It is advisable to book in advance, although it is possible just to turn up and wait. Space is given on a first-come, first-served basis.

The carless alternative

You may want to consider arriving in Britain without your car and renting one once you get here. Airlines and many travel agents can arrange 'fly-drive' packages for you on request. *See* **Getting Around**, p.16, for rental companies in London.

If you're arriving from the Continent, remember to adjust the dip of your headlights for driving on the left. Wearing seatbelts is compulsory in Britain, front seats and back.

By bus

National Express/Eurolines

52 Grosvenor Gardens, London SW1
t 08705 80 80 80
www.nationalexpress.com

Coach trips are both the cheapest and the least pleasant way to travel long distances. National Express do not charge for under-3s, and under-16s travel half-price. They also offer annual family coachcards for £8 (one adult, one child) and £16 (two adults, two children) which allow children to travel free on all services for a year.

Although National Express operates coach routes to all major cities in Britain and Europe, its convoluted routes mean that journeys can take many hours. London's main coach station is at Victoria, 10 mins' walk from the train/Underground station along Buckingham Palace Road.

Passports and visas

From Europe

Although the UK is part of the European Union – which technically gives all union citizens the right to move freely in and between member states – it is still necessary for EU citizens to present their passports or identity cards upon arrival.

From elsewhere

Nationals from the USA, Canada, Australia, New Zealand, South Africa, Japan, Mexico and Switzerland do not need a visa in order to visit Britain for a holiday of up to three months, but must present their passport upon arrival and answer a few routine questions relating to the nature of their visit. Other nationals should check entry requirements with their embassies.

Customs

EU nationals over the age of 17 are no longer required to make a declaration to customs upon entry into another EU country, and so can import a limitless amount of goods for personal use. For non-EU nationals the limits are 200 cigarettes, one litre of spirits, two litres of wine, 60ml of perfume, two cameras, one movie camera and one TV.

Retail Export Scheme

Visitors from non-EU countries can make savings on purchases made in London via the Retail Export Scheme. Pick up a form from participating shops.

Pet Passports

Until recently, no pet could be brought into the country unless it had first spent six months in quarantine to make sure it wasn't carrying any infectious diseases (particularly rabies). The rules have now relaxed slightly allowing visitors from Western Europe, USA, Canada (and certain island states such as Cyprus and Malta) to bring in pets so long as they fulfil strict criteria. The animal must not have been outside the qualifying area at any time; each pet must be fitted with an identification microchip and have been inoculated against rabies, and the owner must carry a document (known as the Pet Passport) proving this. The animal must undergo a further blood test 30 days after entry.

Getting to London from elsewhere in the UK

By air

It is possible to fly to London from most of the UK's main cities, but it isn't a cost- or time-effective option unless you're travelling from the north of England or Scotland. The environmental impact of 'unnecessary' flights should also be considered.

British Airways, **t** 0870 850 9850, **www**.britishairways.com, British Midland, **t** 0870 607 0555, **www**.flybmi.com, and the low-cost airlines easyJet, **t** 0871 244 2366, **www**.easyjet.com, Ryanair, **t** 0871 246 000, **www**.ryanair.com and Bmibaby (British Midland's budget subsidiary), **t** 0871 224 0224, **www**.bmibaby.com, all offer services and a bewildering array of fares. As a simple rule of thumb, the earlier you book your flight, the cheaper it will be. If you book at least

two weeks in advance, you should be able to get a flight from Edinburgh to London on a major carrier for between £70–£100. A flight booked just a few days before departure will rise to £160–£180. easyJet, in particular, operates an escalating fare policy. The first people to book for a particular flight will get the cheapest deal but, as the service fills up, the prices will rise until they are more or less compatible with those of the major carriers.

By rail

You can get to London from anywhere in the UK and, as with air travel, the earlier you book your journey, the cheaper it will be. For the very cheapest deals, you need to book at least 21 days in advance and travel outside peak times. Perhaps the best option is to pick up a family railcard which, for just £20 a year, entitles up to four adults to a 33% saving and up to 4 children to a 60% saving on most services, **www**.family-railcard.co.uk. Contact National Rail Enquiries, **t** 08457 48 49 50, **www**.nationalrail.co.uk, for more information.

The major train companies are:

Central Trains t (0121) 634 2040,
www.centraltrains.co.uk
The Midlands
First Capital Connect t 0845 026 4700,
www.firstcapitalconnect.co.uk
Greater London, East Midlands and the Southeast
First Great Western t 0845 700 0125,
www.firstgreatwestern.co.uk
West of England, including southwest peninsula
First ScotRail t 0845 601 5929,
www.firstgroup.com/scotrail
Scotland
GNER t 0845 722 5225, www.gner.co.uk
East Midlands, Yorkshire, northeast and Scotland
One t 0845 600 7245, www.onerailway.com
East Anglia and the southeast
Silverlink t 0845 601 4867,
www.silverlink-trains.com
The Midlands
Southeastern t 0800 783 4548,
www.southeasternrailway.co.uk
The southeast
South West Trains t 0845 600 0650,
www.southwesttrains.co.uk
The southwest
Virgin t 0870 789 1234, www.virgintrains.co.uk
West coast, West Midlands, northwest and Scotland

Making your way around the maze of London's streets can be tricky. They have neither the block-by-block clarity of New York nor the open accessibility of Paris. The most convenient option, if you are new to the city, is to take the Underground (the 'Tube'). This in itself can be exciting for children, especially if they have never travelled on an underground system before. When you, and they, are a little more at home in London, you'll find that buses make a welcome change, allowing you to see the sights as you travel around, albeit at a more leisurely pace. Other forms of transport, such as London's famous black cabs, are fun, though expensive.

By Underground and DLR

There are 12 interconnecting Underground lines (colour-coded) which crisscross London from Heathrow out to the west to Upminster in the east, and from Barnet in the north to Morden in the south. In central London you're never more than five minutes from a Tube station, though the system becomes more sparse the further from the centre you get. Tube trains run from 5.30am to 12 midnight (7am on Sundays) every day apart from Christmas. Try to avoid travelling at peak times (Mon–Fri 7.30am–9.30am and 5pm–7.30pm). This is especially important if you are using a pushchair.

The Docklands area in east London is served by the DLR (Docklands Light Railway), an overground monorail which links up with ⊖ Bank and ⊖ Tower Gateway. For information, call the DLR customer services t (020) 7363 9700, www.tfl.gov.uk/dlr. Trains run to 12.30am Mon–Sat, 11.30pm Sun.

Tickets and passes

If you are not using a travelcard or Oyster card, which entitle you to significant travel discounts, Tube fares are a flat rate adult £4, child 50p, regardless of the length of the journey. For travelcard and Oyster card holders, fares in London are based on a zonal system. The capital is divided into six concentric rings or 'zones'. Zone 1 is the centre, Zone 6 the outskirts. Your fare is worked out according to the

distance of your journey within and between these zones. For instance, a single Oyster Tube fare within Zone 1 is adult £1.50, whereas a single fare between Zone 1 and Zone 2 rises to adult £2. Children's fares apply between the ages of 5 and 15. After the age of 12 children need to show an age identification photocard (available from any Tube or train station) when they purchase their ticket; under-5s go free.

Follow procedure

Underground tickets must be bought in advance of travel. Travelcards (including weekly and monthly passes) and Oyster cards are available from Tube ticket windows and machines, and from many newsagents.

At most Underground stations you will find an 'Assistance and Tickets' window, plus a bank of electronic ticket machines. You can buy a carnet of 10 tickets or a weekly pass from some machines.

Some stations have ticket inspectors; most, however, have automated barriers. Oyster card users must swipe their cards over the readers on top of barriers, while regular ticket holders should place their ticket (with the black magnetic strip face down) into the slot at the front of the machine. The ticket will reappear from a slot at the top of the machine.

Few Tube stops have lifts, which means taking the stairs or (if you're sensible) the escalator. Pushchairs must be folded up and held on the escalator. It is the custom to stand on the right-hand side and walk on the left and people may get very sniffy with you if you get this wrong. On crowded trains, young, fit passengers are supposed to give up their seats for senior citizens, pregnant women and parents with babies or toddlers. Sometimes this even happens.

By bus

Despite an increase in the number of bus lanes, London's ongoing traffic congestion problems make buses a slow choice of transport. However, it can make a very pleasant alternative to subterranean travel. Bus travel is also a great way of getting to know the city.

Attempts are being made to speed up the bus service and most buses in central London now operate a 'pay before you board' policy. To take a ride on a conductor-less bus, you now have to purchase your ticket in advance from one of the

Question 1

In Paris it's 'le métro', in New York it's the 'subway', so what is it called in London?

answer on p.250

ticket machines located by the bus stop (or from a newsagent) rather than from the driver.

The standard single fare for an adult is £2, children (under 16) travel for free, though photo ID is required if your child looks older.

There are two types of bus stop: white, at which buses must stop, and red, which are request stops. To hail a bus at a red stop, stick your arm out. To alight at a request stop, ring the bell.

Night buses

Standard buses stop operating around midnight, at which point N-prefixed night buses take over until 5am the following morning. There are far fewer night bus routes – you can pick up a night route map from any Underground station and most newsagents. One-day Travelcards are valid on night buses until 4.30am.

By train

For nipping around central London, stick to the Tube. For longer journeys out into the suburbs, however, you may wish to switch to the train. London's rail network links up with the Tube at various points and, unlike the Tube, there are certain services (particularly the airport routes) that run all night. To find out when trains are running throughout Britain call **t** 08457 48 49 50, **www**.nationalrail.co.uk; for details of family railcards *see* p.13. All train and Tube stations have a map, known as a Journey Planner, showing London's combined Tube and train network. If you buy a travelcard or Oyster card, you can chop and change your mode of transport throughout the day, using as many Tubes and buses as you like. Note that Oyster cards are frequently not accepted on mainline trains, so check before you travel.

Taxis

Though undeniably expensive, London's taxis are incredibly efficient and reliable. Cabbies must train for two years and pass a strict test before qualifying for their taxi licences. During this time they must learn every street and major building in the capital, as well as 468 separate routes – a mean feat of learning known simply as 'The Knowledge'.

London cabs are easily recognizable. Most are black although some now sport the coloured livery of advertisers. All have orange 'For Hire' signs on their roofs which light up when the cab is available. Car seats are fitted as standard in all TX1 black cabs. The seats are built into the central arm rest in the rear of the cab and can accommodate children between 22 and 36kg. You may hail a cab on the street (by sticking out your arm) or, if staying at a hotel, you can ask the doorman to do it for you. There are taxi ranks outside all major railway stations and also some Tube stations. Alternatively, call Dial-A-Cab, **t** (020) 7426 3420. To track down that mislaid umbrella or teddy bear, call Black Cab Lost Property on **t** (020) 7918 2000. Black cabs are licensed to carry four people at a time (sometimes five), with space next to the driver for luggage. Most black cabs can accommodate wheelchairs. Bear in mind that fares increase after 8pm when a higher tariff applies.

Minicabs are cheaper, but less reliable and largely unregulated. A driving licence is pretty much all that's required to qualify as a minicab driver. Hiring a minicab can therefore be rather risky and, in general, is best avoided. There are some reputable firms, however, including:

Greater London Hire
t (020) 7490 4222
www.glh.co.uk
Lady Minicabs
t (020) 7272 3000
www.ladyminicabs.co.uk
A specialist service run by women (all the drivers are female) for women.

By car

Driving in central London is recommended only for the very patient or the very rich. A congestion charge was introduced in 2003 as a means of reducing traffic by deterring motorists from making unnecessary journeys and raising revenue to improve the city's public transport system. All drivers entering central London between 7am and 6.30pm Monday to Friday must pay a flat fee of £8.

The Congestion Charging Zone currently stretches around central London from King's Cross in the north to Elephant and Castle in the south, and from Kensington in the west to Tower Bridge in the east. Entry points are clearly marked by a big white 'C' in a red circle painted on the road. The system is enforced by a network of CCTV cameras that monitor number plates. Drivers have until midnight of the day of travel to pay the charge. If payment is left until the following day, the charge rises to £10. After that, if the charge remains unpaid, the driver will be issued with a penalty charge for £100. If it is paid within 14 days, it is reduced to £50 but if it remains unpaid within 28 days, it increases to £150. Payment can be made by phone, t 0845 900 1234, online at **www.cclondon. com** or at shops bearing the 'C' symbol. You can pay on a daily, weekly, monthly or annual basis.

If you do use your car, beware the parking restrictions. Going over the allotted time at a parking meter can result in a wheel clamp or, if you're particularly unlucky, your car may be towed away. To find out which pound to go to to reclaim your car, call TRACE, the Towed Vehicle Tracking Service, t (020) 7747 4747 – the main ones are at Marble Arch, Earl's Court and Camden. The fine will be a staggering £200 – minimum – and will increase each day the car remains unclaimed. Using the car for trips outside London, however, does make a little more sense. Before setting off, buy a copy of the British Highway Code (available from post offices) in order to familiarize yourself with the British way of motoring. You don't need to carry your papers with you but, if stopped, you will usually be asked to present them at a police station within five days. If you are hiring a car, you need to be at least 21 years old (more usually 25), with a year's driving experience.

Car rental companies

Alamo
UK t 0870 400 4562
www.alamo.co.uk
US t (1 800) 462 5266
www.alamo.com
Avis
UK t 0844 581 0147
www.avis.co.uk
US t (1 800) 230 4898
www.avis.com
easycar
UK t 0906 33 33 33 3 (calls charged at 60p per min)
www.easycar.com
Hertz
UK t 0870 844 8844
www.hertz.co.uk

US t (800) 654 3131
www.hertz.com
Thrifty
UK t (01494) 751 540
www.thrifty.co.uk
US t (800) 847 4389
www.thrifty.com

By bike

London is not very cycle-friendly. Extreme congestion, pollution and limited cycle lanes are just some of the hazards. Cycling as part of a large tour-guided group (see below) is a safer option. Here are some rental companies that provide bikes and helmets for families. Hire rates are approximately adult £3 per hour, child £2 per hour. Bikes usually have to be returned by 7pm on the day of hire.

On Your Bike
52–4 Tooley Street, SE1
t (020) 7378 6669
www.onyourbike.com
⊖ London Bridge

London Bicycle Tour Co.
1a Gabriel's Wharf, 56 Upper Ground, SE1
t (020) 7928 6838
www.londonbicycle.com
⊖/⊟ Waterloo
Bike hire from £3 per hour, £18 for first day (£9 per day after that). London tours from £17.95.

Capital Sport Ltd
t (01296) 631 671
www.capital-sport.co.uk
Offers guided tours along the Thames.

Rickshaws

The past few years have seen the introduction of pedal-powered rickshaws, hundreds of which now operate in the centre of town. Though fun-looking, they are not recommended for families for a number of reasons. It is a wholly unregulated industry: no licence is required to set up as a rickshaw driver, which means that no one is sure how many currently operate; drivers are not vetted and are not required to have any knowledge of the capital; the lack of fare-capping structure means that drivers can effectively charge what they like – and many do, with tourists being charged exhorbitant rates for short journeys; finally, rickshaws are not required to have seat belts, and many do not.

IDEAS, IDEAS

TOP TIPS

IDEAS, IDEAS

The best of kids' London

This is our selection of the very best that London has to offer younger visitors: all the best things to see, eat, visit, shop, ride and play with that can be found in England's capital city.

Best animal attraction
The 'Gorilla Kingdom' enclosure at London Zoo, see p.42.

Best annual jamboree
Coin Street Festival, see p.34.

Best café
Café in the Crypt in Trafalgar Square, see p.225.

Best Christmas experience
Skating outdoors at Somerset House, see p.84.

Best church
For views and all round 'wow' factor, St Paul's Cathedral, see p.129.

Best cinema
The big, big screen: Imax 3D Cinema, see p.107.

Best firework display
At the end of the Lord Mayor's Show, see p.36.

Best for gruesomeness
The London Dungeon's grisly tableaux, see p.116, or the Old Operating Theatre, see p.119.

Best interactive fun
The Launch Pad at the Science Museum, see p.140.

Best market
For budding fashionistas: The Stables in Camden Market, see p.49.

Best museum
The Natural History Museum, for its animatronic dinosaurs and sheer number of beasts, see p.138.

Best park
Regent's Park, for the boats, playgrounds, wildfowl, open air theatre and sports facilities, see p.46.

Best restaurant
The Rainforest Café – jungle dining doesn't get any better, see p.74.

Best shop
Daisy and Tom, see p.244, or Benjamin Pollock's Toy Shop, see p.249.

Best sightseeing tour
Sailing down to Greenwich on a Bateaux London-Catamaran Cruiser, see p.29.

Best sports event
The racy to the downright wacky: the Oxford-Cambridge Boat Race, see p.33, the London Marathon, see p.153, or the superannuated vehicles in the London to Brighton Vintage Car Run, see p.36.

Best statue
Nelson on his column, see p.66.

Best toy shop
Hamley's, of course, see p.248.

Best view
From a capsule in the London Eye, see p.107, from Hampstead Heath, see p.174, or from the top floor café of the National Portrait Gallery, see p.73.

Tips for getting around

▶ London has one of the most extensive public transport systems of any city in the world. Trying to get around the city's traffic-filled streets in your own car is both painful and, following the introduction of the Congestion Charge, expensive (see 'By Car', p.15). Using taxis for more than the odd journey is even more pricey and again, you'll often find yourself stuck in traffic.

▶ Under 10s travel free on all London's buses, Tubes and DLR services. 11–16 year olds also travel free on buses, but pay a flat rate of 50p for Tubes and DLR services, and around half the adult fare for rail tickets.

▶Don't buy tickets every time you use public transport. Travelcards and Oyster cards can be used for the Tube (Underground/subway), buses, the DLR and train system. This works out cheaper than single tickets and you won't have to queue to pay your fare every time you travel. See 'Getting Around', p.14.

▶ London offers a wide range of **sightseeing tours**. These are some of the best and most enjoyable ways of getting an idea of the city – since they often involve just sitting and looking from a boat or bus. The classic boat trips on the Thames are among London's don't-miss attractions, but don't pass over less well-known rides like the open-top bus tours, canal trips, the madcap fun of the amphibious Duck Tours or, for the energetic, guided walks. For details, *see pp.28–31.*

Getting more for less

London is one of the wealthiest cities in the world and much of what it has to offer does not come cheap. Even so, it is still possible to have a fun day out without breaking the bank.

Churches

Admission to all the churches in London is free – except for St Paul's Cathedral and Westminster Abbey. Special services take place several times a year, most notably at Christmas and Easter.

City farms

Coram's Fields and Vauxhall City Farm allow families to pet and stroke their animals and engage in a range of country crafts free of charge. *See pp.176–7.*

Entertainment

Free foyer concerts are often given at the Royal National Theatre, Royal Festival Hall and the Barbican in the early evening. Covent Garden plays host to some of the country's top buskers and street performers on a daily basis (*see p.78*). The Covent Garden Festival of Street Theatre takes place every September.

Events & festivals

Various free events take place in London each year. *See p.31* for more details of the London year.

Daily events
Changing of the Guard
Outside Buckingham Palace.

Ceremony of the Keys
The Tower of London.

Hyde Park Gun Salutes
By the Royal Horse Artillery; these take place on 6 February (Accession Day), 21 April (Queen's birthday), 2 June (Coronation Day), 10 June (Prince Philip's birthday) and the State Opening of Parliament in November. Note if any of the above dates fall on a Sunday, the salute will be fired on the following Monday.

Museums & galleries

The number of museums and galleries that don't charge for admission is, believe it or not, actually increasing. Some of the capital's most prestigious collections, including the Natural History Museum, Science Museum, Museum of London, National Maritime Museum and Imperial War Museum, have recently taken the decision to waive their entrance fees.

Bank of England Museum *see p.131*
British Library *see p.58*
British Museum *see p.54*
Bruce Castle Museum *see p.161*
Clowns International Gallery *see p.161*
Geffrye Museum *see p.162*
Horniman Museum *see p.162*
Houses of Parliament *see p.99*
Imperial War Museum *see p.111*
Kenwood House *see p.163*
London International Gallery of Children's Art
    see p.163
Museum of London *see p.130*
National Army Museum *see p.163*
National Gallery *see p.67*
National Maritime Museum *see p.150*
National Portrait Gallery *see p.69*
Natural History Museum, *see p.138*
Petrie Museum of Egyptian Archaeology *see p.57*
Prince Henry's Room *see p.133*
Queen's House *see p.151*
Ragged School Museum *see p.164*
Royal Air Force Museum *see p.164*
Royal Naval College *see p.151*
Royal Observatory *see p.150*

Museum trails
Several museums and galleries produce free leaflets and trails that children can use to make their visit more enjoyable. Ask at the foyer on entry if there are any audio guides, backpacks or free leaflets for kids to use.

Science Museum *see* p.139
Serpentine Gallery *see* p.143
Sir John Soane's Museum *see* p.82
Tate Britain *see* p.100
Tate Modern *see* p.117
V&A Museum of Childhood *see* p.164
Victoria & Albert Museum *see* p.140
Wallace Collection *see* p.47
Wandsworth Museum *see* p.165

Museums free for children

Benjamin Franklin House *see* p.83
Cartoon Museum (Sat only) *see* p.56
Churchill Museum and Cabinet War Rooms
   see p.100
Courtauld Gallery *see* p.84
Design Museum, *see* p.122
Dulwich Picture Gallery *see* p.161
Foundling Museum *see* p.59
Gilbert Museum *see* p.84
Guards' Museum *see* p.93
Handel House Museum (Sat only) *see* p.57
HMS *Belfast see* p.120
Kew Gardens *see* p.172
London Transport Museum *see* p.78
The Museum in Docklands *see* p.153

Parks & views

From elegantly manicured royal gardens to great swathes of ancient woodland, London's parks are all free. Wherever you're staying in London there will be a park, usually with a children's playground, not too far away. *See* **Kids out** p.171 for more information.

For stunning views try Hampstead Heath (*see* p.174), The Mall (*see* p.92), the Oxo Tower (*see* p.110), Westminster Bridge (*see* p.98) or the London Eye (*see* p.107).

On foot

London comes in two different sizes: Greater London, which is huge – 28 miles north to south, 35 miles east to west; and central London, where the majority of the capital's tourist attractions are located, which isn't very big at all. Touring on foot is the best way to get to know the smaller version; you can explore all the hidden nooks and crannies you would miss if you relied exclusively on public transport. A few words of warning, however.

▶ Vehicles travel on the left on Britain's roads, so when crossing remember to look right, then left, then right again, and not vice versa.

▶ Never cross the road except at a designated crossing zone such as a set of traffic lights, a pelican crossing (a green man will light up to tell you when it's safe to cross) or a zebra crossing – a black-and-white striped crossing point with an orange flashing beacon on either side. In theory, traffic should stop as soon as you put your foot on a zebra. But do wait for this to happen before you start to cross.

Travel discounts

With kids travelling for free on buses and for a flat rate of 50p on the Tubes, you might think that London's public transport system is the ideal money-saving way of getting around. And it is – so long as you're under 16. For adults, it's a whole different story. London's grown-up population pays some of the highest transport costs in Europe and fares keep rising year on year. This is one area where it really is worth seeking out what bargains there are. If you're planning a long trip, the best way of saving money is to invest in an Oyster card, a swipe card which you can use to store up to £90 of pre-paid travel credit. There are several advantages to this system. First, Oyster fares are much cheaper. A single Tube ticket for a journey right across London is just £2 with an Oyster card compared with the normal rate of £4. Secondly, bus fares are capped at a maxium £3 per day, regardless of the number of journeys, while combination rail/Tube and bus journeys are capped at £6.20 (50p cheaper than the equivalent travel card). Finally, you can sign up for a free top-up service, which will prevent your card from running out of money and you leaving you potentially stranded. Oyster cards are available at all underground stations, by calling **t** 0845 330 9876 or online at **www.tfl.gov.uk/oyster**. The card requires photo identification, so you'll have to provide a passport-sized photo of yourself. You need to swipe the card over the relevant reader at the Tube, train or bus stops at the start and finish of your journey to ensure that you pay the lowest fare.

If your holiday is not long enough to warrant getting an Oyster card, your best bet is to buy either a weekly or a one-day travelcard. These let you make unlimited journeys on London's Tubes and buses (including night buses until 4.30am,) and also entitle the holder to a 33% discount on most scheduled Thames riverboat services.

Useful London websites

Contact the relevant local borough council for details of local and seasonal events (firework nights in particular), plus free festivals. Council websites are as follows:

www.[nameofborough].gov.uk
eg: **www.barnet.gov.uk**
www.visitlondon.com
The official tourist board site with various attractions, hotel details etc.
www.thisislondon.co.uk
The *Evening Standard*'s website, full of jolly ideas and up-to-the-minute events
www.timeout.com/london/kids
Time Out magazine's website. The kids' section is selective and has some interesting features
www.londonnet.co.uk
This site doesn't have a huge kids' section, but its savvy attitude is appealing
www.kidslovelondon.com
The London Tourist Board's dedicated kids' site with links to top attractions, listings of upcoming events, online games and reviews by primary age children (5–11 years).

At the time of writing, a weekly travelcard covering zones 1 and 2 is adult £23.20, child £11.60 while a travelcard covering all six zones is adult £43, child £21.50 The one-day equivalents are: adult £5.10, child £2 for zones 1–2; adult £6.70, child £2 for a travelcard covering all six zones

Note, that one-day travelcards can only be used after 9.30am Mon–Fri and are valid up until 4.30am of the following morning.

If you travel beyond the limits of your ticket, you will be liable for an on-the-spot penalty fare. This is £20 on Tubes and trains and £10 on buses.

There are also a number of tourist buses plying their trade in the capital. The best is probably the Big Bus Company, **t** (020) 7233 9533. Adult £17, child £8 – for 24hours unlimited travel on BBC buses (*see* p.30).

London Pass

An all-in-one sightseeing ticket, the London Pass gives you free entry to over fifty selected museums, river cruises, historic houses, zoos, cinemas, galleries, guided walks, etc., plus special offers at restaurants, cinemas, theatres and shops. Prices: one day (adult £34, child £20); two days (adult £44, child £31); three days (adult £54, child £36); six days (adult £74, child £50). Tickets including free public transport range from one day (adult £39, child £22) to six days (adult £112, child £70). Holders also receive a free 132-page guide to the capital. Available in person from the British Visitor Centre or by logging on at **www.london-pass.com**

London Rail and River Tour

Gives an overview of the best the capital has to offer both old and new, from historical sights and attractions to the latest shopping and restaurants around Canary Wharf and Docklands. The Rail and River Rover Ticket is valid for one day and allows unlimited travel on the Docklands Light Railway and City Cruises River Boats, which run between Westminster, Waterloo, Tower Hill and Greenwich.

Fares Adult £11, child £5.50, family £27 (2 adults and up to 3 children), **www.citycruises.com**, **t** (020) 7740 0400, **www.tfl.gov.uk/dlr**, **t** (020) 7363 9700.

Fun & games

Just in case the kids have time to be bored, which we very much doubt, here are a few ways to keep them occupied.

Pub cricket

Pubs in London have names like the Dog & Duck and the Red Lion. You can play a game called pub cricket in which you score runs according to the number of legs a pub has, i.e. the Dog & Duck scores six runs (a dog having four legs and a duck two). Just as in cricket, the object of the game is to score as many runs as possible. If you spot a pub with no legs, such as the Crown, then you lose a wicket. Ten wickets and you're out and it is someone else's turn to score a few runs. The game can get a little more complicated with a pub such as the Horse & Hounds – decide for yourself just how many hounds are to be counted.

What am I?

A London version of the guessing game, What Animal Am I?

E.g.:
Q. What London landmark am I?
I am quite tall
I have a pointed roof
I make a noise every hour

I have numbers on my face
A. Big Ben

Quick draw

You will need:
pocket-sized pad of plain paper
a pen that glides easily across the page

This really is the simplest game imaginable, rest the pad on your knee and lightly poise the pen over it. As the vehicle you are in moves around the pen will jump leaving a crazy pattern on the paper. Kids can take turns making the patterns and trying to figure out what the drawings look like. They could even spend time colouring in the shapes should you experience a long delay to your journey.

THEMES

Sometimes children can get madly interested in a particular subject, such as football, animals, film or the theatre. When this occurs, everything else becomes dull and uninspiring and just a little bit pointless. With this in mind, here are a number of suggested days out for excitable kids with abiding passions.

Stagestruck kids

Itinerary 1

Morning Take the Tube to Waterloo for a tour of the National Theatre. *See* p.109.
Lunch At Pizza Express on Belvedere Road. *See* opposite.
Afternoon Walk along the riverside, past Shakespeare's Globe, climb the stairs up to London Bridge and then head down Tooley Street for the Unicorn Theatre where you can watch one of their acclaimed plays for children. These usually start at 1.30pm Mon–Fri and 2pm on Sat.

National Theatre

South Bank, SE1
t (020) 7452 3400
www.nationaltheatre.org.uk
Tour Mon–Sat 3 times a day, tour lasts 1hr 15mins
Adm Backstage tours: £5, concs £4, family £13

Pizza Express

The White House, 9c Belvedere Road, SE1
t (020) 7928 4091
www.pizzaexpress.com
Open 11.30am–12 midnight daily

Unicorn Theatre

147 Tooley Street, SE1
t (020) 7645 0560
www.unicorntheatre.com
Adm Adult £9.50, child £5

Itinerary 2

Morning Take the Tube or train to London Bridge for a tour around the reconstructed Globe Theatre to see how plays were performed in Shakespeare's day. *See* p.168.
Lunch At the nearby Gourmet Pizza Company, just along the riverfront *See* below.
Afternoon Walk further along the riverfront past the South Bank (where a free performance may be taking place on Theatre Square outside the National Theatre) to Waterloo. From Waterloo you can take the train to Wimbledon to catch an afternoon performance at the Polka Theatre, the only purpose-built children's theatre in the country (*see* p.169).

Shakespeare's Globe Theatre

New Globe Walk, Southwark, SE1
t (020) 7902 1400
www.shakespeares-globe.org
Open Performances staged Apr–Oct.
For performance times call in advance; museum 10–5 daily
Adm Museum: adult £6.50, child £4.50 (under-5s **free**), concs £5, family ticket (2+3) £15

Gourmet Pizza Company

Gabriel's Wharf, 56 Upper Ground, SE1
t (020) 7928 3188
www.gourmetpizzacompany.co.uk
⊖/≋ Waterloo
Open 12 noon–10.30

Polka Theatre

240 The Broadway, SW19
t (020) 8543 4888
www.polkatheatre.com
Open Tues–Fri 9.30–4.30, Sat 11–5.30
Adm Tickets for performances range from £5–£10; a one-day workshop is £25

Toy-mad kids

Morning Take the Tube to Oxford Circus, then head down Regent Street to the country's most famous toy emporium, Hamleys, with its six goodie-stuffed floors. *See* p.59.
Lunch At the café on Hamleys' fifth floor or at Pizza Express on nearby Dean Street.
Afternoon A short journey to Covent Garden to enjoy the traditional toys of Benjamin Pollocks' Toy shop (*see* p.80), before, if you've still got the energy, heading to Harrods and its great 4th-floor toy department (*see* p.145).

Hamleys
188–196 Regent Street, W1
t 0800 280 2444
www.hamleys.com
Open Mon–Sat 10–8, Sun 12 noon–6

Pizza Express
10 Dean Street, W1
t (020) 7439 8722
⊖ Tottenham Court Road
www.pizzaexpress.co.uk
Open 12 noon–11.30 daily

Benjamin Pollock's Toy Shop
44 Covent Garden Market, WC2
t (020) 7379 7866
www.pollocks-coventgarden.co.uk
Open Mon–Sat 10.30–6, Sun 12 noon–6

Harrods
87–135 Brompton Road
Knightsbridge, SW1
t (020) 7730 1234
www.harrods.com
Open Mon–Sat 10–9, Sun 12–6

Life at sea

Morning Take a riverboat cruise from Charing Cross Pier to Greenwich with Bateaux London–Catamaran Cruises, to visit the National Maritime Museum with its vast collection of nautical equipment. *See* p.150.
Lunch In the Trafalgar Tavern, Park Row, over-looking the river.

Afternoon Take the train from Greenwich to London Bridge for HMS *Belfast*, a Second World War destroyer moored permanently on the riverfront. *See* p.120.

Bateaux London & Catamaran Cruisers
t (020) 7695 1800
www.bateauxlondon.com
Fares A Circular Cruise (from central London to Greenwich and back): adult return £7, child return £3.50

The Trafalgar Tavern
Park Row, SE10
t (020) 8858 2437
Open Mon–Sat 11.30–11, Sun 12 noon–10.30

National Maritime Museum
Romney Road, Greenwich, SE10
t (020) 8858 4422
Infoline **t** (020) 8312 6565
www.nmm.ac.uk
Open 10–5 daily
Free

HMS *Belfast*
Morgan's Lane, off Tooley Street, SE1
t (020) 7940 6300
http://hmsbelfast.iwm.org.uk
Open Mar–Oct 10–6 daily, Nov–Feb 10–5 daily
Adm Adult £9.95, under-16s **free**, concs £6.15

Gory kids

Morning Take a Tube or train to London Bridge for the London Dungeon, the capital's premier gorefest. *See* p.116.
Lunch At Café Rouge in the nearby Hay's Galleria or Manze's on Tower Bridge Road.
Afternoon If you still feel like grossing out, head either to the Old Operating Theatre, where surgeons gaily butchered people in the early 19th century (*see* p.119), without antiseptics and often without anaesthetic, or the Clink Museum (*see* p.121), built on the site of a former prison, which holds a collection of scary-looking, medieval torture instruments.

London Dungeon
Tooley Street, SE1
t (020) 7403 7221

www.thedungeons.com
Open School hols 9.30–6.30 daily, otherwise 10.30–5 daily
Adm Adult £17.95, child (under 14) £13.95, under-5s **free**, concs £14.25

Café Rouge

Hays Galleria, Tooley Street, SE1
t (020) 7378 0097
www.caferouge.co.uk
⊖/≉ London Bridge
Open Mon–Fri 8.30am–11pm, Sat 9am–11pm, Sun 9am–10.30pm

Manze's

87 Tower Bridge Road, SE1
t (020) 2407 2985
www.manze.co.uk
Open Mon 11–2, Tues–Thurs 10.30–2, Fri–Sat 10–2.45

St Thomas' Old Operating Theatre

9a St Thomas Street, SE1
t (020) 7955 4791
www.thegarret.org.uk
Open 10.30–5 daily
Adm Adult £5.25, child £3 (under-8s **free**), family ticket (2+2) £12.95

Clink Museum

1 Clink Street, SE1
t (020) 7403 6515
www.clink.co.uk
Open 10–6 daily
Adm Adult £5, child £3.50, concs £3.50, family £12

Animal-mad kids

London Zoo (⊖ Camden Town or Baker Street) is still one of the best places for kids to come and learn about animals. *See p.42.*
Morning 'Meet the Monkeys'. Get up close and personal with squirrel monkeys in their own enclosure at the zoo's latest exhibit.
12 noon Walk through a tropical deluge at the Clore Rainforest Biome.
12.30 Lunch at the zoo's 'Oasis' self-service café.
2–2.30 Feeding Time – for the penguins in the Penguin Pool.

2.30–2.45 Animals in Action in the Amphitheatre – leaping lemurs and flying parrots demonstrate their skills.
3pm 'Gorilla Kingdom – enter the land of the great apes at the zoo's latest attraction.
3.30 B.U.G.S. – marvel at giant bird-eating spiders at the Web of Life building.
5pm Watch the giraffes being put to bed at the Giraffe House. (Note: this takes place at 3.15pm in winter).

London Zoo

Regent's Park, NW1
t (020) 7722 3333
www.zsl.org/zsl-london-zoo
Open Mar–Oct 10–5.30 daily; Nov–April 10–4 daily
Adm Adult £16.50, child (under 16) £11, under-3s **free**, concs £13, family £45.50

Movie-mad kids

There's absolutely no way you can mention film any more without reference to the Harry Potter phenomenon. London, of course, features in all the Potter books and on-screen, plus in a number of other movies besides.

Itinerary 1

Morning Take the Tube to Camden Town or Baker Street, then take the 274 bus to London Zoo. Linger around the Reptile House and see if your kids can communicate with the serpents as well as young Harry does. *See p.42.*
Lunch Stroll over to Regent's Park for a picnic and see if you can spot any of Dodie Smith's *One Hundred and One Dalmatians* or head further north to Primrose Hill to re-enact the twilight barking. *See p.46 and p.48.*
Afternoon Hop on the Bakerloo Line down to Waterloo and catch a state-of-the-art film show at the 3D IMAX cinema. *See p.107.*

London Zoo

Regent's Park, NW1
t (020) 7722 3333
www.zsl.org/zsl-london-zoo
Open Mar–Oct 10–5.30 daily; Nov–April 10–4 daily
Adm Adult £16.50, child (under 16) £11, under-3s **free**, concs £13, family £45.50

IMAX 3D Cinema
1 Charlie Chaplin Walk, SE1
t 0870 787 2525
www.bfi.org.uk/imax
Open Mon–Fri 12.30–8, Sat & Sun 10.45–8.45
Adm Adult £8.50, child (5–15) £5, under-3s **free**,
concs £6.25

Itinerary 2

Morning Though not the best spot for hanging
around with the kids, St Pancras (exterior) and
King's Cross (interior) stations are a must for all
Potter-ites, but do try to restrain them from
throwing themselves at the sign for Platform 9³/4,
located next to platforms 9–11. Instead, move
swiftly along to the Piccadilly Line and head to
Leicester Square – the heart of London's movie-
going scene – to watch the latest blockbuster or
gaze at the handprints of famous stars set into the
pavement around the square. *See p.72.*
Lunch On a fine day you can grab a picnic and sit in
Leicester Square. Alternatively, catch a Northern
Line train to Waterloo or Embankment and have a
snack in the BFI Southbanks' Film Café underneath
Waterloo Bridge. *See p.72 and p.112.*
Afternoon Stay in the BFI Southbank for an afternoon screening of an old black and white classic or
a special kids' film. On Saturdays kids can also take
part in a film-related workshop. *See p.109.*

Leicester Square Cinemas
Empire
t 0871 471 4714
www.empirecinemas.co.uk
Odeon Leicester Square
t 0871 224 4007
www.odeon.co.uk
Vue West End
t 08712 240 240
www.myvue.com

BFI Southbank
t 0870 787 2525
www.bfi.org.uk
Adm Family film screenings: child £1,
accompanying adults £8.20, workshops £6.50

Arty kids

Self-expression is vital to a child's creative
development. Thankfully London has plenty of
galleries where children can not only go for
inspiration, but also have a go at making a master-
piece themselves.

Itinerary 1

Morning Take the Tube or train to London Bridge
for the vast Tate Modern, which offers tailor-
made kids' audio guides and organizes weekend
activities for children, including art trails and
creative workshops. *See p.117.*
Lunch The Tate Modern café can get very busy, so
opt for an early lunch. The brasserie-style food is a
bit pricey but it's worth it just for the spectacular
view of the River Thames.
Afternoon Head north on the Northern Line or
walk over the new Hungerford footbridge to
Charing Cross and Trafalgar Square. If it's fine you
can always picnic in the square before stopping off
at the National Gallery for a look at the famous
paintings. The gallery hosts a variety of family
events, including storytelling sessions and drawing
days under the tutelage of a professional artist.
See p.67.

Tate Modern
Bankside, SE1
t (020) 7887 8888
www.tate.org.uk/modern/
Open Sun–Thurs 10–6, Fri and Sat 10–10
Free

National Gallery
Trafalgar Square, WC2
t (020) 7747 2870
www.nationalgallery.org.uk
Open 10–6 daily, Wed 10–9
Free Charges apply for some temporary
exhibitions

Itinerary 2

Morning Ceramics Café. Let your children's imagi-
nations run riot painting plates or designing their
own pots at this popular, creative workshop. *See*
p.166.
Lunch The ICA (⊖ Charing Cross) has a good café
and a shop selling jewellery, gadgets and prints
made by local artists. *See p.92.*

Afternoon Take the Tube or train to Vauxhall for Tate Britain. Families could easily spend a whole day wandering around the galleries here, but it's also good for interactive fun. On Sundays – and daily in the school holidays – look out for the art trolley doing its rounds, packed full of arty materials for kids to try. *See* p.100.

Ceramics Café
6 Argyle Road, West Ealing
t (020) 8810 4422
www.ceramicscafe.com
⊖ West Ealing
Open Tues–Sat 10–6, Sun 11–5
Adm £2 studio fee, £3–£15 for materials

ICA Gallery
The Mall, SW1
t (020) 7930 3647
www.ica.org.uk
⊖ Piccadilly Circus, Charing Cross
Open Galleries 12 noon–7.30
Adm Depends on exhibition

Tate Britain
Millbank, SW1
t (020) 7887 8888
www.tate.org.uk/britain
⊖ Pimlico, Vauxhall, ⇌ Vauxhall
Bus 2, 3, 36, 77A, 88, 159, 185, 507, C10
Open 10–5.50, daily, till 10pm first Fri of each month
Free (charges apply for some temporary exhibitions)

Mini-monarchists

Of course, there are any number of royal exhibits in London – the following is our pick of the bunch.
Morning Take the Tube to St James's Park for the Buckingham Palace tour (summer only). Young royalists won't be happy without it. *See* p.90.
11.27 If you time things well, you could watch the Changing of the Guard after your 45-minute tour of the palace. Allow yourself time to get the children out and find a place to stand.
Lunch Unless Her Majesty has invited you to lunch, it's not so easy to find a royal-themed eatery. You could, however, encounter the royalty of rock (including The Artist Formerly Known as Prince

and, of course, Queen) at the nearby Hard Rock Café. *See* below.
Afternoon Princess Diana's palace in Kensington Gardens (⊖ High Street Kensington) has guided tours through the plush historic apartments and an excellent exhibition of royal clothes. Get there by 2.30 as it closes early: it might be easier (and less exhausting) to skip the Changing of the Guard today. After you've seen the palace, the gardens provide a refreshing break from pomp and ceremony. *See* p.142.

Buckingham Palace
St James's Park, SW1. The ticket office for purchasing tickets on the day is located in Green Park at Canada Gate
t Booking line (020) 7766 7300/1
www.royal.gov.uk
Open Late July–Sept 9.30–6 daily (last entry 3.45)
Adm Buckingham Palace: adult £15, child (under 17) £8.50, under-5s **free**; joint ticket to Buckingham Palace, Queen's Gallery and Royal Mews: adult £27, child £13.50, under-5s **free**, family £69.50.
The tour lasts 45mins

Changing of the Guard
t (020) 7930 4832
www.royal.gov.uk
Times The ceremony takes place every morning between April and August at 11.30 sharp and on alternate days for the rest of the year
Free
The ceremony lasts over 1hr

Hard Rock Café
150 Old Park Lane, W1
t (020) 7514 1700
www.hardrock.com
Open Sun–Thurs 11.30am–12.30am, Fri–Sat 11am–1am

Kensington Palace
t 0870 751 7050
www.hrp.org.uk
Open Mar–Oct daily 10–6, Nov–Feb daily 10–5, last admission 1hr before closing
Adm Adult £12, child £6, concs £10, family £33

SEE IT, DO IT

So you're ready to hit the town, but what to do first? Do you rush headlong at the nearest attraction and proceed in haphazard fashion? Not if you want to preserve a little sanity to go home with at the end of the day. Here are a few ways of getting a snapshot of the city before taking the plunge. Then you can move on to the sightseeing chapters in earnest.

Walks

It may seem an arduous task with kids in tow, but pushchair-bound kids need to limber and stretch. On a clear day there's really nothing nicer than a leisurely stroll along the river, and on a misty morning where better to take a trip than through London's murky past?

The Original London Walks

PO Box 1708
London NW6 4LW
t (020) 7624 3978
www.walks.com

The original and best – there are several companies offering walking tours of London, but this one (London's oldest) is easily the pick of the bunch and certainly the most child-friendly (under-15s **free** if accompanied by an adult, adults £6). As well as organizing tours around several specific areas of London, including the City, Greenwich, Westminster and Hyde Park, London Walks offer various themed treks including 'Shakespeare's London', 'Ghosts of the West End', 'Jack the Ripper Haunts', etc, although your children's pick will no doubt be the new 'Harry Potter Tour'. All the tours are led by knowledgeable, entertaining guides.

London Silver Jubilee Walkway

A 10-mile walk is not every child's idea of a great day out. This walkway is generally more for strong-thighed adults than children, but it's still worth considering for a family trip. The route is split into seven sections – which run from Leicester Square through Westminster across the river to the South Bank and then back through the City to Covent Garden – each topped and tailed by a Tube stop, so you can walk as much or as little as you like. The route is marked by discs set in the pavement (there are 400 in total); kids love being the first one to

'find' the marker. The walk was created in 1977 to commemorate the Queen's Silver Jubilee, hence the name. For more information, visit the London Tourist Information Office at Victoria.

Millennium Mile

London's latest walkway, the Thameside path between Westminster Bridge and Tower Bridge, has been spruced up since the millennium and rechristened (appropriately enough) the Millennium Mile. As a result, what was once one of the city's more tatty districts is now much smarter and one of the best places to come to for a family walk. The route is dotted with some of the capital's best attractions, including the London Aquarium, London Eye, the National Theatre, the Oxo Tower, Tate Modern, the Globe Theatre, HMS *Belfast* and Tower Bridge. You can find out more by visiting **www**.southbanklondon.com.

The Thames Path

For a more ad hoc walking experience, you might like to try a portion of the Thames Path, a designated nature trail along the banks of the Thames. You might have a job finishing the route, however, as it stretches the entire length of the river, all 180 miles of it. For more information contact the Thames Barrier Visitor Centre, **t** (020) 8305 4188.

Blue Plaque Tours

Have you ever noticed that some London houses have blue plaques adorning their walls? These were erected by English Heritage (**www**.english-heritage.org.uk) to indicate that a famous person used to live there.

It can be quite good fun using these plaques as the basis for a walk around the city. It allows you to explore streets and areas not normally covered on official sightseeing itineraries. (*See* box opposite.)

Pub Signs

As you walk around the city, look out for the painted signs hanging up outside pubs, particularly old pubs. The names displayed are often very distinctive, not to say occasionally rather peculiar – Lamb and Flag, Hoop and Grapes, Black Friar, Old Cheshire Cheese, Bleeding Heart Tavern, Red Lion, White Swan, Coach and Horses, etc. These were chosen specially because of the ease with which they could be illustrated on the pub sign. Remember, back in the 17th and 18th centuries, a large proportion of London's population couldn't

Blue plaque tours

If visiting the British Museum, try finding the following, all within 10 minutes' walk:

7 Fitzroy Square: Home of **George Bernard Shaw**, author of *Pygmalion* (which was subsequently used as the basis for the musical *My Fair Lady*) and the modernist writer Virginia Woolf.

110 Gower Street: Home of **Charles Darwin**, one of the world's greatest scientists and the man who, in his book *The Origin of Species*, published in 1859, first put foward the now widely accepted Theory of Evolution. This states that every living creature on the earth has come about as a result of natural selection over millions of years rather than divine creation.

48 Doughty Street: Here, you'll find the former home of **Charles Dickens**, Victorian Britain's most famous and celebrated novelist. His works, including *Oliver Twist*, *Nicholas Nickleby*, *David Copperfield* and *Great Expectations*, are still widely read today and have been filmed on numerous occasions. His house is open to the public and is filled with period furniture and memorabilia relating to his life. *See* p.56.

If shopping on Oxford Street, look out for the following:

15 Poland Street: Home of the romantic poet **Percy Bysshe Shelley**.

28 Dean Street: Home of **Karl Marx**, founder of Marxism (and buried in Highgate Cemetery).

23 Brook Street (it's just off New Bond Street): Home of the legendary rock guitarist **Jimi Hendrix**.

24 Brook Street (next door to the above): Home of the 18th-century composer **George Handel;** among his most famous works is the choral classic *The Messiah*.

If shopping on the King's Road, try and spot the following:

18 St Leonard's Terrace: Home of **Bram Stoker**, author of the first vampire novel, *Dracula*.

23 Tedworth Square: Home of **Mark Twain**, the American author of children's favourites *Tom Sawyer* and *Huckleberry Finn*.

56 Oakley Street: Home of **Captain Scott**, the famous Polar explorer who died in the early 20th century on the return journey following his unsuccessful attempt to become the first man to reach the South Pole.

13 Mallord Street: Home of **A.A. Milne**, creator of the Winnie the Pooh stories and one of the most popular children's authors of all time.

read or write and would have had to rely on such images to make sure they found the right pub.

Look out, in particular, for pubs bearing the name 'The Royal Oak'. If you look closely at the tree depicted in the sign, you should after a while be able to pick out the image of a man hiding in its branches. This is the young Stuart prince Charles (later Charles II) who, after his Royalist army was defeated by the Parliamentarians ('Roundheads') at the the end of the Civil War in 1652, had to hide in an oak tree for a whole day to avoid capture.

Boat trips

The following companies offer sightseeing boat trips along stretches of the Thames. The frequency depends on the time of year. For more details, visit the London River Services website **www.tfl.gov.uk/river**, where you can download a comprehensive Thames Boat Service guide and map, or call t (020) 7941 4500. Note that Travelcard holders (both adults and children) are entitled to a 33% discount on most scheduled riverboat services.

Bateaux London & Catamaran Cruisers

t (020) 7695 1800
www.bateauxlondon.com
Fares London Eye Pass: adult £24.50, child from £12.20 (includes unlimited travel on the hop-on hop-off service for one day and entry to London Eye) Tower Pass: adult £24, child £12.20 (includes unlimited travel on the hop-on hop-off-service for one day and fast track entry to Tower of London) Hopper Pass: adult £9.50, child £4.75 (allows unlimited use of service for one day enabling you to hop on and off at different sites) Circular Cruise (non-stop 50 minute cruise from Westminster Pier): adult return £9.50, child return £4.75, family £23

River cruises on purpose-built vessels with fun, informative commentary. Provides unrivalled views of some of London's best-loved sights.

City Cruises

t (020) 7740 0400
www.citycruises.com
Fares Westminster–Tower Pier: adult single £6.20, return £7.40; child single £3.10, return £3.70, under-5s **free**
Westminster–Greenwich: adult single £7.20,

return £9.40; child single £3.60, return £4.70, under-5s **free**

Rail & River Rover: adult 11, child £5.50, family £27, under-5s **free**

Runs between Westminster Pier, Waterloo Pier, Tower Pier and Greenwich. The huge boats, which seat up to 500, are easily recognized by their bright red livery. City Cruises also offers a 'Rail and River Rover Ticket' allowing unlimited travel for a day on both their boats and the Docklands Light Railway.

Thames Clippers

t 0870 781 5049

www.thamesclippers.com

Fares Tate to Tate: Adult £4, child £2, family £10; River Rover hop-on hop-off service one day: adult £8, child £4, family £18. Travelcard holders are entitled to discounts

Thames Clippers operate the direct boat link between Tate Modern and Tate Britain, which runs every 40 minutes from Bankside Pier to Millbank Pier and back again, stopping off at Waterloo Pier (for the South Bank) en route. The company also runs services to Greenwich and the new O2 Arena.

Thames River Services

t (020) 7930 4097

www.westminsterpier.co.uk

Fares Westminster–Greenwich: adult single £7.20, return £9.40; child single £3.60, return £4.70; family £21; Westminster–Thames Barrier–Greenwich: adult single £8.95, return £11.30; child single £4.50, return £5.65; family £26

Operates services all the way from the Thames Barrier upriver to the west and to Greenwich downriver to the east.

Westminster Passenger Service

t (020) 7930 2062

www.wpsa.co.uk

Fares Westminster–Kew (return): adult £16.50, child £8.25, family £41.25

Westminster–Richmond (return): adult £18, child £9, family £45

Westminster–Hampton Court (return): adult £19.50, child £9.75, family £48.75

Head upriver with some spicy commentary about the occupants of a few well-appointed flats in Chelsea and titbits from the history of London. From Hammersmith onwards the journey becomes more serene and pastoral as you glide towards Kew Gardens, Richmond and Hampton Court.

Canal trips

London Waterbus Company

50 Camden Lock Place

t (020) 7482 2660

www.londonwaterbus.com

Camden Town, Chalk Farm

Bus 6, 46

April–Oct daily service, boats run hourly from 10–5; Nov–Mar weekends only

Fares Adult single £6, return £8.40; child single £4.30, return £5.40, under-4s **free**; combined canal trip and zoo visit adult £16.50, child £13.50, under-4s **free**

Trips aboard traditional, painted narrow boats between Camden Lock and Little Venice, stopping off at London Zoo (*see* p.42) – you get a reduction on the price of admission.

Sightseeing buses

Various companies offer services, but the Big Bus Company – recognizable by its distinctive maroon and cream livery – is perhaps the best. It operates three colour-coded routes: Green, the West End and Bloomsbury; Blue, Knightsbridge and Mayfair; and Red, from Victoria to the Tower of London. Main departure points are Marble Arch, Green Park, Baker Street and Victoria, although you can board at any stop along the route. The company now also offers walking tours.

The Big Bus Company

48 Buckingham Palace Road, SW1

t (020) 7233 9533

www.bigbus.co.uk

Fares Adult £22, child £10

Ticket allows 24hrs unlimited travel on BBC buses

Balloon trips

Adventure Balloons

t (01252) 844 222

www.adventureballoons.co.uk

Fares £175 per person

It's not the most straighforward way of getting to know the capital, it's certainly not cheap and it's only available to over-8s (so long as they stand over 1.4km/4ft 6in high), but if you're up for it (literally), an early morning hot air balloon flight can be an unforgettable experience. The flights take off from sites near Vauxhall Bridge and Tower Hill, last around an hour and go right over the capital. They take place just after dawn on Tuesdays, Wednesdays and Thursdays from May to August, must be booked in advance and are liable to late-notice postponement due to the weather.

Visitor centres

Thames Barrier
1 Unity Way, Woolwich, London, SE18
t (020) 8305 4188
⊖ New Cross, New Cross Gate
≋ Charlton
River Cruise Regular service from Westminster Pier, call Thames River Services t (020) 7930 4097
Open April–Sep 10.30–4, Oct–Mar 11–3.30 daily
Adm Adult £2, child £1
Suitable for ages 8 and over
Allow at least 1hr

One of the marvels of modern London, the Thames Barrier is an astounding piece of engineering. Spanning the river's 1,700-ft width, these 10 huge steel gates (each the size of a five-storey house) are often all that stands between a dry London and one under 10 feet of water. The gates, which lie on 10,000-ton concrete sills on the riverbed, can be raised into position in an astonishing 10 minutes flat in the event of a flood.

The barrier's construction was prompted by a flood in 1953 which killed 300 people. You can find out more about London's battle with its ever-rising river at this small 'Information and Learning Centre'. Here you can see a working model of the barrier, watch a video detailing its construction and look at a map showing which unfortunate parts of London would now be regularly submerged if it wasn't in place. Time it right and you might even get to see the mighty metal behemoth in action – the barrier is tested once a month, and the Centre can provide details of the schedule.

Whatever time of the year you visit London, there's always something going on. From festivals and parades to major sporting events and exhibitions, hardly a week goes by without a noteworthy event. London is always busy, always fun, always buzzing, and if you grow tired of the capital you must be, as Dr Johnson famously said, tired of life.

Daily events

Ceremony of the Keys
Tower of London, EC3
t (020) 3166 6278
www.hrp.org.uk
⊖ Tower Hill
Bus 15, 25, 42, 78, 100, D1
Adm Free. Every day at 9.53pm
The ceremony lasts about 20mins

The nightly locking of the Tower of London is one of the oldest military ceremonies in the world. For free tickets apply in writing at least two months in advance (remember to include a SAE) to The Ceremony of the Keys, HM Tower of London, London EC3N 4AB.

Changing of the Guard
Buckingham Palace, SW1
t (020) 7930 4832
www.royal.gov.uk
Infoline t (020) 7766 7300
⊖ St James's Park, Green Park, Victoria
Bus 7, 11, 139, 211, C1, C10
Free

An hour of pomp and pageantry outside Buckingham Palace beginning at 11.30am sharp every day May–July and on alternate days for the rest of the year, *see* p.90 for further details.

Annual events

January
London Parade
New Year's Day
Parliament Square to Piccadilly by way of Whitehall and Trafalgar Square
t (020) 8566 8586

www.londonparade.co.uk
⊖ Westminster, Embankment, Green Park,
Piccadilly Circus
Adm Free along route
   The estimated 10,000 performers and over a
million spectators make this one of the the biggest
New Year's Day parties in Europe.

National Storytelling Week
Last week of January
t (0118) 9351 3818
www.sfs.org.uk
   The Society for Storytelling organizes readings
and events in bookshops, libraries and museums
across the country for children of all ages.

Chinese New Year Festival
Late January or early February
Gerrard Street, Lisle Street & Newport Place, WC1
www. chinatown-online.co.uk/pages/
new_year/index.html
⊖ Leicester Square
Bus 6, 7, 8, 10, 12, 13, 14, 15, 19, 23, 25, 38, 53, 55, 73, 88,
94, 98, 139, 159, 176, X53
Free
   Chinatown celebrates its annual rebirth with
firecrackers, paper lanterns and papier-mâché
dragons that dance down the street.

February
Accession Day Gun Salute
Accession Day, 6 February, 12 noon
Hyde Park
⊖ Hyde Park Corner, Knightsbridge, South
Kensington, Lancaster Gate, Queensway
Bus 2, 9, 10, 12, 14, 16, 19, 22, 36, 52, 70, 73, 74,
82, 94, 137
Free
   This is the first gun salute of London's year.
The Royal Horse Artillery gallop furiously into
Hyde Park and unleash an extremely noisy 41-gun
salute. The practice is repeated several times: on
the Queen's birthday (21 April), Coronation Day
(2 June), Prince Philip's birthday (10 June) and the
State Opening of Parliament, which takes place in
November. Note that if any of the above dates fall
on a Sunday, the salute will be fired on the
following Monday.

Spitalfields Pancake Race Day
Shrove Tuesday
Spitalfields Market, E1

t (020) 7375 0484
www.alternativearts.co.uk
⊖ Liverpool Street
Bus 5, 8, 26, 35, 43, 47, 48, 67, 78, 149, 242, 344
Free
   Organized by Alternative Arts, this Shrove
Tuesday charity event sees competing teams of
costumed runners racing along Dray Walk, near
Spitalfields Market, tossing pancakes as they go.

March
Ideal Home Exhibition
Mid- to late March
Earl's Court Exhibition Centre, Warwick Road, SW5
t 0870 606 6080
www.idealhomeshow.co.uk
⊖ Earl's Court
Bus 31, 74, C1, C3
Adm Adult Mon–Fri £14, Sat–Sun £16; child Mon–Fri
£9, Sat–Sun £10; all tickets £6 after 5pm, except on
first Fri and last Sun; under-5s **free**
   At Europe's largest consumer show you'll find
designer bathrooms, bedrooms and other house
interiors as well as all the latest labour-saving gizmos
– juicers that cut as they peel and boil an egg, etc.

Easter
Oxford–Cambridge Boat Race
www.theboatrace.org
Saturday before Easter or Easter Saturday
The Thames between Putney Bridge and Mortlake
For start ⊖ Putney Bridge;
for finish ⇌ Mortlake
Bus For start 14, 22, 39, 74 85, 93, 220,265, 414, 430;
for finish 209, 485, R69
Free
   The two teams have been battling it out over the
4.5-mile Thames course for over a century now. The
best viewing points (and the places with the best
atmosphere) are Putney Bridge and Chiswick Bridge.

Easter Parade
Easter Sunday
Battersea Park, SW11
t (020) 8871 7534
www.batterseapark.org
⇌ Battersea Park, Queenstown Road
⊖ Sloane Square
Bus 44, 137, 319, 344, 345
Open Dawn till dusk
Free

Easter Sunday carnival with a fairground, parade and special children's village featuring a bouncy castle, playground, clowns and puppet shows. Special events, such as displays by freefall parachute teams, are often laid on.

April

London Marathon
t (020) 7902 0200
www.london-marathon.co.uk
Sunday in late April. Race starts at 9am
26 miles 385 yards between Blackheath and Westminster Bridge by way of the Isle of Dogs, Victoria Embankment and St James's Park.

Over 30,000 people put mind and body to the test each year over the 26-mile course between Blackheath and Westminster Bridge. There's a mini-marathon for stretching little legs as well.

May

Museums Month
t (020) 7233 9796
www.mgm.org.uk
In participating museums throughout the capital
This annual celebration of the nation's collections and treasure troves is the largest museums promotion anywhere in the world. Organized by the 'Campaign for Museums', hundreds of museums participate, organizing a range of hands-on activities and events (including late openings), many of which are free and family-friendly.

May Fayre and Punch & Judy Festival
Nearest Sunday to 9 May
St Paul's Church, Covent Garden
t (020) 7375 0441
⊖ Covent Garden, Leicester Square
Bus 9, 11, 13, 15, 23, 77a, 91, 176

Free
An annual celebration of puppet marital disharmony in the grounds of St Paul's Church.

June

Trooping the Colour
Second Saturday in June, starts at 10.45am
Buckingham Palace to Horse Guards Parade
www.royal.gov.uk
⊖ Charing Cross, St James's Park
Buses 7, 11, 139, 211, C1, C10
Free along route
Tickets for this top piece of British pageantry are awarded by ballot – you must apply in writing by the end of February. Write to the Brigade Major (Trooping the Colour), Household Division, Horse Guards Parade, SW1A 2AX, enclosing a stamped addressed envelope. There is a maximum of two tickets per application. The ceremony, which marks the official birthday of the Queen (confusingly, her real birthday is actually on 21 April), takes place at Horse Guards Parade and is preceded by a Royal Air Force jet display.

Biggin Hill International Air Fair
Mid-June weekend, starts at 8am
Biggin Hill Airfield, Biggin Hill, Kent
t (01959) 572 277
www.airdisplaysint.co.uk
⇌ Bromley South, Croydon East or West, from where a shuttle bus links with the airfield
Bus 246, 320, 464, R2
Adm Adult £20, child £7, family £45
Every summer, plane enthusiasts from all over the country gather in order to get up close and personal with the truly high-flying machines of the aviation world. Second World War Spitfires and Hurricanes are the biggest draws, but there are lots of other planes to see both on the ground and in the sky. A host of displays, fly-pasts and skydives takes place over the two days, and there's also a funfair and exhibition stands.

Henley Royal Regatta
Wed–Sat late June (sometimes early July)
The Thames at Henley
t (01491) 572 153
www.hrr.co.uk
⇌ Henley
Adm £11 per person in the regatta enclosure, otherwise free

Both a serious athletic competition, which sees a host of international squads taking part in a series of rowing races along the Thames, and a grand society occasion, this is above all a great excuse for a Thames-side picnic .

Wimbledon

Last two weeks in June
All England Lawn Tennis and Croquet Club, Church Road, Wimbledon, SW19
t (020) 8946 2244
www.wimbledon.org
⊖ Southfields, Wimbledon
⇌ Wimbledon
Bus 39, 93 or shuttle bus from any of the above stations
Adm Centre Court tickets start at £38 for the first Monday rising to £91 for the final Sunday. Ground tickets start at £20 for the first Monday (£14 after 5pm), dropping to £8 for the final weekend (£5 after 5pm)

Tickets for the top matches on Centre and No.1 courts of the world's most prestigious tennis tournament are obtainable only by ballot, which must be entered the previous September. You can queue up during the tournament for a ground pass which gives you access to all the courts apart from Centre and No.1. Obviously, the major stars will play most matches on the show courts, but the atmosphere on the outside courts is sometimes more exciting and you should be able to see a few famous faces. From 2pm onwards, you can queue up to buy resale show court tickets from a kiosk on the hill in front of the big screen.

City of London Festival

Late June–mid-July
t (020) 7796 4949
www.colf.org

Musical kids can hit the high notes at this three-week festival of sound held in the magnificent churches and halls of the City. Free lunchtime recitals featuring everything from classical to jazz take place daily.

July

Coin Street Festival

Mid-July–mid-September
The South Bank at the Oxo Tower Wharf, Gabriel's Wharf and the Bernie Spain Gardens
t (020) 7401 2255
www.coinstreetfestival.org
⊖ Waterloo, Westminster, Blackfriars
Bus 4, 68, 76, 77, 149, 168, 171, 176, 188, 211, 501, 505, 507, 521, D1, P11
Free

There's plenty to please the kids at this three-month free arts festival on London's South Bank organized by the Coin Street Community Builders – fancy dress parades, arts and crafts workshops, and stalls selling food from around the world.

Greenwich & Docklands Festival
Ten days in mid-July
Various venues in Greenwich
t (020) 8305 1818
www.festival.org
⊖ North Greenwich
DLR Island Gardens
≋ Greenwich
Bus 177, 180, 188, 199, 286, 386
Free
This popular arts festival combines concerts and theatre as well as children's events, and starts with a bang with an opening night firework display.

August
Notting Hill Carnival
August Bank Holiday Sunday and Monday
Notting Hill and surrounding streets
t (020) 8964 0544
www.rbkc.gov.uk/nottinghill
⊖ Westbourne Park, Ladbroke Grove (due to crowds avoid Notting Hill Gate)
Free
The largest carnival in the world after Rio. Steel bands, floats, costumed dancers, fancy dress, jugglers, face-painting, exotic food: this is one of the year's most intense experiences. In fact, it can be a little hairy for very young children, who might prefer the scaled down junior carnival held in Kensington Memorial Park a fortnight before the main event (mini floats, mini parades, mini fancy dress, etc). Older kids, however, will have a great time. There is a special children's parade on the Sunday.

Marine Week
Second week of August
Various locations around London
t (01489) 774 400
www.southeastmarine.org.uk
Marine-themed events at locations throughout the capital and the southeast (including, inevitably, the London Aquarium) organized by the Wildlife Trust.

August Bank Holiday Funfairs
Funfairs set up for business during the summer's premier bank holiday weekend at many of London's parks including Alexandra Palace Park and Hampstead Heath.

September
Last Night of the Proms
Early September, on final Sat of the Proms
Hyde Park
t 0870 899 8001
www.bbc.co.uk/proms
⊖ Hyde Park Corner
Bus 2, 8, 9, 10, 12, 14, 16, 19, 22, 36, 39, 73, 74, 82, 94
Adm £23, under-3s **free**
Following an afternoon of easy on the ear classical tunes and West End musical sing-a-longs, attention turns to the Big Screen where the BBC Philharmonic will begin the annual celebration of patriotism, leading the crowd through lusty renditions of *Jerusalem* and *Rule Britannia*.

Covent Garden Festival of Street Theatre
Early September
Covent Garden
t (020) 7836 9136
www.coventgarden.org.uk
⊖ Covent Garden, Leicester Square
Bus 9, 11, 13, 15, 23, 77A, 91, 176
Free
Fire-eaters, escapologists, stilt-walkers, unicyclists and comedians put on a week of performances in Covent Garden's Piazza.

Thames Festival
Mid-September on second weekend of autumn school term
Various points on the Thames between Waterloo and Blackfriars Bridge
t (020) 7928 8998
www.thamesfestival.org
⊖ Embankment, Charing Cross, Southwark, Waterloo
Bus 1, 4, 26, 45, 63, 68, 76, 77, 149, 168, 171, 171a, 172, 176, 188, 501, 505, 507, D1, P11, X68, RV1
Free
The Thames really comes to life with a range of events along the banks, from firework displays to lantern processions. There's a food village, artworks and installations, river races, stalls, music and funfair rides. During the day there are craft workshops.

October
Costermongers' Pearly Kings and Queens Harvest Festival
First Sunday in October, starts at 3pm
St Martin-in-the-Fields, Trafalgar Square, WC2
t (020) 7766 1100
⊖ Charing Cross, Leicester Square
Bus 9, 24, 109
Free

A Harvest Festival with added sequins – London's
East-end community of Pearly Kings and Queens
descends on St Martin-in-the Fields (*see* p.70) on
the first Sunday of the month for an old-fashioned
knees-up.

Children's Book Week
First week of October
t (020) 8516 2977
www.booktrusted.co.uk/cbw

The altruistic leanings of the literary charity, the
Book Trust, combine with the more commercial
concerns of the nation's biggest bookshop chain,
Waterstone's, to produce a week of book-related
events across the UK – readings, author visits,
workshops, etc.

November
London to Brighton Vintage Car Run
First Sunday in November, starts 7.30am
Hyde Park to Brighton
t (01327) 856 024
www.lbvcr.com
⊖ Hyde Park Corner, Marble Arch
Bus 2, 8, 9, 10, 14, 16, 19, 22, 36, 73, 82, 137
Free

Entry to the race is free to all so long as you're in
possession of a car built before 1905. This parade of
clunking, clanking contraptions is one of London's
great annual spectacles. It attracts hordes of car
enthusiasts who come to see them off at the
start (and help fix them once they break down
shortly after).

Bonfire Night
5 November
In parks and recreation grounds across London, *see*
www.visitlondon.com for more details.

Remember, remember the fifth of November...
Parks all over London hold firework displays on this
date to celebrate the capture and execution of Guy
Fawkes and his failure to blow up James I and the

Houses of Parliament (*see* p.99). Some of the
best displays take place at Blackheath (*see* p.153),
Wimbledon Park and Alexandra Palace Park
(*see* p.172).

Lord Mayor's Show
Second Saturday in November, starts at 11am
Mansion House to the Old Bailey
t (020) 7606 3030
www.lordmayorsshow.org
⊖ Mansion House, Blackfriars
Free

The ceremonial parade to mark the beginning
of the Lord Mayor of London's year in office starts
at Mansion House and wends its way to the
Old Bailey. The event ends with a spectacular
firework display over the Thames. With over 5,000
participants and 70 floats, this is one of the
largest street parades of the year. The Lord
Mayor rides at its head in the Lord Mayor's Coach
which, for the rest of the year, is on display in the
Museum of London.

Discover Dogs
Second weekend in November
Earl's Court 2, SW5
t 0870 606 6750
⊖ West Brompton
Bus 190
www.the-kennel-club.org.uk

A sort of more informal version of the Crufts
dog show where you can watch police dog agility
displays, meet 190 different pedigree breeds of dog
and, just to distinguish it from its more illustrious

Still in its relative infancy, having begun in 2005, this is fast becoming a major event offering a mixture of film screenings from around the world (many by young film makers), creative workshops, hands-on events and singalongs. Children also get the chance to judge the films and pick their favourites.

December

Carol Services

December–early January
Trafalgar Square, WC1
⊖ Charing Cross, Leicester Square
Bus 9, 24, 109
Free

Carol singing takes place around the huge Trafalgar Square Christmas tree every evening from early December to early January. The tree itself is lit from dusk till midnight until the twelfth day of Christmas (6 January).

Pantomime Season

Mid-November to mid-February
All over the capital

Come December, a motley collection of retired sportsmen, soap stars and TV magicians will join forces with a host of actors to produce a very old, corny and British institution. For details of performances check out the listings section of the *Evening Standard* or *Time Out*.

Royal Institution Christmas Lectures for Young People

Between Christmas and New Year
21 Albemarle Street, W1
t (020) 7409 2992
www.rigb.org/events/christmaslecture
⊖ Green Park
Bus 8, 9, 14, 19, 22, 38

This prestigious series of lectures has been informing and entertaining schoolchildren (aged 11 and over) on a variety of scientific subjects since the 1820s.

New Year's Eve in Trafalgar Square

The traditional venue for London's end of year bash, Trafalgar Square is within easy listening distance of Big Ben's 12 bongs at midnight. The celebrations can get a little crowded and boisterous and it isn't recommended for young children. Fun though if you can get a babysitter.

rival, watch (or even take part) in the Scruffts Family Cross Breed competition.

The Christmas Lights

Mid-November
Oxford Street, Regent Street and Bond Street

The elaborate street illuminations are turned on in mid-November by a celebrity *du jour* – usually a soap star or pop singer.

Tutankhamun and the Golden Age of the Pharaohs

15 November 2007–30 August 2008
O2 Centre, Drawdock Road, SE10
t (01753) 565 656
www.kingtut.org
⊖ North Greenwich
Boat Thames Clippers run services from Central London to the O2, **t** 0870 781 5049

The glittering treasures of the boy pharaoh – including his golden coffin and lapis lazuli inlaid death mask – are going on display in this country for the first time in over 30 years. The organizers, National Geographic, are hoping that the show will match the hysteria of its early 1970s predecessor when tens of thousands queued up outside the British Museum.

London Children's Film Festival

Third week in November
Barbican, Silk Street, EC2
t (020) 7638 8891
www.londonchildrenfilm.org.uk
⊖ Barbican, Moorgate
Bus 8, 22B, 56
Times Sat 10.30am

CENTRAL LONDON

2 miles

3 kms

HACKNEY

BETHNAL GREEN

SHOREDITCH

WHITE CHAPEL

WAPPING

KINGSLAND RD

WHITE CHAPEL ROAD

COMMERCIAL ROAD

CITY ROAD

CLERKENWELL

ISLINGTON

CALEDONIAN ROAD

THE CITY

Liverpool Street

Museum of London

St Paul's Cathedral

Fenchurch Street

Cannon Street

TOWER BRIDGE ROAD

Tower Bridge

Tower of London

London Bridge

London Dungeon

Globe Theatre

Tate Modern

SOUTHWARK

National Theatre

Royal Festival Hall

Waterloo

Elephant & Castle

GREENWICH

Greenwich Park

National Maritime Museum

Royal Observatory

KENNINGTON

The Oval

LAMBETH

BLOOMSBURY

King's Cross

St Pancras

Euston

British Museum

COVENT GARDEN

Covent Garden

Theatre Museum

London Transport Museum

Charing Cross

National Portrait Gallery

National Gallery

Trafalgar Square

County Hall

London Aquarium

Big Ben

Houses of Parliament

Westminster Abbey

Tate Britain

VAUXHALL BRIDGE RD

PIMLICO

EUSTON RD

OXFORD STREET

SOHO

Piccadilly Circus

PICCADILLY

MAYFAIR

St James's Park

Green Park

Buckingham Palace

Victoria

WESTMINSTER

CAMDEN ROAD

CAMDEN

ST JOHN'S WOOD

AVENUE RD

Primrose Hill

London Zoo

Regent's Park

ALBANY ST

MARYLEBONE RD

Madame Tussaud's/London Auditorium

Paddington

PADDINGTON

BAYSWATER ROAD

KNIGHTSBRIDGE

Kensington Gardens

Hyde Park

KENSINGTON

Science Museum

Victoria & Albert Museum

Natural History Museum

SOUTH KENSINGTON

CHELSEA

CHELSEA EMBANKMENT

Battersea Park

FULHAM ROAD

Regent's Park to Baker Street

Some of the capital's best-loved attractions are grouped around Regent's Park. To the north is London Zoo, which has undergone a thoroughly modern makeover in the past few years in its attempts to provide its inhabitants with nicer living accommodation. To the south is Madame Tussaud's, London's most popular fee-paying attraction, filled with the frozen famous. And you don't need to be a super-sleuth to find the little Sherlock Holmes Museum on Baker Street or the Wallace Collection's imposing frontage in Manchester Square. Then, of course, there's the park itself, where the whole family could easily idle away a whole day boating on the lake, making friends in the playgrounds, or watching a performance at the Open Air Theatre.

Highlights

The Wallace Collection's wheely cart

Watching a show aboard the Puppet Theatre Barge

Mingling with the great apes at London Zoo's Gorilla Kingdom

Key

Numbers correspond to restaurants in 'Where To Eat', p.50

Chalk Farm

CHALK FARM ROAD

Camden Stables

Camden Lock Market

Camden Buck Street Market

London Waterbus Company

CAMDEN HIGH STREET

KENTISH TOWN ROAD

Camden Town

Primrose Hill

AVENUE ROAD

PRINCE ALBERT ROAD

OUTER CIRCLE

London Zoo

Playground

PARKWAY

ALBANY STREET

OUTER CIRCLE

St John's Wood

WELLINGTON ROAD

Regent's Park

Lord's Cricket Ground

ST JOHN'S WOOD ROAD

PARK ROAD

OUTER CIRCLE

Boating Lake

Open Air Theatre

Queen Mary's Gardens

Playground

LISSON GROVE

Sherlock Holmes Museum

GLOUCESTER PL

BAKER STREET

Baker Street

OUTER CIRCLE

Regents Park

EUSTON ROAD

Portland Street

PORTLAND PL

Marylebone

MARYLEBONE ROAD

Madame Tussaud's/ London Auditorium

500 metres
500 yards

Edgware Road

EDGWARE ROAD

PADDINGTON ST

WEYMOUTH STREET

MARYLEBONE HIGH ST

BLANDFORD ST

Wallace Collection

BAKER STREET

SUSSEX GARDENS

London Zoo

Regent's Park, NW1
t (020) 7722 3333
www.zsl.org/zsl-london-zoo
⊖ Camden Town or Baker Street, then 274 bus
Bus 274, C2
Open Mar–Oct 10–5.30 daily; Nov–April 10–4 daily
Adm Adult £16.50, child (under 16) £11, under-3s
free, concs £13, family £45.50
*Wheelchair accessible for most areas, adapted
toilets, disabled parking bays by the entrance
First-aid post in the centre of the zoo
Suitable for all ages
Allow a morning or afternoon, or even a whole day*

London Zoo is home to thousands of animals –
lions, giraffes, pythons, meerkats, komodo dragons,
zebras, anteaters, hippopotamuses, penguins,
camels ... the list goes on – and has been a main-
stay of school trips and family outings for years.
However, it has been undergoing something of a
transformation of late, redesigning many of its
enclosures with the aim, not just of giving the
animals more and better space, but of recasting
the relationship between the zoo's inhabitants and
its visitors. To this end, the zoo has, where possible,
tried to remove (literally) the barriers separating
animals from humans. At its hugely popular 'Meet
the Monkeys' exhibition, visitors are invited to
come inside a 1,500-square-metre squirrel monkey
enclosure to watch the hyperactive mammals
scamper, jump and climb their way around from
close quarters. At the Clore Rainforest biome, you
can enter the damp jungle environment itself
(contained beneath a transparent roof) to get the
best view of marmosets and golden tamarins in
the canopy. However, the best example of the 'New
London Zoo', is undoubtedly the new multi-million
pound Gorilla Kingdom, where a sizable swathe of
prime zoo real estate has been transformed into an
'African jungle clearing' inhabited by three gorillas
and a troop of colobus monkeys. Visitors observe
the gorillas by following a path through the enclosure, thus gaining unobstructed views of the great
apes as they go about their lives in (so it's hoped)
as natural a way as possible. It's the zoo's expecta-
tion that these more comfortable surroundings
will in time help the gorillas do what comes
naturally, and make more gorillas. After all, this
is ultimately the zoo's best way of justifying its
existence in the modern world.

The zoo has run a very successful captive
breeding programme for some time now and has
played an important part in reintroducing many
endangered species back into the wild. This doesn't
mean that the zoo has become dry and scientific,
however. It takes its role as an educator very seriously and understands that the best way to get
children interested in something is by entertaining
and involving them.

The Original Jumbo

Perhaps London Zoo's most famous inmate
was Jumbo the elephant, who in the 19th
century became an international star. He was
brought to the zoo from Africa in 1865, as a
baby, but by the 1870s had transformed into a
mighty beast standing some 4m high and
weighing over 6 tonnes – the largest elephant
in captivity. You might think that he had quite
an appropriate name, but, in fact, at that time
the word 'Jumbo' didn't mean anything at all.
It was simply a misspelled version of the
Swahili word 'Jambo', which means 'hello'.
Such was Jumbo's fame (and, of course, his
size) that soon anything overwhelmingly large
came to be known as 'Jumbo-sized'. In 1882 the
zoo sold him to the American Circus owner, P. T.
Barnum, but Jumbo died a few years later when
he refused to get out of the way of a train.

Jumbo still draws the crowds today, however
– his huge skeleton is on display at the
Museum of Natural History in New York.

Every day the zoo organizes demonstrations and talks. Turn up at feeding time and you can watch pelicans and penguins gobbling their way through buckets of fish or a snake slowly swallowing a rat – whole.

Spectacular animal shows are held in three special demonstration areas: you can see lemurs and parrots leaping, climbing and flying during the Animals in Action presentations in the Amphitheatre (usually at 2.30pm) while, on the display lawn, there are regular exhibitions (usually at 2pm) of aerobatic skill by the zoo's birds of prey – keepers will throw pieces of meat into the air for them to swoop down and catch. At the new Happy Families area you can watch animals who live in large groups – meerkats, otters, marmosets etc – playing together in a terribly cute way. Look out, in particular, here for the pygmy marmoset, which, at just 11–15cm tall, is the world's smallest monkey.

It's all very impressive, but your children will no doubt be itching to get involved in a more hands-on way. Take them to the Children's Zoo where, in the Touch Paddock, they can stroke and pet the resident sheep, goats and wallabies and help feed the pigs. To really get into the swing of things, kids can even have their faces painted to look like a lizard, a butterfly or (easily the most popular choice) a tiger. Be sure to visit the tiger enclosure in the main zoo. Stand at the round window when they're on the prowl and you may find yourself just a few inches away from these fearsome beasts.

Even on rainy days, the zoo is still worth visiting. While the animals in the outdoor enclosures take cover, you can do the same at the Aquarium, the Reptile House or B.U.G.S., an imaginative exhibition which aims to demonstrate how various animals and organisms combine to form ecosystems. You can see examples of different habitats from around the world and discover how the resident animals have adapted themselves to their surroundings; how butterflies camouflage themselves against tree bark; how dung beetles use the material other animals reject – watch them carefully rolling their precious balls of dung – and how leafcutter ant societies operate with military-like precision. Even the tanks housing the exhibits are interesting. Several have magnifying lenses built into the glass to allow you to look at tiny organisms in greater detail, while others are shaped like helmets, enabling you to immerse yourself in the animals' environment. Kids are specially catered for at the Activity Den where they can take part in a broad range of crafts including brass rubbing and badge making.

The zoo has a central relaxation area with a café, gift shop, fountain and a small children's carousel. There are also several playgrounds dotted about

Can you spot?
Many of the animals in the zoo have managed to adapt themselves to their surroundings. Just as a chameleon will subtly change the colour of its skin, so other creatures have learned to blend in with the environment around them. Can you find any examples at the zoo?

with slides and climbing frames. In the summer there's usually a bouncy castle.

Regent's Canal Trip

Perhaps the most novel way to arrive at London Zoo is aboard a canal boat. The London Waterbus Company runs a service from Little Venice along Regent's Canal to Camden Lock, stopping off at the Zoo on the way. You get a reduction on the price of admission with your ticket.

London Waterbus Company

50 Camden Lock Place
t (020) 7482 2660
www.londonwaterbus.com
⊖ Camden Town, Chalk Farm
Bus 6, 46
April–Oct daily service, boats run hourly from 10–5; Nov–Mar weekends only
Fares Adult single £6, return £8.40; child single £4.30, return £5.40, under-4s **free**; combined canal trip and zoo visit adult £16.50, child £13.50, under-4s **free**

Jason's Traditional Canal Boat Trips

opposite 60 Blomfield Road, Little Venice
t (020) 7286 3428
www.jasons.co.uk
⊖ Warwick Avenue
Bus 6, 46
Daily service at 10.30, 12.30 and 2.30, with an extra service at 4.30 on weekends June–Aug
Fares Adult single £6.50, return £7.50; under-14s single £5.50, return £6.50, under-4s **free**

Jenny Wren

250 Camden High Street, NW1
t (020) 7485 4433
www.walkersquay.com/jennywren.html
⊖ Camden Town, Chalk Farm
Bus 24, 27, 29, 31, 74, 134, 135, 168, 214, 253, C2
Apr–Oct daily service 12.30, 2.30 and 4.30; extra service at 10.30 during Aug
Fares Adult £8, child £4, under-3s **free**, family £20

Madame Tussaud's

Marylebone Road, NW1
t 0870 999 0293
www.madame-tussauds.co.uk
⊖ Baker Street
Bus 3, 13, 18, 27, 30, 74, 82, 113, 274
Open 9–5.30 daily (till 6 weekend and school hols)
Adm Prices vary according to the time of day, ranging from adult £17.50, child (under-16) £10 for late entry (after 5pm) to adult £22.50, child £18.50 for early entry (9–5). Under-5s **free**
No pushchairs allowed; baby carriers are provided.
Wheelchair accessible, although advance booking is recommended, adapted toilets
Suitable for all ages, apart from Chamber of Horrors, which is only suitable for older children (over 8)
Allow at least 1hr

It's strange how this collection of waxen doppelgängers has become one of London's most popular tourist attractions. As famous as it is, with queues that regularly stretch right round the block, it's difficult not to come to the conclusion that it's all a little bit stupid – it's just a load of mannequins, after all, dolled up to look like famous people. It doesn't pay to be too snooty about Madame Tussaud's, however. Whatever its unfathomable attractions may be, your kids understand them and will undoubtedly have a whale of a time, running around pointing at all the famous faces and demanding to have their

Did you know?
If you buy a ticket on the web, you can bypass the massive queues that are always standing outside Madame Tussaud's with a fast-track timed entry ticket. You can also get a fast-track combination ticket for Mme Tussaud's and the London Eye at www.ba-londoneye.com, which includes a £3 discount.

picture taken with David Beckham, Tom Cruise or the Queen.

To their credit, the organizers have done their best to invest proceedings with a little excitement with lots of interactive computer screens, a replica Big Brother diary room and a music zone where kids can warble along with the stars (including Robbie Williams and Christina Aguilera). The authorities also show a commendably relaxed policy towards guests interacting (i.e. groping) the waxworks, a practise which tends to be at its most blatant in the 'Blush, A-List celebrity party', an event at which you can mingle with the frozen doubles of Brad Pitt, J-Lo and Leonardo DiCaprio.

The nature of the exhibition means the displays are constantly changing with new waxworks of rising stars regularly added, while those of celebrities whose fame is on the wane are ruthlessly axed. Recent additions include Johnny Depp, Orlando Bloom and Keira Knightley in a 'Pirates of the Caribbean' exhibition and a fourth incarnation of Kylie Minogue, now complete with smell (of her own perfume). The most well thought out section is probably the Spirit of London Ride where you are carried in a mock-up 'Time Taxi' through representations of London history from Elizabethan times to the present day, although your kids' favourite section will inevitably be the Chamber of Horrors, with its collection of grisly exhibits (for some reason yet to be explained, all children are fixated

Tell me a story: Max wax

Madame Marie Tussaud was born in France in 1761. When just six years old she was taken by her uncle to Paris, where he instructed her in the art of modelling anatomical figures. By her early twenties, Marie had become so accomplished that she was hired to give art lessons to Louis XVI's children at Versailles; something which, in any other era, would have set her up for life. Unfortunately for her, in 1789 France underwent the Revolution – the monarchy was abolished, the King was executed and Marie, suspected of having Royalist sympathies, was thrown into jail and only released on condition that she attend public executions and sculpt the death masks of the Revolution's more celebrated victims.

In 1802, following a failed marriage, she emigrated to England, taking her two children and 35 of her models with her. To make ends meet, she was forced to tour her waxwork gallery of heroes, rogues, victims and confidence tricksters around the country until, in 1835, a permanent home was found for them in London's Baker Street. By 1850, the year Madame died, 'Tussaud's' was sufficiently well known for the Duke of Wellington to have become a regular visitor. He was especially taken with the Chamber of Horrors and left instructions that he should be informed whenever a new figure was added to its gruesome ranks.

By 1884 the exhibition (now managed by Madame's sons) had grown to over 400 models, forcing it to move to new premises in Marylebone Road, where it has stayed ever since. Madame's last work, a rather eerie self-portrait, is still on display in the Grand Hall.

with blood, gore and mayhem) where 'live shows' are now put on featuring an array of gruesomely attired actors.

The adjacent Stardome (formerly the London Planetarium), set beneath a distinctive green dome, has been revamped over the past year and has now been incorporated into the

Question 2
Can you name the eight planets that orbit our sun, starting with the nearest?
answer on p.250

main Madame Tussaud's site. Its latest show, 'The Wonderful World of Stars' was produced by Aardman Animations, who were also responsible for the Wallace and Gromit films. It's a 'comic' look at aliens visiting Earth which will probably appeal to kids, but will hold less interest for parents than the old virtual reality rides through the cosmos which used to be shown here.

Regent's Park

t (020) 7298 2000
www.royalparks.gov.uk/parks/regents_park
✆ Baker Street, Great Portland Street, Regent's Park, Camden Town and then 274 bus
Bus 2, 13, 18, 27, 30, 74, 82, 113, 135, 139, 159, 189, 274, C2
Open 5am to dusk daily
Free
Suitable for all ages

One of London's great parks, Regent's Park has masses going on. There's the boating lake, home to a mass of wildfowl including ducks, moorhens and black swans, where you can hire a rowing boat and take to the water yourself. There are four play-grounds (open daily from 10.30am), complete with toilets solely for the use of children (facilities for parents are separate, usually grouped around a refreshment kiosk or café), sand pits, swings and play equipment. Sporty types, meanwhile, can make use of the tennis courts and several cricket and football pitches. In the centre are the neatly

manicured Queen Mary's Gardens, best visited in summer when you'll find bed upon bed of wonderful, colourful roses. The gardens also house the Open Air Theatre (one of the most enlivening places to introduce your children to the works of Shakespeare), an ornamental lake, a sunken garden and a fountain depicting a man blowing water out of a conch shell. As a further attraction, the park authorities have special activities for families, including 'peregrine falcon watch' days (a pair nest each year on top of a tower block next to the park) and late night 'bat walks' and 'owl prowls' (the park is home to a couple of dozen nesting pairs). For more details **t** (020) 7298 2000.

Open Air Theatre

Regent's Park, NW1
t 0870 060 1811
www.openairtheatre.org
Adm tickets for daytime performances start at £10 (rising to £31); tickets for family shows are a flat rate £12

This respected theatre company celebrated its 25th anniversary in 2007 and usually puts on a child-friendly show during the summer holidays (in 2007, it was the 'Fantastic Mr Fox') as well as a selection from Shakespeare (it's home to the New Shakespeare Company) and a quality musical.

Sherlock Holmes Museum

221b Baker Street, NW1
t (020) 7935 8866
www.sherlock-holmes.co.uk
✆ Baker Street
Bus 13, 18, 27, 30, 74, 82, 113, 159, 274
Open 9.30–6 daily
Adm Adult £6, child £4. Under-5s **free**
No disabled facilities. Suitable for all ages although older children will get the most out of it
Allow at least 30mins

It all depends whether your children know who Sherlock Holmes is. The older ones (10 and over) may well and if, by chance, they are actually fans of Conan Doyle's classic detective, they will be completely bowled over by this little museum. It is a fictional address, of course, No.221 is actually the Abbey Building Society, where a secretary is employed purely to tackle the thousands of letters sent to the great detective each year.

On entering the museum you are met by a 19th-century 'Bobby' and shown round the house by a

Victorian maid. The rooms have been faithfully recreated (or should that be 'created') according to the descriptions in the book. Afterwards you can have a cream tea at Mrs Hudson's Old English Restaurant next door (Mrs Hudson was Holmes's housekeeper in the books). Opposite the museum is a memorabilia shop.

The Wallace Collection

Hertford House, Manchester Square, W1
t (020) 7563 9500
www.wallacecollection.org
⊖ Bond Street, Marble Arch
Bus 2, 10, 12, 13, 30, 74, 82, 94, 113, 137, 274
Open 10–5 daily
Free
Wheelchair accessible. Suitable for children over 5, under-8s must be accompanied at all times. Allow at least 1hr

Hertford House, the former home of the Wallace family – 19th-century art collectors *extraordinaire* – is probably not the first place that springs to mind when thinking of somewhere to take the family. After all, looking at one of the country's most important collections of French 18th-century art is not every child's idea of a great day out. However, you'd be surprised. The conservators have made a real effort to involve children in the gallery, offering trails (with titles such as 'Warrior Kings' and 'Looking for the Owners') and running a full programme of holiday activities. So, while parents

examine the Sèvres porcelain, priceless furniture and suits of armour, kids may be able to enjoy a puppet show, take an art tour, try on a suit of armour or try their hand at papier-mâché mask making, mobile-hanging or collage-making. The gallery also organizes various themed special events (such as their 'Taste of Tudor London Day') where kids can try on historical costumes and handle some of the gallery's extensive collection of weapons (under supervision).

The museum underwent a millennial refurbishment resulting in four new galleries, a new education centre, a new restaurant, Café Bagatelle, which offers a children's menu, and, its most stunning feature, a new glass roof spanning its central courtyard which has been turned into an all-weather sculpture garden and looks a bit like a miniature version of the British Museum's Great Court.

London Canal Museum

12–13 New Wharf Road, N1
t (020) 7713 0836; www.canalmuseum.org.uk
King's Cross
Bus 10, 17, 30, 45, 46, 63, 73, 91, 205, 214, 259, 390, 476, A2
Free mooring is available outside the museum for canal boats
Open Tues–Sun 10–4.30 (last entry 3.45), open Bank Hol Mons, till 7.30 first Thurs of month
Adm Adult £3, child £1.50, under-5s **free**
Wheelchair accessible, with adapted toilets. Suitable for children aged 6 and over. Allow at least 1hr

That rare thing, a museum that makes children appreciate their parents! In the 19th century, 'canal kids' put in 18-hour days leading barge horses along tow paths, opening locks and cleaning the boats. At night, they slept on rough wooden benches. This evocative museum tells their story and the story of everyone who tried to make a living ferrying cargo along London's industrial canals. Kids can explore a painted narrow boat, find out about canal life on touch-screen computers and explore the Activity Zone on the ground floor. On a different tack, they can also see a display on the history of ice cream – the museum is housed in a Victorian warehouse that was used to store ice cream, frozen in the basement on huge blocks of ice imported from Norway.

The museum can provide free trails, which get the kids hunting all over the museum for images of 'Henrietta the Horse', and organizes occasional activity days for children aged 6–12, usually involving painting or model-making, when kids may be able to take a boat trip on the canal.

Lord's Cricket Ground

St John's Wood Road, NW8
t (020) 7676 8500; www.lords.org
St John's Wood then bus
Bus 13, 46, 82, 113, 139, 189, 274
Tour April–Sept 10am, 12 noon and 2pm daily, Oct–Mar 12 noon and 2pm daily. No tours during Test Matches or Cup Finals
Adm Tickets for matches from £10; tours: adult £10, child £6, under-5s **free**, family £27
Limited wheelchair access, call above number. Suitable for all ages. The tour lasts 1hr 30mins

If your children like cricket, they'll enjoy a tour of Lord's (or the Marylebone Cricket Club, to give it its official title), cricket's official HQ. Take a walk through the famous longroom, find out about the great

Question 3
What are the Ashes?
answer on p.250

W. G. Grace and look at the Ashes Urn, the Holy Grail of cricket (which, despite having been won by Australia nine times out of the last ten, remains permanently in English hands). You can also visit the Real Tennis Court.

Puppet Theatre Barge

Blomfield Road, Little Venice, W9
t (020) 7249 6876
www.puppetbarge.com
Warwick Avenue
Bus 6, 46
Open Varies, phone ahead
Adm Adult £8.50, child £8
Some wheelchair access by arrangement. Suitable for all ages

A small puppet theatre on an old Thames barge. From October to May, you can see a show at Little Venice, to the south of Regent's Park. In summer it sails the Thames putting on performances.

Primrose Hill

If you didn't manage to get your fill of green spaces down in Regent's Park, walk up the hill for some fantastic views over the city. The summit was

the setting for the twilight barking in Dodie Smith's *One Hundred and One Dalmatians*, and the area is very popular with families, both canine and human. Regent's Park Road runs adjacent and is good for browsing in book and gift shops.

WHERE TO SHOP

Camden's markets

⊖ Camden Town, Chalk Farm
Bus 24, 27, 29, 134, 135, 168, 214, 253, 274, C2

Older children will enjoy a visit to Camden's bustling weekend markets. The Camden Stables is a casbah-like warren of clothes and fashion stalls; the Lock is craft-based, while Camden (Buck Street) Market is probably the least interesting – it sells an assorted mixture of clothes, jewellery and general whatnots. In between the markets themselves is an assortment of funky fashion shops, restaurants, pubs and music venues. Come early before the crowds arrive, unless you are willing to let your children mingle with the broadest cross-section of society imaginable spilling out from Camden Town Tube station.

Camden Stables

Off Chalk Farm Road, opposite junction with Hartland Road, NW1
t (020) 7485 8355
www.camdenlock.net/stables
Open Sat, Sun 8–6, though some shops stay open throughout the week

Sells secondhand and designer clothes, jewellery, antiques, books, crafts, furniture, candles, souvenirs, games, memorabilia and old toys. It pays to have a good rummage, for within this extremely popular mishmash of stalls and huts are ones dedicated to musical instruments, street fashions and accessories, plus plenty of places to get yourself tattooed or pierced (over-18s only, of course). There's also a great maze of food stalls selling noodles, curry, falafel and more noodles.

Camden Lock

Camden Lock Place, off Chalk Farm Road, NW1
t (020) 7284 2084
www.camdenlock.net
Open Sat, Sun 10–6; some stalls stay open throughout the week

Situated on the riverbank, this collection of yards sells craft goods, books, designer clothes, jewellery, food, mirrors, furniture, musical instruments, hand-made soaps, didgeridoos, hand-woven hammocks and sculptures. Thursdays and Fridays see an influx of bric-a-brac, and there's fresh farm produce in abundance on Fridays, too.

Camden (Buck Street) Market

Camden High Street, at junction with Buck Street, NW1
t (020) 7938 4343
Open 9–5.30, daily

The seventies revivalist's dream – the market stalls are brimming with secondhand clothes, plus jewellery, leather belts, handbags and CDs, fruit and veg, as well as a good selection of leather and suede jackets.

Did you know?
The Regent's Canal was opened in 1820 to link the Grand Junction Canal at Paddington with the River Thames at Limehouse, enabling goods to be moved more easily from the industrial Midlands to the London docks. A bridge used by the barge horses to cross the canal still survives and is one route into the market.

WHERE TO EAT

Picnics & snacks

There's no better spot for a picnic than **Regent's Park**. Supplies can be picked up south of the park, from **Waitrose**, 98–101 Marylebone High Street, W1, t (020) 7935 4787, ⊖ Baker Street; and north of the park, from the organic store **Fresh and Wild**, at 49 Parkway, NW1, t (020) 7428 7575, ⊖ Camden Town.

For a quick bite and a drink, there's **Patisserie Valerie**, 105 Marylebone High Street, W1, t (020) 7935 6240, ⊖ Baker Street, a French-style café serving sticky treats; the **Bagatelle Café** in the Wallace Collection, which offers a children's menu, Manchester Square, W1, t (020) 7563 9500, ⊖ Bond Street, and, located in the terribly grand surrounds of the Royal Institute of British architects, the **RIBA Café**, 66 Portland Place, W1, t (020) 7631 0467, ⊖ Regent's Park, which has a nice (and safe) roof terrace. There are also a couple of good cafés in **Regent's Park** itself, including the **Garden Café** in Queen Mary's Gardens, W1, t (020) 7935 5729, ⊖ Baker Street, and **Honest Sausage**, on the central boardwalk, which serves tasty organic sausage and bacon rolls, as well as a decent self-service café, **Oasis**, in London Zoo. **The Stables** in Camden Market also houses stalls offering takeaway Thai, Chinese and Indian food.

Restaurants

1 Belgo Noord
72 Chalk Farm Road, NW1
t (020) 7267 0718
⊖ Chalk Farm
Open Mon–Fri 12 noon–3 and 5.30–11, Sat 12 noon–11.30, Sun 12 noon–10.30

2 Daphne
83 Bayham Street, NW1
t (020) 7267 7322
www.belgo-restaurants.com
⊖ Camden Town
Open Mon–Sat 12 noon–2.30 and 6–11.30

3 The Engineer
65 Gloucester Avenue, NW1
t (020) 7722 0950
www.the-engineer.com
⊖ Chalk Farm

Open Mon–Fri 12 noon–3 and 7–11, Sat–Sun 12.30–3.30 and 7–11

4 Giraffe
6–8 Blandford Street, W1
t (020) 7935 2333
www.giraffe.net
⊖ Baker Street
Open 8am–11.30pm daily

5 Manna
4 Erskine Road, NW1
t (020) 7722 8028
www.manna-veg.com
⊖ Chalk Farm
Open Mon–Sat 6pm–11pm, Sun 12.30–3 and 6–11

6/7/8 Pizza Express
Branches at 133 Baker Street, t (020) 7486 0888, ⊖ Baker Street
Open daily 11.30am–12 midnight
85 Parkway, t (020) 7267 2600, ⊖ Camden Town
Open Sun–Thurs 11.30am–11pm, Fri–Sat 11.30am–12 midnight
13–14 Thayer Street, W1, t (020) 7935 2167, ⊖ Baker Street
Open Mon–Sat 11.30am–11pm, Sun 12 noon–10pm
www.pizzaexpress.com

9 Royal China
40 Baker Street, W1
t (020) 7487 4688
www.royalchinagroup.co.uk
⊖ Baker Street
Open Mon–Thurs 12 noon–11pm, Fri & Sat 12 noon–11.30pm, Sun 11–10

10 Seashell
49–51 Lisson Grove, NW1
t (020) 7224 9000
www.seashellrestaurant.co.uk
⊖ Marylebone
Open Mon–Fri 12 noon–2.30 and 5–10.30, Sat 12 noon–10.30

See **Eat** pp.224–36 for more details on the above restaurants.
See map on p.41 for the locations of the restaurants numbered above.

British Museum to Oxford Street

There's a huge amount to see and do here. To the east is the British Museum, filled with antiquities from around the globe, while to the west lies London's main shopping hub – Oxford Street, Regent Street and Bond Street – one of the best retail districts in Europe. Be sure to time your trip carefully, however. This whole district is fiercely popular, and on summer weekends or at Christmas the streets can become choked with people.

Thankfully, there are a few well-placed small museums, such as Pollock's Toy Museum, to nip into if you need to escape the throng. All in all, there really are few better places to come for an informative day out or a frenzied shopping spree.

Highlights

Exploring the British Museum's Egyptian galleries

Discovering a world of vintage toys at Pollock's Toy Museum

Watching the new toy demonstrations in Hamleys

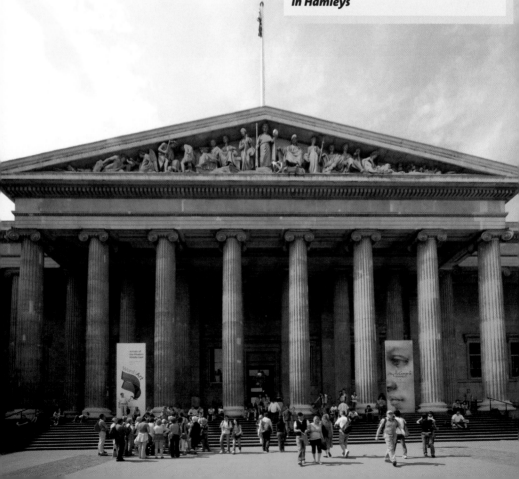

53

Key

Numbers correspond to restaurants in 'Where To Eat', pp.61–2

British Museum

Great Russell Street, WC1
t (020) 7323 8000
Access information **t** (020) 7323 8506
www.thebritishmuseum.ac.uk
⊖ Tottenham Court Road, Russell Square, Holborn
Bus 1, 7, 8, 10, 14, 19, 24, 25, 29, 38, 55, 59, 68, 73, 91, 98, 134, 168, 188, 242, 390, X68
Open 10–5.30 daily, till late Thurs and Fri
Free a £2 donation is recommended; charges apply for some temporary exhibitions
Wheelchair accessible, with adapted toilets. Suitable for all ages, but particularly older children, museum shops (see p.61)
Allow at least a couple of hours

With a collection built up largely during the days of empire when Britain controlled (and considered it her right to plunder the property of) much of the globe, this is one of the world's great museums. In fact, there's so much to look at here that you couldn't hope to do it all in one, or even two, trips. Instead, it's probably best to plan your route around a few must-see exhibits, rather than trying to see everything. Your journey begins at the grand neoclassical entrance on Great Russell Street, from where it's a short walk to the bright, wide open expanse of the museum's central courtyard, known as the Great Court. Topped with a 6,000 square metre glass roof, this is the largest covered public square in Europe and provides a fittingly impressive introduction to the wonders ahead. From here, you can choose from a number of routes into the main galleries: head west for Egyptian Sculpture, east for the impossibly huge King's Library and north for the Wellcome Wing of Ethnography. Inside the courtyard, two massive staircases lead up to the restaurant from where a bridge takes you into the museum's upper galleries.

Did you know?
The British Museum is now over 250 years old. It was the first museum in the country ever to open its doors to members of the general public.

Did you know?
In the early years of the ancient Egyptian kingdom, only the rich could afford to be mummified but, in later times almost everyone was able to afford it. So many mummies were dug up in Egypt in the 1800s that people started using the bodies as fuel and the bandages to make paper.

Whatever route you choose, however, you won't go far wrong if you take your children to the ever-popular Ancient Egyptian Galleries (rooms 62–66) on the first floor. Here, they'll immediately be captivated by the huge gold sarcophagi, the brightly coloured frescoes and, of course, the mummies. The Egyptians, it seems, had a bit of a thing about mummification and these 2,000-year-old dead bodies hold a strange fascination for kids. As well as people, you'll find mummified cats, fish and cattle.

Elsewhere, look out for the enormous (11-m high) early 19th-century totem pole that stands by the North Stairs; Lindow Man, the perfectly preserved, leathery remains of a 2,000-year-old Briton (room 35); and the great fat, smiling, ceramic Buddhas in the Oriental gallery (room 33).

The British Museum's other famous exhibits include the controversial Elgin Marbles (room 8), the frieze reliefs from the Parthenon in Athens which, depending on whom you believe, were either rescued or stolen by Lord Elgin, British Ambassador to the Ottoman Empire, in 1802; the

Rosetta Stone (room 25), an ancient tablet with the same decree inscribed upon it in three languages, which allowed Egyptian hieroglyphics to be deciphered for the first time; and the Sutton Hoo Treasure (room 41), a jewel-encrusted collection of Saxon swords, helmets, bowls and buckles.

The museum produces a number of free trails and activity backpacks on subjects such as 'Ancient Egypt' and 'Roman Britain', which are available from the Paul Hamlyn Library on the ground floor. You can also pick up a 'family audio tour' from here, featuring the voice of Stephen Fry. The museum organizes free events for families throughout the year, including 'Family eye-opener tours' for ages six and over, which are held during the school holidays.

Do remember, when planning your trip, that the British Museum is a vast place and there's always the danger it can turn into a huge blurry mass for many children, especially the younger ones. So be sure to reserve some time for quiet contemplation in the courtyard. And, before you even set off, it's well worth taking a few minutes to explore the museum website as it has a number of resources for children, including puzzles and games, and runs drawing competitions with the best entries displayed on the website.

How to make a mummy

The ancient Egyptians believed that every human was made up of a *ka* (spirit) and a *ba* (body). When a person died, they could only enter the afterlife if their body had not decayed – hence the fascination with preservation through mummification.

The key to a successful mummification is to dry out the body as quickly and as thoroughly as possible. Remember, the body is 75 per cent water and, in a hot climate such as Egypt's, anything wet or damp rots very quickly. Embalmers used natron, a chemical that occurs naturally in Egypt, to suck the moisture out of the body. The eyes and most of the internal organs, including the brain, kidneys and liver, were taken out. The brain was removed through a nostril, a chisel having first been wiggled around inside the skull cavity to mash it into small pieces. The brain would then be thrown away (for some reason the Egyptians didn't think it would be particularly useful in the afterlife). All the other organs, however, were stored safely inside jars and buried with the body, ready for the post-life journey. The skull and body cavities were filled with a mixture of natron and plaster, and the eyes

The Olympics: Then and Now

The Olympic Games, one of the world's most popular sporting events which will be coming to London in 2012, originated thousands of years ago in Greece. In the British Museum's Greek and Roman Antiquities Galleries, several items (including pots, statues and friezes) show images of the ancient games, giving you the chance to see how similar and how different they were from today's games.

▶ As with the modern games, the ancient games were held every four years. Although other cities held their own games, the most renowned were always held in the same location – Olympia.

▶ The modern games have been going for a long time. When the games are held in London, in 2012, it will be 116 years since the first of the modern Olympics. The ancient games, by comparison, went on for a really long time. The first took place in 771 BC, the last in AD 393. In other words, the ancient games were in continuous existence for 1,164 years.

▶ The modern games feature many of the same events as the old, including sprinting, long jump, discus, javelin, wrestling, etc., albeit with the odd rule change. For instance, in Ancient Greece long-jumpers took off from a standing start and swung heavy weights in their hands to build up momentum. Now jumpers are allowed a run-up (but no weights).

▶ Women were not only banned from competing in the ancient games, but could be put to death if caught watching.

▶ The modern Olympics has seen the introduction of gold, silver and bronze medals awarded for 1st, 2nd and 3rd place. Ancient athletes were awarded a simple laurel wreath, although songs were also sometimes written and performed in their honour.

▶ As important as winning is to the modern athlete, it was much more important in ancient Greece. Winners were exempt from local taxes and often had statues erected in their honour, while losers could be whipped if their performance was particularly bad.

▶ The modern Olympics prides itself on spectacle, but there were certain sights available to ancient eyes that the modern games will never match. For one, all athletes in Ancient Greece competed in the nude. Today, athletes do the next best thing and cover their bodies in the most figure-hugging, aerodynamic material available.

Make friends

The Museum's youth club, 'Young Friends of the British Museum', meets every Sunday. Members are entitled to free entry to all exhibitions and access to a special 'Friends and Family' room, plus preferential admission to a range of special events. These include walking tours through the city and behind-the-scenes visits to see items not usually seen by the public, as well as the hugely popular 'Sleepover' nights, which take place four times a year, when kids (up to four plus one adult) can spend the night in amongst the museum's treasures enjoying games, workshops and bedtime stories. Each night is themed around a part of the collection – 'African Sleepover', 'Egyptian Sleepover', etc. Kids will also receive the museum's youth magazine 'ReMus' three times a year. Annual membership costs £20.

replaced with small stones (or, in the case of the unlucky Rameses IV, with two small onions) in order to stop them from becoming sunken. Only the heart was left inside the body; this would have to be weighed in the afterlife against the 'Feather of Truth'. If the feather proved heavier, the heart would be eaten by a monster known as the

'Devourer' and the dead person would be prevented from completing their journey.

Once the body was dry, it was wrapped in bandages. Sometimes over 300 yards of bandages were used, with charms written on pieces of papyrus slipped between the folds. The mummy would then be put into its coffin or sarcophagus and entombed, but not before its mouth had been opened to make sure it could breathe and talk in the afterlife – although, without a brain, conversation was presumably limited.

Cartoon Museum

35 Little Russell Street, WC1
t (020) 7580 8155
www.cartooncentre.com
Θ Tottenham Court Road, Holborn
Bus 8, 25, 59, 68, 91, 168
Open Tues–Sat 10.30–5.30, Sun 12–5.30
Adm Adult £4.50, child £2 (**free** on Saturdays and for family events), concs £3.50
Drop-in cartoon workshops £12 per child

Don't get too excited. This new museum is primarily dedicated to showcasing still cartoons – and political cartoons at that (Hogarth, Steadman etc), rather than the big screen Disney-style extravaganzas your children may be expecting. However, kids will like the displays of Britsh comics – there are examples going back to the 1930s – and the museum organizes workshops and events for would-be caricaturists and animators (aged 8 and up) in the school holidays. The best examples go on display in the Young Cartoonists gallery.

Charles Dickens Museum

48 Doughty Street
t (020) 7405 2127
www.dickensmuseum.com
Θ Chancery Lane, Russell Square
Bus 7, 17, 19, 38, 45, 46, 55, 243
Open Mon–Sat 10–5, Sun 11–5, closed Bank Holidays
Adm Adult £5, child (5–15) £3, family £14

Despite Dickens being a bit of a gadabout – much of the south coast lays more or less spurious claim to a pub where he once supped or scribbled, – he did manage to write a fair bit within the walls of this house, now a museum to his literary life. Although only his home for the first two years of his marriage, it was here that Dickens finished *The*

Pickwick Papers, and went on to write *Oliver Twist*, *Nicholas Nickleby*, *The Old Curiosity Shop* and *Barnaby Rudge*. As the sole survivor of Dickens' London residences, the museum is chock-full of memorabilia and paintings, and the drawing room has been restored to its mid-1800s state. Special family events are organized throughout the year. Some are craft-based – kids can learn how to write with a quill pen – while others take the form of storytelling sessions, often featuring tales from one of the author's lesser-known works, 'A Child's History of England'. Trails can be picked up from the front desk.

Handel House Museum

25 Brook Street, W1
t (020) 7495 1685
www.handelhouse.org
⊖ Bond Street, Oxford Circus
Open Mon–Sat 10–6, (till 8pm Thurs), Sun 12–6
Adm Adult £5, child £2, under-5s **free** (all children go **free** on Saturdays)
Wheelchair accessible, with disabled toilets.
Audio guide, shop

This was the home of the composer from 1723 until his death in 1759. He used the house as a recital room and a ticket office, besides writing *The Messiah* and many operas on the premises. The house contains works of art relating to the composer's life and times and has been refurbished with items of furniture based on an inventory of his possessions. A handling collection, a children's activity pack (ages 6–12) and costumed actors (some weekends, call for details) are all on hand to bring Handel's world to life and give young visitors a taste of 18th-century living. Musical workshops, storytellings and recitals aimed at a family audience are also put on during the school holidays. Rock fans take note, the next-door house was the London home of the legendary guitarist, Jimi Hendrix. His flat has been incorporated into the museum.

Petrie Museum of Egyptian Archaeology

Malet Place, WC1
t (020) 7679 2884
www.petrie.ucl.ac.uk
⊖ Goodge Street

Bus 10, 29, 73, 134
Open Tues–Fri 1–5, Sat 10–1
Free

Part of University College, London, this hidden gem may well inspire your children to get digging out in the back garden. The assembled artefacts were bequeathed to the University by Sir Flinders Petrie in 1933, following his excavations in Egypt. Among them are assorted pieces of jewellery and the oldest piece of cloth in the world (*c.* 2800 BC). Mummy enthusiasts will love the 4,500-year-old pot burial and the Egyptian version of a Barbie makeover mannequin – complete with real eyebrows, lashes and a big hairdo. In summer, families can pick up a backpack and follow the trail back in time to the ancient Valley of the Kings.

Pollock's Toy Museum

1 Scala Street, W1
t (020) 7636 3452
www.pollockstoymuseum.com
⊖ Goodge Street, Warren Street
Bus 10, 24, 29, 73, 134
Open Mon–Sat 10am–5pm; last entry 4.30pm
Adm Adult £3, child (under 18) £1.50
No disabled facilities. Suitable for all ages
Allow at least an hour

This captivating collection of Victorian toys and trinkets is housed in two interlinked 18th-century houses. It's named after Benjamin Pollock, one of Victorian London's leading toy-makers, and is stuffed full of wonderfully crafted historic play-things: handmade paper and card miniature stage sets (Pollock's speciality), tin toys, board games, puppets and dolls' houses; as well as folk toys from Russia, Poland and the Balkans. The museum shop is a good source of stocking fillers – pick up one of the theatre kits based on Pollock's original designs and bring your own version of *Cinderella* or *Aladdin* to life.

British Library

96 Euston Road, NW1
t 0870 444 1500
www.bl.uk
⊖/⇌ King's Cross, Euston
Bus 10, 30, 73, 91
Open Mon, Wed–Fri 9.30–6, Tues 9.30–8,
Sat 9.30–5, Sun 11–5
Free
*Wheelchair accessible, with adapted toilets. Suitable
for older children (over-8s). Allow at least 1hr*
It was completed 10 years behind schedule and
cost a mere £511 million (or £350 million more than
it was meant to), but it's still been hailed as a
great success. The new British Library looks rather
ordinary (almost supermarket-like) from the
outside, but inside it's quite magical, with huge,
bright reading rooms. Although many of the public
displays are confined to the (rather dingy) basement, the library is still well worth a visit. It holds
many of the country's most precious manuscripts,
including the Lindisfarne Gospels, the Magna Carta
and Shakespeare's First Folio (look out for Lewis
Carroll's notebook version of *Alice's Adventures
in Wonderland*, complete with hand-drawn
illustrations). During the school holidays, the
library organizes craft and creative workshops for
children aged 5 and upwards in which they can try
their hand at calligraphy, block-printing and book-
binding, or perhaps meet a writer or artist. Ring or
check the website for details.

Camley Street Natural Park

12 Camley Street, NW1
t (020) 7833 2311
www.wildlondon.org.uk
⊖/⇌ King's Cross
Bus 10, 30, 73, 91
Open Summer Mon–Thurs 9–5, Sat–Sun 11–5,
closed Fri; winter 10–4, closed Fri
Free
Do not let the sight of King's Cross waste-
transfer station's steely towers put you off. This
hidden two-acre site has been teeming with flora
and fauna since it became a nature reserve at the
hands of the London Wildlife Trust in 1983 with
areas of woodland, marshland and meadows as
well as several ponds. Supervised activities

for children take place on weekends all year
round, from pond-dipping and bat walks and
mask-making.

Coram's Fields

93 Guilford Street, WC1
t (020) 7837 6138
www.coramsfields.co.uk
⊖ Russell Square
Bus 17, 45, 46
Open Summer 9–7 daily, winter 9–dusk
Free
Wheelchair accessible, with adapted toilets
This lovely little park has had a long association
with children. It was here that the eponymous
Thomas Coram established a foundling hospital in
1747 which, following the building's demolition in
1920, was turned into a dedicated children's park.
Today, adults can only visit Coram's Fields in the
company of a child. As well as being very safe (it's
permanently staffed), it's also exremely well-
equipped – in addition to lawns, sandpits, a
paddling pool, a basketball court, a helter-skelter
and a supervised playground, you'll find the park's
undoubted highlight, a small farm home to goats,
sheep, pigs, chickens, geese, rabbits and guinea

pigs. Year-round events are laid for kids both to participate in (dance competitions, football matches, flower plantings) and watch (circus performances) and there's a small youth centre offering free IT resources for 13–19-year-olds as well as a very nice vegetarian café.

Dominion Theatre

269 Tottenham Court Road, W1
t 0870 169 0116
Ө Tottenham Court Road
Bus 7, 8, 10, 14, 14A, 22B, 24, 25, 29, 38, 55, 73, 134, 176
Open Tues–Sat 10–6, Sun 12 noon–6
Prices £13.50–£55

A great place to introduce children to the joys of the stage in true Technicolor musical fashion. Its productions are nearly always child-friendly and have, in recent years, included such classics as *The Phantom of the Opera*, *Grease* and *We Will Rock You*.

Foundling Museum

40 Brunswick Square, WC1
t (020) 7841 3600
www.foundlingmuseum.org.uk
Ө Russell Square
Bus 17, 45, 46
Open Tues–Sat 10–6, Sun 12 noon–6
Adm Adult £5, child **free**

You can combine a trip to Coram's Fields (*see* p.58) with a visit to the Foundling Museum next door. It tells the story of London's first hospital for abandoned children, focusing both on the men who founded it (who, in addition to Thomas Coram himself, included such notables as the composer Handel, who provided much of the money, and the artist Hogarth, one of the hospital's original patrons who donated many pictures to the hospital) and the poor destitute children who lived their desperate lives here. There are activity packs for children to guide them round the collection.

Oxford Street, Regent Street and Bond Street together make up one of the busiest shopping districts in the country. For visitors, immersing yourself in the West End crowds is all part of the London experience. And, who knows? Your visit may coincide with one of the area's occasional VIP ('Very Important Pedestrians') days, when the streets are closed to traffic giving shoppers a little extra room to manoeuvre.

You'll find lots of clothes and book shops, all with sections for kids, as well as some well-stocked department stores. There are also a number of shops, like Hamleys and Niketown, which will call to your children like sirens from a rock.

If you're keen on browsing for something to read, Borders on Oxford Street, a massive book, CD and magazine shop, will appeal equally to adults and children. It's one of the capital's most innovative bookstores, organizing storytellings for children on Saturday mornings – with a roster of costumed characters on hand to enliven proceedings.

Otherwise, head to Charing Cross Road, London's unofficial book centre, and particularly Foyle's, one of the largest bookstores in London. This charming, sprawling shop has a superb collection of children's books. It also has an unfathomable layout but then looking is half the fun. The branch of Waterstone's at Piccadilly is the largest bookshop in Europe.

If your kids are comic fans try Gosh! on Great Russell Street where you can pick up all your Marvel and DC favourites such as *Superman* and *The Incredible Hulk* (and compilations of news-paper strip cartoons like *Peanuts* and *The Far Side*), or Forbidden Planet on Shaftesbury Avenue, full of sci-fi comics, books and models. See **Shop** p.239.

Hamleys

188–196 Regent Street, W1
t 0800 280 2444
www.hamleys.com
Ө Oxford Circus
Bus 3, 6, 12, 13, 15, 23, 53, 88, 94, 139, 159, X53
Open Mon–Sat 10–8, Sun 12 noon–6

Hamleys is one of the largest and most famous toy shops in the world. You can find every toy imaginable on its six floors. In fact, if Hamleys don't stock it, it probably doesn't exist (or possibly it's the day before Christmas and they've run out).

Briefly, this is what you can expect to find. The basement is where to go for computer games. Part of the floor has also been turned into an arcade

called 'Cyberzone', filled with dozens of video games. On the ground floor you'll find thousands of soft toys plus all the latest stocking fillers. The first floor is the place for science kits and board games. On the second floor are pre-school toys and books while the third floor is dedicated to dolls: rag dolls, porcelain dolls and, of course, Barbie. The fourth floor is packed with more cerebral games: jigsaw puzzles, model kits and computer programmes, as well as an enormous collection of remote-controlled vehicles. The fifth and final floor, which is overlooked by a giant, swinging fibreglass superman, holds, appropriately enough, action figures from all the greatest and latest blockbusters – *Star Wars*, *Pirates of the Caribbean*, etc.

Niketown

236 Oxford Street, W1
t (020) 7612 0800
http://niketown.nike.com
⊖ Oxford Circus

Bus 6, 7, 8, 10, 12, 13, 15, 23, 25, 55, 73, 94, 98, 113, 135, 137, 139, 159, 176, 189
Open Mon–Wed 10–7, Thurs–Sat 10–8, Sun 12 noon–6

The biggest sports name in town, the giant Niketown is more than just a sports shop. It's a theme store, a mini-museum, an 'experience' – or so the hype would have us believe. It's certainly fascinating, the shop treating sport almost as a religion. Each dedicated section (football, golf, tennis, running, etc.) is enhanced by video images and memorabilia and it's sometimes difficult to remember that it is basically just somewhere to buy trainers – and not particularly cheap ones. Still, if your kids are insisting on the latest Air Zooms, then this is definitely the place to come.

Question 4
Which London football club has a claret and blue home strip?
answer on p.250

The Disney Store

360–66 Oxford Street, W1
t (020) 7491 9136
www.disneystore.co.uk
✆ Oxford Circus
Open Mon–Sat 10–8, Sun 12 noon–6

Videos, play figures, mugs, costumes: the store holds a vast array of merchandise relating to Disney's roster of cartoon characters. The video screen belting out singalong classics never fails to attract a gaggle of warbling children. A selection of toddler's merchandise is in the basement.

The Apple Store

235 Regent Street, W1
t (020) 7153 9000
www.apple.com/uk/retail/regentstreet
✆ Oxford Circus
Open Mon–Sat 10–9, Sun 12 noon–6

The Macintosh Corporation's flagship London store is full of all the latest gadgets and gizmos – iPods, iMacs, iPhones, etc – as well as all the relevant accessories and paraphernalia. The store stages regular in-store events – including performances by musicians to promote its Itunes products – and offers tutorials on digital photography, movie- and music-making. Visit the website or see in store for details.

British Museum Shops

22 Bloomsbury Street WC1
t (020) 7637 9449
Open Mon–Sat 9.30–6, Sun 12 noon–6

There are four outlets which, in total, make up the British Museum shopping experience: a

Question 5
How many square metres does the roof of the British Museum's Great Court cover? answer on p.54 or see p.250

souvenir and guide shop on the west side of the Great Court, selling souvenir mugs, books, T-shirts, etc. (the place to pick up that all-important Rosetta Stone pencil sharpener or mummy T-shirt); the slightly more fancy Grenville shop, next to Room 3 by the entrance, which specializes in expensive reproductions of museum exhibits – replica sculptures, jewellery, clothes, etc.; a book-shop on the north side of the Great Court; and, last but not least, a specialist children's shop on the east side of the Great Court, filled with pocket money-priced souvenirs for young visitors. You can also shop online at **www.**britishmuseum.co.uk.

Can you spot?

The Telecom Tower? One of London's most distinctive landmarks, the great cylindrical tower (it looks a bit like a huge spark plug) is clearly visible from the north side of Oxford Street. Standing some 580ft high, this was the tallest building in London when it opened in 1964 – it needed to be so tall in order to broadcast clear radio and TV signals over the city's rooftops. The views from the top are said to be fantastic. Sadly, members of the public have been barred from the top of the tower since the closure of the revolving restaurant (yes, a revolving restaurant) in the 1970s for security reasons.

Picnics & snacks

Green picnic spots are a bit thin on the ground in this most central of locations. However, **Phoenix Gardens** is a little oasis of nature that rose from the rubble of a former car park – hence the name – just off Shaftesbury Avenue. It was created with the aim of giving the capital's wildlife some much-needed respite from the area's relentless urban sprawl, and performs the job just as well for the city's human inhabitants. **Coram's Fields** on the outskirts of the area is another good picnic spot and has a great vegetarian café. You can also take food into the Great Court of the **British Museum** which provides a sort of all-weather picnic venue (you can't, however, eat your own food at the café tables). Supplies can be picked up from: the French delicatessen/bakery/pâtisserie/restaurant **Truc Vert**, 42 North Audley Street, W1, **t** (020) 7491 9988, ⊖ Bond Street; **Carluccio's** (see p.227), 8 Market Place, W1 **t** (020) 7636 2228, ⊖ Oxford Street; **Fresh and Wild** organic food halls, 69–75 Brewer Street, W1, **t** (020) 7344 3179, ⊖ Tottenham Court Road; **Tesco Metro**, 2–4 Dean Street, W1, **t** 0845 677 9863, ⊖ Tottenham Court Road; or, if you really want to splash out, **Selfridges** magnificent food halls, 400 Oxford Street, W1, **t** 0870 837 7377, ⊖ Bond Street.

There are lots of snack bars, sandwich shops, fast-food outlets and chain restaurants where you can grab a quick bite before returning to the dizzying world of retail. Snacks, sandwiches and sticky treats are available from **Patisserie Valerie** (see p.231), 44 Old Compton Street, W1, **t** (020) 7437 3466 ⊖ Tottenham Court Road, and the venerable **Maison Bertaux**, 28 Greek Street, W1, **t** (020) 7437 6007 ⊖ Tottenham Court Road, which opened way back in 1871. Burgers (and, of course, happy meals) can be picked up at **McDonald's** at 8–10 Oxford Street, W1, 120 Oxford Street, W1, 185 Oxford Street, W1, 291b Oxford Street, W1, 40 New Oxford Street, W1, 310–312 Regent Street, W1, and 134 Tottenham Court Road, W1. If you fancy sampling some slightly more upmarket burgers try **Hamburger Union**, 22–25 Dean Street, W1, **t** (020) 7437 6004 ⊖ Leicester Square, and **Tootsies** (see p.235), 35 James Street, W1, **t** (020) 7486 1611 ⊖ Bond Street, a brightly-coloured diner-style bar.

Restaurants

1 Ask Pizza
74 Southampton Row, WC1

t (020) 7405 2876
www.askcentral.co.uk
⊖ Holborn, Russell Square
Open 11.30–11.30 daily

2 Bodeans Smoke House
10 Poland Street, W1
t (020) 7287 0506
www.bodeansbbq.com
⊖ Oxford Circus
Open Mon–Fri 12 noon–3 & 6–11, Sat 12 noon–11.30, Sun 12 noon–10.30

3 Masala Zone
9 Marshall Street, W1
t (020) 7287 9966
www.realindianfood.com
⊖ Oxford Circus
Open Mon–Sat 12 noon–2.30 and 5.30–11.30, Sun 12.30–3

4/5 Pizza Express
7 Charlotte Street, W1
t (020) 7580 1110
⊖ Goodge Street
10 Dean Street, W1
t (020) 7437 9595
⊖ Tottenham Court Road
www.pizzaexpress.com
Open daily 12 noon–11.30

6/7 Wagamama
10a Lexington Street, W1
t (020) 7292 0990
⊖ Oxford Circus
101 Wigmore Street, W1
t (020) 7409 0111
⊖ Oxford Circus
www.wagamama.com
Open Mon–Sat 12 noon–11, Sun 12 noon–10

8 Yo! Sushi
52 Poland Street, W1
t (020) 7287 0443
www.yosushi.com
Open Mon–Sat 12 noon–11, Sun 12 noon–10
⊖ Oxford Circus, Tottenham Court Road

See **Eat** p.224–36 for more details on the above restaurants.
See map on p.53 for the locations of the restaurants numbered above.

Trafalgar Square to Piccadilly

The much-improved Trafalgar Square, with its happy gurgling fountains and newly pedestrianized north side, provides the centrepiece of this area. Overlooked by a spruced-up Nelson's Column (the square's hundreds of pigeons have had their numbers drastically cut), the square is home to two of the city's great art galleries: the National Gallery and the National Portrait Gallery. Nearby is Leicester Square, London's cinematic heart, and the neon-lit Piccadilly Circus, site of the Trocadero centre where many a teenage adventurer has strayed to sample the arcade rides and games.

Highlights

Trafalgar Square's cooling fountains

The latest arcade thrills at the Trocadero

Eating with chopsticks in Chinatown

Key

Numbers correspond to restaurants in 'Where To Eat' pp.73–4

Trafalgar Square

⊖ Charing Cross, Leicester Square, Embankment
Bus 3, 6, 9, 11, 12, 13, 15, 23, 24, 29, 53, 88, 91, 109, 139, 159, 176, 184, 196

Until recently, Trafalgar Square often came as a bit of a letdown to visitors. True, it had many attractions, but the traffic that filled the outskirts of the square, and the huge flocks of pigeons that occupied its centre, made it a noisy, congested and, in truth, rather dirty place. Things, however, have changed. The north side has been pedestrianized and prettified, while the pigeons have (for the most part) been sent on their way. The result is a very pleasant public space. It could do with a bit more greenery to make it compare with Europe's best city squares, but it's certainly moving in the right direction. The grand staircase at the square's northern end provides a great place to sit and admire the views, which are of course dominated by the 185-ft granite bulk of Nelson's Column. Kids will instinctively roll their heads back in an attempt to catch a glimpse of the one-eyed, one-armed British hero perched on its summit. Lord Horatio Nelson (for it is he) was Britain's greatest naval commander. The square and column were built in the early 19th century to commemorate his victory over the combined Franco-Spanish fleet at the Battle of Trafalgar back in 1805. Unfortunately, Nelson was fatally wounded during the course of the battle and was brought home to Britain for a hero's funeral, his body having been preserved during the journey in a barrel of brandy.

The friendly-looking iron lions at the base were sculpted by Edwin Landseer. They were unveiled in 1870, some 25 years after the construction of the column. Children always fall madly in love with them and will expend remarkable amounts of energy trying to clamber aboard the beasts' great shiny backs. A photo of your kids sitting between a pair of giant protective forepaws is one of the classic snapshots of London. Alternatively, you

Did you know?
Just before the 40ft statue of Nelson was erected in Trafalgar Square, 14 stonemasons had a celebratory dinner perched on top of the column – 145ft in the air. Did you also know that the statue of Charles I (on the south side of the square) is the precise point from which all distances from London are measured?

could pose them in front of one of the square's great gushing, gurgling fountains which spring into life at 10am or by the new statue of Nelson Mandela. The stairs also provide a fittingly grand approach to the National Gallery, one of the world's finest collections of paintings, which sits next to the National Portrait Gallery, the nation's artistic scrapbook.

Christmas and New Year

Trafalgar Square is particularly popular in winter. Every year the Norwegian government donates a huge Christmas tree to Britain as a thank you for help during the Second World War. The tree is erected in the square next to Nelson's Column. Carol singing takes place around the tree every evening from early December to Christmas Eve. Every 31 December (New Year's Eve) thousands of people cram into Trafalgar Square to celebrate the New Year – waiting for the 12 o'clock chimes of Britain's most famous clock, Big Ben, to ring out.

Can you spot?
Trafalgar Square is home to the world's smallest police station. See if you can find it. Hidden in a lamp post, in the southeast corner of the square, it has room for one police officer.

National Gallery

Trafalgar Square, WC2
t (020) 7747 2870
www.nationalgallery.org.uk
⊖ Charing Cross, Leicester Square, Embankment
Bus 3, 6, 9, 11, 12, 13, 15, 23, 24, 29, 53, 88, 91, 109, 139, 159, 176, 184, 196
Open 10–6 daily, Wed 10–9
Free Charges apply for some temporary exhibitions
Wheelchair accessible, with adapted toilets, loop system for hard of hearing. Suitable for children aged 8 and over. Allow at least 2hrs

Lots and lots of pictures. Rooms and rooms of paintings. Over 2,300 canvases covering the last eight centuries of Western European art – and you don't have to pay a penny to see them (although a donation is always appreciated).

All the great artists are here: Cézanne, Constable, Leonardo da Vinci, Picasso, Turner, Van Gogh ... think of a famous painter and it can be pretty much guaranteed that you'll find an example of their work here. The sheer size and scope of the gallery can make the prospect of a visit seem daunting for adults, let alone children.

> **Did you know?**
> The gallery's collection was begun in 1824 when the government bought 38 pictures from a wealthy merchant, John Julius Angerstein, for £57,000.

To get the best out of the gallery, it's often a good idea to pick perhaps a dozen or so pictures in advance and then plan your tour accordingly. That way you can turn the experience into a sort of treasure hunt. Fortunately, the wonderful resources of the National allow you to plan your trip in exactly this fashion. Your first mission should be to find an 'ArtStart' screen. These are located in the Sainsbury Wing foyer, in the Espresso Bar in the East Wing and in the special ArtStart room in the Sainbury Wing. Here you can explore the gallery's entire collection on touch-screen computer terminals and print out your own personalized tour. For very young children, however, it's probably best just to let them wander and point, rather than structuring your trip too rigorously – you'll be surprised at what catches their eye.

The collection is divided into four colour-coded wings: the Sainsbury Wing (blue) shows paintings from 1260 to 1510; the West Wing (green) paintings

Tell me a story: Nelson v Napoleon

By 1805 Napoleon, the Emperor of France, had conquered Spain and Italy and was making plans to invade Britain. To this end, he had assembled a fighting fleet of some 33 fearsomely armoured Spanish and French ships which he stationed at Cadiz Harbour under the command of Admiral Pierre de Villeneuve. In September, Villeneuve was ordered to sail the fleet to Italy to prepare for the invasion. The British, however, had different ideas and instructed the Royal Navy's premier commander, Admiral Horatio Nelson, to lead his own fleet of 27 warships in an ambush against Napoleon's ships. Nelson intercepted the enemy at Cape Trafalgar off the Spanish coast, whereupon he gave orders, using a system of flag signals, for his fleet to divide itself into two squadrons, each of which was to attack half the Franco-Spanish fleet. Nelson, meanwhile, would lead the fighting from aboard his flagship, the *Victory*.

At 11.50am, Nelson signalled his now legendary message: 'England expects that every man will do his duty', and then ordered the fighting to commence. It soon became clear that the British forces would win the day as they quickly smashed through the enemy lines, their heavy cannon causing widespread devastation. A brief counter-attack by the Franco-Spanish forces had little effect and, by 5pm, the battle was over. Twenty enemy ships had been sunk and 7,000 men, including Villeneuve himself, taken prisoner.

It would have have been a time of great rejoicing among the British ranks had it not been for the fact that, at 4.30pm, Nelson, whilst commanding operations from the deck, had been mortally wounded by an enemy sniper. He died, at least knowing that victory was assured. His final words, spoken to his second in command, Hardy, were supposedly either '*kismet*' (which means fate) or 'kiss me' (which means something else entirely).

Nelson's legacy proved to be a lasting one. Not only did his final naval victory thwart Napoleon's plans, but it assured Britain's naval supremacy in Europe for the next hundred years.

from 1510 to 1600; the North Wing (yellow) paintings from 1600 to 1700 and the East Wing (red) paintings from 1700 to 1900.

The Gallery also produces special themed audio guides (including 'A Right Royal Tour' and 'Tell Me a Picture') and paper trails (including 'Winged Things' and 'Chinese Zodiac') for children, both of which are available for free from any information desk. A range of family events are organized throughout the year including art workshops for 5–11 year olds and storytellings for under-5s on the Gallery's 'magic carpet'. A full programme is available on the Gallery website where kids can also enjoy some online artistic activities at the 'Art Action Zone'. Most events are free and do not require pre-booking, although you'll need to arrive early to ensure your place.

There's a decent self-service café and a more expensive restaurant where they've recently introduced a children's menu (burgers, macaroni cheese, boiled eggs with soldiers etc) or you can bring your own picnic to eat in the Education Centre's sandwich rooms. The gallery's three shops are all well worth a visit, selling lots of good introductory art books as well as a variety of art products including pens, drawing pads, CD-ROMs, videos, slides, Renoir umbrellas, Van Gogh backpacks etc. They're located by the main entrance, by the Sir Paul Getty entrance and in the Sainsbury Wing. The last operates the gallery's popular 'print-on-demand' poster service, which allows you to have a poster printed while you wait of any picture in the gallery's collection. They cost: A4 £10, A3 £20, A2 £25.

The pictures

There are certain pictures in the National that will especially appeal to children. The colour and vibrancy of many of the Renaissance canvases (to be found in the Sainsbury and West Wings) often touch a nerve with kids, and the subjects – St George killing the Dragon, St Sebastian shot full of arrows, John the Baptist's head on a silver platter – are usually gory enough to impress. Paintings that employ overt forms of visual trickery also often grab children's attention. Here are five paintings they may enjoy.

Hans Holbein

The Ambassadors (above, left; West Wing)
This is a wonderfully bright and colourful picture of two very grand 16th-century courtiers. Everything seems quite normal apart from a strange stretched shape at the bottom of the picture. Get your kids to go as close to the wall on the right hand side of the picture as possible and then look back at the picture. By changing the point of view in this fashion, the stretched shape should now have transformed itself into the picture of a skull.

Can you spot?
Hidden among the fruit and flowers of Jan van Os' picture are the following creatures and objects. How many can you find? There are two butterflies, three flies, a snail, a dormouse, a dragonfly and a bird's nest.

Jan van Eyck

The Arnolfini Portrait (opposite; Sainsbury Wing)

This 15th-century Dutch picture of a couple holding hands seems quite unremarkable on first glance. But if you look closely at the mirror hanging on the wall behind the couple, you should be able to see the reflection of the back of the couple stretching out their hands towards a visitor. The visitor is van Eyck himself, come to paint the couple's portrait. Van Eyck seems to have been very keen for the viewer to know who painted the picture. The words 'Van Eyck fuit hic, 1434' appear on the wall above the mirror. Roughly translated they mean 'Van Eyck made this, 1434'.

Andrea Mantegna

The Introduction of the Cult of Cybele at Rome (Sainsbury Wing)

A 15th-century painting made to look like a sculpture. Mantegna painted this so that, from a distance, it looks carved out of stone.

Samuel van Hoogstraten

Peepshow (North Wing)

Created in the 17th century, this isn't a conventional painting at all, but a wooden box mounted on a plinth. In the side of the box is a peephole. If you look through the hole, you'll see what looks like a miniature house filled with what appears to be 3D furniture. It is, in fact, a 2D painting which cleverly uses perspective to make you think you are seeing things which aren't really there.

Jan van Os

Fruit, Flowers in a Terracotta Vase (East Wing)

This picture, from the late 18th century, is so realistic that it almost looks like a photograph. The trick is in the composition rather than the representation. Although the fruit and flowers in the picture appear quite fresh, in fact they couldn't possibly have all appeared together at the same time as they all ripen at different times of year. The painting was therefore painted over the course of a year, each new fruit and flower being added as it came into season.

National Portrait Gallery

St Martin's Place, WC2
t (020) 7306 0055
www.npg.org.uk
⊖ Charing Cross, Leicester Square, Embankment

Can you spot?
Young visitors to the National Portrait Gallery will probably be less concerned with artistic merit than with spotting some famous faces.
See if they can find portraits of the following: Princess Diana, David Beckham, Michael Owen, Barbara Windsor and Ozzy Osbourne.

Bus 3, 6, 9, 11, 12, 13, 15, 23, 24, 29, 53, 88, 91, 109, 139, 159, 176, 184, 196
Open Mon–Wed, Sat–Sun 10–6, Thurs–Fri 10–9
Free Charges apply for some temporary exhibitions
Wheelchair accessible, with adapted toilets. Suitable for older children (8 and over). Allow at least 1hr

If history is, as Sir Thomas Carlyle once claimed, merely the 'biographies of great men', then the National Portrait Gallery is its picture album. Over 2,000 portraits of the greatest figures from the last 700 years of British history are on display here. The collection is arranged more or less chronologically, so it's best to start at the top (there's a lift) with the Tudors (look out for the clever picture of Edward VI by William Scrots which requires you to look at it from an acute angle in order to see the perspective) before making your way slowly down through the centuries via the Balcony Gallery to the 20th-century works on the ground floor – which is also where most of temporary exhibitions are held. On the way children will find themselves putting faces to names they had previously only read about in textbooks or heard in history lessons: kings, queens, soldiers, statesmen, scientists, politicians, artists and sculptors, they're all here. Kids might enjoy tracking down the picture of Edwin Landseer carving the lions that would eventually go on display outside in Trafalgar Square. The Gallery has also introduced some new family trails

as well as Rucksack tours for 4–12 year olds. Themed according to a section of the exhibition (i.e. 'Tudors', 'Victorians' or 'Twentieth Century'), each tour contains eight different activities relating to the displays – puzzles, quizzes, drawing tasks, etc. The rucksacks are free to borrow and are handed out on a first-come, first-served basis.

Because the Gallery's pictures have been chosen on the basis of identity rather than ability, the quality and style of the works varies enormously. Note how most of the older paintings have been painted in a very traditional, formal style, while the more modern works have been rendered using a great mishmash of different techniques.

Once you've finished your tour, catch the lift back up to the top-floor café, which has wonderful views out over Trafalgar Square.

Elsewhere on Trafalgar Square

On the northeast edge of Trafalgar Square stands the church of **St Martin-in-the-Fields** (currently hidden behind scaffolding while it is renovated) so named because when it was first built in the 12th century, it stood amid rolling fields. The church you see now was built in 1722 on the site of an earlier Tudor construction (itself a replacement for the original Norman church), making it the square's oldest building. Its churchyard hosts a rather touristy bric-a-brac market, while inside the church proper, free classical concerts are given every Tuesday lunchtime – there are paid ones most other days as well. Check the website at **www**.stmartin-in-the-fields.org. Children may particularly enjoy the Christmas carol offerings. Down in the eeriest crypt, you'll find the London Brass Rubbing Centre and the Café in the Crypt.

Piccadilly

Piccadilly Circus is London's neon heart and unofficial tourist hub. It's a strange place; too small to be grand, too big to be unobtrusive. In truth, there's not much here, beyond a small fountain statue and some rather ordinary neon signs. But for decades it's been a focal point for visitors to the capital, who constantly pack out the small pedestrianized area around the statue. Despite its own lack of attractions, the square gives the appearance of being at the centre of things, with roads going off every which way – to Trafalgar Square, Soho, Leicester Square, Regent Street and Piccadilly. It's a place to pause a while and work out what you're going to do next.

The statue in middle of Piccadilly Circus is called *Eros*, although this is a misnomer. The man who designed it, Sir Alfred Gilbert, had intended it to be the Angel of Christian Charity and wanted it to be placed above a cascading fountain. But funds ran low and plans changed. Gilbert was so angry that he boycotted the opening ceremony.

Incidentally, the square gets its name from its first inhabitant, a wealthy tailor called Robert Baker who built a mansion on fields here in 1612. Baker's friends thought his wealth had gone to his head, and so christened his new house 'Piccadill', meaning 'shirt-cuff', in order to remind him of his humble origins.

Trocadero

Piccadilly Circus, WC1
t (020) 7439 1791
www.londontrocadero.com
Piccadilly Circus, Leicester Square
Bus 3, 12, 14, 19, 22, 38
Open Sun–Thurs 10am–12 midnight, Fri–Sat
10am–1am
Free
Some wheelchair access. Suitable for ages 10–15.
Allow at least 2hrs

   Originally a plush hotel, the Trocadero has
been revamped in recent years into a large and
very noisy arcade-cum-electronic entertainment
centre. It is filled with souvenir shops and fast-food
restaurants, not to mention a seven-screen cinema
and its biggest draw, Funland – six floors of the
latest computer games. Definitely fun for
computer-mad kids but perhaps not for you.

Question 6
Other than being next to each other, what do
Piccadilly Circus, Coventry Street and Leicester
Square have in common?
answer on p.250

Funland

t (020) 7292 3642
www.funland.co.uk
Open Daily 10am–1am
Free, to the building, the cost of the individual
rides and games vary
Fast-food restaurants

   It may advertise itself as a giant indoor theme
park, but Funland is essentially just a giant
amusement arcade with six floors of video games
to explore – shoot-'em-ups, fighting games, flight
simulators and racing games – interspersed with
various 3-D simulator rides as well as a few more
traditional attractions such as pool tables, air-
hockey, 10-pin bowling, dodgems, etc.

   Don't be fooled by the free entry signs. Each
video game costs at least £1 and each of its large
3-D rides, £2-£3 (there are small savings to be made
by buying a combined ticket to several rides).
Tip *The very loud noise and flashing lights may*
make it a little overwhelming for very young
children. Older children (teenagers in particular),
however, will love it.

St James's Church

196 Piccadilly, W1
t (020) 7734 4511
www.st-james-piccadilly.org
Green Park, Piccadilly Circus
Bus 6, 9, 2, 14, 15, 19, 22
Open 8–7 daily
Free
Wheelchair accessible, with adapted toilets. Suitable
for older children (8 and over).

   The leafy tree-lined garden of this Sir Christopher
Wren-designed church plays host to a lively arts
and crafts market from Wednesday to Saturday.
There's also a small antique market held here on
Tuesdays. The church makes a nice, quiet spot
away from the hurly-burly of Piccadilly Circus just
down the road. Lunchtime performances of
classical music are regularly put on and there's
a decent café.

Fortnum and Mason

181 Piccadilly, W1
t (020) 7734 8040
www.fortnumandmason.co.uk
⊖ Green Park, Piccadilly Circus
Bus 6, 9, 12, 14, 15, 19, 22
Open Mon–Sat 10–6.30, Sun 12–6
Suitable for older children (8 and over).

This is a big, important, grown-ups sort of a shop really, with its elegant halls filled with gourmet food, but kids should enjoy browsing the lavish chocolate boxes and tins of traditional sweets – and older ones might like a meal in the Fountain Room (*see* p.231). They will all like the clock outside, when mechanical figures of Mr Fortnum and Mr Mason come out and bow to each other when it chimes every hour.

Royal Academy

Burlington House, Piccadilly, W1
t 0870 848 8484
www.royalacademy.org.uk
⊖ Green Park, Piccadilly Circus
Bus 9, 14, 19, 22, 38
Open 10–6 daily, Fri till 10pm
Adm Depends on the exhibition
Wheelchair accessible for all areas, wheelchair hire available in advance. Suitable for older children (10 and over). Younger kids may enjoy it but only for short bursts. Allow at least 1hr

The Royal Academy specializes in blockbuster temporary art exhibitions, such as its recent 'Impressionists by the Sea' and 'Aztec' extravaganzas. It also holds an annual Summer Exhibition (and has done since 1769, making it the world's longest-running art exhibition) of works submitted by the public. Anyone can enter, although only a fraction of the hundreds of entries are chosen. The Academy organizes various family events – including gallery talks and art and music workshops – to tie in with the Summer Exhibition. A free activity art tray and worksheets, called the 'Art Detective's Guide', are available from reception. Kids are encouraged to create their own artwork on the sheet with the best examples going on display on the gallery's website.

Leicester Square

Flanked by four giant cinemas, Leicester Square is where all the major film premieres are held and big releases get their first runs. Once a fashionable 19th-century meeting place with a Turkish bath, music and dance halls, it is now (if we're honest) a bit tacky with its souvenir shops, chain restaurants, portrait painters and buskers. Still, the central garden offers some shade on a sunny day and you can buy half-price tickets for West End shows at the TKTs booth in the square's southeast corner.

Leicester Square Cinemas
Empire
t 0871 471 4714
www.empirecinemas.co.uk
Odeon Leicester Square
t 0871 224 4007
www.odeon.co.uk
Vue West End
t 08712 240 240
www.myvue.com

> **Can you spot?**
> Engraved on a series of brass plaques in Leicester Square's garden (central cobbled area) are the distances in miles from London to all the Commonwealth countries.
> See who's the quickest to find the distance to the following:
> ▶ Ottawa in Canada – 3,332 miles
> ▶ Jamaica – 4,684 miles
> ▶ Kenya – 4,237 miles

Picnics & snacks

Though the featured area is chock-a-block full of fast-food restaurants, cafés and pizza bars, do also remember (particularly if it's a sunny day) that it's also within walking distance of two of the city's best picnic spots – **Green Park** and **St James's Park**. St James's in particular boasts an excellent self-service café, '**Inn the Park**', **t** (020) 7451 9999, ✚ **St James's Park,** set in an eco-friendly building (it has a turf roof) with a terrace overlooking one of the wildfowl ponds, which sells pre-packed picnic hampers.

Upmarket supplies, befitting a picnic in a royal park, can be picked up from **Fortnum & Mason's** terribly grand food halls, 181 Piccadilly, W1, **t** (020) 7734 8040, ✚ **Piccadilly Circus**. Less expensive fare is available from **Lina's Stores** Italian delicatessen, 11 Brewer Street, W1, **t** (020) 7437 6482, ✚ **Tottenham Court Road**; the French delicatessen/bakery/patisserie **Truc Vert**, 42 North Audley Street, W1, **t** (020) 7491 9988, ✚ **Bond Street**; **Fresh and Wild** organic food halls, 69–75 Brewer Street, W1, **t** (020) 7344 3179, ✚ **Tottenham Court Road**; and **Marks and Spencer**, 173 Oxford Street, W1, **t** (020) 7437 7722, ✚ **Oxford Street**. You can also bring a picnic to eat in the National Gallery's Education Centre's sandwich rooms.

In **Leicester Square**, try **Café Fiori** on the corner of Leicester Square and Charing Cross Road, while if in or around **Trafalgar Square** head either up to the very posh top-floor café of the **National Portrait Gallery**, St Martin's Place, WC2, **t** (020) 7306 0055, ✚ **Leicester Square**, which offers wonderful views of the square, or down to the **Café in the Crypt** (*see* p.225) below St Martin-in-the-Fields church, **t** (020) 7839 4342, ✚ **Charing Cross**. Piccadilly Circus can offer little except a very crowded branch of **Burger King**, although if you're in the area, you might want to make your way to the **Fortnum & Mason Fountain Room** (*see* p.231), 181 Piccadilly, **t** (020) 7734 8040, ✚ **Piccadilly Circus**, a wonderfully elegant tea room set in the basement of the Queen's grocers. It's a haven of old-fashioned style and charm, suitable for older children, or you could splash out on tea at the **Ritz Hotel** (*see* p.231), 150 Piccadilly, W1, **t** (020) 7493 8181, ✚ **Green Park**. Burgers and happy meals are available at various branches of **McDonald's** at 5 Swiss Court, Leicester Square, ✚ **Leicester Square**, 57–60 Haymarket, ✚ **Piccadilly Circus**, 69–73 Shaftesbury Avenue, ✚ **Leicester Square**, and 34–35 The Strand (next to Charing Cross Station).

Restaurants

1 Benihana
37–43 Sackville Street, W1
t (020) 7494 2525
www.benihana.co.uk
✚ Charing Cross, Leicester Square, Embankment
Open Mon–Sat 12 noon–3 & 5.30–10.30, Sun 5–10

2 National Dining Rooms
Level 1, Sainsbury Wing, National Gallery, Trafalgar Square, W1
t (020) 7747 2525
www.nationalgallery.org.uk
✚ Charing Cross, Leicester Square
Open Thurs–Tues 10–5, Wed 10–8.30

3/4 Pizza Express
20 Greek Street, W1
t (020) 7734 7430
✚ Leicester Square
Open 11am–12 midnight daily
6 Upper James Street, Golden Square, W1

t (020) 7437 4550
⊖ Piccadilly Circus
Open Mon–Sat 11.30–11.30, Sun 12 noon–9.30pm
www.pizzaexpress.com

5 Planet Hollywood
13 Coventry Street, W1
t (020) 7734 6220
www.planethollywoodlondon.com
⊖ Leicester Square, Piccadilly Circus
Open 11.30am–1am daily

6 Rainforest Café
20 Shaftesbury Avenue, W1
t (020) 7434 3111
www.therainforestcafe.co.uk
⊖ Leicester Square, Piccadilly Circus
Bus 3, 12, 14, 19, 22, 38
Open 12 noon–11 daily, Fri–Sat 12 noon– 12 midnight

7 Texas Embassy Cantina
1 Cockspur Street, SW1
t (020) 7925 0077
www.texasembassy.com
⊖ Charing Cross
Open Mon–Thurs 12 noon–11, Fri–Sat 12 noon–
12 midnight, Sun 12 noon–10.30pm

8 TGI Friday's
29 Coventry Street, W1
t (020) 7379 6262
www.tgifridays.co.uk
⊖ Piccadilly Circus
Open 12 noon–11 daily

9/10 Wagamama
14a Irving Street, WC2
t (020) 7839 2323
⊖ Leicester Square
Open Mon–Thurs 12 noon–11, Fri–Sat 12 noon–
12 midnight, Sun 12 noon–10
8 Norris Street, Haymarket, SW1
t (020) 7321 2755
⊖ Piccadilly Circus
Open Mon–Sat 12 noon–11, Sun 12 noon–10
www.wagamama.com

11 Yo! Sushi
St. Albans House, 57 Haymarket, SW1
t (020) 7930 7557
⊖ Piccadilly Circus
www.yosushi.com
Branches open 12 noon–12 midnight daily

Chinatown
The pedestrianized Gerrard Street, just north of Leicester Square, along with the adjacent Lisle Street, makes up London's Chinatown district.

It's a fascinating place to go for a meal or just to explore with its decorative lamps and phone boxes made up to look like oriental pagodas. Every Chinese New Year (late January or early February) paper dragons dance down the street as part of a week of traditional celebrations.

12 Royal Dragon
30 Gerrard Street, W1
t (020) 7734 1388
⊖ Leicester Square

13 Chuen Cheng Ku
17 Wardour Street, W1
t (020) 7437 1398
www.chuenchengku.co.uk
⊖ Leicester Square

14 New World
1 Gerrard Place, W1
t (020) 7734 0396
⊖ Leicester Square

See **Eat** p.224–36 for more details on the above restaurants.
See map on p.65 for the locations of the restaurants numbered above.

Covent Garden

Covent Garden combines being both lively and entertaining with being rather cultured and sophisticated. In other words, children will enjoy themselves and parents won't feel guilty about letting them.

There's lots for kids to do here; they can clamber aboard a vintage bus at the newly revamped London Transport Museum, dodge the dancing fountains at Somerset House or enjoy the ad hoc entertainment provided by the buskers outside in the Piazza. Spend a Saturday morning here and you're bound to encounter at least one impromptu performance from the army of mime artists, fire-eaters, comedians and opera singers that frequent the area. There are also various toy and gift shops designed to attract the fancy of children, as well as the wallets of their indulgent parents.

Highlights
Somerset House's fountains/ice rink
Buskers on Covent Garden's Piazza
Messing around on the buses at London's Transport Museum

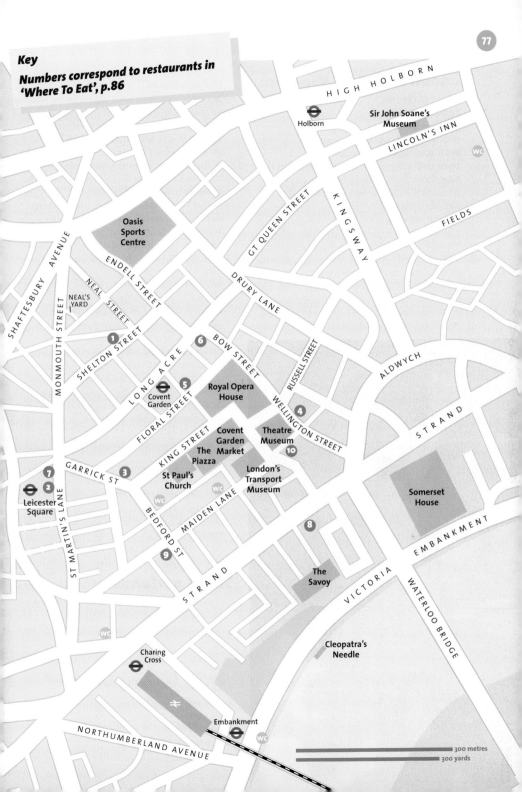

London Transport Museum

Covent Garden, WC2
t (020) 7379 6344
www.ltmuseum.co.uk
⊖ Covent Garden/Leicester Square
Bus 6, 9, 11, 13, 15, 23, 77A, 91, 176
Open 10–6 daily, except Fri when it opens at 11am
Adm Adults £5.95, children **free**, concs £4.50
Wheelchair accessible, with adapted toilets
Suitable for all ages
Allow at least 2hrs

At the time of writing, this great child-friendly museum was still closed for a major renovation, though reopening is scheduled for November 2007. In its previous incarnation the Transport Museum provided one of the capital's very best family day's out with lots of exhibits tracing the history of public transport from its inception in 1829 to the present day. It possessed a wonderful, colourful

collection of horse-drawn and motorized trams, buses and trolley cars, which were interspersed with a number of dedicated kids zones offering lots of buttons to push, levers to pull and exhibits to clamber over. The people in charge have promised that the new version will be even better with more exhibition space and greater interactivity, as well as a new shop, café and theatre.

Street performers

Some of the capital's most talented and exuberant street performers strut their stuff at Covent Garden. The approach to the Tube station is

Question 7
How many bus stops are there in London?
a) 1,000?
b) 7,000?
c) 17,000?
answer on p.250

usually occupied by a spray-painted mime artist or two, while on the lower levels of the shopping area you will often encounter highly skilled classical and jazz musicians belting out tunes with merry abandon. The proximity to the newly refurbished Royal Opera House means you'll also occasionally find a plain-clothes Carmen or two warbling powerfully. Children who've never heard opera in the raw before will be impressed by the sheer volume of noise produced by these sturdy divas.

The main performing space, however, is the Piazza, in front of St Paul's Church, where some of London's great physical comedians come to ply their trade. You may even spot a star of the future wobbling on his or her unicycle or juggling with fire. This was where comedian and actor Eddie Izzard made his living before he became famous.

On weekends large crowds gather to watch a steady stream of jugglers, mime artists, fire-eaters, unicyclists and escapologists. All the children stream to the front, eager to help out by throwing a juggling club, secure some handcuffs or take part in a seemingly death-defying stunt. The masses on the balcony of the Punch and Judy pub overlooking the Piazza offer constant encouragement (and criticism). Remember, these people are not paid to perform and depend on the generosity of the audience. A £1 coin (around $1.50) is usually considered an appropriate donation.

St Paul's Church

Open Mon 9.30–2.30, Tues–Fri 9.30–4.30 and for services on Sunday. The entrance is around the corner through the rose garden

Bordering the Covent Garden Piazza, this is one of the few major buildings in London to survive the Great Fire of London in 1666. Its proximity to the theatres of the West End has gained it the nickname of the 'Actors' Church' and if you go inside you will find plaques to actors and actresses such as Charlie Chaplin, Noel Coward and Vivien Leigh. If you've seen the film *My Fair Lady*, take a look at the front of St Paul's Church, the place where the film's two principal characters, Professor Henry Higgins and the Covent Garden flower-seller Eliza Doolittle, are meant to have first met.

Royal Opera House

Bow Street, WC2
t (020) 7304 4000
www.royaloperahouse.org

> ### Question 8
> What were decency boards and where would you find them?
> answer on p.250

⊖ Covent Garden/Leicester Square
Bus 6, 9, 11, 13, 15, 23, 77A, 91, 176
Open Tours: Mon–Fri at 10.30am, 12.30pm and 2.30pm, Sat at 10.30am, 11.30am, 12.30pm and 1.30pm
Adm Tours: adult £8, child £7
Wheelchair accessible, with adapted toilets

The magnificently revamped Royal Opera House probably doesn't rank too highly on most families' 'must-visit' list. Most kids, however, enjoy exploring buildings, which is exactly what they can do (provided they're eight or over) on a backstage tour given three times a day during the week and five times on Saturday (allow an hour). These take in the magnificent concert hall itself, the orchestra pit, the dressing rooms and the costume production department. Though not exactly Disneyland, the Royal Opera House is a degree more family-friendly than it once was. In an effort to welcome more of the population to opera, public exhibitions and free classical concerts are now staged in its foyer on Monday lunchtimes, and family-friendly shows are often put on at Christmas time.

Tell me a story: Covent Garden

Covent Garden was once part of a great estate owned by the Earls of Bedford. Formerly a convent garden (hence the name, the 'n' ceased to be pronounced over time), it came under the ownership of the first Earl during the dissolution of the monasteries in 1552, and was turned into the city's very first square in 1630 by the fourth Earl, who instructed his architect, Inigo Jones, to ape the design of a classical Italian piazza.

Initially inhabited by high society, it became home, for much of its existence, to the capital's great wholesale 'fruit 'n' veg' and flower markets. In 1974, however, the markets relocated to Vauxhall and the square underwent a genteel facelift. The market buildings were transformed into alfresco cafés, chic boutiques and stylish museums, while the square's pedestrianized confines were reborn as a sort of semi-bohemian crafts centre. Today, these gently cobbled streets and shopping arcades are perhaps London's closest approximation of European café culture.

WHERE TO SHOP

Its museums and street performers aside, Covent Garden is known principally for its shopping. It boasts a number of places that will appeal to families, including Peter Rabbit & Friends (a shop dedicated to Beatrix Potter's furry creations), the Australia Shop (for all your down-under needs – boomerangs, koala bear soft toys and, of course, Vegemite), Cybercandy (which stocks sweets from all over the world, as well retro British classics, such as Moondust and Spangles), and a branch of the Disney Store.

Apple Market

Open 9–5, daily

This cheerful weekday market occupies part of the old central market building. You'll find a wide variety of craft produce including hand-painted jewellery, knitwear and candles, and on Mondays there's a small antique market.

The Australia Shop

27 Maiden Lane, WC2
t (020) 7836 0646
www.australiashop.co.uk
Open Mon–Sat 10.30–7.30, Sun 10.30–6

Benjamin Pollock's Toy Shop

44 Covent Garden Market, WC2
t (020) 7379 7866
www.pollocks-coventgarden.co.uk
⊖ Covent Garden/Leicester Square
Bus 6, 9, 11, 13, 15, 23, 77a, 91, 176
Open Mon–Sat 10.30–6, Sun 12 noon–6

This lovely little shop, full of olde worlde toys and games, is a great place to take the kids in order to show them that not all toys need batteries and joysticks. Here you'll find hand-painted puppets, carved yo-yos, butterfly kites, dragon mobiles, intricate paper planes and flying machines powered by ingenious rubber-band technology. There are also kaleidoscopes, die-cast soldiers and musical boxes. Pride of place, however, goes to some exquisite replica paper theatre sets, complete with scale scenery and actors. You can buy home assembly kits – suitable for older, more dextrous children.

Cybercandy

3 Garrick Street, WC2
t 0845 838 0958
www.cybercandy.co.uk
Open Mon–Sat 10–10, Sun 11–8

The Disney Store

9 The Piazza, Covent Garden, WC2
t (020) 7836 5037

Can you spot?

The French-born Claude Duval was one of 17th-century London's most successful and famous highwaymen, holding up hundreds of stage-coaches during his career. He was particularly renowned for the daring nature of his robberies and the gallantry and charm he displayed toward his female victims – many of whom were said to have fallen in love with him. He was hanged in 1670. See if you can find the floor stone in St Paul's on which is written a four-line poem dedicated to this dandy highwayman. It reads:

Here lies Du Vall: Reader, if male thou art,
Look to thy purse, if female to thy heart...
Old Tyburn's glory, England's
illustrious thief,
Du Vall, the ladies' joy, Du Vall
the ladies' grief...

www.disneystore.co.uk
Open Mon–Sat 10–8, Sun 10–7

Jubilee Market

Jubilee Hall
Open 9.30–6, daily

Rebuilt in the 1980s on the site of the old foreign flower market, this deals mainly in tourist fare – Union Jack tea towels and the like. It is, however, a good place to hunt for cheap versions of the latest must-have toys.

Peter Rabbit & Friends

42 The Market, Covent Garden, WC2
t (020) 7497 1777
www.peterrabbit.com
Open Mon–Sun 10–6

Neal Street and Neal's Yard

North of the square past the Tube station and Long Acre lies the real heart of Covent Garden's shopping district. Neal Street and its surrounding roads have, in recent years, become an attraction in their own right, with a flourishing collection of funky fashion boutiques, health food stores and novelty shops. This whole area has a distinctly bohemian vibe attracting a motley collection of punters (not to mention buskers and street performers) on weekends, when it has an atmosphere more akin to a thriving market than a traditional shopping street. It's particularly good for hobbies and sports. It's especially good for The Kite Store, at no. 48, which sells just about every shape and colour kite imaginable, from super-speedy stunt numbers to novelty kites; Slam City Skates at 16 Neal's Yard, for skateboards in a million different colours and clothes of a myriad different styles (so long as they're baggy) and, at no. 41, Speedo, the place for goggles, swimwear and other aquatic essentials. You might also like to pay a visit to Neal's Yard, just around the corner. The Tintin Shop, dedicated to the comic adventures of the Belgian boy detective, is a couple of roads away at 34 Floral Street.

Other notable stores in the area include a branch of Baby Gap/Kids Gap on Long Acre and, should you need that little extra adornment, the the the Bead Shop at 21a Tower Street (behind Cambridge Circus), whose shelves are filled with coloured baubles and necklaces.

If you (or perhaps more pertinently your kids) need to take rest from shopping, head to the north end of Neal Street, past Shaftesbury Avenue to Stacey Street where you'll find Phoenix Garden, a lovely little park built on the site of a car park and filled with flowers and wildlife.

The Bead Shop

24 Earlham Street, WC2
t (020) 7379 9214

www.londonbeadshop.co.uk
Open 10.30–8 daily

Gap Kids

121–123 Long Acre, WC2
t (020) 7836 0646
www.gapkids.com
Open Mon–Sat 10–8, Sun 12 noon–6

The Kite Store

48 Neal Street, WC2
t (020) 7836 1666
Open Mon–Sat 10–6 (till 7 Thurs)

Slam City Skates

16 Neal's Yard, WC2
t (020) 7240 0928
www.slamcity.com
Open Mon–Sat 11–7, Sun 12–5

Speedo

41 Neal Street, WC2
t (020) 7497 0950
www.speedo.com
Open Mon–Sat 9.30–7, Sun 12–5

The Tintin Shop

34 Floral Street, WC2
t (020) 7836 1131
www.thetintinshop.uk.com
Open Mon–Sat 10–5.30
See **Shop** p.237–49 for more details on the above
shops.

> **Did you know?**
> The world's first postage stamp, the Penny
> Black, was introduced in 1840. Previously, the cost
> of sending a letter was born by the recipient
> rather than the sender. You can see an example of
> a Penny Black in the well-stocked Stanley
> Gibbons stamp emporium (see p.85).

AROUND & ABOUT

Drury Lane & Bow Street

You could pay a visit to the Drury Lane Gardens, a
small enclosed open space for the under-5s with
various climbing frames and soft rubbery floors.
There are several benches where parents can sit
and watch their charges – recommended on sunny
days. Built in 1877, this was one of London's first
public gardens and was constructed, on the
recommendation of the public health reformer
Edwin Chadwick, on a former burial ground. Bow
Street, one of London's most famous streets, is
just east of Covent Garden, while nearby is the
architectural oddity of Sir John Soane's Museum,
home to a bizarre collection of art and curiosities.
After a heavy day's sightseeing, you could cool off
with a dip in the Oasis Sports Centre Pool, just to
the north of Covent Garden, at 32 Endell Street,
WC2, **t** (020) 7831 1804 (see p.187).

Sir John Soane's Museum

12–14 Lincoln's Inn Fields, WC2
t (020) 7405 2107
www.soane.org
♦ Holborn
Open Tues–Sat 10–5, until 9pm on first Tues of
each month
Free
*Limited wheelchair access, call (020) 7440 4263 for
information and assistance*

Situated on Lincoln's Inn Fields, this wonderful
museum is made up of three interlinked houses
that were once the home of Sir John Soane, the
celebrated 18th-century architect (he designed the
original Bank of England building) and collector
extraordinaire. Inside, it's a real treasure trove. You'll
find statues, Egyptian relics, toys, models of buildings, artworks (including a collection of lively

Hogarth cartoons – follow the 'Rake's Progress' from wealthy young ne'er-do-well to the madhouse) and jewellery. Everything, in fact, that caught Sir John's eye. Indeed, inveterate hoarder that he was, his collection grew so big that he was eventually forced to turn his house into a museum, in which he created a set of ingeniously elaborate unfolding cabinets to better display his effects.

The museum recently opened an education room where events and activities are laid on for families. Guided tours of the museum are available on Saturdays at 11am and cost £5. On the first Tuesday evening of each month, you have the chance to see the house as Soane himself would have experienced it, illuminated by candlelight.

Note, the house is not very big and extremely popular, which can mean long queues. If visiting at the weekend, aim to get there first thing.

The Strand and Embankment

⊖ Embankment, Charing Cross
Bus 6, 9, 11, 13, 15, 23, 77a, 91, 176

The Strand, one of London's most famous thoroughfares, runs east from Trafalgar Square just to the south of Covent Garden. Here you'll find the world-famous Savoy Hotel with its elegant tea room, the newly restored Benjamin Franklin House and the riverside museums of Somerset House, as well as the Stanley Gibbons stamp emporium – a must for young stamp collectors everywhere. Determined accumulators should also consider paying a visit to the Charing Cross Collectors' Fair, which is held every Saturday from 8.30am–5pm in the basement of the PriceWaterhouseCoopers car park on Villiers Street behind Charing Cross Station. Here, as well as stamps and first day covers, you'll find hordes of ancient Roman and British coins for sale.

Until 1860, the great mansions on the Strand's southern side faced on to the Thames. The constant threat of flooding and disease, however (in 1849 over 2,000 people a week were dying of cholera), forced the authorities to construct the Victoria Embankment as a buffer. Today, the Embankment is flanked by a four-lane carriageway and is, in truth, rather gloomy, although its sightseeing potential has been considerably increased by the creation of the Hungerford Footbridge a few years ago which links the Charing Cross end of the Embankment with the South Bank Centre and offers great views up and down the river. It stands next to Cleopatra's Needle, a 50-ft-tall, 1,500-year-old Egyptian monument erected here in 1879 (see p.85). There is also an embarkation point for a sightseeing catamaran here that will take you east along the river as far as Greenwich.

Benjamin Franklin House

36 Craven Street, WC2
t (020) 7925 1405
www.benjaminfranklinhouse.org
⊖ Embankment, Charing Cross
Open 12 noon–5 daily
Adm Adult £7, under-12s **free**

Restored historical residences are often of only limited appeal to children, no matter how illustrious their former occupants. And they don't get much more illustrious than the American founding father, scientist and philosopher, Benjamin Franklin. The people behind the recent restoration of Franklin's only surviving UK residence seem to have understood that there's only so much fun to be had from beautifully preserved period furniture, and have taken a more 'dramatic' approach to their task. You're guided around the house by an actress playing the part of Polly Hudson, the daughter of Franklin's landlady, who tells stories of the great man's life, using the exhibits as props for her tales. The museum also has a special Discovery Room for children and organizes workshops and events for families throughout the year.

Somerset House

The Strand, WC2
t (020) 7845 4600
www.somersethouse.org.uk
⚩ Temple, Charing Cross, Embankment, Covent Garden
Bus 6, 9, 11, 13, 15, 23, 77a, 91, 176
Open 10–6 daily
Adm Entry to Somerset House, the Courtyard and the River Terrace is **free**; Courtauld Gallery: adult £5, child **free**, concs £4; Gilbert Collection: adult £5, child **free**, concs £4, joint ticket (any two collections) adult £8; Hermitage Rooms: adult £5, child £4
Wheelchair accessible, with adapted toilets

There has been a building on this site since at least Tudor times, although the terribly grand structure you see today was erected in the 18th century for the Duke of Somerset, and has, over the course of its history, served a variety of functions. It was home to the Navy Board and Inland Revenue and, most famously of all, was for a long time occupied by the Register of Births, Marriages and Deaths. Following a multi-million-pound refurbishment for the millennium, its grand wings now provide venues for three outstanding artistic attractions: the Courtauld Gallery, which has a large collection of Impressionist and post-Impressionist paintings (including Van Gogh's *Bandaged Ear*); the Hermitage Rooms, where Russian imperial treasures from the State Hermitage Museum in St Petersburg are displayed; and the Gilbert Collection of jewellery, silverware and other assorted treasures donated by the late American collector and philanthropist, Arthur Gilbert. Interesting though these are, it's the building itself which is the real attraction, with its wonderful river views (particularly from the River Terrace, which is linked by a walkway to Waterloo Bridge) and glorious courtyard set with dozens of water jets that have been specially programmed to put on choreographed displays. Dotted with benches, it's a great place to have a picnic. At Christmas, the New York-style ice rink that is installed here on an annual basis is a lovely, atmospheric treat for adults and children alike.

Refreshment is available at the very grand (and expensive) Admiralty restaurant, the much more

relaxed River Terrace Café Bar or the takeaway delicatessen next to the Seaman's Hall. The Courtauld Institute organizes free, art-based family workshops on Saturdays from 2–3.30pm, when children aged 6–12 can take part in a range of activities, such as 'making a silver goblet' and 'animal safaris'. You can also meet strolling players in the courtyard, take part in tours or simply pick up a free family trail guide at the main desk.

Cleopatra's Needle

Cleopatra's Needle, a 50-ft-tall, 1,500-year-old Egyptian obelisk, is one of London's odder monuments. When first you see it, plonked somewhat haphazardly in the gloomy surrounds of the Victoria Embankment, your immediate thought is 'why couldn't they have found somewhere nicer to put it?' But, truth be told, it's a wonder they got it here at all. Bequeathed to Britain in 1819, by Mohammad Ali, the Turkish Viceroy of Egypt, it took over 59 years to get to its present site. At first, no one could work out how to move it and then, when an engineer did devise a means of transport using an iron cylindrical pontoon, it very nearly sank. The intended site for the obelisk, near the Houses of Parliament, turned out to be unsuitable because of subsidence, forcing the Board of Works, whose responsibility the Needle had become, hurriedly to find a new spot for it on the Victoria Embankment. To top it all, the sphinxes sitting at the Needle's base are facing the wrong way.

Buried beneath the Needle are two time capsules. They contain a picture of Queen Victoria, several newspapers, four Bibles, a railway guide and photographs of (allegedly) the 12 prettiest girls in Britain at the time.

Stanley Gibbons

399 The Strand, WC2
t (020) 7836 8444
www.stanleygibbons.com
Open Mon–Fri 9–5.30, Sat 9.30–5.30

The world's oldest stamp dealer's is a collector's paradise, selling everything imaginable for the philatelist.

Boat trips

Bateaux London & Catamaran Cruisers

t (020) 7695 1800
www.bateauxlondon.com
Times Apr–Oct cruises depart every 30mins from 10.30–4, Nov–Mar cruises depart every 45mins between 10.30–3

River cruises with recorded commentary in purpose-built catamarans sailing between Embankment Pier, Waterloo Pier and Westminster Pier, as well as out to Greenwich and the Thames Barrier, passing some of the river's most famous landmarks – including the Houses of Parliament, St Paul's Cathedral, Tate Modern and the Tower of London – en route. See p.29 for fare details.

Picnics & snacks

It is possible to find the odd nook and cranny suitable for an alfresco meal in the area. Good spots include **Embankment Gardens** (there's also a small café), **Phoenix Gardens**, just off Shaftesbury Avenue, the churchyard of **St Paul's Church** and the courtyard at **Somerset House**. For supplies, go to **Neal's Yard**, WC2, just north of Covent Garden for **Neal's Yard Bakery**, at no.6, t (020) 7836 5199, and **Neal's Yard Dairy** nearby at 17 Shorts Gardens, WC2, t (020) 7240 5700, ➔ **Covent Garden**. There are also branches of **Marks & Spencer** at 107–115 Long Acre, WC2, t (020) 7240 9549, ➔ **Covent Garden**, and a **Tesco Metro** at 22–25 Bedford Street, t 0845 677 9173, ➔ **Covent Garden**.

Restaurants and cafés to try include **Fuel**, t (020) 7836 2187, which can offer ringside seats for the daily entertainment on the Piazza. More wholesome fare can be found at **Food for Thought** (see p.233), 31 Neal Street, WC2, t (020) 7836 0239, a cheap and friendly vegetarian café (it can get crowded, so turn up early for lunch) and the **World Food Café**, 14 Neal's Yard, WC2, t (020) 7379 0298. For fast food, try the **Rock and Soul Plaice** (see p.227), 47 Endell Street, WC2, t (020) 7836 3785, ➔ **Covent Garden**, the oldest fish and chip shop in the capital, serving large portions of battered fish and chunky chips. Sticky treats are available from fancy, French patisserie, **Paul**, at 29 Bedford Street, WC2, t (020) 7836 5321, ➔ **Covent Garden**.

Restaurants

1 Belgo Centraal
50 Earlham Street, WC2
t (020) 7813 2233
www.belgo-restaurants.com
➔ Covent Garden
Open Mon–Thurs 12 noon–11, Fri and Sat 12 noon–11.30, Sun 12 noon–10.30

2 Brown's
82–84 St Martin's Lane, WC2
t (020) 7497 5050
www.browns-restaurants.com
➔ Leicester Square, Covent Garden
Open Mon–Wed 9am–11pm, Thurs & Fri 9am–11.30pm, Sat 10–11.30, Sun 10–10.30

3 Café Pasta
2 Garrick Street, WC2
t (020) 7497 2779
www.cafepasta.com
➔ Leicester Square, Covent Garden
Open Mon–Sat 11.30am–12 midnight, Sun 11.30-11

4 Café Rouge
34 Wellington Street, WC2
t (020) 7836 0998
www.caferouge.co.uk
➔ Covent Garden
Open Mon–Sat 9am–11pm, Sun 9am–10.30pm

5 Maxwell's
8/9 James Street, WC2
t (020) 7836 0303
➔ Covent Garden, Embankment, Leicester Square
Open Mon–Sat 10am–12 midnight, Sun 10am–11.30pm

6/7 Pizza Express
Branches at: 9 Bow Street, WC2, t (020) 7240 3443, ➔ Covent Garden; 80–81 St Martin's Lane, WC2, t (020) 7836 8001, ➔ Covent Garden, Leicester Square
www.pizzaexpress.com
Open Mon–Sat 11.30am–12 midnight, Sun 11.30-11 (11.30pm at Bow St branch)

8 Smollensky's
105 The Strand, WC2
t (020) 7497 2101
www.smollenskys.co.uk
➔ Embankment, Charing Cross
Open Mon–Wed 12 noon–12 midnight, Thurs–Sat 12 noon–12.30am, Sun 12 noon–5.30 and 6.30–11

9 TGI Friday's
6 Bedford Street, WC2
t (020) 7379 0585
www.tgifridays.co.uk
➔ Covent Garden, Leicester Square, Charing Cross
Open 12 noon–11.30 daily

10 Wagamama
1 Tavistock Street, WC2
t (020) 7836 3330
www.wagamama.com
➔ Covent Garden, Charing Cross
Open Mon–Sat 12 noon–11, Sun 12 noon–10

See **Eat** p.224–36 for more details on the above restaurants.
See map on p.77 for the locations of the restaurants numbered above.

Buckingham Palace

This is picture-postcard London at its finest – an elegant, tree-lined boulevard leading down to the magnificent regal architecture of Buckingham Palace where, as every schoolchild knows, the Queen lives, and where you can take a guided tour in summer. Afterwards, why not have a picnic and run around in one of the two great parks flanking the palace, or head to Horse Guards Parade to see the Queen's chocolate-box soldiers parading up and down, before taking a stroll along the nearby King's Road with its fabulous shops and restaurants?

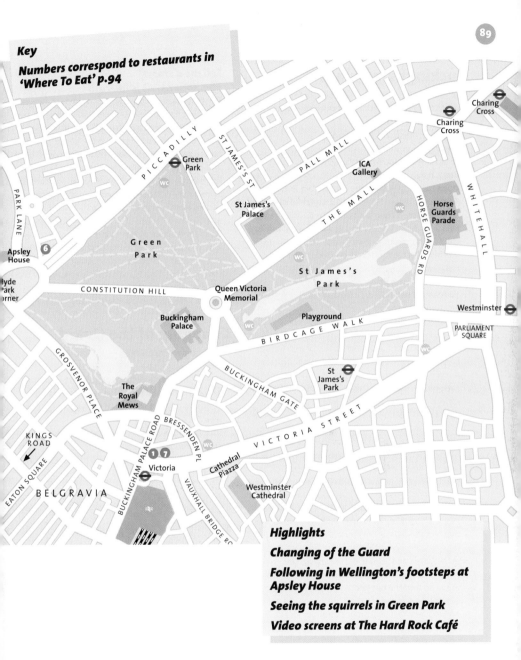

Highlights

Changing of the Guard

Following in Wellington's footsteps at Apsley House

Seeing the squirrels in Green Park

Video screens at The Hard Rock Café

Buckingham Palace

St James's Park, SW1. The ticket office for purchasing tickets on the day is located next to the palace entrance

t Booking line (020) 7766 7300/1
www.royal.gov.uk
St James's Park, Green Park, Victoria
Bus 7, 11, 139, 211, C1, C10
Open Late July–Sept 9.30–6 daily (last entry 3.45)
Adm Buckingham Palace: adult £15, child (under 17) £8.50, under-5s **free**; joint ticket to Buckingham Palace, Queen's Gallery and Royal mews: adult £27, child £13.50, under-5s **free**, family £69.50. There is a £1 booking fee for tickets booked online or over the phone
Wheelchair accessible
Suitable for older children (10 and over)
The tour lasts 45mins

During the Queen's two-month summer holiday, when she ups sticks (or, perhaps more accurately, has her royal retinue up her sticks for her) for the crown estates in Balmoral, Scotland, her more famous London residence throws its doors open to the public. Or at least some of its doors; in fact the official guided tour takes in just the state rooms plus a small section of the gardens, rather than any of the private quarters. These include the Grand Hall, the Throne Room, the State Dining Room, the Music Room, the Royal Picture Gallery and the Silk Tapestry Room. All are splendid in a formal, rather haughty sort of way, although the Throne Room is a bit of a disappointment as it doesn't even contain a throne, just two pink and yellow chairs marked EIIR (Elizabeth Regina) and P (Philip). To be honest, much of the palace will probably prove a little dull for most children, although there is now a family activity area and a small nature trail in the gardens. Many of the more interesting areas are roped off and the rarefied 'don't touch' atmosphere is a little restrictive.

The Queen's Gallery on Buckingham Palace Road is a lot more fun with loads of jewels and crowns on display as well as plenty of Old Master paintings, which take the form of rotating displays taken from the extensive royal collection, plus occasional touring exhibitions.

Remember, if the Union Flag is raised the Queen is at home; if it's lowered, she's out.

Tell me a story:
The house that John built
The first house on this site was a modest dwelling built by John Sheffield, Duke of Buckingham in 1702, which was bought by the Royal Family in 1762. George IV decided to improve the house, but then he and architect John Nash decided to knock it down and start again. So grand was the scheme that by the time George died in 1830, the new palace wasn't even finished. Parliament, worried about the cost, sacked Nash and gave the job to Edward Blore, who finished the job at the lowest price possible. Nearly the whole of Nash's work was covered with a new façade and his gateway, the Marble Arch, was moved to its present position at the bottom of Oxford Street. Finally, in 1913, a new façade by the architect Sir Aston Webb replaced Blore's to produce the famous building we see today.

Changing of the Guard

St James's Park, Green Park, Victoria
Bus 1, 16, 24, 52, 73
Times The ceremony takes place every morning between April and August at 11.30 sharp, and on alternate days for the rest of the year
Free
Suitable for all ages
The ceremony lasts about 40mins

This daily costume drama has become a veritable symbol of Britishness attracting hundreds of

tourists every day, and yet, it has to be said, it's just a teensy bit dull. To begin with it'll probably capture your interest – the rows of bearskinned, red-coated soldiers, the barked orders, the military band, the complex, regulated marching patterns but, after an hour of the stuff, you could be forgiven for wishing that they'd get to the point (which, in case you're wondering, is to replace the 40 men guarding Buckingham Palace with another contingent from Wellington Barracks). Nonetheless, it's extremely popular, and the views from outside Buckingham Palace can quickly become obscured. Even perched on your shoulders, kids may have trouble seeing. Your best bet for a glimpse of the marching soldiers is to take up one of the alternative vantage points at St James's or Birdcage Walk.

Horse Guards

London's own toy soldiers, the Horse Guards, are perhaps the most photographed military personnel in the world. Sitting astride their horses in full dress uniform of red tunic, breastplate and sword, it's an image that has graced a million postcards. The stillness of the soldiers – both horse and man are trained not to move and to look straight ahead – fascinates children, who will try hard to pull the funniest face and break the soliders' concentration. At 11am every summer morning you can see them move as they march to Buckingham Palace for the changing of the Guard. They also take part in a great military show in front of the

Can you spot?

A famous London monument. It's fairly hard to miss. It's 124-ft tall and supports a statue of George III's son Frederick, the Commander-in-Chief of the British forces during the Napoleonic Wars or, as he's more famously known, the Grand Old Duke of York – yes, that Grand Old Duke of York.

Queen in early June known as Trooping the Colour. See 'London's Year' p.33.

Royal Mews

Buckingham Palace Road, SW1
t (020) 7766 7302
www.royal.gov.uk
⊖ St James's Park, Green Park, Victoria
Bus 1, 16, 24, 52, 73
Open Mar–July and Oct 11–4 (last admission 3.15), Aug–Sept 10–5 (last admission 4.15)
Adm Adult £7, child (under 18) £4.50, concs £6, family £18.50
Wheelchair accessible, but call in advance. Suitable for ages 7 and over. Allow at least 1hr

These are the stables where the horses that work for the Royal Family are kept. As you would expect, the stalls themselves are rather magnificent, with tiled walls and gleaming horse brasses. You can touch and pet the horses and admire the beautiful gold coach used for coronations – it's so heavy, it takes eight horses to pull it!

Question 9
How did Birdcage Walk, which borders
St James's Park to the south, get its name?
answer on p.250

The Mall

The capital's most majestic avenue was built in the early 20th century as a memorial to Queen Victoria. It runs from Trafalgar Square to Buckingham Palace. Note the Victoria Memorial in front of the Palace gates. The views from Admiralty Arch at the Trafalgar Square end, down the beautiful tree-lined sweep, are particularly impressive.

Double indemnity

In 1842, as Queen Victoria rode through crowds lining the Mall with her husband, Prince Albert, by her side, a man stepped forward out of the crowd and attempted to fire a shot at the Queen. Luckily for Victoria, the gun misfired. The police were unable to catch the culprit, so the incident was dropped. The very next day, however, the same thing happened again, except this time the gun did go off ... fortunately, the bullet was a blank and caused no damage. The gunman, a John Francis, was arrested and sentenced to death, but was then granted a reprieve before execution.

ICA Gallery

The Mall, SW1
t (020) 7930 3647
www.ica.org.uk
◉ Piccadilly Circus, Charing Cross
Bus 3, 6, 9, 11, 13, 14, 15, 19, 22, 23, 38, 77a, 88, 91, 139, 159, 176
Open Galleries 12 noon–7.30
Adm Depends on exhibition

The Institute for Contemporary Arts (known as the ICA) is generally more concerned with presenting arthouse films than entertaining families, but come the summer there's plenty for 11–16-year-olds to do. The institute runs a number of courses in web design, movie-making and computer game creation for younger visitors, as well as half-term workshops in drawing, sculpture, dance, animation and art history. The shop is good for arty bits and bobs, including original jewellery designs and gifts made by local artists. There's also a very good café although you have to become a day member in order to make use of it.

Apsley House: The Wellington Museum

Hyde Park Corner, 149 Piccadilly, W1
t (020) 7499 5676
www.english-heritage.org.uk
◉ Hyde Park Corner
Bus 2, 8, 9, 10, 14, 16, 19, 22, 36, 38, 73, 82, 83, 137
Open Apr–Oct Mon–Sat 10–5, Nov–Mar 10–4 daily
Adm Adult £5.30, under-18s £2.70, English Heritage Members **free**
Free entry to all on Waterloo Day (18th June). Sound guides, access via steps to house and lift

London's most singular address (it's officially known as No.1 London) was built by Robert Adam between 1771 and 1778 and was home to the first Duke of Wellington (he of the famous boots and, indeed, famous defeat of Napoleon). It's still the family's London residence.

Ten rooms have been lovingly restored under the auspices of the Victoria & Albert Museum and, since 2004, English Heritage. The collection, assembled by the Duke following his triumphant return from the Battle of Waterloo, includes paintings by Goya, Velasquez, Van Dyck, Landseer and Rubens, as well as medals and memorabilia. Themed sound guides and trails for children (on subjects such as 'servants', 'society parties' and, of course, 'The Battle of Waterloo') are available throughout the year and there are special family-friendly activities organized for Museums and Galleries Month in May, on Waterloo Day in June and at Christmas. You can also purchase a ticket here to visit the nearby Wellington Arch at Hyde Park Corner, which you can climb for great views of the area.

Green Park

Piccadilly W1 & The Mall, SW1
t (020) 7298 2000
www.royalparks.gov.uk/parks/green_park/
◉ Green Park
Bus 2, 8, 9, 14, 16, 19, 22, 38, 52, 73, 82
Open Dawn till dusk, daily
Free

This a lovely serene place and very popular with London's children. Every spring, for a few weeks, it becomes a Yellow and Green Park when hordes of daffodils pop up. If you walk across it from Buckingham Palace you come to Piccadilly.

St James's Park

The Mall, SW1
t (020) 7298 2000
www.royalparks.gov.uk/parks/st_james_park/
⊖ St James's Park
Bus 3, 11, 12, 24, 53, 77A, 88, 109, 159, 211, X53
Open Dawn till dusk, daily
Free

A must for all bird-lovers. In the 17th century the park held several aviaries (hence the name of the road that runs alongside the park, Birdcage Walk) and today is home to one of London's finest wild-fowl ponds, a great stretch of water where you can find more than 20 species of bird including ducks, geese and even pelicans (you can watch them being fed between 2 and 3pm each day). There's also a playground with a sandpit and a teashop. If your kids have seen the film *One Hundred and One Dalmatians* (the live action version, not the cartoon), they may recognize certain parts of the park – it was the scene of the bicycle chase where poor old Pongo gets thrown into the lake. See if you can spot the black swans that nest on the pond's central island. Brass, concert and military bands play on the park's bandstand on Saturday, Sunday and Bank Holiday afternoons throughout the summer.

Guards' Museum

Wellington Barracks, Birdcage Walk, SW1
t (020) 7414 3271
www.theguardsmuseum.com
⊖ St James's Park
Bus 3, 11, 12, 24, 159
Open 10–4, daily
Adm Adult £2, under-16s **free**

The museum traces the history of British troops from Cromwell's New Model Army and Charles II's five regiments to the present day. There's also an excellent toy soldier shop. You can compare these mini uniforms with the ones at the Changing of the Guard (*see* p.90).

King's Road

⊖ Sloane Square

King's Road is one of London's best shopping streets. Here you'll find the Early Learning Centre at no.36, the children's clothes shops Brora (no.344), Gap Kids (no.122), Iana (no. 186), Jigsaw Junior (just off the King's Road on Duke of York Square) and Trotters (no.34) as well as the main branch of Daisy and Tom's (no.181), a dedicated kids' department store filled with toys, games, books and clothes.

See **Shop** p.238–49 for details of the above stores.

Picnics & snacks

With two of the city's finest parks within easy reach, you really are spoiled for choice. There are few nicer areas to enjoy a picnic than **St James's Park** and **Green Park**. For supplies, head to Elizabeth Street, SW1, ⊖ **Sloane Square**, where there's an excellent collection of quality food shops. Try **Poilâne**, a French bakery at no. 46, **t** (020) 7808 4910; the bakery/delicatessen **Baker & Spice** at no.54, **t** (020) 7730 3033, or the **Chocolate Society**, a chocolate shop-cum-café, at no. 36 **t** (020) 7259 9222. More great organic fare is available further west on Upper Tachbrook Street, where there's the Italian deli **Gastronomica Italia** at no.8, **t** (020) 7834 2767, and the **Rippon Cheese Stores** at no.26, **t** (020) 7931 0628. A food market is held on the street every day except Sunday and a farmer's market on nearby Orange Square, just off Pimlico Road, every Saturday from 9am–1pm. Less fancy fare can be picked up at **Tesco Metro** at 18 Warwick Way, SW1, **t** 0845 677 693, near Victoria Station.

Other than the **Inn the Park** café set by one of the lakes in St James's Park, **t** (020) 7451 9999, ⊖ St James's Park, which sells pre-packed picnic hampers, there's not much close to Buckingham Palace itself. For details of cafés in the **Trafalgar Square** area, see p.73–4. Otherwise, your best bet is to head to the **King's Road**. Look out for the **Chelsea Kitchen** (see p.225) at no. 98, SW3, **t** (020) 7589 1330, ⊖ Sloane Square, an old-fashioned café selling sandwiches, salads and pasta dishes. There are branches of **McDonald's** at 155 Victoria Street, SW1 and in the Victoria Place Shopping Centre in Victoria Station.

Restaurants

1 Ask Pizza
160–162 Victoria Street, SW1
t (020) 7630 8228
www.askcentral.co.uk
⊖ Victoria
Branches open 11.30am–11.30pm

2 Benihana
77 King's Road, SW3
t (020) 7376 7799
www.benihana.co.uk
⊖ Sloane Square
Open Mon–Sat 12 noon–3 & 5.30–10.30, Sun 5–10

3 Blue Elephant
3–6 Fulham Broadway, SW6
t (020) 7385 6595
www.blueelephant.com
⊖ Fulham Broadway
Bus 11, 14, 28, 211, 295, C4
Open Mon–Thurs 12 noon–2.30 & 7–11.30,
Fri & Sat 12 noon–2.30 & 6.30–11.30, Sun 12 noon–3
& 7–10.30

4 The Blue Kangaroo
555 Kings Road, SW6
t (020) 7371 7672
www.thebluekangaroo.co.uk
⊖ Fulham Broadway
Open 9.30–8.30 daily

5 Chutney Mary
535 King's Road, SW10
t (020) 7351 3113
www.chutneymary.com
⊖ Fulham Broadway
Open Mon–Sat 12.30–2.30 and 5.30–11.30,
Sun 12.30–3 and 7–10.30

6 Hard Rock Café
150 Old Park Lane, W1
t (020) 7514 1700
www.hardrock.com
⊖ Hyde Park Corner
Open Mon–Thurs & Sun 11.30am–12.30am, Fri and
Sat 11.30am–1am

7/8 Pizza Express
154 Victoria Street, SW1
t (020) 7828 1477
⊖ Victoria
152 King's Road, SW3
t (020) 7351 5031
⊖ Sloane Square
www.pizzaexpress.com
Open Mon–Sat 11.30–12 midnight, Sun 11.30–11.30

See **Eat** p.224–36 for more details on the above restaurants.
See maps on pp.88–89 for the locations of the restaurants numbered above.

Westminster

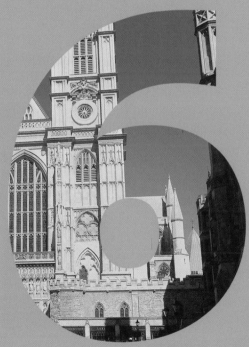

Westminster, the nation's political heartland, is likely to be of most interest to older children, those with some knowledge and understanding of history, rather than youngsters and toddlers who, once they've finished pointing excitedly at the big clock, will quickly grow bored. Remember, a tour of this area can easily be combined with a trip to Trafalgar Square, or a foray across the Thames to the South Bank.

You could describe Westminster as the very epicentre of Englishness. It's the home of Big Ben, the world's most famous big clock, whose bongs are relayed around the country at midnight every New Year's Eve. Adjoining it are the Houses of Parliament, where the great and good of the country come to thrash out the issues of the day, while across Parliament Square is the 900-year-old Westminster Abbey where the coronation of all British monarchs takes place.

Take a quick walk along Parliament Street and you'll find Downing Street, where the Prime Minister lives, the Cenotaph, the country's most important war memorial, and the Churchill Museum and Cabinet War Rooms, where Britain's Second World War campaign was formulated. It's all very serious stuff and yet, at the same time, also quite touristy. Should you decide to pay the area a visit, you'll no doubt be accompanied on your travels by hordes of camera-wielding tourists, furiously clicking at everything in sight.

Remember, Tate Britain, one of the nation's pre-eminent art galleries and home of the ever-controversial Turner Prize, is just a short walk south along the river.

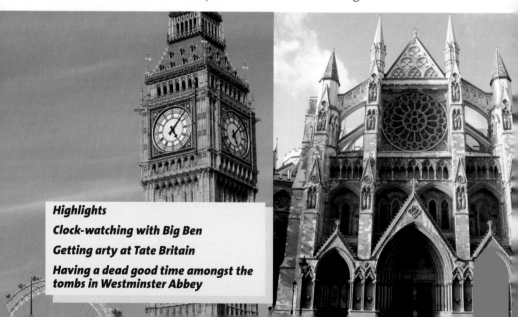

Highlights

Clock-watching with Big Ben

Getting arty at Tate Britain

Having a dead good time amongst the tombs in Westminster Abbey

RECENT

HAYMARKET

Trafalgar Square

Charing Cross

Embankment

PALL MALL

NORTHUMBERLAND AVE

THE MALL

WHITEHALL

VICTORIA EMBANKMENT

WC

2

Horse Guards Parade

Banqueting House

St James's Park

WC

HORSE GUARDS RD

10 Downing Street

Cenotaph

KING CHARLES ST

WC

Cabinet War Rooms

Westminster

BIRDCAGE WALK

WESTMINSTER BRIDGE

St James's Park

PARLIAMENT SQUARE

Big Ben

VICTORIA STREET

GREAT SMITH STREET

Westminster Abbey

Houses of Parliament

MILLBANK

Victoria Tower Gardens

1

Westminster Cathedral (off map)

GREAT PETER STREET

MARSHAM STREET

ROCHESTER

HORSEFERRY ROAD

Key
Numbers correspond to restaurants in 'Where To Eat' p.102

VINCENT SQUARE

VINCENT STREET

JOHN ISLIP STREET

ATTERBURY STREET

MILLBANK

Tate Britain

3

VAUXHALL BRIDGE RD

ALBERT EMBANKMENT

Pimlico

VAUXHALL BRIDGE

500 metres
500 yards

Vauxhall

Vauxhall

Westminster Abbey

Broad Sanctuary, SW1
t (020) 7222 5152
www.westminster-abbey.org
Westminster, St James's Park
Bus 3, 11, 12, 24, 53, 88, 109, 159, 211, X53
Open Mon–Fri 9.30–4.45 (last admission 3.45,
Wed till 8, last admission 7), Sat 9–2.45 (last
admission 1.45)
Adm Adult £10, child £7, family £24
Wheelchair accessible for most of the abbey; entry
ramp at the north door. Audio guides are available.
Suitable for ages 6 and over. Allow at least 1hr

Kids are not always interested in churches, even
ones as famous and important as this, and you
may feel disinclined to subject them to the Abbey,
whatever its history or however lovely the stained
glass. But, then, it all depends on how you
approach it. Left to their own devices your kids will
probably have seen enough here in three minutes
flat, but point out the fact that the stones they are
touching and, often as not, walking over conceal
dead bodies, regale them with a few choice stories
(*see below*) and they'll find the whole experience
much more interesting.

The Abbey could be described, if you were feeling
a little disrespectful, as a great indoor graveyard
filled with the remains, relics and reminders of the
last thousand years of British history. You enter
through Statesmen's Aisle, which features memorials
to three of the country's most famous past Prime
Ministers: Gladstone, Disraeli and Palmerston.
Continue on around the Abbey and you'll find the
tombs of Elizabeth I and her cousin Mary, Queen of
Scots, whom she beheaded, and what is thought to
be the last resting place of the two young princes,
Edward V and his brother Richard, who were
supposedly murdered by their uncle (later Richard III)
in the Tower of London in 1483. Explore further and
you'll find the centrepiece of the Abbey – the
shrine of St Edward, the king (then Edward 'The
Confessor') who had the whole thing constructed
nearly a thousand years ago. The Abbey's muddled
layout just makes it more interesting for kids who
happily wend their way through the assorted
statues, stones, memorials and shrines. See if they
can find Poets' Corner where Geoffrey Chaucer was
buried in 1400. Ever since, some of the country's
most famous poets and writers have ended up
here including Dryden, Samuel Johnson, Sheridan,
Browning and Tennyson. Others, such as
Shakespeare, Shelley and Keats, are memorialized
without actually being interred here.

The Abbey is a very beautiful place with great
vaulted ceilings and richly coloured stained glass
windows, but the best thing about it is that it
manages to engage the macabre interest of
children while, at the same time, offering a more
serene, reflective air which adults will appreciate.

There's a café and a souvenir shop in the cloisters,
the area where the monks who resided in the
Abbey until the middle of the 16th century lived
and worked. Audio guides are available for £4 at
the front desk.

Tell me a story: Emperors' new clothes

Supertunica and Imperial Mantle may sound like
good titles for a couple of glam-rock songs, but
actually they are the names given to the Royal
Coronation Robes which, when worn together,
weigh in at a hefty 23lbs. The Imperial Mantle was
made for the coronation of George IV, whose
overall ensemble – including a specially made
crown bearing 12, 314 diamonds and 204 pearls –
was so heavy that he very nearly fainted.
Throughout the five-hour ceremony his estranged
wife Queen Caroline hammered angrily on the doors
of the Abbey in an attempt to gain admittance.
She was refused, however, much to the displeasure
of the crowd assembled outside, most of whom
despised the flashy 'show-off' George.

Can you spot?

The statues in Parliament Square of three of Britain's most famous Prime Ministers: Palmerston, Disraeli and Winston Churchill. How is Churchill's statue different to the others? It is, how shall we put it, cleaner than the other statues. This is because it's heated from the inside to stop pigeon droppings from sticking.

Houses of Parliament

Parliament Square, SW1. The ticket office is opposite the St Stephen's entrance
t (020) 7219 3000
www.parliament.uk &
www.explore.parliament.uk
⊖ Westminster
Bus 3, 11, 12, 24, 53, 77a, 88, 109, 159, 184, 211, X53
Open To watch a debate from the House of Commons Visitors' Gallery, you must queue from 2.30pm onwards Mon–Wed, from 11.30am Thurs and from 9.30am Fri. Seats for Prime Minister's Question Time, which takes place on Wed at 12 noon, are available to UK residents only, who must write to their local MP. Guided tours of the palace when the house is sitting are again available only to UK residents (they take place on Mon, Tues and Wed mornings) and again only via written application to your local MP. In the summer recess (July–Sept) daily guided tours, given by qualified blue badge guides, are available to all visitors (both UK and overseas).
Adm Tours: adult £12, child £5, family £30, under-5s **free**; it is **free** to watch a debate
Wheelchair accessible
Suitable for ages 12 and over

Its official name is the Palace of Westminster, but politicians refer to it simply as 'the House'. Whatever you call it, it is one of the unmistakable sights of London. Most of the huge building dates from the 1830s, the original medieval structure

having burned down in a fire in 1834, although parts of the interior, including Westminster Hall, were built at the end of the 11th century.

This is where the British government goes about its daily business, and where the ruling party of the day debates policy with the opposition. Despite its importance, however, it was, until recently, very difficult for members of the public to take a look inside the beautiful, neogothic palace. Happily, guided tours are now available from July to September to all visitors (and to UK residents for the rest of the year via written application to your local MP). The tour includes the House of Commons chamber where the country's most important debates take place. It's surprisingly small, the chamber's plush leather benches having room for just 437 MPs (forcing many of the current 659 MPs to stand during popular debates).

From here it's on to the 'Noes Lobby', where MPs come to vote on legislation. Other places of interest on the tour include the Royal Gallery and Queen's Robing Room, where the Monarch prepares for the State Opening of Parliament; the House of Lords Chamber, and the very grand Westminster Hall, the oldest part of the whole palace. Though now only used for ceremonial occasions, the hall was once the setting for important state trials. Both Charles I and the Gunpowder plotters were tried (and found guilty) here.

Children wanting to find out more about parliament and its role in British society should visit the special family-friendly website **www**.explore.parliament.uk, which aims to make what is often thought quite a dry and dusty subject interesting for young people.

Big Ben

Big Ben, the great clock tower, completed in 1859, was named after a Mr Benjamin Hill, the portly commissioner of works at the time. Big Ben is actually the name of the bell rather than the tower – its distinctive sound is due to a crack that appeared

during its installation. Tours of the clock tower are occasionally available to UK residents (no children under 11) via written application to your local MP.

Churchill Museum & Cabinet War Rooms

Clive Steps, King Charles Street, SW1
t (020) 7766 0120
http://cwr.iwm.org.uk/
ǝ Westminster, St James's Park
Bus 3, 11, 12, 24, 53, 87, 88, 109, 148, 159, 184, 211
Open 9.30–6 daily (last admission 5pm)
Adm Adult £11, child **free**, concs £9, half-price entry for disabled visitors
Free audio guide available, wheelchair accessible, lift to museum ground floor, adapted toilets
Suitable for ages 6 and over
Allow at least 1hr

This is a great place to take children provided they have some knowledge of the Second World War. It contains both the Cabinet War Rooms – 21 cramped, low-ceilinged chambers 17 ft underground that were, for the last few years of the conflict, the nerve centre of the British war effort – and the country's only museum dedicated to the great wartime leader. The museum is divided into five sections covering Churchill's entire life, not just his wartime career, with exhibits ranging from his baby rattle and school reports to the periscope he used while on active service in the trenches of the First World War as well as many Second World War documents. There are also audiovisual and interactive displays giving a wealth of detail about the life story and legacy of the man recently voted the 'Greatest Briton' ever.

The war rooms themselves were, for a few years, the most important place in the entire country, for it was here that Churchill and his ministers made decisions that changed the course of history. To visit these rooms today is to take a step back into the past; they have remained untouched since the final days of the war in 1945. They are wonderfully evocative, their very smallness (Churchill's office was a converted broom cupboard) giving some sense of the desperate pressure of the times. Each individual detail, so ordinary in itself, becomes, in this context, charged with significance. You can even see Churchill's bedroom from where he made his legendary radio broadcasts. For the full effect, make use of the free, self-paced audio guides, on

which you can hear several of Churchill's rousing speeches accompanied by period music. There are also child-orientated audio guides available using children's memories of war, sound effects and recordings of conversations to bring the museum, and its role in the war, alive for younger visitors. The website also has family trails and information sheets which you can download before you visit.

Tate Britain

Millbank, SW1
t (020) 7887 8888
www.tate.org.uk/britain
ǝ Pimlico, Vauxhall ⇌ Vauxhall
Bus 2, 3, 36, 77A, 88, 159, 185, 507, C10
Open 10–5.50, daily, till 10pm first Fri of each month
Free (charges apply for some temporary exhibitions)
*Lift, buggy storage, wheelchair accessible via the entrances in Atterbury Street and John Islip Street; disabled parking spaces can be booked on **t** (020) 7887 8888*
Suitable for ages 6 and over
Allow at least 1hr 30mins

Can you spot?
The big beige office building with green windows opposite Tate Britain, on the other side of the river. This is the HQ of MI6, Britain's secret service. Until recently, the British government denied that this service existed, which meant that, officially, the building also didn't exist – and neither did the people who worked in it.

Question 10
What did Henry Tate invent that made him rich enough to pay for the Tate Gallery to be established in 1897?

answer on p.250

The Tate was originally intended as a showcase for British art when it opened in 1897. Unfortunately, over the next century, it built up such a large collection of international works that the amount of space being given over to British art was continually being reduced and, indeed, much of the Tate's collection sat permanently locked away in dark vaults. Something needed to be done. That something took the shape of a disused power station on Bankside which was opened in 2000 as Tate Modern (*see* p. 117). The old Tate, meanwhile, was reborn as Tate Britain, a gallery once again devoted solely to British art.

As with its younger sibling, Tate Britain now organizes its collection according to themes as well as chronology. So within the major sections, British Art 1500–1900 and British Art 1900– 2005, you'll find sections named 'Victorian Spectacle', 'Family Value', 'Intimate Interiors' and 'Devastation', as well as no less than seven rooms dedicated to the works of William Turner himself.

Families are very well catered for at Tate Britain, whose curators have long understood that children can quickly grow bored staring at painting after painting, and so provide plenty of activities to keep them amused (most of which are, happily, free). In addition to offering a variety of family workshops and tours, including its 'Secret Tate' explorations behind the scenes of the gallery, the gallery provides audio guides and trails which aim to bring pictures to life through stories, quizzes, riddles and sound effects. The 'Spot the Circle' discovery trail is a particular favourite inviting children to spot circles, not just in the paintings, but in the walls, doors and ceilings of the building, and even in the café. All are available from the information desk.

The ever-popular art trolley is wheeled out on weekends, bank holidays, and occasionally during the school holidays between 12 noon and 5pm. Designed for adults and children to work on together, all you have to do is turn up to choose from a range of games and activities related to the many works of art on display.

Tate Britain is linked to Tate Modern by a ferry service (*see* p.30 for more details).

Banqueting House

Whitehall, SW1
t 0870 751 5178
www.hrp.org.uk/banquetinghouse/
⊖ Westminster, Charing Cross
Bus 3, 11, 12, 24, 53, 77a, 88, 159
Open Mon–Sat 10–5
Adm Adult £4.50, child £2.25, concs £3.50
Pushchairs can be used on the ground floor and left in the cloakroom before ascending the stairs to the main hall. Suitable for ages 10 and over
Allow at least 30mins

Next to Horse Guards, this grand old building will be of more interest to parents than children with its magnificent ceiling paintings by Rubens. It does, however, hide one secret that may get the young ones pricking up their ears. Charles II was beheaded here, just outside the great dining hall in 1649, following his army's defeat by the forces of Parliament.

Downing Street

You can catch a glimpse of Number 10, the house where the Prime Minister lives, through a pair of great black iron railings at the end of the road. Unfortunately, you are no longer allowed to go and have a close-up look. Britain's official centre of power is certainly not as grand as the White House in Washington or the Elysée Palace in Paris. But then, the man who built it, George Downing, never meant it to be more than a simple residential house. When Robert Walpole moved here in the mid-18th century (once the preceding tenant, the improbably-named Mr Chicken, had moved out) he had no idea that all the Prime Ministers would follow in his footsteps, and to this day no one really knows why they have.

Near the junction of Downing Street and Whitehall stands the **Cenotaph**, the nation's chief memorial to the dead of the two World Wars. An official ceremony of remembrance takes place here each year on the Sunday nearest Armistice Day, 11 November, when wreaths of poppies are laid at the memorial.

Westminster Cathedral

Victoria Street, SW1
t (020) 7798 9055
www.westminstercathedral.org.uk
⊖ St James's Park, Victoria
Bus 11, 24, 148, 211, 507

WHERE TO EAT

Open to the cathedral: Mon–Fri 7am–7pm, Sat 8am–7pm; *Campanile:* Apr–Nov 9.30–12.30 & 1–5 daily, Dec–Mar Thurs–Sun 9.30–12.30 & 1–5
Free to the cathedral; *Campanile:* adult £5, child £2.50, family £11
Wheelchair/pushchair accessible, café, audio guide (£2.50, £1.50 concs), worksheets, tours by arrangement
Suitable for ages 8 and up
Allow at least 30mins

Principally worth visiting for the fantastic views from the platform at the top of the newly restored St Edward's Tower, some 280 ft up – you can see right into the gardens of Buckingham Palace. Built in 1903, Westminster is London's main Roman Catholic Cathedral and has the widest nave in Britain. Its green pillars were hewn from the same stone as the 6th-century Basilica of St Sophia in Istanbul. It took over two years to transport them all the way to London. Worksheets for children are available from the cathedral shop.

Picnics & snacks

The closest spot for a picnic is **Victoria Tower Gardens** (1), a relatively quiet and unvisited stretch of park next to Parliament and overlooking the river. You're also within easy reach of **St James's Park** (2), which has a good café, **Inn the Park**, just to the west, and if it's raining you can use the picnic area by the **Tate Britain café** (3) (half portions and baby-changing facilities available).

Otherwise, you're not exactly spoiled for choice in the immediate vicinity. Your best bet is to head either up Victoria Street towards the station or to Trafalgar Square and the West End, where you'll find a vast number of eateries. For more details, *see p.94 and pp.73–4.*

See map on p.97 for the locations of the picnic spots numbered above.

The South Bank

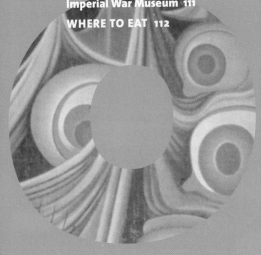
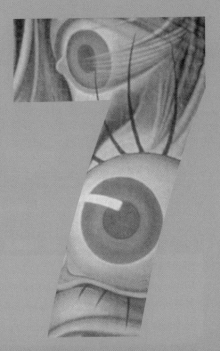

There's a tremendous concentration of attractions in this area, which has seen more revamps, renovations and facelifts than almost anywhere else in London over the past decade. Starting at Westminster Bridge, just across from the Houses of Parliament, is County Hall, home to the London Aquarium, with its thousands of sea creatures, the Dalí Museum and a giant Arcade, the Namco Station. Standing proudly in front by the river is the London Eye, the biggest big wheel in the world, which takes passengers on a fantastic 30-minute tour, high up above the London skyline. Back down on the ground there are river walks to enjoy, plus live music events, theatre performances and festivals at the South Bank Centre's plethora of venues. Budding movie buffs are spoilt for choice with the newly restored and expanded BFI Southbank and the IMAX 3D cinema right on the doorstep.

Highlights
Driving into the Thames on a Duck Tour
Watching the London Aquarium sharks
Elevated gazing from the London Eye

Temple

EMBANKMENT

BLACKFRIARS BRIDGE

Blackfriars

Oxo
Tower
3 **5**

Gabriel's Wharf
2

Embankment

Queen
Elizabeth
Hall

National
Theatre

STAMFORD STREET

ROAD

WATERLOO BRIDGE

BFI Southbank

Hayward
Gallery

1 **6**

Royal
Festival
Hall
4

IMAX 3D
Cinema

HUNGERFORD RAIL
AND FOOT BRIDGE

Jubilee
Gardens

Waterloo
East

Southwark

THE CUT

London
Eye

Waterloo

WC

BLACKFRIARS

County Hall/
London
Aquarium,
Dali Universe,
Saatchi Gallery **6**

Waterloo

Waterloo

WC

WATERLOO ROAD

BELVEDERE ROAD

YORK ROAD

WESTMINSTER BRIDGE

Florence
Nightingale
Museum

WC

WESTMINSTER BRIDGE ROAD

KENNINGTON ROAD

ST GEORGE'S ROAD

LONDON ROAD

LAMBETH PALACE ROAD

Lambeth
Palace

LAMBETH ROAD

Imperial
War Museum

WC

Elephant
& Castle

BROOK DRIVE

400 metres
400 yards

Key
*Numbers correspond to restaurants in
'Where To Eat' p.112*

THE SIGHTS

County Hall and close by

⊖ Waterloo, Westminster ⇌ Waterloo
Bus 11, 12, 24, 53, 76, 77, 159, 211, 341, 381, X53

For much of its existence County Hall, the beautiful Edwardian building that sits on the South Bank opposite the Houses of Parliament, was home to London's premier administrative body, the Greater London Council (GLC). Following the council's abolition in 1986, however, the building sat empty for many years, with no one quite sure what to do with it – there was even talk of knocking it down. Thankfully, it has once again found a purpose. The political animals may have long gone, but there are still many weird and wonderful creatures to be found swimming in the vast tanks of the London Aquarium, which now occupies the building's basement. Here, too, can be found Namco Station, a sort of giant video-game arcade and Dali Universe, a museum dedicated to the great, Spanish Surrealist artist, as well as numerous restaurants and hotels.

London Aquarium

County Hall, Riverside Building, Westminster Bridge Road, SE1
t (020) 7967 8000
www.londonaquarium.co.uk
Open 10–6 daily
Adm Adult £13.25, 15–17 year olds £11.25, under 15s £9.75 (under-3s **free**), family £44, concs (including registered disabled) £11.25
Wheelchair accessible, with adapted toilets.
Suitable for all ages
Allow at least 1hr

In the decade since it opened, the London Aquarium has become firmly established as one of the capital's premier animal attractions. Its vast tanks are home to thousands of sea creatures, from water-spitting archer fish and gruesome-looking eels to multi-coloured corals and translucent floating jellyfish. It's arranged according to habitat and region, with displays on freshwater rivers, coral reefs, tidal mangrove swamps and rainforests, as well as the Indian, Pacific and Atlantic Oceans. The prime attractions, of course, are the sharks, which swim in lazy circles around the Pacific tank (they are fed at 2.30pm on Tuesday, Thursdays and Saturdays).

More serene pleasures can be found at the touch pool where visitors can stroke the resident rays. Children love this, but do make sure that they treat the rays gently.

Dotted in among the tanks are a number of interactive terminals where more can be learnt about the aquarium's inhabitants. There are touch-screen quizzes and short-play videos in which cartoon sea creatures explain themselves and their environment to children. More information can be gleaned at the free daily talks given by the aquarium's keepers at 2pm and 4pm at the Coral Reef and Pacific Tank (where the sharks live), and kids can pick up activity trails from the front desk.

Dali Universe

County Hall, Riverside Building, Belvedere Road, SE1
t 0870 744 7485
www.daliuniverse.com
Open Daily 10–5.30
Adm Adults £12, child (8–16) £8, under-8s £5, under-4s **free**, concs £10, family £30
Shop, wheelchair accessible

> **Did you know?**
> The world's biggest fish is the whale shark which can grow to over 70 ft in length. Unlike some other sharks, it is perfectly harmless, feeding only on plankton.

Question 11
What do lobsters and the Royal Family have in common?
answer on p.250

This museum is filled with bizarre sculptures and paintings by the Spanish Surrealist. In particular, look out for the sofa designed to resemble an enormous pair of red lips (it was modelled on the Hollywood actress Mae West) and the lobster telephone. An audio guide and activity sheets for children are available from the front desk.

Namco Station

County Hall, Riverside Building, Westminster Bridge Road, SE1
t (020) 7967 1066
www.namcoexperience.com
Open 10am–12 midnight, daily
Free, although each game costs £1–2

Love it or hate it, this noisy, arcade-ridden labyrinth is packed with hundreds of video games and simulators as well as a full-size car racing game, bowling, dodgems and pool tables. The downstairs section is for over-18s only.

IMAX 3D Cinema

1 Charlie Chaplin Walk, SE1
t 0870 787 2525
www.bfi.org.uk/imax
⊖/ ≷ Waterloo
Bus 1, 4, 26, 59, 68, 76, 77, 168, 171, 176, 188, 211, 243, 341, 381, 501, 505, 507, 521, RV1

Open Mon–Fri 12.30–8, Sat & Sun 10.45–8.45
Adm Adult £8.50, child (5–15) £5, under-3s **free**, concs £6.25
Wheelchair accessible, lifts, adapted cinema seats and toilets
Suitable for all ages
Shows last approximately 1hr each

Britain's largest cinema screen is housed in a seven-storey glass cylinder in the middle of the Waterloo bullring. The screen itself is the height of five double-decker buses, the sound system transmits 11,000 watts and the films are recorded and projected using the most up-to-date 3D format available – it's a pretty all-encompassing experience. The programme changes regularly, but you can be confident of seeing some kind of sci-fi/wildlife spectacular plus the odd effects-laden Hollywood blockbuster. *See* p.139 for the IMAX cinema in the Science Museum.

British Airways London Eye

Next to County Hall, South Bank, SE1
General information and advance booking **t** 0870 500 0600
www.ba-londoneye.com
Open Oct–May 10–8 daily, June–Sep 10–9 daily
Adm Adult £15, child (5–16) £7 (under-5s **free**), concs £11. Tickets must be purchased in advance. 10% online discounts available
Wheelchair accessible, disabled guests **t** *0870 990 8886*

One of the few Millennium projects to have stood the test of time, this 453-ft rotating observation wheel perched on the south bank of the Thames has provided both tourists and London residents alike with a whole new way of looking at the capital. Night rides are particularly spectacular, especially when the Christmas lights go on.

Officially the fourth-highest structure in the capital, each of the Eye's 32 enclosed glass-sided capsules (they hold up to 25 people each) takes around 40 minutes to complete its circuit. Don't worry though, it moves so slowly and smoothly there's little chance of travel sickness and there's a central seating area for passengers to sit down. Combination river cruises and London Eye trips are available. See p.29 for more details.

London Duck Tours

County Hall, Belvedere Road, SE1
t (020) 7928 3132
www.londonducktours.co.uk
Open Feb–Dec 10–dusk daily
Adm Adults £17.50, children £12, concs £14, family £53

A novel approach to sightseeing – London Duck Tours have adapted a number of former Second World War amphibious vehicles into bright yellow sightseeing 'ducks' capable of tackling London by both road and river. Each duck begins its 80-minute tour on land at County Hall, before crossing Westminster Bridge and making its way to Lacks Dock in Vauxhall, by way of some of the city's major sights, including the Houses of Parliament, Downing Street, Trafalgar Square, Hyde Park Corner and Buckingham Palace. Following 'splashdown' into the Thames, you are taken on a half-hour sightseeing cruise down the river to the starting-point opposite Dali Universe. It's a different and fun way of navigating through London and the plunge into the river is truly exciting. It may be advisable to wear waterproofs.

South Bank Arts Centre

The South Bank, SE1
t 0871 663 2501
www.southbankcentre.org.uk
⊖ Waterloo, Embankment

⇄ Waterloo
Bus 1, 4, 26, 68, 76, 77, 168, 171, 172, 176, 188, 211, 341, 381, 501, 507, 521, RV1, X68
Wheelchair accessible, facilities for hearing/visually-impaired visitors

One of the world's great art complexes, the South Bank comprises, at present, the Royal Festival Hall, the Queen Elizabeth Hall, the BFI Southbank (the successor to the National Film Theatre), the Hayward Gallery and the Royal National Theatre. Together, they put on a range of events suitable for families throughout the year including dance classes, concerts by youth orchestras, ballet performances, theatre shows and poetry sessions.

Royal Festival Hall

t 0871 663 2500
www.southbankcentre.co.uk
Open 10am–10.30pm daily

Along with the adjacent Purcell Room and the Queen Elizabeth Hall, the recently revamped and remodelled Royal Festival Hall is one of the top venues for classical music in the country. Look out, in particular, for the National Festival of Music for Youth, which takes place every summer, and the drumming festival 'Rhythm Sticks', which features open days and workshops aimed at younger visitors. Free concerts and exhibitions are often put on in the Festival Hall foyer.

Can you spot?
The country's one and only floating police station, just to the side of Waterloo Bridge?

BFI Southbank

t 0870 787 2525
www.bfi.org.uk
Adm Family film screenings: child £1, accompanying adults £8.20, workshops £6.50

After years of delays, the National Film Theatre finally underwent its long-awaited tranformation, and has now emerged, reborn, as the BFI Southbank, a very grand and glossy environment in which to watch the best of British and world cinema. It now boasts four screens, lots of bars, cafés and sit-down areas, and stages regular temporary art exhibitions and installations. There's also a new facility called 'Mediateque', which allows visitors to browse the BFI's vast archive of film entirely free of charge. Best of all, for children, are the Saturday morning family film screenings. The programme is made up of a mixture of time-less classics and modern blockbusters – think 'Thief of Baghdad' to 'The Incredibles' – usually with an accompanying workshop.

Hayward Gallery

t 0871 663 2500
www.southbankcentre.co.uk
Open 10–6 daily, until 8pm on Wed and Thurs
Adm Varies, depending on the exhibition

The Hayward has no permanent exhibition, but puts on a series of temporary shows throughout the year, with children's art trails and activities attached wherever possible. It often organizes art and photographic workshops for children in the holidays as well (usually for over-12s). The Hayward shop can be accessed via the foyer and stocks a large and impressive range of art and activity books for children, from board books and bath books to project-based art boxes.

National Theatre

t (020) 7452 3400
www.nationaltheatre.org.uk
Open 10am–11pm daily
Adm Backstage tours: £5, concs £4, family £13
Wheelchair accessible

Three theatres in one: in descending size, these are the Olivier, the Lyttleton and the Cottesloe. All offer a year-round programme of drama. For a taster, pop along to Theatre Square, just outside, where free performances are staged throughout the year. Inside, free concerts are put on in the foyers during the early evening. Backstage tours of all three stages take place three times a day, Monday to Saturday; you can see how the costumes are created, how the scenery is shifted around and how even the stages themselves can be moved during a performance. For more details, call **t** (020) 7452 3400. There's also an excellent bookshop.

Coin Street Community Builders

The Coin Street Community Builders (CSCB) is the name given to the non-profit organization that manages Gabriel's Wharf, the Bernie Spain Gardens, the Oxo Tower Wharf and organizes the three-month free Coin Street Arts Festival every summer. From near-dereliction in the early 1980s, the CSCB has transformed the area into a thriving arts centre. Contact **t** (020) 7401 2255 or check out the website, **www**.coinstreet.org

Gabriel's Wharf

Just down from the South Bank is Gabriel's Wharf, a bohemian collection of shops, restaurants and snack places. Look out for the **London Bicycle Tour**

Company, who will rent you bikes to ride around the capital or arrange a guided bike tour.

London Bicycle Tour Company

1A Gabriel's Wharf, SE1
t (020) 7928 6838
www.londonbicycle.com
Bike hire Adult £3 per hour, £18 per day (for the first day, £9 per day after that), tours £17.95

Oxo Tower

Barge House Street, SE1
t (020) 7401 2255
www.oxotower.co.uk
Blackfriars, Waterloo
Bus 63, 149, 172, 455, D1, P11
Open Studios Tues–Sun 11–6; bars and restaurants every day until late

Topped by its famous Art Deco tower (one of the capital's great landmarks), the Oxo Tower Wharf is now an artsy shopping arcade housing designer boutiques, art studios and fashionable eating places, most notably its celebrated rooftop restaurant, which offers fantastic views out across the city – there's also a free viewing gallery next door. In the 1930s, when the Oxo Tower was first commissioned by the famous stock-cube company, it was their intention to have the company's name spelled out in lights on the top. Unfortunately, the strict advertising laws of the time forbade this, forcing the company to come up with an ingenious alternative. They instructed the architect to incorporate the Oxo logo into the design of the tower's windows, thus enabling them to claim that it was an architectural feature rather than an advert.

It's nice to walk by the river along Millennium Mile (see p.28), either from Waterloo, which is nearest, or London Bridge, passing plenty of sights and a good view of the Thames along the way.

The Coin Street Festival

t (020) 7401 2255
www.coinstreetfestival.org
Three months each summer, usually June–Aug

For three months every summer, the Oxo Tower Wharf, Gabriel's Wharf and the Bernie Spain Gardens play host to a range of art, music and dance events from across the globe.

Although the programme changes each year, the festival usually features a whole host of children's events including creative workshops and a special children's fancy-dress parade.

Tell me a story: **Evacuation**

When Britain declared war on Germany on 3 September 1939, Londoners began preparing for the worst. It would surely only be a matter of time, they reasoned, before the German air force began bombing raids on the city (it actually took over a year) and it was therefore crucial that the capital's children (up to age 15) were quickly evacuated to safer parts of the country. Of course, finding places for all the children to stay (not to mention people with disabilities, teachers and helpers) proved to be no easy task. The sheer numbers involved meant that there was no way of guaranteeing which child went where, with the result that many middle-class kids found themselves in labourers' cottages while slum children were billeted in stately homes. In this way, the evacuation process helped to foster a level of social integration that would have been impossible outside wartime. For some it proved to be a frightening and unhappy experience, although others, with fresh food to eat and space to run around in, saw it more as a holiday.

AROUND & ABOUT

Florence Nightingale Museum

2 Lambeth Palace Road, SE1
t (020) 7620 0374
www.florence-nightingale.co.uk
/ Waterloo
Bus 12, 53, 76, 77, 148, 159, 211, 341, 381, 507
Open Mon–Fri 10–5, Sat, Sun 10.30–4.30, last admission one hour before closing
Adm Adult £5.80, child and concs £4.20, family £13
Wheelchair accessible
Suitable for ages 6 and over
Allow at least 1hr

A wonderful place to bring aspiring medics. The museum tells the story of Florence Nightingale, the founder of modern nursing, using reconstructions, such as the ward scene from the Crimean War where 'the lady with the lamp' tends to the wounded, videos and articles from her life, including several of her letters. The museum is very much geared towards kids, so there are lots of interactive consoles and audio visual displays including a 20-minute film

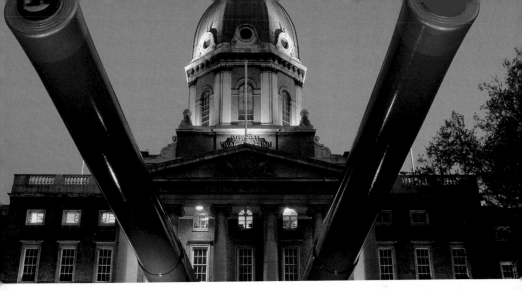

on Florence's achievements in health care. Free family events – dressing up, trails, storytellings etc – are put on during the second weekend of each month, and activity trails are available from the front desk.

Imperial War Museum

Lambeth Road, SE1
t (020) 7416 5320
http://london.iwm.org.uk/
⊖ Lambeth North, Elephant & Castle
Bus 1, 3, 12, 45, 53, 59, 63, 68, 100, 159, 168, 171, 172, 176, 188, 344, C10
Open 10–6, daily
Free
Wheelchair accessible
Suitable for ages 6 and over
Allow at least 1hr

On catching sight of the huge 15-inch naval guns by the entrance, you could be forgiven for thinking that this is a place that glorifies war and treats it as some gung-ho 'Boys Own' adventure. Quite the opposite – the museum is largely dedicated to exploring and demonstrating the human experience of war; the lives of the ordinary men and women charged with settling the arguments of nations on the battlefield. There are some fantastic machines to look at in the large central hall, including tanks, planes, one-man submarines and even a 30-ft Polaris missile, but the museum never loses sight of the very real cost of conflict. For every piece of dazzling equipment, there's a more sobering exhibit – the Trench Experience, for instance, is recreation of the life of a foot soldier on the Western Front in the First World War, while the Blitz Experience lets you see what conditions were like for Londoners during the Second World War, huddled in shelters under the streets as Hitler's bombs rained down overhead.

The Holocaust exhibition on the third floor is perhaps the most affecting of all, but is not recommended for children under 14. It charts the rise of Hitler and the Nazi party through to the horror of the Final Solution.

Until 2010, the museum will be hosting 'The Children's War', an exhibition that aims to explore the experience of the Second World War, as recalled by the children who lived through it. So the displays deal with matters that most affected children – evacuation (the mass evacuation of children at the start of the war was Britain's largest migration of people), rationing (kids were allowed just 57g of sweets a week – the equivalent of one small chocolate bar) and school. There's also a replica wartime house to explore.

There's a good proportion of interactive exhibits – you can clamber around the cockpits of some of the fighter planes, take the controls of a fighter plane simulator or watch some archive footage on one of the touch-screen TV terminals that dot the museum floor. Children's trails are available at reception and the museum organizes activity workshops in the school holidays, including their very popular 'In their Shoes' days when kids (under supervision) are invited to handle artefacts from the collection in order to try and work out the stories behind them.

Afterwards, it may be a relief to take a walk to the Tibetan Peace Garden just outside, which was opened by His Holiness the Dalai Lama in 1999.

WHERE TO EAT

Picnics & snacks

There's not much greenery on the South Bank. The main 'park', **Jubilee Gardens**, is little more than a scrubby lawn next to County Hall, although it is set to be redeveloped. There are plenty of benches lining the Millennium Walkway (see p.28) next to the river-front, but these aren't very picnic-friendly as there is a constant flow of pedestrians, joggers, cyclists, roller bladers and skateboarders.

However, as one of the busiest places on the London arts scene, the **South Bank** has more than its fair shaire of fast food outlets and cafés. There's the Royal Festival Hall's **Festival Café**, t (020) 7486 6154, ⊖/≋ Waterloo, on Festival Terrace, which serves pastas, salads, sandwiches and drinks throughout the day and has a nice outdoor terrace; as well branches of the **Eat Café** on the ground floor of the Oxo Tower, t (020) 7401 2255, ⊖/≋ Waterloo, Blackfriars, and the riverside level of the Royal Festival Hall, t (020) 7401 2989, ⊖/≋ Waterloo, Blackfriars, where you can pick up home-made breads, tortilla wraps and smoothies; and, perhaps the pick of the bunch, the **Film Café**, at the BFI Southbank, ⊖/≋ Waterloo, t (020) 7928 3232, under Waterloo Bridge, by the Riverside Book Market. While children tuck into pizzas and jacket potatoes, adults can look through the stalls or listen to the buskers along this vibrant stretch of the river. Slightly further afield, the **Imperial War Museum Café**, Lambeth Road, SE1, t (020) 7820 9817, ⊖/≋ Lambeth North, Elephant & Castle, provides special lunchboxes for kids with sandwiches, cake, a piece of fruit and a fruit drink. Gabriel's Wharf also has several places including **House of Crêpes** and **Sarnis**, ⊖/≋ Waterloo, which specializes in continental sandwiches made from panini, ciabatta, focaccia and baguettes. There's also a **McDonald's** in County Hall, ⊖/≋ Waterloo.

Restaurants

1 Giraffe
Unit 1 & 2, Riverside Level 1, Royal Festival Hall
t (020) 7928 2004
www.giraffe.net
⊖/≋ Waterloo
Open 8.30am–11.30pm daily

2 Gourmet Pizza Company
Gabriel's Wharf, 56 Upper Ground, SE1
t (020) 7928 3188
www.gourmetpizzacompany.co.uk
⊖/≋ Waterloo
Open 12 noon–10.30

3 Oxo Tower Restaurant
Oxo Tower, Barge House Street, South Bank, SE1
t (020) 7803 3888
www.harveynichols.com
⊖/≋ Waterloo, Blackfriars
Open Mon–Sat 12 noon–2.30 and 6–11,
Sun 12 noon–3 and 6.30–10

4 Pizza Express
The White House, 9c Belvedere Road, SE1
t (020) 7928 4091
www.pizzaexpress.com
⊖/≋ Waterloo
Open 11.30–12 midnight daily

5 Tamesa@Oxo
2nd Floor, Oxo Tower, Barge House Street, SE1
t (020) 7633 0008
www.oxotower.co.uk/tamesa
⊖/≋ Waterloo
Open Mon–Sat 12 noon–3.30 & 5.30–11.30, Sun
12 noon–4

6 Wagamama
Unit 7, Riverside Level 1, Royal Festival Hall, SE1
t (020) 7021 0877
www.wagamama.co.uk
⊖/≋ Waterloo
Open Mon–Sat 12 noon–11, Sun 12.30–10

7 Yo! Sushi
County Hall, Belvedere Road, SE1
t (020) 7928 8871
www.yosushi.com
⊖/≋ Waterloo
Open Mon–Tue 12 noon–10, Wed–Sat 12 noon–11,
Sun 12 noon–8

See **Eat** p.224–36 for more details on the above restaurants.
See map on p.105 for the locations of the restaurants numbered above.

Southwark

There really isn't much that you can't do here. From London Bridge Station it's a short walk down to the river, where you'll find some of London's best-loved attractions. Here stand the giant art gallery, Tate Modern, the adjacent Shakespeare's Globe, where you can see the bard's plays, as his contemporaries would have done, out in the open air, and the fearsome World War II destroyer, HMS *Belfast*, not to mention that postcard perfect emblem of London, Tower Bridge. The river doesn't get all the fun, however. The backstreets have plenty of gems of their own. Look out for the ghoulish London Dungeon, the Old Operating Theatre, the Design Museum and the newly opened Unicorn Theatre.

Highlights

Quoting Shakespeare at The Globe

Feasting on art at Tate Modern

Views from atop the Tower Bridge Exhibition

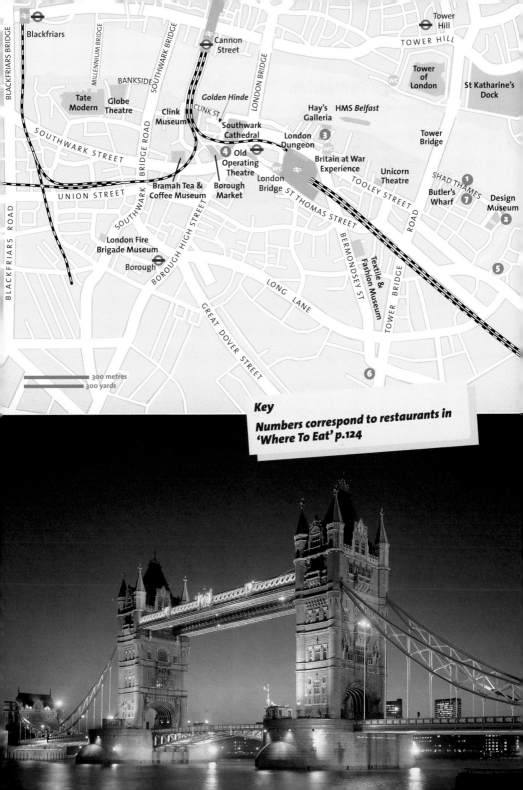

Blackfriars

BLACKFRIARS BRIDGE

MILLENNIUM BRIDGE

SOUTHWARK BRIDGE

BANKSIDE

Tate Modern

Globe Theatre

SOUTHWARK BRIDGE ROAD

SOUTHWARK STREET

Clink Museum

CLINK ST

Golden Hinde

Southwark Cathedral

Cannon Street

LONDON BRIDGE

4 Old Operating Theatre

Bramah Tea & Coffee Museum

Borough Market

SOUTHWARK BRIDGE ROAD

BOROUGH HIGH STREET

UNION STREET

BLACKFRIARS ROAD

London Fire Brigade Museum

Borough

London Bridge

ST THOMAS STREET

London Dungeon

3

WC

Hay's Galleria

HMS *Belfast*

Britain at War Experience

WC

WC

Tower Hill

TOWER HILL

WC

Tower of London

St Katharine's Dock

Tower Bridge

Unicorn Theatre

TOOLEY STREET

BERMONDSEY ST

Textile & Fashion Museum

SHAD THAMES

1

Butler's Wharf

7

Design Museum

2

5

TOWER BRIDGE ROAD

LONG LANE

GREAT DOVER STREET

6

300 metres
300 yards

Key

Numbers correspond to restaurants in 'Where To Eat' p.124

Tower Bridge Exhibition

London Bridge, Fenchruch Street
t (020) 7403 3761
www.towerbridge.org.uk
⊖ Tower Hill, London Bridge
Bus 15, 25, 40, 42, 78, 100, D1, P11, RV1
Open April–Sep 10–6.30, Oct–Mar 9.30–6, last
entry 1hr before closing
Adm Adult £6, child £3, concs £4.50, under-5s **free**,
family ticket (2+2) £14
Wheelchair accessible for all public areas
Suitable for ages 6 and over
Allow at least 1hr

With its fairytale turrets and huge decks, which
raise to let tall ships pass through, this is easily
London's most recognizable and popular bridge. At
the Tower Bridge Exhibition you can see the steam-
powered machinery that was used to raise the
decks in Victorian times (these days the bridge
relies on hydraulics and electricity), play with some
interactive models and climb the 200 or so steps
(or if you're sensible, take the lift) to the covered
walkway that runs along the top of the bridge
some 150 ft above the Thames. From here you can
enjoy spectacular views up and down the river and
out across London. Look out, in particular, for the
new Greater London Authority building next to the
bridge, which looks a bit like an enormous glass
paperweight. The bridge is still raised at least once
a day; you can find out exactly when by calling
t (020) 7940 3984, or by looking at the notice board
near the bridge. Family activities, such as 'Victorian

Capers' and 'Summer Kids' Trails' as well as storytelling sessions, are put on throughout the year.

London Dungeon

Tooley Street, SE1
t (020) 7403 7221
www.thedungeons.com
⊖ / ≷ London Bridge
Bus 21, 35, 40, 43, 47, 48,49, 133
Open School hols 9.30–6.30 daily, otherwise
10.30–5 daily
Adm Adult £17.95, child (under 14) £13.95, under-5s
free, concs £14.25
Wheelchair accessible
Suitable for ages 8 and over
No unaccompanied children allowed
Allow a couple of hours

The concept behind the London Dungeon is
rather odd but it's one that seems perfectly
attuned to the interests of children, who often
harbour a strange desire to be scared in a 'safe' way.

In the dark, candlelit 'dungeon' (actually a series
of railway arches next to London Bridge Station),
you'll be taken on a one and a half hour tour past a
series of gruesome waxwork tableaux depicting
some of the more grisly episodes from British
history and legend: mingle with the blotchy,
bloated victims of the great plague; escape from
the Great Fire of London and walk the shadowy
streets where everyone's favourite serial killer, Jack
the Ripper used to prowl. Costumed actors are on
hand to up the fright levels. Indeed, the dungeon
has greatly increased the level of interactivity in
recent years. There's now a mirror Maze, 'Labyrinth
of the Lost', a 'traitor's' boat ride to the Tower and,
the *pièce de résistance*, 'Extremis: Drop Ride of
Doom!', which is essentially a fairground-style
vertical drop ride dressed up in some slightly
dubious 'replicating the experience of hanging'

Did you know?

▶ That each bridge deck weighs an astonishing
1,000 tonnes? That's as much as 200 elephants.
▶ That the 'proper' name for one of the bridge's
decks is a 'bascule'.
▶ That in 1952 a double-decker bus had to jump
a three foot gap between the opening bridge
decks when the traffic lights didn't turn red?
▶That the bridge took eight years to be built? It
was completed in 1894.
▶That the bridge was deliberately designed to
look 'ancient', so as not to look out of place next
to the very old Tower of London?

dodginess. You'll have to judge for yourselves whether you consider this sort of fare suitable for children. It's probably not a good idea to take very young ones (those under 8) or anyone (young or old) susceptible to nightmares.

Tip The London Dungeon is very popular, particularly on weekends and school holidays, when enormous queues can tail back as far as London Bridge Station. Booking online will allow you to jump straight to the front.

Tate Modern

Bankside, SE1
t (020) 7887 8888
www.tate.org.uk/modern
⊖/ ⇌ London Bridge, Blackfriars
Bus 45, 63, 76, 100, 344, 381, RV1
Open Sun–Thurs 10–6, Fri and Sat 10–10
Free
Wheelchair accessible, hearing facilities, free touch tours
Suitable for ages 8 and over
Allow at least a couple of hours

Tate Modern, the country's pre-eminent modern art gallery, has been packing them in ever since it opened around the time of the Millennium. Housed in the striking setting of the former Bankside power station, the collection is arranged around a vast, vaulted turbine hall that serves as both entrance and exhibition space. It is here that

a series of giant temporary installations have been erected, some of which, such as the 2006 Carsten Holler Slides (essentially a helter-skelter) have been as much fun for kids as for art aficionados.

The museum has a mighty 100,000 square feet of display space dedicated to modern international works from the 19th century to the present day. That's a lot of art, but don't be put off. The permanent collection takes up just four (albeit very large) wings, and there are lightweight collapsible stools available for you to take round for when your legs start to get tired (plus plenty of comfy sofas, strategically placed around the galleries).

All the major movements of twentieth century art – Surrealism, Minimalism, Cubism, Abstract Expressionism etc – are explored and explained in easy, accessible terms, using umbrella topics, such as 'Poetry and Dream', 'Idea and Object' and 'States of Flux' to trace links and resonances between artists who might otherwise seem to have little in common. Much of the work on show, such as Marcel Duchamp's *Fountain* (actually a toilet) and Carl Andre's *Equivalent VIII* (a pile of bricks), are the kind of works of art that the British public love to hate, although there are also many famous works by more 'traditional' artists such as Bacon, Dali, Freud, Hockney, Matisse, Picasso, Pollock, Rothko, Spencer and Warhol.

As with Tate Britain, its sister gallery, Tate Modern provides plenty of resources to help families understand and involve themselves in the collection. After all, modern art, perhaps more than any art form, often needs to be explained (to both adults and children) in order to be properly appreciated and enjoyed. Free activity trails, called 'Tate Teasers', which offer themed routes around the collection, are available from the information desks on levels 1 and 2, encouraging kids to draw their own impressions of the artworks. You can also hire a multimedia guide – a hand console on which you can listen to music, watch videos and play art-related games. The gallery organizes a programme of art-related activities for children including 'Start', a drop-in event on Sundays between 11–5 (and on certain weekdays during the school holidays) aimed at providing a basic introduction to art for the over-5s.

Before leaving, head up to the top floor where the café offers wonderful views of the river, the Millennium Bridge and St Paul's. And save time for the shop on the ground floor, where you can pick

Tell me a story: **The Blitz**

The deliberate and systematic bombing of London by the German air force, or 'Luftwaffe', began on the afternoon of Sunday 7 September 1940. Squadron after squadron hit the East End where the warehouses at Surrey Docks, filled with rubber, paint and rum, were soon ablaze. That night the Luftwaffe struck again and by the dawn of 8 September, 448 Londoners had lost their lives. The 'Blitz', as it came to be known, had begun and continued unabated for the next 76 days, during which time vast swathes of the capital were flattened and thousands of lives lost. There were, however, some miraculous escapes along the way. Buckingham Palace was hit but escaped relatively undamaged, while St Paul's Cathedral, despite the destruction around it, survived the bombing virtually intact and became a symbol of London's defiance. Night after night, Londoners took cover in steel shelters or on the platforms of the Underground stations as the German planes attempted to crush their morale in preparation for a land invasion. Much to the Nazis' chagrin, however, the bombing, if anything, served to stiffen British resolve to resist the enemy at all costs. Even so, London paid a heavy price for its brave resistance. Over the next four years 20,000 people were killed in the air raids and a further 25,000 were wounded.

up T-shirts, mugs, umbrellas and a stationery box in the shape of the Bankside building which includes a magnetic 'lightbeam lid'.

Tate Modern is linked to its sister gallery, Tate Britain, by a ferry service (*see* p.30 for more details).

Winston Churchill's Britain at War Experience

64–66 Tooley Street, SE1
t (020) 7403 3171
www.britainatwar.co.uk
⊖/≷ London Bridge
Bus 47, 381, RV1
Open Apr–Sept 10–6 daily,
Oct–Mar 10–5 daily
Adm Adult £9.95, child (under 16) £4.85, under-5s
free, concs £5.75, family £25
Wheelchair accessible
Suitable for ages 6 and over
Allow at least 1hr

On Tooley Street, under the same set of arches as the London Dungeon, is one of the best places for kids to come and find out what life was like in this country during the Second World War. You start by taking a lift down to a replica underground shelter of the type hidden in by Londoners during the Blitz, when bombs rained down on the city, night after night. In order to get a real sense of the times, children can dress up in period costume complete with gas masks, tin helmets and ARP (air-raid patrol) uniforms. A mixture of sounds, smells and visual effects are used along with archive footage, radio broadcasts and music to conjure up a period atmosphere. The overall effect is fun and exciting, but also informative, successfully conveying a little of the reality of the time: the desperate fear that must have been felt by the people sheltering here, as well as the community spirit that helped them to get through. You finish the tour by walking through a replica bombed street as sirens wail and spotlights criss-cross overhead. It's a great interactive museum where kids can get their hands dirty finding out about what war was like in the past.

Question 12
What is a groundling?
answer on p.250

Shakespeare's Globe Theatre

New Globe Walk, Southwark, SE1
t (020) 7902 1400
www.shakespeares-globe.org
⊖/≋ London Bridge
Bus 11, 15, 17, 23, 26, 45, 63, 76, 100, 344, 381, RV1
Open Performances staged Apr–Oct,
for performance times call in advance; museum
10–5 daily
Adm Museum: adult £6.50, child £4.50 (under-5s
free), concs £5, family ticket (2+3) £15, Saturday
'Child's Play' Workshops **adm** £10
Limited wheelchair access, call disabled access
information on (020) 7902 1409
Suitable for ages 8 and over
Allow at least 1hr to see the museum
Performances can last a few hours

The Globe is a perfect modern recreation of the
Elizabethan theatre where Shakespeare premiered
many of his most famous plays, including *Othello*,
Macbeth and *Romeo and Juliet*. The original theatre
burnt down in 1613 during a performance of *Henry
VIII*, when an ember from a stage cannon set fire to
the thatched roof.

You can take a guided tour of the new Globe
(which, begun in the early 1980s, was finally
completed in the mid-1990s), visit the multimedia
museum which explains the history of the Globe
(old and new), or watch a performance of a
Shakespeare play almost as his contemporaries
would have done: seated on wooden benches or
standing in the open in front of the stage. This can
add to the atmosphere at performances, but can
also serve to obscure children's views.

On certain Saturdays, children aged between 8
and 11 can take part in Saturday afternoon 'Child's
Play' sessions at the Globe's Education Centre.
While parents watch a matinée performance, kids
are treated to storytelling sessions and art and
drama workshops before joining the groundlings
(*see* question opposite), in front of the stage for the
final act (£10 per child, booking essential).

Shakespearean theatre

Welcome to the bad side of town... In the 16th
century, when the first Globe theatre was built, this
was the area of town frequented by the city's
reprobates and ne'er-do-wells – where people
came to indulge in bawdy, rowdy entertainments
such as drinking and gambling, bear and bull

Did you know?
*The Globe's roof is the first thatched roof to top
a London building since the Great Fire of 1666. In
order to prevent another disaster, the thatch sits
on an insulating layer of fibreglass and is dotted
with sprinklers.*

baiting, cock and dog fighting (any sort of mayhem
with animals seems to have been particularly
popular) and, of course, going to the theatre. While,
today, we often regard theatre-going as something
rather refined and elegant, in Shakespeare's day it
was a much more rough and ready form of entertainment. During the summer months, children
can find out more about the decadent history of
Southwark on a Globe Walkshop; a guided tour
taking in the sites of the prisons, inns, brothels and
theatres which used to make up the bulk of the
area's buildings (10–12 noon Saturday; adm £7,
concs £5, student £4; call **t** (020) 7902 1433).

Old Operating Theatre

9a St Thomas Street, SE1
t (020) 7188 2679
www.thegarret.org.uk
⊖/≋ London Bridge
Bus 17, 21, 35, 40, 43, 47, 48, 133, 149, 343, 521, RV1
Open 10.30–5 daily
Adm Adult £5.25, child £3 (under-8s **free**), family
ticket (2+2) £12.95
*No wheelchair or pushchair access. Museum is
reached via narrow staircase, young children
must be carried*
Suitable for ages 8 and over
Allow at least 1hr

Just think what it would be like to have your
tonsils taken out here, in the country's only
surviving example of an early 19th-century
operating theatre. These days we tend to think
of surgery as a skilled job involving the delicate
repair of internal organs by trained professionals.

Did you know?
*In the early 19th century, surgeons were
regarded by the medical establishment as being
little better than butchers. Even today, when they
are among the most highly skilled of all medical
practitioners, they do not take the title 'Dr' but
remain a simple 'Mr'.*

That wasn't the case in the early 1800s when a surgeon's main task was amputations – the removal of damaged or diseased limbs with a fine-toothed saw. The patient wouldn't have had an anaesthetic (this wasn't cruelty, it hadn't been invented yet). Surgeons relied instead on speed and the bravery of the patient. Patients could actually watch while someone sawed off their leg – imagine what that must have felt (and looked) like. There was also no antiseptic and standards of hygiene were poor – surgeons often didn't clean their instruments between operations. A third of all amputees died from infections that they caught during surgery; the museum cheerily explains that surgeons often performed operations 'stinking with pus and blood'.

It's a fantastic place, thick with atmosphere. You can see the gruesome medical equipment (almost indistinguishable from the tools of torture at the nearby Clink Museum, *see* p.121), the operating table and pickled bits of unlucky patients in jars.

The theatre itself has had a fascinating history. It was housed in a medieval tower that acted as a herb garret (drying room) for the old St Thomas' hospital. When the hospital relocated to Lambeth in 1860, the old building was demolished and only the tower was left standing. The operating theatre within was forgotten for nearly a century until it was rediscovered by chance and turned into a museum in 1956.

Unicorn Theatre

147 Tooley Street, SE1
t (020) 7645 0560
www.unicorntheatre.com
⊖/ ≉ London Bridge
Bus 17, 381, RV1
Open Performance times vary, call in advance
Adm Adult £9.50, child £5
Wheelchair access, adapted toilets, café

This award-winning children's theatre only recently relocated to the Southbank, where it enjoys snazzy new premises – all glass and steel – and two new theatre spaces: the Weston Theatre, seating 300, and the Clore Theatre, which seats 120. Its productions, though always child-size in terms

of scope, length and price, are always of a very high standard. The theatre runs workshops for wannabe young actors throughout the year.

HMS *Belfast*

Morgan's Lane, off Tooley Street, SE1
t (020) 7940 6300
http://hmsbelfast.iwm.org.uk
⊖/ ≉ London Bridge
Bus 21, 35, 40, 43, 47, 48, 133, 381
Open Mar–Oct 10–6 daily, Nov–Feb 10–5 daily
Adm Adult £9.95, under-16s **free**, concs £6.15
Wheelchair accessible for main deck, but not for many below-deck areas. Suitable for ages 6 and over
Allow at least 1hr

This huge, heavily armed, heavily armoured cruiser was used during the D-Day landings in 1944. These days it is a floating nautical museum, moored permanently between London Bridge and Tower Bridge. Children love running around the ship's clunking metal decks, looking down the barrels of the huge naval guns, manoeuvring the lighter anti-aircraft guns and exploring the seven floors of narrow corridors. Children's trails, available at the entrance, send kids all over the ship for clues, and there are also audio guides for hire. Hands-on activities are laid on for families on the first weekend of every month.

The *Golden Hinde*

Pickfords Wharf, Clink Street, SE1
t 0870 011 8700
www.goldenhinde.org
⊖/ ≷ London Bridge
Bus 17, 21, 22a, 35, 40, 43, 44, 47, 48, 95, 133, 149, 214, 501, 505, 510, 513, D1, P3, P11
Open Call in advance (the ship is only open to casual sightseeing when there are no pre-booked groups visiting)
Adm Adult £6, child £4.50, family £10. Overnight Living History Experiences: £39.95 per person. Pirate Fun Days adult £7, child £5
No wheelchair access
Suitable for ages 6 and over

This full-size replica of the 16th-century ship on which Sir Francis Drake became the first Englishman to circumnavigate the globe sits in dry dock, just back from the river front. There are five levels to explore including Drake's cabin and a 14-cannon gun deck. As the children roam the ship, the crew, dressed in Tudor costume, will entertain them with tales of the high seas.

Although a replica, this fully functioning vessel has sailed the Atlantic several times since it was built in 1973, clocking up over 10,000 miles at sea. It's available for children's parties, and school groups or families are invited to attend the ship's **Overnight Living History Experiences**, which run from 5pm until 10am the next day. During this time the whole family can assume the roles of a crew of Tudor sailors: performing shipboard tasks, eating Tudor food and sleeping in the cabins on the lower decks. 'Pirate Fun Days' are also available.

Clink Museum

1 Clink Street, SE1
t (020) 7403 0900
www.clink.co.uk
⊖/ ≷ London Bridge
Bus 17, 95, 149, 184
Open Mon–Fri 10–6, Sat & Sun 10–9
Adm Adult £5, child £3.50, concs £3.50, family £12
No wheelchair access
Suitable for ages 8 and over
Allow at least 30mins

If your kids aren't quite up to the big frights of the London Dungeon, try them on the smaller fun-size frights offered here. The museum has attempted to recreate many of the scenes and settings of the

> **Did you know?**
> Medieval prisoners were expected to pay for the privilege of being manacled and tortured. They had to contribute towards their food, their cells and the wages of the men who kept them locked up. They even had to pay for their own ball and chain!

medieval Clink Prison which stood on this spot in the Middle Ages. Although the prison building was demolished in 1780, the name 'the Clink' has survived to this day as a nickname for all prisons. It hasn't got the budget of other big-name horror attractions such as the London Dungeon (*see* p.116) or the Chamber of Horrors at Madame Tussauds (*see* p.44) and many of its supposedly gory effects are actually a bit ordinary. Even so, it boasts a unmatched historical authenticity and manages to convey something of the eerie gruesomeness of these primitive and brutal forms of punishment.

It's divided into a number of cells, each inhabited by rather unhappy-looking mannequins undergoing some of the various forms of torture that were popular during the Middle Ages. There are the Stocks, which are basically two wooden planks used to hold a prisoner's head and hands fast; the Fure, a hole in the ground where trussed-up prisoners were left to rot; and the Cage, a wire contraption fitted to the head of 'scolds and gossips' – in other words women who, in the eyes of their husbands, talked too much. In one particular cell you'll find a torture chair to which a victim would be strapped before being forced to confess by use of pincers (for tooth extractions), knives and foot crushers. The section detailing the history of the Stews (medieval brothels) is for over-18s only.

The prison closed soon after the Great Fire of London in 1666. City merchants and investors started moving in, putting the brothels, drinking houses and gambling dens that had provided most of the prison's clientele out of business. For a while the building continued to be used as a warehouse before finally being knocked down in 1780.

The Millennium Bridge

Designed by Norman Foster, Anthony Caro and the engineering firm Arup, this elegant walkway linking Tate Modern with St Paul's on the other side of the river provides great views up and down the Thames, not to mention easy access between the City and Southwark.

Bramah Tea & Coffee Museum

40 Southwark Street, SE1
t (020) 7403 5650
www.teaandcoffeemuseum.co.uk
⊖/ ⇌ London Bridge
Bus 15, 25, 42, 78, 100, 381, RV1
Open 10–6 daily
Adm Adult £4, child, £3.50, concs £3.50, family ticket (2+4) £10
Suitable for ages 8 and over
Allow at least 30mins

This charming little museum details the history of the country's two favourite (non-alcoholic) beverages.

You can find out how the drinks were introduced to Britain in the 17th century, how public tastes have changed since then and how the ritual of drinking coffee, and particularly tea, has become such a part of British life. Children will like the extraordinary collection of over 1000 teapots and coffee-makers, which come in all shapes and sizes:

dragons, monsters, lions, pillarboxes and even policemen. Perhaps the most interesting section (for adults) is devoted to the way in which the drinks have been advertised since the beginning of the 20th century. If all this talk of tea and coffee gets you thirsty, you can always head for the café and sample one of the museum's own blends.

Design Museum

28 Shad Thames, Butler's Wharf, SE1
t 0870 909 9009
www.designmuseum.org
⊖ London Bridge, Tower Hill
Bus 15, 42, 47, 78, 100, 188, P11
Open 10–6, daily
Adm Adult £7, child £4, under-12s **free**, family £16
Suitable for ages 10 and over
Allow at least an hour

This museum aims to explain why various ordinary, everyday objects – such as telephones, vacuum cleaners, toothbrushes and cars – look the way they do, examining them from both a functional and an aesthetic perspective.

You can sit in some of the outlandish chairs of yesteryear and there's a very good shop selling books and gadgets as well as a standard café on the ground floor selling sandwiches, quiche and salad, etc. and the more upmarket, attractive (but expensive) Conran-run, Blueprint café, which is more of a restaurant really. Younger visitors are specifically catered for with 'Design Action Packs', available for free at reception, which provide games and trails based on the collection, as well as a 'Spot the Building' game inviting kids to identify some of the famous surrounding landmarks (St Paul's, the Gherkin, etc.). Kids' workshops for 5-11 year olds are offered on Sunday afternoons where kids can turn their hands to anything from hat- and mask-making to animation (£4 per child).

Fashion & Textile Museum

83 Bermondsey Street, SE1
t (020) 7403 0222
www.ftmlondon.org
⊖/ ⊅ London Bridge
Bus 42, 47, 78, 149, 188, 381, RV1
Wheelchair accessible, with adapted toilets; café
Suitable for ages 10 and over

Currently closed for major refurbishment, the country's only dedicated fashion museum is due to re-open in late 2007. There will be a whole new set of exhibitions detailing the development of fashion and textile production, together with new 'event spaces' and a 'fashion café'. As before, fashion workshops for kids will be run in the summer holidays.

Hay's Galleria

London Bridge, Tooley Street, SE1
t (020) 7940 7770
www.haysgalleria.co.uk
⊖/ ⊅ London Bridge
Bus 10, 44, 48, 70, 133
Open 10-6 daily

A rather nice shopping arcade. Its main entrance is on Tooley Street, almost directly opposite the London Dungeon, and it can be used as a quick short-cut to the Thames riverside path. Should you decide to linger you'll find lots of well-to-do shops, restaurants (including branches of Café Rouge and the Bagel Factory) and craft and jewellery stalls, while the kids' attention will no doubt be caught

by the great statue-cum-fountain, *The Navigators*, which stands at the riverside end of the arcade.

London Fire Brigade Museum

94a Southwark Bridge Road
t (020) 7587 2894
www.london-fire.gov.uk
⊖ London Bridge, Borough
Bus 344
Open Mon–Fri, pre-booked tours only at 10.30am, 2pm
Adm Adult £3, child £2, under-7s £1
Suitable for ages 7 and over

Once upon a time, every small boy who didn't want to be a train driver wanted to be a fireman. Times have changed, of course, but today's would-be astronauts, pop stars and internet gurus may like to pay a visit (by appointment only) to this museum of firefighting to see what they're missing out on. You'll see some 20 historic fire engines ranging from 18th-century hand-pumped affairs to the latest super hi-tech models and find out how the fire service has developed in the 300-odd years since the Great Fire of London in 1666 when huge swathes of the city burned down. Best of all, kids can try on some of the uniforms. Space travel pales in comparison.

Southwark Cathedral

Montague Close, SE1
t (020) 7407 3708
www.southwark.anglican.org
⊖/ ⊅ London Bridge
Bus 17, 21, 35, 40, 43, 48, 133, 149, 501, D1
Open Cathedral: 8–6 daily; exhibition: Mon–Sat 10–6, Sun 11–5
Free to the cathedral; exhibition: adult £3, child £1.50, under-5s **free**, family £12.50
Wheelchair accessible, call in advance; restaurant, shop, lifts

The Cathedral's landscaped grounds are practically crying out for a picnic. There's also a new interactive museum, 'The Long View of London' with touch-screen computers, a camera obscura mounted on the Cathedral tower showing panoramic views of the city, plus a variety of medieval, Roman and Victorian artefacts.

Picnics & snacks

As with the South Bank, its adjacent area, Southwark, doesn't really go in for inviting expanses of greenery. Its one small park, the **William Curtis Park** by the new GLA building, offers great views of Tower Bridge and is a pleasant enough spot for a picnic, although you can feel a bit hemmed in. The newly landscaped gardens of **Southwark Cathedral** are much more welcoming and you're also welcome to picnic in the Tate Modern's Clore Education Centre.

Supplies can be picked up from **Borough Market**, (just south of Southwark Cathedral, off Borough High Street) which sells a huge array of farmer's market produce: fruit and veg, cheeses, meat etc. and also has a number of delicatessen counters.

There's plenty of choice. The **Hays Galleria**, SE1, ⊖ London Bridge, has numerous eateries including **Absolutely Starving**, a delicatessen-cum-sandwich shop, **t** (020) 7407 7417; the **Bagel Factory**, **t** (020) 7407 7616, which serves American-style bagels, cookies and brownies; and **Schulers**, **t** (020) 7378 6968, which serves made-to-order sandwiches and salads. Several of the area's attractions also have good cafés including **Southwark Cathedral**, **t** (020) 7407 3708, where there's outside seating; **Tate Modern**, **t** (020) 7887 8000, which has a café on the second floor, an espresso bar on Level 4 and a very grand restaurant on Level 7 (the latter offers great views of the river).

Restaurants

1 Ask Pizza
Spice Quay, 34 Shad Thames, Butlers Wharf, SE1
t (020) 7403 4545
www.askcentral.co.uk
⊖/≋ London Bridge, ⊖ Tower Hill
Open 11.30–11.30

2 Browns
Shad Thames, SE1
t (020) 7378 1700
www.browns-restaurants.com
⊖ London Bridge, Tower Hill
Open 12 noon–12 midnight

3 Café Rouge
Hay's Galleria, Tooley Street, SE1
t (020) 7378 0097

www.caferouge.co.uk
⊖/≋ London Bridge
Open Mon–Fri 8.30am–11pm, Sat 9am–11pm, Sun 9am–10.30pm

4 Fish!
Cathedral Street, SE1
t (020) 7407 3803
www.fishdiner.co.uk
⊖ London Bridge, Borough
Open Mon–Thurs 11.30am–11pm, Fri & Sat 11–11, Sun 12 noon–10.30

5 La Lanterna
6–8 Mill Street, SE1
t (020) 7252 2420
www.pizzerialalanterna.co.uk
⊖ Tower Hill
Open 12 noon–11pm

6 Manze's
87 Tower Bridge Road, SE1
t (020) 2407 2985
www.manze.co.uk
⊖ London Bridge, Tower Hill
Open Mon 11am–2pm, Tues–Thurs 10.30am–2pm, Fri 10am–2.30pm, Sat 10am–2.45pm

7 Pizza Express
Cardamom Building, Shad Thames, SE1
t (020) 7403 8484
www.pizzaexpress.com
⊖ London Bridge, Tower Hill
Open Mon–Thurs & Sun 11.30–11, Fri & Sat 11.30–12 midnight

See **Eat** p.224–36 for more details on the above restaurants.
See map on p.115 for the locations of the restaurants numbered above.

The City

Old Street

300 metres
300 yards

FARRINGDON ROAD

CLERKENWELL ROAD

GOSWELL ROAD

OLD STREET

⑫

Farringdon ⑥

Barbican

CHISWELL STREET

Barbican Centre ⑦

Liverpool Street

CHARTERHOUSE STREET

ALDERSGATE STREET

Moorgate ⑩

Smithfield Market

KING ED STREET

Museum of London

④

LONDON WALL

WC

SHOPSGATE

FARRINGDON STREET

St Pauls

⑧

Bank of England Museum

THREADNEEDLE STREET

FLEET STREET

②

St Paul's Cathedral

CHEAPSIDE

Bank

①

Mansion House

KING WILLIAM STREET

Blackfriars

QUEEN VICTORIA STREET

⑨

Cannon Street

Monument

UPPER THAMES STREET

The Monument

WC

BLACKFRIARS BRIDGE

MILLENNIUM BRIDGE

SOUTHWARK BRIDGE

LONDON BRIDGE

Key

Numbers correspond to restaurants in 'Where To Eat' p.134

Highlights

Gazing at the Crown Jewels

The view from the top of St Paul's Cathedral

Staring at the gold bars in the Bank of England Museum

London's monied heart, the City, is home to the Bank of England, the Stock Exchange and the Royal Mint as well as dozens of other seriously rich institutions. Millions and millions of pounds change hands here every day at the blink of an eye.

It's the most commercial area of London and the least residential. In the Middle Ages, when the City *was* London, people would come here from miles around to sell their goods and livestock at market, as surviving street names, such as Bread Street, Wood Street and Poultry, can testify.

It's an area both filled with history and in a permanent state of reinvention. Dotted with cranes all year, the City skyline is constantly being reshaped. So, alongside such grand old landmarks as St Paul's Cathedral and the 900-year-old Tower of London, you'll find some of London's newest creations – places like the Swiss Re building, a stunning giant glass cylinder nicknamed the 'Gherkin' by the press.

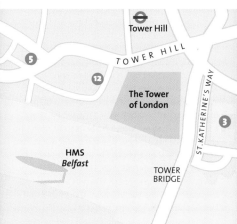

Tower of London

Tower Hill, EC3 (the entrance, while the Tower Hill area is being redeveloped, is via Tower Moat – follow the signs from Tower Hill Underground)
t 0870 756 6060
www.hrp.org.uk/toweroflondon/
⊖ Tower Hill
Bus 15, 42, 78, 100, RV1
Open Mar–Oct Tues–Sat 9–6, Sun 10–6; Nov–Feb Tues–Sat 9–5, Sun–Mon 10–5
Adm Adult £16, child £9.50, concs £13, family (2+3) £45
*Very limited wheelchair access to much of the castle, but the Jewel House and Crown Jewels are fully accessible, call **t** 0870 751 5191 for access guide. The entrance for pushchairs and wheelchair users is via the Tower's West Gate on Lower Thames Street.*
Tours, family trail guides, audio guides
Suitable for ages 7 and over
Allow at least 3hrs

Murders, executions, assassinations, conspiracies and betrayals – the Tower of London has seen them all. So that kids get the most out of their visit here, it's important that they know a little of the history. An old building is not particularly interesting in itself, but if children are told that this is the building in which two princes were murdered and bricked up behind a wall, perhaps by their wicked uncle so that he would become king instead of them, it suddenly becomes much more exciting. The famous Yeoman Warders or 'Beefeaters' come in very handy in this regard, as they are generally more than willing to regale children with tales of intrigue and murder.

At around 900 years old, the Tower is one of London's oldest major landmarks, and also one of the best-preserved medieval castles in the world. The White Tower, at its heart, was built by William the Conqueror soon after his invasion of England in 1066 in order to shore up his position and provide a stronghold against future rebellions. It was to prove a great success; its massive 15-ft walls have never been breached. The Tower has not always served a purely defensive role, however. In the 16th and 17th centuries it proved just as good at keeping people in as it had been at keeping them out. You can visit the spot on Tower Green where the teenage Lady Jane Grey, Walter Raleigh and Anne Boleyn all met their grisly ends – and grisly, in this instance, really means grisly. The sword blow that killed Anne Boleyn, Henry VIII's second wife, was

> ### *Tell me a story:* A Bloody coup
> Today the crown jewels are protected by sophisticated security devices, but in 1671 the fantastically named Irish adventurer and Civil War veteran Colonel Thomas Blood almost succeeded in stealing them from the Tower. On the day in question, Blood disguised himself as a clergyman and, accompanied by his wife and nephew, went to the Tower where his wife pretended to faint. When the Keeper of the Jewels came to help, Blood knocked him out with a mallet. He then grabbed the crown, which he bent to fit under his cloak, while his nephew put the orb in his pocket. The nephew then tried to file the royal sceptre in half to hide it under his coat. He took so long, however, that the keeper's son was able to raise the alarm and the two men were captured and thrown into a dungeon. Charles II was apparently so impressed by the daring shown that he not only granted Blood a pardon, but also gave him a pension of £500 a year (a fortune in those days). Sometimes, it seems, crime really does pay.

Question 13
What was the name of the king who is said to have had his nephews killed in the Tower?
answer on p.250

delivered with such speed that her lips supposedly continued to recite a prayer after her head had been removed.

The Tower's fantastic security record led to it being entrusted with the safekeeping of the nation's most precious treasure – the Crown Jewels. You can see them at the Jewel House, where you are carried past the priceless crowns, sceptres and orbs on a moving walkway. Look out for the Cullinans I and II, the largest top-quality cut diamonds in the world.

Elsewhere in the Tower you'll find Edward I's medieval palace, where guides dressed in period costume will demonstrate crafts such as calligraphy and quill-making; the Armouries, where there's a display of miniature suits of armour made for royal children (presumably the medieval equivalent of a modern millionaire giving their child a miniature Ferrari), and the White Tower where there's a display of grisly torture instruments. It was here that Guy Fawkes confessed to having tried to blow up James I (only after his legs and arms were almost pulled off on the rack). Do also look out for the Tower's most famous residents, the shiny black ravens which live in the Tower Gardens (although

be sure to keep your distance as they can get a bit grumpy). According to legend, if the ravens ever leave the Tower, it, and the country, will topple.

The Tower is one of the most popular sites in London which means that, if you're visiting in summer, you're going to have to queue. It can also be quite hard on the legs, especially for young children, but it does provide a memorable day out. Free children's activity trails are available from the Welcome Centre and the Tower organizes a whole range of free family activities.

St Paul's Cathedral

St Paul's Churchyard, EC4
t (020) 7236 4128
www.stpauls.co.uk
⊖ St Paul's, Mansion House
Bus 4, 11, 15, 23, 25, 26, 100, 242
Opening times Mon–Sat 8.30–4.30
Adm Cathedral only: adult £9.50, child £3.50, family (2+2) £22.50, concs £8.50
Wheelchair accessible for all areas except galleries
Suitable for ages 5 and over
Allow at least 1hr

Finally free of the scaffolding that has obscured its exterior for the past few years, St Paul's is clean and spruce and ready to celebrate its 300th anniversary in 2008, its great plump dome once again dominating the city skyline.

This is a great place for kids to come and burn off some excess energy. The 521-step climb, though hard on the thighs, is well worth it. The panoramic views from the top of the dome, 365 ft up, are stupendous. You can see more or less the whole of London stretched out before you like a great 3D tapestry.

Designed by Sir Christopher Wren, and built in the late 17th century after the original, wooden cathedral burnt down in the Great Fire in 1666, St Paul's is arguably London's most beautiful church. The fantastically decorated interior is almost as impressive as the view from the top of the cathedral, particularly the massive domed ceiling. About halfway up the inside of the dome is the Whispering Gallery. You can put it to the test by doing the following: stand on one side of the Gallery while a friend goes over to the other. Now, providing it's quiet enough, you should be able to whisper something to the wall on your side and have your friend hear it quite clearly on the other, 107 ft away.

In the crypt, which is the largest in Europe, you'll find the tombs of many of Britain's greatest military leaders – Admiral Nelson (his coffin is made out of the main mast of the flagship of the French fleet that was defeated at the Battle of Trafalgar in 1805) and the Duke of Wellington (who beat Napoleon at the Battle of Waterloo in 1815) among them – as well as one of Wren's original models of the cathedral – he made three designs before the final one was accepted, although, even then, he made changes as the work progressed. There's also a shop, restaurant, and a great, child-friendly café.

Museum of London

London Wall, EC2
t 0870 444 3852
www.museumoflondon.org.uk
↔ Barbican, Bank, St Paul's
Bus 8, 22b, 56
Open Tues–Sat 10–5.50, Sun 12 noon–5.50
Free
Wheelchair accessible. Suitable for all ages
Allow at least an hour

This fascinating museum, which tells the story of life in London from prehistoric camps to internet cafés, is currently undergoing an £18 million refit. This means that, until 2009, you'll only be able to follow the story up until 1666 and the Great Fire. All the modern stuff is getting a 21st-century

Can you spot?

The following landmarks, visible from the top of St Paul's. The Thames is due south.
▶ To the west: the British Telecom Tower (formerly the Post Office Tower), a tall, thin, round building that looks like an enormous spark plug. Its sides are covered in transmitters and satellite dishes.
▶ To the northwest: The Old Bailey (the colloquial name for the Central Criminal Courts), which looks a bit like St Paul's but with a much smaller dome. Perched on top is a golden statue of a woman holding a sword in one hand and a pair of scales (representing the balance of justice) in the other.
▶ To the south, across the river: Tate Modern – formerly a power station, this is a huge square brick building with a tall central square tower.
▶ To the east: London's three tallest buildings – Canary Wharf (812 ft), Tower 42 (600 ft) and the Swiss Re Building, more commonly known as 'The Gherkin' (590 ft). Canary Wharf is so tall it has to have a winking light on its triangular-shaped roof to prevent low-flying aircraft from hitting it
▶ Tower Bridge (*see* p.116), with its two great turrets and raising decks.

makeover. There's still plenty to enjoy, however, including some wonderful scale models – a prehistoric mammoth hunt, Shakespeare's Rose Theatre etc – and a number of restored and reconstructed interiors. Look out for the Roman kitchen.

The revamp has been prompted in part by the museum's ever-expanding collection, much of which has been derived from the local area, thanks to big business' need to constantly dig up and rebuild the city. By law, no new development can be undertaken within the 'Square Mile' until there's been a thorough architectural excavation of the site. Recent digs at Spitalfields and Gresham Street have uncovered hoards of Roman antiquities (including tombstones, jewellery, kitchenware and even the remains of a waterwheel), many of which have gone on display in the museum a few weeks after being discovered.

The museum tries hard to make history come alive for its younger visitors. The curators allow families to attend artefact handling sessions on weekends. During the school holidays the museum also organizes a number of workshops, demonstrations and performances for children on a range of subjects from metalwork to preparing Roman food.

Question 14
The Lord Mayor's gold coach resides in the museum for 364 days of the year. Where is it on the remaining day?
answer on p.250

Bank of England Museum

Threadneedle Street, EC2. The entrance is on Bartholomew Lane
t (020) 7601 5545
www.bankofengland.co.uk
⊖ Bank, Cannon Street
Bus 9, 11, 22
Open Mon–Fri 10–5
Free
Wheelchair accessible
Suitable for children aged 10 and over
Allow at least 1hr

Take a trek through the monetary world to see how financial transactions have developed from paper IOUs to whizzing numbers on a computer screen. The curators have obviously thought long and hard about how to make what is a rather dry subject interesting for children. So you'll find a recreation of an 18th-century bank office inhabited by be-wigged waxwork bankers; lots of interactive video screens where you can find out the history of the bank and, the highlight, a large perspex pyramid filled with gold bars – the kids glued permanently to its side are not part of the exhibit.

The museum also has displays on more modern currency matters – the Stock Exchange, financial trading, etc. – which include a (very difficult) interactive currency trading game. Activity worksheets for kids (there are versions for 5–8-year-olds, 9–12-year-olds and 13–16-year-olds) available from the front desk. Monetary themed activities for children (banknote design etc) are organized in the summer holidays.

The Monument

Monument Street, EC3
t (020) 7626 2717
⊖ Monument
Bus 15, 22a, 35, 40, 48
Open 9.30–5, daily
Adm Adult £2, child £1, under-5s **free**
No wheelchair access
Suitable for ages 4 and over
Allow at least 30mins

Did you know?
▶ That the first St Paul's Cathedral was built by the Saxons way back in AD 604?
▶ That the present cathedral took 35 years to build at a cost of £721,552 (over £50 million in today's money) and was paid for by a tax put on coal coming into the city?
▶ That the cathedral clock tower 'Great Tom' houses Britain's heaviest bell (17 tonnes) and that the dome itself weighs a staggering 65,000 tonnes?
▶ That when the medieval cathedral caught fire in 1666, it generated such a tremendous amount of heat that the 250-year-old corpse of the former Mayor of London, Robert Braybrooke, was blasted out of his grave and thrown clear of the churchyard?

If the Monument were to fall over, its top (provided it fell in the right direction) would land on the very spot in Pudding Lane where the Fire of London broke out in the early hours of 2 September 1666, more than 300 years ago. It was designed by Sir Christopher Wren as a memorial for the victims of the Fire. He also rebuilt many of the churches that were destroyed in the fire, including Old St Paul's Cathedral (see p.129). At 202 ft high it was, on completion in 1677, the tallest free-standing column in the world. Of course, by modern standards, 202 ft isn't very tall at all, and today the monument is rather obscured by the medium-sized buildings surrounding it. You can climb the 311 steps to the top where you get a close-up look at the great bronze urn that sits a the summit of the monument, spouting shiny metallic flames. The views are good, albeit not as good as those from the top of St Paul's, but kids will enjoy sending themselves dizzy running down the spiral staircase, and they receive a certificate to commemorate having made the climb.

Barbican Centre

Silk Street, EC2
t (020) 7638 4141
www.barbican.org.uk
⊖ Barbican, Bank, St Paul's, Moorgate
Bus 4, 8, 11, 21, 76, 100, 141, 153, 214, 271
Wheelchair accessible

Question 15
The Bank of England Museum has a collection of British coins. However, the bank only issues notes. Who issues British coins?
answer on p.250

Nobody could describe the Barbican as beautiful, but it is one of the capital's major arts centres and, as such, always has a lot going on. These great concrete tower blocks and labyrinthine corridors are home to several of the country's most prestigious artistic bodies including the London Symphony Orchestra and the English Chamber Orchestra as well as three cinemas, an art gallery and a semitropical garden. Special children's events and performances are put on in the school holidays as part of the centre's 'Barbican Family' programme. These include the annual LSO Discovery Concert (see p.165), the Discovery Creative Music Workshops, which offer informal instrument tuition for 7–12-year-olds, and the London Children's Film Festival (see p.39). There's also a Family Film Club for 5–11-year-olds which meets every Saturday morning at 10.30.

Smithfield, the capital's largest meat market, was a popular site for jousting in the Middle Ages and also witnessed the bloody conclusion of the Peasants' Revolt (see below). Opposite the market, on the wall of St Bartholomew's Hospital, is a blue plaque marking the spot where another revolt came to an end when William Wallace (as featured in the film *Braveheart*), the leader of the Scots, was hung, drawn and quartered by the English in the 13th century.

Further afield, on Fleet Street, is Prince Henry's Room (see opposite), while just off King Edward Street is one of the City's few pieces of greenery, Postman's Park. It has a memorial wall dedicated to people who have sacrificed their lives for others.

The peasants are revolting

In 1381 a band of commoners marched on London demanding the repeal of the newly imposed Poll Tax (which charged everyone the same amount, regardless of their ability to pay). Once in the City, they stormed the Debtors' Prison and slaughtered as many lawyers and tax collectors as they could. The 14-year-old king, Richard II, met them at Smithfield to discuss their grievances. At first it seemed that the king would agree to a number of concessions, including the repeal of the tax and the abolition of serfdom. However, the Mayor of London became so incensed at the protesters' presumption that he stepped forward and stabbed the rebel leader Wat Tyler, fatally wounding him. Rather than continue their protest, the rebels decided to accept the word of the king and disband. Bad move – once they had turned for home, Richard's troops captured and killed as many of them as they could find. A picture of the dagger used to stab Tyler was subsequently incorporated into the City of London's coat of arms.

Prince Henry's Room

17 Fleet Street, EC4
t (020) 7936 2710
Temple, Blackfriars
Open Mon–Sat 11–2
Free

This ornately decorated room provides a glimpse of a London that no longer exists, being one of the few structures that survived the fire of 1666. It's filled with memorabilia relating to the life of Samuel Pepys, who famously documented the fire and was also a regular patron of the tavern, known as the Prince's Arms, that used to occupy the rest of the building.

Picnics & snacks

There aren't many green spaces in the City. A few small courtyards aside, the best is **Postman's Park** on King Edward Street, which is nice for a picnic (although it gets busy at sunny lunchtimes). Picnics and packed lunches can also be eaten in the school rooms of the **Museum of London** and, if the weather's fine, the museum's **Barber Surgeon's Gardens**, which are bordered by the remains of a Roman fort.

Leadenhall Market on Gracechurch Street, EC3, has plenty of grocers and delicatessens; the **Deli Bar** at 117 Charterhouse Street, EC2, **t** (020) 7253 2070, Farringdon, and **Tesco Metro** at 80B Cheapside, EC1, **t** 0845 677 9148, Bank are both two useful examples.

The primary function of the City's food outlets is to feed its thousands of day workers. Consequently you'll find plenty of fast food, sandwich bars and cafés (although many of these are closed on week-

---

Tell me a story: Filthy lucre

Have you heard the one about the man who got into the Bank of England's gold vaults by way of the sewers? It's no joke.

In 1836 the directors of the Bank are said to have received an anonymous letter stating that the writer had discovered an underground passage to the bullion. He offered to meet them there to prove his claim at any hour they chose. Although initially sceptical, the directors were persuaded to assemble one night in the vault. At the agreed time, they heard a noise under the floor and a man appeared from below merely by displacing a few floorboards.

This man turned out to be a sewerman who, during repair work to the tunnels, had discovered an old drain that ran directly under the bullion vault. He might have carried away enormous sums but he resisted the urge and for his honesty the Bank is said to have rewarded him with a gift of £800.

Following the incident, the directors decided to take precautions against further intrusions. Several letters were sent to George Bailey, Curator of the Soane Museum*, asking for the architect's plans of the drains under the Bank premises to be returned to the Bank, just in case of other passages.
* Sir John Soane was the Bank of England's architect from 1788 to 1833. See p.82 for more on his extraordinary house, now a museum.

ends). There are numerous eateries lining **Ludgate Hill** by the west front of St Paul's including a **Starbuck's** and **Fresh Italy** at no.38, **t** (020) 7329 5629, ⊖ St Paul's, a sort of fast-food Italian café where you can pick up simple pasta dishes, salads and focaccia sandwiches. **St Katharine's Dock**, next to Tower Bridge, is also a good source of cafés and restaurants. Otherwise look out for **The Place Below**, an excellent vegetarian café under the church of St Mary le Bow, Cheapside, EC2, **t** (020) 7329 0789, ⊖ St Paul's, Bank; **Smiths of Smithfield** at 67–77 Charterhouse Street, EC1, **t** (020) 7251 7950, ⊖ Farringdon, which does a very good all-day breakfast; and the self-service **Crypt Café** of St Paul's Cathedral, St Paul's Courtyard, EC4, ⊖ St Paul's, which is cool on a sunny day and is not restricted to cathedral visitors. There are also branches of **McDonald's** at 143 Cannon Street, ⊖ Cannon Street, 41–42 London Wall, ⊖ Moorgate, 12 Tower Hill Terrace, ⊖ Tower Hill and 50 Liverpool Street, ⊖ Liverpool Street.

Restaurants

1/2 Café Rouge
Hillgate House, Limeburner Lane, EC4
t (020) 7588 3008
www.caferouge.co.uk
⊖ Blackfriars
Unit 5, Condor House, St Paul's Churchyard, EC4
t (020) 7489 7812
⊖ St Paul's
www.caferouge.co.uk
Open Mon–Sat 8.30am–11pm, Sun 9am–10.30pm

3 Dickens Inn
St Katherine's Way, E1
t (020) 7488 2208
www.dickensinn.co.uk
⊖ Tower Hill, Tower Gateway
DLR London Bridge

4/5/6 Pizza Express
Branches at: 125 Alban Gate, London Wall, EC2, **t** (020) 7600 8880, ⊖ Barbican, St Paul's **Open** Mon–Fri 11.30–11, Sat 12 noon–10, Sun 12 noon–8; 1 Byward Street, EC3, **t** (020) 7625 5025, ⊖ Tower Hill; 26 Cowcross Street, EC1, **t** (020) 7490 8025, ⊖ Farringdon **Open** 11.30–11, daily
www.pizzaexpress.com

7 Searcy's
Level I, Barbican Centre, EC2
t (020) 7588 3008
⊖ Barbican
Open Mon–Fri 12 noon–2.30 and 6–10.30, Sat–Sun 12 noon–3 and 5–6.30

8/9/10/11 Wagamama
22 Old Broad Street, EC2, **t** (020) 7256 9992
⊖ Liverpool Street, Bank
4 Great St Thomas Apostle, EC4, **t** (020) 7248 5766
⊖ Mansion House
1a Ropemaker Street, EC2, **t** (020) 7588 2688
⊖ Moorgate
2b Tower Place, Tower Hill, EC3, **t** (020) 7283 5897
⊖ Tower Hill
www.wagamama.com
Branches open Mon–Sat 12 noon–11, Sun 12.30–10

12 Yo! Sushi
95 Farringdon Road, Clerkenwell, EC1
t (020) 7841 0785
www.yosushi.com
⊖ Farringdon
Open Mon–Sat 12 noon–11, Sun 12 noon–10.30

See **Eat** p.224–36 for more details on the above restaurants.
See maps on pp.126–7 for the locations of the restaurants numbered above.

Museumland

There are few better places than this to come for an exciting day out. In the morning, start with a quick tour around one of the capital's great museums. You can choose from the Natural History Museum, the Science Museum or the Victoria & Albert Museum. All are within spitting distance of each other on the Cromwell Road, all offer guaranteed entertainment with a huge range of family-friendly exhibits and facilities and, as an added bonus, all are free. From here it's a five minute walk to Hyde Park for a picnic and a quick jaunt in a rowing boat on the Serpentine, before finishing the day with some souvenir and gift shopping in the unforgettable halls of Harrods.

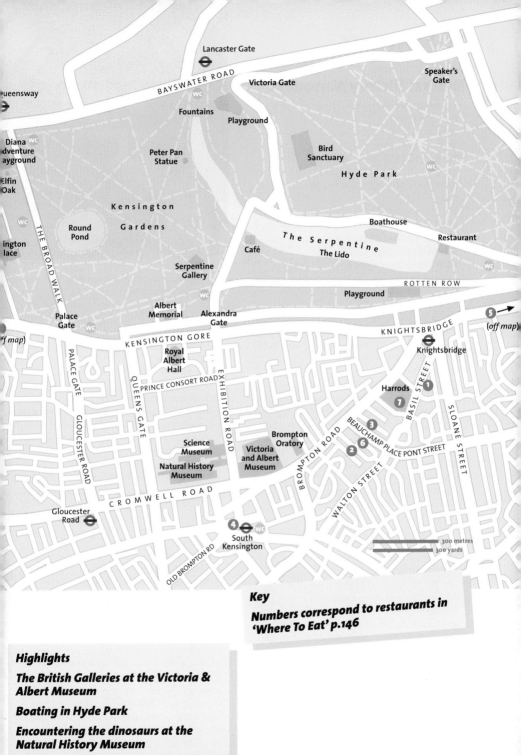

Lancaster Gate

BAYSWATER ROAD

Victoria Gate

Speaker's Gate

Queensway

WC

Fountains

Playground

Diana
Adventure
Playground

WC

Peter Pan
Statue

Bird
Sanctuary

Hyde Park

WC

Elfin
Oak

Kensington Gardens

WC

Round
Pond

Boathouse

The Serpentine

Restaurant

Kensington
Palace

THE BROAD WALK

Café

The Lido

WC

Serpentine
Gallery

ROTTEN ROW

Palace
Gate

Albert
Memorial

Alexandra
Gate

Playground

KNIGHTSBRIDGE

5→

(off map)

WC

(off map)

KENSINGTON GORE

Royal
Albert
Hall

Knightsbridge

PALACE GATE

QUEENS GATE

PRINCE CONSORT ROAD

EXHIBITION ROAD

Harrods

1

7

BASIL STREET

SLOANE STREET

GLOUCESTER ROAD

Science
Museum

Natural History
Museum

Victoria
and Albert
Museum

Brompton
Oratory

BROMPTON ROAD

BEAUCHAMP PLACE

3

2

6

WALTON STREET

PONT STREET

CROMWELL ROAD

Gloucester
Road

OLD BROMPTON RD

4

South
Kensington

WC

300 metres
300 yards

Key
**Numbers correspond to restaurants in
'Where To Eat' p.146**

Highlights

**The British Galleries at the Victoria &
Albert Museum**

Boating in Hyde Park

**Encountering the dinosaurs at the
Natural History Museum**

Natural History Museum

Cromwell Road, SW7
t (020) 7942 5000
www.nhm.ac.uk
⊖ South Kensington
Bus 9, 10, 14, 49, 52, 70, 74, 345,
414, C1
Open Mon–Sat 10–5.50, Sun 11–5.50
Free
*Wheelchair accessible for most galleries, with
adapted toilets. The entrance for wheelchair users is
in Exhibition Road. Three shops*
Suitable for all ages
Allow a morning or afternoon

One of the must-see sights in London for both
children and adults, the Natural History Museum
is, quite simply, a fabulous place. Huge monsters,
replica volcanoes, earthquake simulators, creepy-
crawlies, precious stones, big things, small things,
shiny things – there's so much to look at. This is
the sort of museum where kids tend to rush off
pointing at everything.

The museum is split into four colour-coded
sections: green, blue, red and orange. Here, briefly,
is what you can expect to find in each. The green
zone is your introduction to the museum. You
arrive through the main Cromwell Road entrance
into the central hall where you'll be confronted by
the great swooping head of a fossil diplodocus
looming down above you, sadly only a replica. This
zone also contains the Learning Zone as well as
displays of prehistoric marine reptiles, although
not the main dinosaur exhibits, which, somewhat
confusingly, are in the adjacent blue zone. Here
you'll find all the superstar fossils – triceratops,
allosaurus etc – models of dinosaur nests and, the
main attraction, a two-thirds size, animatronic
Tyrannosaurus Rex – it growls, it slavers, it snaps
its jaws, it really is rather excellent. The blue zone
also has displays of modern vertebrates – fishes,
amphibians, reptiles and mammals. Look out,
in particular, for the full-size replica blue whale,

the largest creature to have ever lived, suspended
from the gallery ceiling.

The red zone is best accessed via the Exhibition
Road entrance, where you'll find yourself walking
through a guard of honour made up of bizzare
futuristic statues, before riding an escalator up into
a huge clunking, clanking metal globe. The displays
here are primarily concerned with geological
processes, i.e. lots of stuff about volcanoes and
earthquakes. There are videos of exploding craters,
models of lava flows, plastercasts of the Pompeii
victims frozen in mute agony and, best of all, an
earthquake simulator – every five minutes you can
stand inside a mock-up Japanese supermarket as it
undergoes a minor tremor.

The final zone, the orange zone, is the setting
for the Darwin Centre and the Wildlife Garden.
The former was built a few years ago at a cost of
£30 million and covers some 10,000 square metres.
It provides a showcase for the museum's vast
collection of preserved animal species (of which
there are around 22 million, although the centre
only has space for a mere 450,000). The centre's
walls are lined with shelves on which sit hundreds
and hundreds of preserving jars, each containing a
different animal. There are monkeys, birds, sharks,
tortoises, lizards, plus countless others. Several
seem to have been put (or rather stuffed) into jars
a little too small for them, their distorted features
creating grotesque visages against the sides of
the glass. Amazingly, some of the creatures were
actually collected by the great naturalist Charles
Darwin himself during his mid-19th-century
travels to the Galapagos Islands, and provided
the evidence for his world-changing theories of
evolution via natural selection.

Did you know?
The Natural History Museum is every collector's
idea of paradise. It contains a staggering 68
million plants, animals, fossils, rocks and minerals
from all regions of the world.

Question 16

The word 'dinosaur' itself means 'terrible lizard' in Latin. What do the following dinosaur names mean?

a) Triceratops
b) Deinocheirus
c) Baronyx

answer on p.250

Free behind-the-scenes 'Explore' tours to see the thousands of specimens not on public display, as well as the laboratory facilities used to examine them, are given daily (available to ages 10 and over only).

Interesting though the centre is, it offers little in the way of interaction and kids itching to get involved in a more hands-on way should head to the Investigate Centre in the Clore Education Centre. Here 7–14-year-olds are invited to take an item (such as a fossil, plant or preserved bird or insect) from the 'Specimen Wall' and examine it at one of several workstations, which come equipped with computer terminals, microscopes, magnifiers and measures. The Wildlife Garden houses a display of living creatures – insects, carniverous plants and the like.

Even if the Education Centre is closed or busy – it's set aside for school visits during the week in term time – there's still plenty on offer for families in the museum. Free discovery guides, aimed at all ages from 7–16, and Explorer backpacks (a £25 refundable deposit is required), aimed at under-7s, are available. The museum organizes family workshops for both under-7s (storytelling, puppet shows, etc.) and 7–12-year-olds (hands-on activities, beast hunts in the new museum courtyard, etc.) on Saturdays and Sundays and some school holiday weekdays. The workshops are free, but can only be booked on the day at the information desk in Gallery 10. The museum also organizes special events and family talks year round.

If it gets the funding, the museum hopes to open yet another extension in 2009 in which it will display some of its collection of 6 million preserved plants and 22 million preserved insects.

Nature-mad kds can even become members of the museum, which entitles them to free entry to special exhibitions, a free nature magazine, 'Second Nature', four times a year, use of a special members' room and discounts in the museum shop. It costs adult £50, child £30, family £68 per year. More details can be found on the kids section of the museum website, **www**.nhm. ac.uk/kids-only/

Science Museum

Exhibition Road, London SW7
t 0870 870 4868
www.sciencemuseum.org.uk
⊖ South Kensington
Bus 4, 14, 30, 49, 52, 70, 74, 345, 360, 414, C1
Open 10–6, daily
Free IMAX: adult £8, child £6
Wheelchair accessible, with adapted toilets. An 'Access and Facilities Guide' is available from the information desk
Suitable for all ages
Allow a morning or afternoon

The Science Museum, perhaps more than any other museum, understands children. It understands that children like to be involved with the exhibits. Nowhere is this better demonstrated than in the 'Who am I?' exhibition on the first floor, which looks at how science has helped us to understand what it means to be human. You can morph your features on a computer to make yourself look older or younger, or even switch gender. In 'In Future', you can play an interactive game to decide which technologies you think will be most relevant in the decades to come. There is also an IMAX film theatre showing science-related films on huge, four-storey-high screens (usually on a spectacular nature- or space-related theme), a simulator ride, SimEx, which takes you on a journey through the land of the dinosaurs and then out into space (adult £4, child £3), and the Pattern Pod where under-8s can find out about patterns in the natural world through simple experiments.

Short of time?

There's far too much in the museum to be covered in a single day and you may prefer to plan your tour around a few headline exhibits. Here are some suggestions:

▶ A 1903 Burnley mill engine. This is the showpiece of the Energy Gallery on the ground floor, dedicated to the great machinery of the Industrial Revolution.

▶ The Black Arrow. Britain's first and only satellite launch rocket. The enormous craft is in the Exploring Space gallery on the ground floor.

▶ The Apollo 10 Command Module. In 1969 it flew three astronauts into space as a rehearsal for the moon landing mission later in the year. Note the scorch marks on the craft, which were caused when it re-entered the earth's atmosphere at great speed. It is in the Making the Modern World gallery on the ground floor.

▶ Charles Babbage's Difference Engine. This collection of cogs, gears and levers was the world's first-ever computer. It is in Making the Modern World on the ground floor.

▶ A replica of one of the earliest telescopes through which in 1610 the great Italian astonomer, Galileo, became the first man to see the rings of Saturn (which he called the planets 'ears'). It is in Exploring Space on the ground floor.

▶ The Gloster-Whittle E.28/39, which in 1941, became the first plane to fly without requiring a propellor to power it. Instead, it used the newly invented jet engine, the creation of the British air-force officer, Sir Frank Whittle. It's located in the Flight gallery on the third Floor.

Impressive though all this stuff is, you'll want to save some time for some of the museum's other exhibits, several of which are specifically designed for children. These include a revamped Launch Pad in the basement where there are various games and pieces of equipment through which kids can learn a few basic scientific principles. They can create a giant bubble, touch a plasma ball and see electricity following their fingers, build a rubber bridge or perhaps try and tiptoe past the vibration detector. Staff are on hand to guide the youngsters through the apparatus. The basement is also the location for 'The Garden', aimed at 3–6-year-olds, which gives children the chance to experiment with water, using pumps, dams and buckets. Also try not to miss the Secret Life of the Home. This takes a humorous look at domestic gizmos and gadgets from vacuum cleaners and washing machines to WCs, fridges and heaters.

Of course, there are plenty of other galleries which, while not specifically designed for children, will nonetheless appeal. These include the Flight Gallery, filled with a century's worth of flying contraptions, from biplanes to jump jets, Exploring Space with its spacecraft and space paraphernalia (including space food) and Making the Modern World, which showcases life-changing inventions from the past two hundred years, from lawnmowers and orreries to moon rockets and personal computers.

Before leaving, make sure you check out the museum shop which is filled with 'science' toys and games – junior astronomy kits, rainbow Slinkies, holograms, binoculars, models, kaleidoscopes and the like. Themed children's trail guides are available both here and at reception for £2.

Science Nights

Kids will like the museum so much that they'll probably wish they could spend the night. Well, guess what? The museum runs Science Nights every month when children aged between 8 and 11 (plus an accompanying parent) can come and camp overnight. They are treated to midnight tours of the museum, workshops and bedtime stories. The sleepovers, which are only available to groups of 5–9 children, are very popular and need to be booked well in advance. They cost £30 per child.

Victoria & Albert Museum

Cromwell Road, SW7
t (020) 7942 2000
www.vam.ac.uk
⊖ South Kensington
Bus 14, 49, 70, 74, 345, 414, C1
Open Mon–Thurs, Sat & Sun 10–5.45, Fri 10–10
Free
Wheelchair accessible. Wheelchair users should use Exhibition Road entrance where there are also 4 designated disabled parking bays
Suitable for ages 10 and over
Allow at least 2hrs

Dedicated to the decorative arts, the Victoria & Albert Museum (or the V&A as it is known) has, over its long history, gathered together a huge collection of treasures from all over the world: silverware from European royal palaces, ceramics from eastern temples, sculptures by African tribes and vast hoards of jewellery, furniture, textiles, tapestries and paintings – it's like an enormous magpie's nest, full of the world's most gaudy, glittery things. The Dress Gallery usually appeals to clothes-conscious teens. It traces the evolution of fashion from the 17th century to the present day, from ruffs and crinolines to miniskirts and trainers.

For something to gasp at, head to the Cast Court where you'll find plaster casts of some of the world's greatest (and biggest) statues and monuments – Michelangelo's *David* and Trajan's Column (in two huge pieces) are among them.

The British Galleries 1500–1900 are a welcome addition, with play areas where kids can try on Victorian clothes or attempt to rebuild the Crystal Palace using perspex blocks, as well as touch-screen information points, reconstructed room sets and banks of computer workstations.

There's not much to push or pull in the other galleries, though the museum organizes plenty of kids' activities. These are usually themed according to the gallery – origami in the Japanese Gallery, paper clothes-making in the Dress Gallery and jewellery-making in the Silver Gallery. Free themed family trails are available from the information desk daily, and activity backpacks full of jigsaws, stories, puzzles and construction games can be

Tell me a story: Tudor tales

The V&A is home to a number of rare and precious objects, among them Charles Dickens' pen case and manuscript for *Oliver Twist*, as well as Joseph Paxton's first sketch for the Crystal Palace, built for the Great Exhibition of 1851. Here are a selection of Tudor curios, each with its own story. Try and find them on your way round this eclectic museum.

▶ The Great Bed of Ware – over 11ft long and 10ft wide, the bed is mentioned in Shakespeare's *Twelfth Night* and in a poem by Lord Byron. Charles Dickens is said to have tried to buy it. It was, in fact, a Tudor marketing ploy, to attract visitors to The White Hart Inn at Ware in Hertfordshire. The bed is also supposed to be haunted.

▶ A rare 16th-century Standing Salt, or ceremonial salt cellar. In the Tudor period salt was a luxury commodity and was kept in a precious container called simply a 'salt'. Distinguished guests sat 'above the salt' at the table and had the choice of the best dishes.

▶ The beautiful hanging panels from Oxburgh Hall were embroidered by, amongst others, Mary Queen of Scots when imprisoned (1569–85).

▶ A fine 16th-century Silver Tankard. These were introduced during the reign of Henry VIII and soon became fashionable gifts at court. They could be engraved with the individual's heraldic insignia, and were used to drink warm beer or ass's milk.

picked up from the Grand Entrance on Saturday afternoons (1–4.30). Designed for ages 5–12, there are seven themed packs to choose from (themes include 'Chinese Treasures', 'Antique Detective' and 'Magic Glasses'). On Sundays and in the school holidays a roving activity cart tours the museum's seven miles of corridors, while on the first Sunday of each month the museum organizes drop-in events for 5–12-year-olds, based around the current temporary exhibitions and usually involving some artistic activity such as drawing or photography.

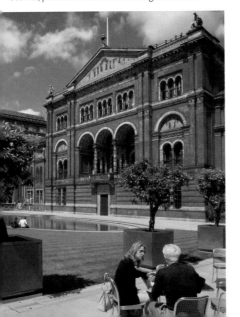

Question 17
How many years did it take to build the V&A Museum's current home and in what year was it finished?
answer on p.250

Hyde Park/Kensington Gardens

t (020) 7298 2000
www.royalparks.gov.uk/parks/hyde_park/
⊖ Hyde Park Corner, Knightsbridge, South
Kensington, Lancaster Gate, Queensway,
Marble Arch
Bus 2, 8, 9, 10, 12, 14, 16, 19, 22, 36, 39, 73, 74, 82, 94
Free
*Suitable for all ages, although only children aged 5
and over can go boating on the Serpentine*

A wonderful expanse of greenery, Hyde Park
provides a welcome oasis of calm in the hectic,
bustling city. In fact, only the eastern side is officially
called Hyde Park; the western side is known as
Kensington Gardens, but there is no official border
and it's really just one big park. In the middle is
the Serpentine – a great, snake-shaped lake as
the name suggests – populated by swans, ducks,
geese and other wildfowl. You can hire rowing
boats – a great way to spend a lazy summer
afternoon. Alternatively, if the kids would rather
play on the grass, help yourself to one of the many
green and white striped deckchairs that dot the
park – an attendant will eventually find you and
charge you the required £1. You can also swim in
the Serpentine Lido (adult £4, child £1, under-3s
free, family £9), paddle in the children's pool
(between May and September) and clamber
aboard the giant model pirate ship in the Princess
Diana Adventure Playground. This is located near
the famous Elfin Oak (a tree decorated with dozens

of tiny elf sculptures). The park's famous Peter Pan
statue is also near here. Author J. M. Barrie lived at
100 Bayswater Road, not 500 yards from the park,
and erected the statue secretly in the middle of
the night.

Because of its location, Hyde Park is extremely
popular, but it is also, owing to its sheer size, serene
and quiet. Furthermore, it's clean and largely free
of dogs. The only real problem is the footpaths,
which seem to be the favoured thoroughfares of
London's roller-skating and jogging community,
and if the weather's fine you may be better off
walking on the grass. For more information on the
park's flora and fauna, head to the former police
observation point in the centre of the park, which
has been turned into an education post. The staff
organize occasional beast hunts, pond dippings
and nature walks, call **t** (020) 7706 3990. Circus
workshops (learn how to juggle or spin a plate) and
arts and crafts activities are also laid on at the lido
in the summer.

Did you know?

Rotten Row, the name of the bridle path
running along the southern edge of the park,
is a corruption of the French 'route de roi' (king's
way). It became the first road in London to
have street lighting when William III hung
300 lanterns from the trees along its route in
order to deter highwaymen.

Do also remember that Hyde Park is one of the very few places in central London where you can go horse-riding (although you'll have to pay quite handsomely for the privilege). Hyde Park Stables, on the north side of the park, offer lessons for all abilities, see p.183 for Hyde Park details.

Speaker's Corner

London's more passionate citizens have, since 1872, been allowed to let off steam every Sunday at Speaker's Corner, which is located at the north-eastern end of the park. People can say whatever they want here and, standing on a makeshift plat-form, attempt to rally passers-by to their cause (be it Buddhism, Marxism or the uses and abuses of potting compost) – providing they can make themselves heard above the traffic on Park Lane.

Kensington Palace

The State Apartments, Kensington Gardens, W8
t 0870 751 7050
www.hrp.org.uk
⊖ High Street Kensington, Notting Hill Gate, Queensway
Bus 9, 10, 12, 52, 73, 94
Open Mar–Oct 10–6, daily, Nov–Feb 10–5, daily, last admission 1hr before closing
Adm Adult £12, child £6, concs £10, family £33
Limited wheelchair access, adapted toilets. Suitable for ages 8 and over, audio tour guides
Allow at least 1hr

On the western edge of Kensington Gardens, this rather reserved-looking palace is where Diana, Princess of Wales lived following her divorce from Prince Charles. The gardens outside were covered in 1.5 million bunches of flowers in the week following her untimely death just over a decade ago. There are guided tours between 10am and 3.30pm, when you can walk through the plush historic apartments and see the Royal Ceremonial Dress Collection. This features a rotating display of items taken from the royal wardrobe – everything from flouncy 18th-century creations and early 20th-century debutante dresses to (always prompting the most interest) some of Princess Diana's glamourous outfits. The palace's very fancy Orangery restaurant offers a children's menu.

Serpentine Gallery

Kensington Gardens, W2
t (020) 7402 6075
www.serpentinegallery.org
⊖ South Kensington, Knightsbridge, Lancaster Gate
Bus 9, 10, 12, 52, 73, 94
Open 10–6, daily
Free
Wheelchair accessible. Suitable for ages 8 and over

The Serpentine Gallery stages temporary exhibitions of modern art. In summer it organizes 'family Sundays' with exhibitions, activities and workshops.

Can you spot?
Can you find the Pet Cemetery by the Victoria Gates in Hyde Park's northwest corner?

Royal Albert Hall

Kensington Gore, SW7
t (020) 7589 8212
www.royalalberthall.com
⊖ High Street Kensington, Knightsbridge
Bus 9, 10, 52, 360
Wheelchair accessible, but wheelchair users are advised to call in advance, so that they can be allocated appropriate seats

A great red barrel of a building, it sits across from the Albert Memorial (*see* opposite) on Kensington Gore. Despite its indifferent acoustics and legendary echo, the Albert Hall is well-loved. Visually, it is one of the more successful Victorian buildings in London, both an echo of the colosseums of antiquity and a bold 19th-century statement on progress and learning. The high frieze around the outside depicts the Triumph of Arts and Sciences – a most Albertian theme. The hall is huge (capacity 7,000 or more) and remarkably versatile: through the year it hosts symphony orchestras, rock bands, conferences, tennis tournaments and boxing matches. Each summer, it plays host to 'the Proms' – a series of innovative classical concerts that have become a national institution.

The Albert Memorial

This huge gold statue set in an elaborate 175 ft stone frame was built in the 1860s on the orders of Queen Victoria as a memorial to her late husband, Prince Albert. Around its carved stone sides are tributes to all the important men of letters, arts and sciences of the Victorian era. Women are somewhat few and far between. The statue itself was considered so bright that the gilding was removed during the war to stop it attracting the attention of enemy planes. It has recently been renovated to stunning effect. There are guided tours every Thurs, Fri, Sat–Sun at 2pm and 3pm, adult £3, concs £2.50, **t** (020) 7495 0916.

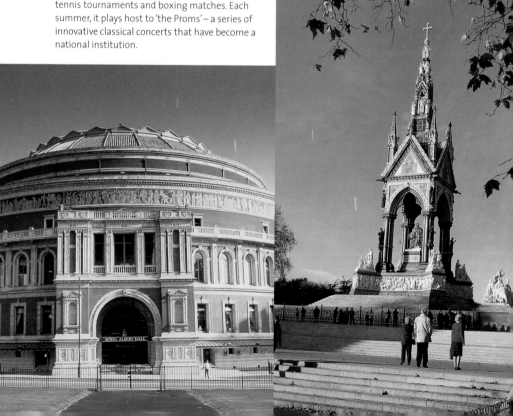

WHERE TO SHOP

There's Knightsbridge, of course, home to two of the world's most famous department stores – the ultra-chic Harvey Nichols and legendary Harrods, with its enormous toy department and magnificent food halls – as well as the nursery equipment and children's clothes shops of Walton Street, particularly Dragons at no.23 (which also has a concession in Harrods) and Nursery Window at no.83. If you've got the shopping bug, however, remember that you're just a Tube stop or two away from two of London's best shopping areas: the King's Road (see p.93) and High Street Kensington – look out for the Early Learning Centre at no.174, the computer game store Game at no.185, a branch of the Virgin Megastore at no.64, the children's clothes stores H&M (no.103–11) and Trotters (no.127). See Shop p.237–41 for details of the above stores.

Harrods

87–135 Brompton Road
Knightsbridge, SW1
t (020) 7730 1234
www.harrods.com
☐ Knightsbridge
Bus 10, 19, 52, 74, 137
Open Mon–Sat 10–9, Sun 12–6

Harrods, the capital's best-known department store, is famous for its luxurious interiors. The food halls, in particular, are fabulously opulent – children may well take a passing interest in the exotic fruit displays, fresh fish sculptures and straw-boatered shop assistants as they drag you towards the toys on the fourth floor. Here you can find everything, from limited edition Steiff teddies and one-third-size Ferraris with full leather interior to the latest video games. There's also a children's book department and (parents, at least, might like to know) a children's-wear section (with separate sections for formalwear, designerwear and international designerwear, of course). There are places to eat on each of the four floors including a tapas bar, an oyster bar, a crêperie, a sea grill, a pizzeria, a diner and a sushi bar. Your kids will probably insist on dining at Planet Harrods, however, next to the toy department, where cartoons play constantly on big screens. The toy department organizes various events and activities for children, including Teddy Bear days and Easter Egg hunts.

Harvey Nichols

109–125 Knightsbridge, SW1
t (020) 7235 5000
www.harveynichols.com
☐ Knightsbridge
Bus 10, 19, 52, 74, 137
Open Mon–Sat 10–8, Sun 12 noon–6

Young children will probably not like this as much as Harrods, but for fashion-conscious teenagers, this can be little short of an ultra-hip wonderland (indeed, you may have trouble tearing them away). It's long been renowned as London's most fashionable department store and always stocks the latest high fashions for men, women and children. Its food halls on the fifth floor are, in their own way, just as impressive as those to be found at Harrods, and offer some great views of the Knightsbridge skyline, especially in the evening.

Did you know?

One of the largest bank robberies ever, happened in Knightsbridge in July 1987, when a gang of thieves stole £40 million from the Knightsbridge Security Deposit Centre in broad daylight. One finger print was found and traced to an Italian, Valerio Viccei. He and his accomplices were arrested in August 1987.

Picnics & snacks

There's plenty of choice. **Hyde Park**, of course, offers a grand swathe of picnic-friendly greenery, but you should also be aware that the area's three great museums each have designated picnic areas. You can lunch alfresco in front of the **Natural History Museum**, in the **Pirelli Gardens** of the **V&A** or, if the weather has taken a turn for the worse, in the **Science Museum's 'Megabyte'** picnic area on the first floor. Supplies can be picked up from the grand food halls at **Harrods** and **Harvey Nichols** or from the Italian delicatessen, **La Picena**, at 5 Walton Street, **t** (020) 7584 6573, SW3, both ✆ Knightsbridge. It's also worth checking out the **Whole Foods Market**, The Barkers Building, 63 Kensington High Street, W8, **t** (020) 7368 4500, ✆ High Street Kensington, a vast department store of organic food. The basement and first floor are filled with fresh produce and there's a food court upstairs.

All three Kensington museums have good cafés. The pick of the bunch is probably the **Science Museum's Deep Blue Café**, which can be found on the ground floor of the Wellcome Gallery. Otherwise try **Café Crêperie**, just around the corner at 2 Exhibition Road, SW7, **t** (020) 7589 8947, ✆ South Kensington. If shopping in Knightsbridge, be aware that the **Brompton Road**, SW3, is lined with pavement cafés, patisseries and fast-food restaurants – look out for branches of **Gloriette Patisserie** (see p.231) at no.128, **t** (020) 7589 4750, and **McDonald's** at no.177, ✆ South Kensington. Though there isn't much in the immediate vicinity of Hyde Park, you can get excellent toasted sandwiches at the **Kensington Gardens Café** on the Broad Walk, ✆ South Kensington, and the **Kensington Kiosk** near the Princess Diana Memorial Playground, ✆ Queensway.

Restaurants

1 Café Rouge
27–31 Basil Street, SW3
t (020) 7584 2345

See **Eat** p.224–36 for more details on the above restaurants.
See map on p.137 for the locations of the restaurants numbered above.

www.caferouge.co.uk
✆ Knightsbridge
Open Mon–Sat 8.30am–11pm, Sun 9am–10.30pm

2 Monza
6 Yeoman's Row, SW3
t (020) 7591 0210
✆ South Kensington, Knightsbridge
Open Tues–Sun 12 noon–2.30 and 7–11.30, Mon 7pm–11.30pm

3 Pizza Express
6–7 Beauchamp Place, SW3
t (020) 7589 2355
✆ Knightsbridge
Open Mon–Sat 11.30am–12 midnight, Sun 11.30am–11.30pm

4 Pizza Organic
20 Old Brompton Road, SW7
t (020) 7589 9613
www.pizzapiazza.co.uk
✆ South Kensington
Open 11.30am–12 midnight daily

5 Pizza on the Park
11 Knightsbridge, SW3
t (020) 7255 5273
www.pizzaexpressclub.com
✆ Hyde Park Corner, Knightsbridge
Open Mon–Fri 8.15am–12 midnight, Sat–Sun 9.30am–12 midnight

6 Pizza Pomodoro
51 Beauchamp Place, SW3
t (020) 7589 1278
www.pomodoro.co.uk
✆ Knightsbridge
Open 12 noon–1am daily

7 Planet Harrods
Fourth Floor, Harrods, 87–135 Brompton Road, SW1
t (020) 7730 1234
✆ Knightsbridge
Open Mon–Sat 10–7, Sun 12 noon–6

8 Sticky Fingers
1a Phillimore Gardens, W8
t (020) 7938 5338
www.stickyfingers.co.uk
✆ High Street Kensington, Holland Park
Bus 9, 10, 27, 28, 31, 49, 94
Open 12 noon–12 midnight daily

Greenwich

Greenwich is just a hop and a jump on the DLR from central London, but it has an entirely different ambience. It's as relaxed, cultured and stately as the city is brash, racy and commercial.

Of course, elegance and beauty don't always cut it with children. They want action, not elegantly crafted buildings and parks. Thankfully, Greenwich can also offer plenty of fun.

The National Maritime Museum is stuffed full of ships and nautical equipment for kids to clamber over, while the nearby Royal Observatory has been thoroughly overhauled in recent years and now offers lots of space age exhibitions, as well as spectacular state-of-the-art star shows in its new planetarium. Located on the Prime Meridian, the observatory also offers the singular pleasure of allowing you to stand above a line marked on the ground with one foot planted firmly in the world's western hemisphere and one foot in the east.

The surrounding park has a children's boating lake and playground, as well as lots of green, grassy spaces to run around on, not to mention great views of the capital.

And should you tire of doing, you can always turn your attention to buying at the town's various craft and antique markets.

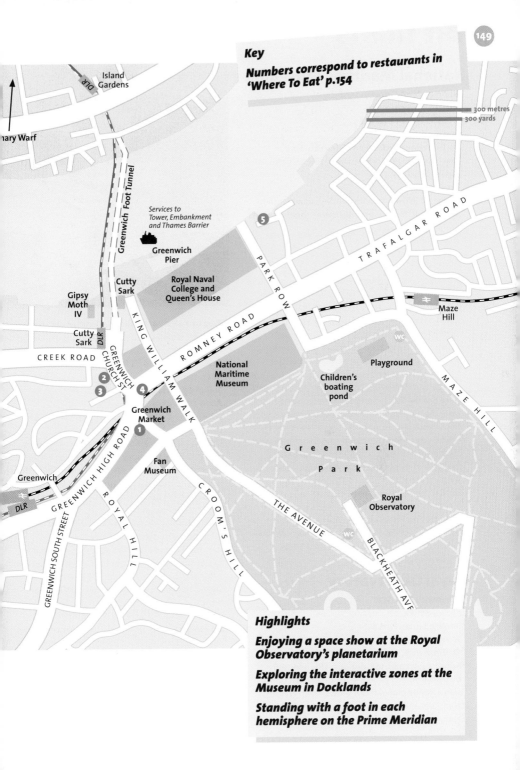

Key

Numbers correspond to restaurants in 'Where To Eat' p.154

300 metres
300 yards

Island Gardens

DLR

nary Warf

Greenwich Foot Tunnel

Services to Tower, Embankment and Thames Barrier

Greenwich Pier

5

TRAFALGAR ROAD

PARK ROW

Royal Naval College and Queen's House

Cutty Sark

Gipsy Moth IV

Cutty Sark

DLR

Maze Hill

KING WILLIAM WALK

ROMNEY ROAD

CREEK ROAD

GREENWICH CHURCH ST

WC

MAZE HILL

National Maritime Museum

Children's boating pond

Playground

2

3

4

Greenwich Market

1

Fan Museum

GREENWICH HIGH ROAD

GREENWICH SOUTH STREET

ROYAL HILL

Greenwich

DLR

CROOM'S HILL

G r e e n w i c h

P a r k

THE AVENUE

Royal Observatory

WC

BLACKHEATH AVE

Highlights

Enjoying a space show at the Royal Observatory's planetarium

Exploring the interactive zones at the Museum in Docklands

Standing with a foot in each hemisphere on the Prime Meridian

National Maritime Museum

Romney Road, Greenwich, SE10
t (020) 8858 4422
Infoline **t** (020) 8312 6565
www.nmm.ac.uk
⇌ Greenwich, **DLR** Greenwich, Cutty Sark
Bus 53, 54, 177, 180, 188, 199, 202, 286, 380, 386
Open 10–5 daily
Free
Bosun's Café with outdoor seating, souvenir shop
Wheelchair accessible for all floors – ramps and lifts
Suitable for all ages
Allow 1hr

The National Maritime Museum is one of the nation's favourite family museums, probably because it puts so much effort into entertaining its younger visitors. The history of the nation's relationship with the surrounding sea – a subject that could, for want of a better word, be a little dry – is instead covered with much wit and verve, and no little interactivity. In addition to all the museum's historic ships and nautical paraphernalia, there are two special children's galleries on the third floor, 'All Hands' and 'The Bridge', where kids can can experience 'pulling flags', 'firing cannons', sending morse code messages and learning how to steer a ship. For a touch of gore, pop into the Nelson Gallery where you can see the bloodstained uniform worn by the famous Admiral during his final battle at Trafalgar in 1805. *See* p.67 for more on this famous nautical encounter. Other galleries deal with ocean exploration, map making and warships.

Activity trails for ages 5 and over are available from the front desk and the museum runs regular events and activity sessions for both the over-fives and under-fives – the latter are called 'Little Explorer' sessions.

Royal Observatory

Greenwich Park, SE10
t (020) 8858 4422
Infoline **t** (020) 8312 8565
www.nmm.ac.uk/astonomy/index.html
⇌ Greenwich, **DLR** Greenwich, Cutty Sark
Bus 53, 54, 177, 180, 188, 199, 202, 286, 380, 386
Open Astronomy galleries: 10–5 daily, last admission 4.30pm; planetarium shows: Mon–Fri 1pm, 2pm, 3pm and 4pm, Sat & Sun 11am, 12pm, 1pm, 2pm, 3pm and 4pm

Free to astronomy galleries. Planetarium shows: adult £6, child £4
Limited wheelchair access owing to the age of the building. Guided tours by prior arrangement
Baby-changing room
Suitable for all ages
Allow 1hr 30mins

Just behind the Royal Naval College, the Royal Observatory stands on the Greenwich Meridian, the official dividing line between east and west, declared to be 0° degrees longitude. The line is marked out so you can stand with one foot in the western hemisphere and the other in the east. In 1884 the observatory was given the task of setting the time for the whole world, and Greenwich Mean Time (GMT) is still the standard against which all other times are measured. Every day at exactly 1pm, a red timeball on the Observatory roof drops to allow passing ships to set their clocks accurately.

Built in the late 17th century by Sir Christopher Wren, the observatory has in the past few years been given a 21st century makeover at a cost of some £15 million. The result is a number of new astonomical galleries filled with hands-on gizmos and gadgets designed to bring the heavens into sharper focus, as well as an exhibition detailing the history of timekeeping since the Middle Ages. The highlight, however, is the new 120-seater planetarium in which spectacular star shows, suitable for ages six and up, are projected onto its domed roof using the latest digital technology.

Tell me a story: Mean time

Since the late 19th century, the Prime Meridian at Greenwich has been used to calculate GMT or 'Greenwich Mean Time'. Before this, almost every town in the world kept its own local time. However, with the vast expansion of the railway and communications networks in the mid-19th century, it became necessary to come up with an international time standard.

In 1884, the International Meridian Treaty established in law that 'every new day begins at mean midnight at the cross-hairs of the Airy Transit Circle telescope at the Royal Observatory'. Forty-one delegates from 25 nations met in Washington DC for the International Meridian Conference and decided 22 to one that Greenwich had won the prize of Longitude 0°. The decision, essentially, was based on the argument that by naming Greenwich as Longitude 0°, it would inconvenience the least number of people.

The observatory organizes free 'drop-in' science events for children between 2–4pm every Saturday, as well as longer summer workshops where they can learn about astronomy and astronomical techniques and have a go at making basic astronomical equipment.

The search for longitude

Until the late 18th century nobody knew how to measure longitude – the distance east or west around the earth. People could work out latitude (the distance north or south) using the position of the pole star, but no such system existed for longitude. In 1754, the government put up a reward of £20,000 for anyone who could come up with a solution. The reward was finally claimed, in 1772, by a clockmaker called John Harrison. He constructed a clock which could measure time accurately at sea, and so permit navigators to calculate a ship's east-west position to within 30 miles.

Royal Naval College

King William Walk, SE10
t (020) 8269 4747
www.oldroyalnavalcollege.org
≥ Greenwich, **DLR** Greenwich, Cutty Sark
Bus 53, 54, 177, 180, 188, 199, 286, 380, 386
Open 10–5, daily
Free

Coffee shop, souvenir shop
Limited wheelchair facilities. Call in advance
Suitable for ages 10 and over

With its grand classical façades overlooking the river, the Royal Naval College (now home to the University of Greenwich) provides a wonderfully elegant first sight of Greenwich to anyone arriving from the riverside.

The building is the work of three of Britain's most famous architects: Sir Christopher Wren, Nicholas Hamilton and Sir John Vanbrugh, and was originally used as a hospital for disabled sailors before being turned into a college in 1873. It's now home to a visitors' centre, the Greenwich Gateway, with exhibitions on the history of the borough, and provides information on local attractions. It's located in the Pepys Building. Of the rest of the site, only the chapel and Painted Hall are open to the public. Their fabulously painted interiors were designed by James Thornhill, who also decorated the dome of St Paul's (see p.129).

Queen's House

Romney Road, SE10
t (020) 8312 6565
≥ Greenwich, **DLR** Greenwich, Cutty Sark
Bus 53, 54, 177, 180, 188, 199, 286, 380, 386
Open 10–5, daily (last entry 4.30)
Free
Wheelchair accessible

In between the Royal Naval College's façades stands the Queen's House, an earlier Italianate palace designed by Inigo Jones. The interiors are just as sumptuous as the college, adorned with frescoes and paintings, but it's a touch more child-friendly and organizes regular holiday activities and workshops for children.

Can you spot?

The self-portrait of James Thornhill on the wall of the Painted Hall in the Royal Naval College? Despite being paid £1 per foot for decorating the walls and £3 per foot for the ceilings – which, in the early 18th century, was quite a lot of money – Thornhill still decided to paint himself with his hand outstretched as if asking for more cash.

Cutty Sark

King William Walk, SE10
t (020) 8858 2698
www.cuttysark.org.uk
⇌ Greenwich, **DLR** Greenwich, Cutty Sark
Bus 53, 54, 177, 180, 188, 199, 286, 380, 386
Open 11–5, daily
Free
Souvenir shop
Wheelchair accessible
Suitable ages 7 and over

Following a devasting fire, the *Cutty Sark* is currently closed to visitors while restoration takes place, which it is estmated will take several years. You can still visit the adjacent visitor centre to learn about the famous tea clipper who, in her day, was the world's fastest sailing ship, able to sail the round-Africa journey from Shanghai to London in a record 107 days.

Greenwich markets

Greenwich is home to three excellent weekend markets: a small **antique market** off Greenwich High Road, between junctions with Stockwell Street and Royal Hill (**open** weekends 9–5), where you can often pick up good old toys; **the central market** on Stockwell Street, opposite the Hotel Ibis, **t** (020) 8766 6844 (**open** weekends 9–5; organic food market Sat only; village market **open** Fri, Sat 10–5, Sun 10–6); and the South London Book Centre, with its huge collection of comics; and a covered **craft market** on

Question 18
How long did it take Sir Francis Chichester to sail around the world?
answer on p.250

College Approach, with entrances on Turpin Lane (off Greenwich Church Street) and Durnford Street, **t** (020) 7240 7405, **www**.greenwich-market.co.uk (**open** Fri–Sun 9–5).

Fan Museum

12 Croom's Hill, Greenwich, SE10
t (020) 8305 1441
www.fan-museum.org
⇌ Greenwich, **DLR** Greenwich, Cutty Sark
Bus 177, 180, 188, 199, 286, 380, 386
Open Tues–Sat 11–5, Sun 12 noon–5
Adm Adult £4, child £3, under-7s **free**
Shop, baby-changing room
Wheelchair accessible, with adapted toilet
Suitable for all ages

Housed in a beautiful 18th-century townhouse, this is a delightful collection of over 2,000 fans from the 17th century to the present day. It holds regular demonstrations of fan-making.

Did you know?
The name Cutty Sark is a corruption of the French phrase 'courte chemise' meaning 'short shirt', the garment worn by the ship's figurehead.

Thames Tunnel

Open 24hrs daily. Lift open 5am–9pm
Wheelchair and pushchair accessible when lift open

It's a simple pleasure, standing in a tunnel under the River Thames, but one that never fails to enthral kids. The glass-domed entrances to the tunnel are easy to spot on the south side of the river by the *Cutty Sark* and on the north in Island Gardens.

Greenwich Park

Charlton Way, SE3
t (020) 7928 2000
www.royalparks.gov.uk/parks/greenwich_park/
Open Dawn till dusk daily
Free

Everything in Greenwich Park has been touched by the brush of elegance, from the flower gardens and stately avenues to the ornate Ranger's House and landscaped heights offering stunning views over the Thames. Created as a hunting ground by Henry VI in 1433 – it still has a small deer enclosure on its south side – it was landscaped in the 17th century by the great French gardener André Le Nôtre.

The park also has a boating lake, well-equipped playground and picnic tables. Events for families, including circus performances and puppet shows, are put on in summer, usually in the playground. A carousel also sets up for business here in August (£2 per ride).

Blackheath

Blackheath, SE3
t (020) 8854 8888
≋ Blackheath
Bus 53, 177, 180, 286
Open 24hrs a day
Free

A great windswept piece of common next door to Greenwich Park, Blackheath is popular with kite flyers. Each year, it holds one of London's best Guy Fawkes night firework displays. It's also the start of the London Marathon's 26 miles of annual hell.

Museum in Docklands

No.1 The Warehouse, West India Quay, Hertsmere Road, E14
t 0870 444 3852
www.museumindocklands.org.uk
⊖ Canary Wharf
DLR West India Quay
Bus 15, 115, 277, D3, D6, D7, D8
Open 10–6, daily
Adm Adult £5, concs £3, under-16s **free**; all tickets are valid for a year
Wheelchair accessible,with adapted toilets; shop, café
Suitable for all ages

This museum, housed in a Georgian warehouse on the West India Quay where tea clippers once used to dock, traces 2,000 years of trade on the River Thames, from early Celtic riverside settlements to the dock's post-war decline and rejuvenation. Five floors and 12 galleries provide a wealth of detail about dock-yard life – you can walk through a reconstruction of a Victorian sailors' settlement, see how the Thames has changed (highlights include a scale model of the old London Bridge and the Rheinbeck Panorama, a rare painting showing a bird's eye view of London c.1810) and find out about the penalties meted out to smugglers and pirates.

The museum makes full use of modern technol-ogies and offers close-up details of the exhibits. Best for families is the 'Mudlarks' gallery made up of 12 zones, each offering hands-on experiments to perform. You can winch and weigh cargoes, make a scale model of Canary Wharf and discover archaeo-logical finds in the 'Foreshore Discovery Box'. There's also a separate soft-play area for under 5s.

WHERE TO EAT

Picnics & snacks

Greenwich Park is the obvious choice with its rolling vistas and wide open spaces, but there are also plenty of nice spots by the river overlooking the 02 Arena (formerly the Millennium Dome) and the far from defunct **Canary Wharf**. Supplies can be picked up from **La Salumeria** delicatessen at 184 Trafalgar Road, SE10, **t** (020) 8305 2433, **DLR** Greenwich, the nearby **Cottage Pantry**, SE10, **t** (020) 8858 1734, **DLR** Greenwich, and, for a great selection of cheeses, the **Cheeseboard**, 26 Royal Hill, SE10, **t** (020) 8305 0401, **DLR** Greenwich. Across the river, there's a branch of the upmarket supermarket **Waitrose** at Canada Place, Canada Square, Canary Wharf SE10, **t** (020) 7719 0300.

Although there are less places to eat than in Central London, Greenwich has plenty of village-style cafés and riverside inns. There's a small café, near the entrance to the National Maritime Museum with a garden at the rear, **St Mary's Gate Café**, **t** (020) 8858 9695, **DLR** Greenwich, and a very nice tea house, named, appropriately enough, **The Pavilion Tea House**, in Greenwich Park itself, near the Observatory. It serves lovely cream teas and makes a welcome afternoon pit stop, **t** (020) 8858 0803, **DLR** Greenwich. In town, at 39 Greenwich Church Street, SE10, is **Tai Won Mein**, a great, fast-moving noodle house where you eat at Wagamama-style long tables, **t** (020) 8858 2688, **DLR** Greenwich.

Restaurants

1 Café Rouge
Ibis Hotel, Stockwell Street
t (020) 8293 6660
www.caferouge.co.uk
⇌ Greenwich, **DLR** Greenwich, Cutty Sark
Open Mon–Sat 7am–7pm, Sun 7am–10.30pm

2 Gourmet Burger Kitchen
45 Greenwich Church Street, SE10
t (020) 8858 3920
⇌ Greenwich, **DLR** Greenwich, Cutty Sark
Open Mon–Fri 12 noon–11, Sat 11–11, Sun 11–10

3 The High Chaparral
35 Greenwich Church Street, SE10
t (020) 8293 9143
⇌ Greenwich, **DLR** Greenwich, Cutty Sark
Open Mon–Sat 12 noon–11, Sun 12 noon–10

4 Pizza Express
4 Greenwich Church Street, SE10
t (020) 8853 2770
www.pizzaexpress.co.uk
⇌ Greenwich, **DLR** Greenwich, Cutty Sark
Open Mon–Sat 11.30–11, Sun 11.30–10.30

5 The Trafalgar Tavern
Park Row, SE10
t (020) 8858 2437
⇌ Greenwich, **DLR** Greenwich, Cutty Sark
Open Mon–Sat 11.30am–11pm, Sun 12 noon–10.30

See **Eat** p.224–36 for more details on the above restaurants.
See map on p.149 for the locations of the restaurants numbered above.

Kids in

Rain, rain, go away, come again another day! London is famous for many things, one of which is the unpredictable weather. It rains here – a lot. Thankfully, there is so much to do when the rain comes that it hardly matters.

Adventure Playgrounds

Indoor play areas are a very good option if you want to give the kids a chance to let off steam. Parents are usually expected to stay on the premises while their children play. Below is a selection of venues in the London area. Alternatively, you could try your nearest shopping centre or leisure complex.

Bramley's Big Adventure

136 Bramley Road, W10
t (020) 8960 1515
www.bramleysbig.co.uk
⊖ Ladbroke Grove, Latimer Road
Bus 7, 23, 52, 74, C1
Open 10–6.30, daily
Adm term-time weekdays: under-2s £3, under-5s £4.50, over-5s £5; weekends, school and bank holidays: under-2s £3.50, under-5s £5, over-5s £5.50 for two-hour session. Accompanying adults free
Ages up to 11

One of London's biggest playgrounds offering slides, inflatables, monkey ropes and ball pools galore for ages 5–11. There's also a separate area for under-5s and a café for flagging parents (organic food offered). It's a popular venue for parties with play session, meal, goody bags and balloons.

Clown Town

222 Green Lanes, N13
t (020) 8886 7520
www.clowntown.co.uk
⊖ Manor House
≈ Palmers Green
Bus 121, 329, W6
Open 10–7 daily
Adm Child Mon–Fri £3.75, Sat, Sun and School Hols £4.25, accompanying adult free
Ages 2–14
Height restriction is 4 ft 9 in

Clown-themed adventure playground with a 2000 sq ft three-level adventure frame, slides, aerial runways, ball pools and 'spook room', as well as separate toddler and 'crawler' areas.

Sobell Safari

Sobell Leisure Centre, Hornsey Road, N7
t (020) 7609 2166
⊖ Finsbury Park, Holloway Road
www.aquaterra.org/Islington/Softplay
Bus 43, 271
Open Mon–Fri 9–5.15, Sat–Sun 9–4
Adm Over 1m tall £3.30, under 1m £2.50

This is a great place for kids to come and play at being pirates with three levels of ropes, slides and punchbags for them to clamber over. There's also a separate soft play area for under-5s.

Snakes & Ladders

Syon Park, Brentford, Middlesex
t (020) 8847 0946
www.snakes-and-ladders.co.uk
≈ Gunnersbury
⊖ Kew Bridge
Bus 235, 237, 267
Get off the bus at Brentlea Gate opposite the Royal Mail sorting office. Look for the sign for Syon Park about 15 metres from the bus stop. Follow the pedestrian pathway for 30 metres and then turn left following the signs for Snakes and Ladders.
Open 10–6, daily (last entry 5.15)
Adm Before 4.30: over-5s £5.50, under-5s £4.50, under-2s £3.50; after 4.30: over-5s £4.50, under-5s £3.50, under-2s £2.50
Ages 2–12
Maximum height 4 ft 8 in
Socks must be worn

In the grounds of Syon Park, this is the place to come to use up the last of your kids' energy after a hard day's butterfly hunting or go-karting. There's a 3-tiered climbing frame with slides, ball pools and ropes as well as an outdoor playground in the garden. And if that's not enough noise for you, the centre also hosts kiddy karaoke parties.

Zoomaround

46 Milton Grove, Stoke Newington, London N16
t (020) 7254 2220
www.zoomaround.co.uk
≈ Canonbury
Bus 73, 141, 236, 341, 393, 476
Open 10–6 daily
Adm under-1s £2, under-4s £3.50, over-4s £4.50
Ages 0–11

A multi-level play frame, an 'action zone' full of games, a separate toddlers' area and a garden with rabbits and guinea pigs for children to feed are the main attractions. Parties offered.

Cinemas

London is a great place to see a film. It may not have as many screens as it used to – the days when every high street had an Odeon are now, sadly, long gone – but the cinemas that remain are bigger and better equipped than ever. The biggest and best can be found in Leicester Square, London's cinematic heart, where star-studded premieres take place and all the major blockbusters have their first runs. For a full, up-to-date list of what's on where and when, check the weekly listings magazine *Time Out* or the *Evening Standard*'s *Metro Life* – a free listings magazine which accompanies its Thursday edition.

Leicester Square

Empire
t 0871 471 4714
www.empirecinemas.co.uk
Odeon Leicester Square
t 0871 224 4007
www.odeon.co.uk
Vue West End
t 08712 240 240
www.myvue.com

Both the Odeon and Vue Cinemas run special offers for kids at any of their branches apart from Leicester Square. Call for details.

Cinema clubs

If you consider Leicester Square's cinematic big boys a bit brash and commercial, and find yourself longing for the halcyon days of Saturday matinées, you could be in for a very pleasant surprise. There are several smaller picture houses that run kids' Saturday morning film

Can you spot?
The pavement surrounding Leicester Square's garden is adorned with the handprints of famous actors and directors. See who can be the first to spot them all.

clubs, usually offering a mix of Disney cartoons and family favourites. Additional entertainments, such as workshops, competitions and seasonal events, are also often laid on.

Barbican Centre

Silk Street, EC2
t 0845 120 7528
www.barbican.org.uk/familyfilmclub
⊖ Barbican, Moorgate
Bus 8, 22B, 56
Times Sat 10.30am
Adm Annual membership £7.50, films £4.50 non-members, £3 members
Ages 5–11

The Barbican's Family Film Club meets at 10.30am each Saturday. Here kids can enjoy a family classic and take part in some film-related activities from the 'Movie Cart' in the foyer. Workshops on movie-related skills – animation, make-up, set design, etc. – are held on the last Saturday of the month.

Clapham Picture House

76 Venn Street, SW4
t 0871 704 2055
www.picturehouses.co.uk
⊖ Clapham Common
Bus 88, 137, 155, 345, 355
Times Club meets Sat 11.15am, film starts at 11.45am
Adm Members £2, non-members £3, accompanying adult £3; annual membership £4; all children must be accompanied by an adult
Ages 3–10

At the weekly pre-screening craft workshops, kids can get in the mood by designing their own space-ship, making a cartoon picture book or moulding plasticine, plus a variety of other activities.

Electric Cinema

191 Portobello Road, W11
t (020) 7908 9696
www.electriccinema.co.uk/kids.php
⊖ Notting Hill Gate
Times Sat, films at 11am and 1pm
Adm £3.50 members, £4.50 non-members, accompanying adults
Ages 4–12

Games and activities inspired by the screenings, plus birthday party specials. Also a Parents & Babies club on Thursdays when parents of young babies can go to a special session without dreading that they will start to cry.

BFI Southbank

South Bank, SE1
t (020) 7928 3232
www.bfi.org.uk
⊖ /⇄ Waterloo
Bus 1, 4, 26, 68, 76, 168, 171, 176, 188, 341, 501, 505, 521, X68
Times Sat afternoon, workshop time varies, call ahead
Adm Family film screenings: child £1, accompanying adults £8.20, workshops £6.50
Ages 6–12

The BFI Southbank shows a range of classic family films and organizes movie workshops on the first Saturday of the month, in which kids can learn more about the techniques of film-craft. Supervised by experts, they can try creating animation, making props and costumes or writing their own short film script.

Phoenix Cinema

52 High Road, East Finchley, N2
t (020) 8444 6789
www.phoenixcinema.co.uk/families/
⊖ East Finchley
Bus 102, 143, 263
Times Club meets bi-weekly Sat 11am, film starts at 12 noon
Adm Under-12s £5.50, under-8s £4.50, film only £3; 'Bringing up Baby' screenings £5
Ages 6–11

Combining screenings with hands-on activies such as painting and model-making, 'Freddie's Film Club' aims to introduce children to the wonders of World Cinema. The Phoenix also puts on 'Bringing up Baby' screenings on Tuesday mornings for parents with babies under one year old.

Ritzy Cinema

Brixton Oval, Coldharbour Lane, SW2
t (020) 7733 2229
www.picturehouses.co.uk
⊖ Brixton
Bus 35, 37, 118, 196, 250, P4, P5
Times Sat, films start at 10.30am
Adm Child £1, accompanying adult £3
Ages 3 to 12

Shows two separate programmes: one for 7s and under and the other for 8s and over. In truth, this is done more for reasons of social bonding than anything else, and either age group may attend either programme. There are special kids' club

events organized and free tea, coffee and newspapers provided for parents.

Tricycle Theatre

269 Kilburn High Road, NW6
t (020) 7328 1000
www.tricycle.co.uk
⊖ Kilburn
Bus 16, 31, 32, 98, 189, 206, 316, 328
Times Sat, films start at 1pm
Adm Adult £4, child £3

In addition to its theatre performances and kids' drama workshops (*see* p.170), the ever-versatile Tricycle also runs a Saturday afternoon film club for families, with accompanying workshop.

IMAX 3D Cinema

1 Charlie Chaplin Walk, SE1
t 0870 787 2525
www.bfi.org.uk/imax
⊖ Waterloo, Westminster
Bus 11, 12, 53, 76, 77, 109, 211, 507, D1, P11
Open Mon–Fri 12.30–8, Sat & Sun 10.45–8.45
Adm Adult £8.50, child (4–14) £5, under-3s **free**, concs £6.25
Wheelchair accessible, with lifts, adapted cinema seats and toilets
Suitable for all ages
Shows last approximately 1hr each

Britain's largest cinema screen is housed in a seven-storey glass cylinder in the middle of the Waterloo bullring (a fancy name for what is essentially a roundabout). The screen itself is the height of five double-decker buses, the sound system transmits 11,000 watts and the films are recorded and projected using the most up-to-date 3D format available – it's a pretty all-encompassing experience. The programme changes regularly, but you can usually be confident of seeing some kind of outer space/wildlife-type spectacular, plus the occasional effects-laden Hollywood Blockbuster. See p.139 for the IMAX cinema in the Science Museum.

Internet cafés

If your kids are clamouring to email their mates back home or you fancy sending a cyber postcard, there are plenty of web cafés in London, albeit not quite the variety of outlets there once was now that Easy Internet has begun to dominate the market. You'll also find internet points in most public libraries, main branch post offices and, increasingly, in some fast-food outlets.

Easy Internet Café
Branches at 1160 Kensington High Street; 358 Oxford Street, W1, 9–16 Tottenham Court Road, W1; 456/459 Strand, WC2
www.easyEverything.com
Open 10am–12 midnight
Cost The minimum payment is 50p, but the exact price depends on the time of day and how busy the café is (the busier, the more expensive)

Museums & galleries

Central London
Please *see* the main sightseeing chapters for details of these establishments.

Apsley House: The Wellington Museum
Hyde Park Corner, 149 Piccadilly, W1
t (020) 7499 5676 (*see* p.92)

Bank of England Museum
Threadneedle Street, EC2
t (020) 7601 5545 (*see* p.83)

Benjamin Franklin House
36 Craven Street, WC2
t (020) 7925 1405 (*see* p.xx)

Bramah Tea & Coffee Museum
40 Southwark Street, SE1
t (020) 7403 5650 (*see* p.122)

British Museum
Great Russell Street, WC1
t (020) 7323 8000 (*see* p.54)

Cartoon Museum
35 Little Russell Street, WC1
t (020) 7580 8155 (*see* p.56)

Churchill Museum and Cabinet War Rooms
Clive Steps, King Charles Street, SW1
t (020) 7766 0120 (*see* p.100)

Clink Museum
1 Clink Street, SE1
t (020) 7403 0900 (*see* p.121)

Dalí Universe
County Hall, Riverside Building, Belvedere Road, SE1
t 0870 744 7485 (*see* p.106)

Design Museum
28 Shad Thames, Butler's Wharf, SE1
t 0870 909 9009 (*see* p.122)

Charles Dickens Museum
48 Doughty Street
t (020) 7405 2127 (*see* p.56)

Fashion and Textile Museum
83 Bermondsey Street, SE1
t (020) 7403 0222 (*see* p.123)

Florence Nightingale Museum
2 Lambeth Palace Road, SE1
t (020) 7620 0374 (*see* p.110)

Foundling Museum
40 Brunswick Square, WC1
t (020) 7841 3600 (*see* p.59)

The *Golden Hinde*
Pickfords Wharf, Clink Street
t 0870 011 8700 (*see* p.121)

Guards Museum
Wellington Barracks, Birdcage Walk, SW1
t (020) 7414 3271 (*see* p.93)

Handel House Museum
25 Brook Street, W1
t (020) 7495 1685 (*see* p.57)

HMS *Belfast*
Morgan's Lane, off Tooley Street, SE1
t (020) 7940 6300 (*see* p.120)

ICA Gallery
The Mall, SW1
t (020) 7930 3647 (*see* p.92)

Imperial War Museum
Lambeth Road, SE1
t (020) 7416 5320 (*see* p.111)

London Canal Museum
12–13 New Wharf Road, N1
t (020) 7713 0836 (*see* p.48)

London Dungeon
Tooley Street, SE1
t 0871 360 2049 (*see* p.116)

London Fire Brigade Museum
94a Southwark Bridge Road
t (020) 7587 2894 (*see* p.123)

London Transport Museum
Covent Garden, WC2
t (020) 7565 7299 (*see* p.78)

Madame Tussaud's
Marylebone Road, NW1
t 0870 999 0293 (*see* p.44)

Museum of London
London Wall, EC2
t 0870 444 3852 (*see* p.130)

National Gallery
Trafalgar Square, WC2
t (020) 7747 2870 (*see* p.67)

National Portrait Gallery
St Martin's Place, WC2
t (020) 7306 0055 (*see* p.69)

Natural History Museum
Cromwell Road, SW7
t (020) 7942 5000 (*see* p.138)

Old Operating Theatre
9a St Thomas Street, SE1
t (020) 7188 2679 (*see* p.119)

Petrie Museum Of Egyptian Archaeology
Malet Place, WC1
t (020) 7679 2884 (*see* p.57)

Pollock's Toy Museum
1 Scala Street, W1
t (020) 7636 3452 (*see* p.57)

Queen's Gallery
Buckingham Palace Road, SW1
t (020) 7766 7300 (*see* p.90)

Royal Academy
Burlington House, Piccadilly, W1
t 0870 848 8484 (*see* p.72)

Science Museum
Exhibition Road, London SW7
t 0870 870 4868 (*see* p.139)

Serpentine Gallery
Kensington Gardens, W2
t (020) 7402 6075 (*see* p.144)

Shakespeare's Globe Theatre
Bear Gardens, Bankside, New Globe Walk,
Southwark, SE1
t (020) 7902 1400 (*see* p.119)

Sherlock Holmes Museum
221b Baker Street, NW1
t (020) 7935 8866 (*see* p.46)

Sir John Soane's Museum
12–14 Lincoln's Inn Fields, WC2
t (020) 7405 2107 (*see* p.82)

Somerset House
The Strand, WC2
t (020) 7845 4600 (*see* p.84)

Tate Britain
Millbank, SW1
t (020) 7887 8888 (*see* p.100)

Tate Modern
Bankside, SE1
t (020) 7887 8888 (*see* p.117)

Tower of London
Tower Hill, EC3
t 0870 756 6060 (*see* p.128)

Victoria & Albert Museum
Cromwell Road, SW7
t (020) 7942 2000 (*see* p.140)

Wallace Collection
Hertford House, Manchester Square, W1
t (020) 7563 9500 (*see* p.47)

Winston Churchill's Britain at War Experience
64–66 Tooley Street, SE1
t (020) 7403 3171 (*see* p.118)

Outer London

London is a huge, sprawling city, and can prove quite daunting for visitors. You might think you've got more than enough to cope with visiting the attractions in the centre of town, never mind the outskirts. However, it's well worth giving the suburbs some consideration. Not only can they offer smaller crowds and less congestion, they are also home to some great local museums. To follow is a selection of places that are, in general, a lot less touristy than their central London counterparts, and able to provide you with a much calmer day out. Most are extremely family-orientated and, best of all, many are free.

Bruce Castle Museum

Church Lane, off Lordship Lane, N17
t (020) 8808 8772
⊖ Wood Green
Bus 123, 243
Open Wed–Sun and bank hols 1pm–5pm
Free
Wheelchair accessible, with adapted toilets

This lively local history museum is housed in a listed Tudor building. In addition to its art, history and postal history exhibitions, it has a special 'Inventor Centre' filled with interactive experiments for kids to play with and is surrounded by 20 acres of parkland – there's a tree trail. Free activities for children are laid on on Sundays in term-time and on Wednesdays, Thursdays and Fridays in the school holidays.

Clowns International Gallery

All Saints Centre, Haggerston Road, E8
t 0870 128 4336
www.clowns-international.co.uk
≈ Dalston Kingsland, London Fields
Bus 38, 236, 243
Open 12 noon–5 first Fri of month
Free
Wheelchair accessible. Suitable for all ages

It's a serious business – wearing large shoes and red noses, driving a collapsible car and having custard pies stuffed down the front of your over-sized trousers – which is why this gallery, dedicated to exploring and explaining the noble art of clowning (the only such gallery in the world) re-opened a few years back. Run by volunteer clowns (in plain clothes while on museum duty), the museum traces the history of making people laugh by falling over a lot, from its origins in the 16th century to the present day. Exhibits include clown costumes, clown props (including a collapsible car) and a collection of painted eggs, each showing a different clown's make-up – as with finger prints, no two clowns' make-up is the same. It's fun, in an oddly reverential way.

Dulwich Picture Gallery

Gallery Road, Dulwich Village, SE21
t (020) 8693 5254
www.dulwichpicturegallery.org.uk
≈ North Dulwich
Bus 3, 37, P4
Open Tues–Fri 10–5, Sat, Sun and Bank Hol Mon 11–5

Adm Adult £4, child **free**, senior citizens £3, **free** to all on Fridays
Wheelchair accessible. Suitable for ages 10 and over
Allow at least 1hr

Following an extensive period of refurbishment and rebuilding – which saw a whole new wing added – this is once again one of the finest galleries to be found anywhere in the country outside central London. Formerly owned by Dulwich College, a private boys' school, and now owned by an independent charitable trust, the collection includes Rembrandt's *Girl at a Window* and Gainsborough's *Linley Sisters*, as well as works by Rubens, Poussin, Canaletto and Raphael – child-orientated audio guides are available. The gallery hosts a range of events, including cartoon work-shops and readings during their annual Children's Book Festival. Free, drop-in art workshops (for ages 4 and over) are held on the last Sunday of each month and on Wednesday afternoons during the school holidays, when children can take part in a range of activities, such as collage design, T-shirt decoration and badge-making. There's also a Saturday morning art school for 11–14-year-olds and an after-school art club for 10–13-year-olds. The gallery's park makes a pleasant picnic spot.

Firepower Museum

Royal Arsenal, SE18
t (020) 8855 7755
www.firepower.org.uk
≈ Woolwich Arsenal
Bus 96, 161, 180, 472
Open Nov–Mar Fri–Sat 10.30–5, Apr–Oct Wed–Sun 10.30–5, also open Tues during the school hols
Adm Adult £5, child (5–16) £2.50, family £12
Suitable for all ages, some images may distress
Allow at least half a day

Housed in a former arsenal, the Firepower Museum is like a more whizz-bang version of the Imperial War Museum. It's got a similarly impressive range of military hardware – including a gallery filled with huge tanks and enormous guns – but perhaps places less emphasis in its displays on the human cost of war than its more famous rival. It's certainly a very noisy affair, with battle-field re-enactments and hands-on computerized simulators used to trace the development of military firepower from the slingshot to computer-guided missiles. With opening times arranged around the school holidays, the museum unsurprisingly aims most of its temporary exhibitions and activities directly at families. Kids will like the Command Post on the first floor with its paintball range and climbing wall.

Geffrye Museum

Kingsland Road, E2
t (020) 7739 9893
www.geffrye-museum.org.uk
⊖ Old Street (south exit 2) , Liverpool Street
⇌ Dalston Kingsland
Bus 67, 149, 242, 243, 394
Open Tues–Sat 10–5, Sun 12 noon–5
Free
Suitable for all ages, under-8s must be accompanied by an adult
Allow at least 1hr

This charming little museum, housed in a row of 18th-century almshouses, is dedicated to the evolution of Britain's living rooms. It contains dozens of reconstructed interiors from Tudor times to the present day. Though you can't actually go into the rooms, it's still fun to nose around the strange archaic furniture and find out interesting nuggets of domestic history. There is also a collection of period garden rooms, a restored 18th-century almshouse (restricted opening times, phone ahead) and an aromatic herb garden (open Apr–Oct). On the first Saturday of each month, the museum holds imaginative workshops (known as 'Saturday Specials') for kids, which have included such diverse topics as wig-making, landscape gardening, living room design, Tudor sweet-making, cookery, block printing and mask-making, and also organizes occasional storytelling sessions for young children. Live jazz is sometimes staged on the museum lawn in summer. The website has a dedicated 'kidszone'.

Horniman Museum

100 London Road, SE23
t (020) 8699 1872
www.horniman.ac.uk
⇌ Forest Hill
Bus 122, 176, 185, 197, 356, 363, P4, P13
Open 10.30–5.30 daily
Free (charges apply for temporary exhibitions)
Suitable for all ages
Allow at least a couple of hours

A day spent here is easily as rewarding as a day spent in one of the great Kensington collections. Founded in the early 19th century by the tea

> **Did you know?**
> The museum's founder, Frederick Horniman, was the first man to think of selling tea in small cup-sized packets. These are today known simply as teabags.

magnate Frederick Horniman, it defies classification. It's not really an anthropology museum, although it does contain a vast ethnographic collection including South American tribal masks, African headdresses and Egyptian mummies. Equally, it's not really a natural history museum, but still boasts a fantastic array of animal exhibits – look out for the Goliath beetle, the largest insect in the world – as well as a huge aquarium filled with frogs and fish. Neither is it a museum of music, but it nonetheless holds one of the country's most important collections of musical instruments (*see* p.166 for details of music workshops for children) It also has a wonderful interactive music display where, using touch-screen computers and headphones, kids can find out about (and listen to) some of the world's more obscure instruments. In fact, considering its many wonders, it's perhaps best to describe the museum simply as South London's premier treasure trove.

Thoroughly revamped in recent years with a new layer of interactivity (not to mention a new education centre) added, the museum is now better than ever. As useful as all the new computer terminals and push-button technologies are, however, it's still the sheer clutter and variety of the museum that enthrals. The trails and activity sheets available at the front desk will help put the collection in some sort of order, while, at the 'Hands-on Base', kids have a chance to touch and examine over 4,000 miscellaneous items. There's also a 'Book Zone' for under-5s.

The museum gardens, which have also been completely overhauled, are equally wonderful, offering great views out over South London and containing nature trails, an exhibition on caring for the environment, a small animal enclosure (home to goats, rabbits and turkeys) and a family picnic area.

The Horniman stages a whole host of family events throughout the year including storytellings, arts and crafts sessions (learn how to make an Ancient Egyptian mummy case, an African mask or an Indonesian shadow puppet) and handling activities with puppets, toys and even animals.

Kenwood House

Hampstead Lane, NW3
t (020) 8348 1286
www.english-heritage.org.uk
⊖ Archway
Bus 210
Open April–Oct Sat–Tues & Thurs 10–5, Wed & Fri 10.30–5; Nov–Mar Sat–Tues & Thurs 10–4, Wed & Fri 10.30–4
Free
Wheelchair accessible

Houses a wonderful collection of art including works by Rembrandt, Gainsborough and Vermeer. It also has a rather nice tearoom. Nature-themed events for families, including bat- and butterfly-spotting days, are put on in summer.

Kew Bridge Steam Museum

Green Dragon Lane, Brentford, Middlesex, TW8
t (020) 8568 4757
www.kbsm.org
⇌ Kew Bridge Station
⊖ Gunnersbury, Kew Gardens
Bus 65, 237, 267, 391
Open Tues–Sun & Bank Hols 11–5
Adm Mon–Fri adult £5, Sat–Sun adult £7, Cornish engine steaming weekends adult £8, under-16s **free**
Wheelchair accessible for most of the museum – no access to viewing platform above beam engines
Suitable for all ages

Just across the river from the gardens (*see* p.172), Kew Bridge Steam Museum offers a nice, down-to-earth contrast to all those flowerbeds and neatly sculpted lawns. It focuses on the development of London's water supply and sewage system from Roman times to the present day, and houses a wonderful collection of Victorian water-pumping machinery, including the two largest beam engines in the world. In their prime, these noisy behemoths would have pumped six and a half million gallons of water every day into London's reservoirs. You can get some idea of the power involved when the great Rotative engine is switched on at weekends. The even bigger Cornish engine is set in motion only on certain weekends and bank holidays. Providing water is one thing, but it's the means of taking the waste away that brings the best out of the museum. Kids love the replica London sewage

system; spying through peepholes at sewer rats and mice, hunting for subterranean creatures with a radio-controlled sewer robot, and sieving for sewage treasure, like the 'toshers' – 19th-century sewer workers who made their living in quite the most smelly way imaginable. The museum's Water of Life exhibition has plenty of levers and buttons to push and pull to keep children amused, and there's a full programme of family events put on during the summer months.

London International Gallery of Children's Art

O² Centre, 255 Finchley Road, NW3
t (020) 7435 0903
www.ligca.org
⊖ Finchley Road
Bus 13, 46, 82, 113
Open Tues–Thurs 4–6, Fri–Sun 12 noon–6
Free
Suitable for all ages
Allow at least 30mins

London's only gallery devoted to works of art by children. The collection contains paintings from round the world and organizes free Sunday art workshops for children aged 5–12 (involving such activities as wire sculpting, calendar making and bookmark design), as well as special 'Little Artists' sessions for under-5s. Three-week Saturday art courses are also offered for £30 per child.

National Army Museum and Royal Hospital

Royal Hospital Road, Chelsea, SW3
t (020) 7730 0717
www.national-army-museum.ac.uk
⊖ Sloane Square
Bus 11, 19, 22, 137, 211, 239
Open 10–5.30, daily
Free
Suitable for ages 10 and over
Allow at least 1hr

Telling the story of British army life from the 16th century to the present day, the museum is well laid out and thoughtful. Although parts of it might be a little dry for younger children – the recreation of the Battle of Waterloo using some 75,000 toy soldiers aside – there is a new interactive zone where kids can play on a mini assault course and dress up in soldiers' uniforms. A soft play area is also provided for toddlers. Family trails are available from reception and family events – often involving dressing up, arts and crafts and storytellings – are put on each month. The museum sits next to the Christopher Wren-designed Royal Hospital, founded by Charles II in the 17th century as a home for army veterans and still home to 400 red-coated Chelsea pensioners. Each May, the grounds host the Chelsea Flower Show, the country's premier gardening event.

Ragged School Museum

46–50 Copperfield Road, E3
t (020) 8980 6405
www.raggedschoolmuseum.org.uk
⊖ Mile End
Bus 25, 277, 309, D6, D7
Open Wed–Thurs 10–5, first Sun of every month 2–5
Free
Suitable for all ages
Allow at least a couple of hours

In the late 19th century, thousands of children in London lived in abject poverty. There was no free education system or health care as there is today, and many children had to work for a living, often in dangerous conditions. It was an appalling state of affairs and one that Dr Barnardo, a young missionary, decided to do something about. During his life he founded over 90 homes for London's destitute children. He also ran this 'Ragged School', which provided free education for the poorest children of London's East End. Today, it is a museum. Kids can walk through the classrooms, sit at the old desks and write on the slates. The museum also organizes a range of period activities, including parlour games and sweet-making sessions, for children up to the age of 12 on Wednesdays and Thursdays during the school holidays.

Royal Air Force Museum

Grahame Park Way, NW9
t (020) 8205 2266
www.rafmuseum.org.uk
⊖ Colindale
⇌ Mill Hill Broadway
Bus 204, 303
Open 10–6, daily
Free
Suitable for ages 5 and over, under-16s must be accompanied by an adult
Allow at least a couple of hours

On the site of the former Hendon Aerodrome, the museum is made up of two huge hangars stuffed full of aeronautical hardware. In the 'Milestones of Flight' Hall you'll find fighter planes from right through the 20th century – from biplanes and Battle of Britain Spitfires to the awesome vertical take-off Harrier jump jet. Once you've finished marvelling at these fearsome machines, try some of the interactive exhibits in the Aeronauts Gallery, guaranteed to get your and your kids' combative juices flowing. You can clamber inside the cockpit of a Lockheed Tristar, take the controls in a Jet Provost and find out whether you've got the reactions needed to be the 'best of the best' at the Pilot Skills test. You can even line up the sights to send a bouncing bomb crashing through a dam at a special display on the life of the inventor of the bouncing bomb, Barnes Wallis. The highlight is the flight simulator in which you get to take the controls of a Tornado, though it certainly isn't recommended if you've had a heavy lunch.

The museum organizes a number of family events throughout the year when kids may be able to try on RAF uniforms, experience life in a mock-up wartime classroom or listen to actors retelling the story of the Battle of Britain, the nation's 'finest hour'.

V&A Museum of Childhood

Cambridge Heath Road, E2
t (020) 8983 5200
www.vam.ac.uk/moc/
⊖ Bethnal Green
Bus 8, 26, 48, 55, 106, 254, 309, 388, D6
Open Mon–Thurs, Sat–Sun 10–6
Free (donations welcome); under-5s' soft play area costs £1.80 for 40mins
Suitable for all ages, under-8s must be accompanied
Allow at least 1hr

Following extensive refurbishment, this East London branch of the Victoria and Albert Museum now presents itself better than ever. It contains a wonderful collection of historic childhood artefacts, including clothes, toys (it holds the country's largest collection), nursery furniture and baby equipment. Pride of place, however, goes to the collections of antique dolls' houses (three centuries' worth of miniature homes) and dolls – from 17th-century porcelain beauties to plastic Barbies. As fascinating as they are, the problem with these displays of collectible playthings is that you can't actually play with them – they're far too rare and delicate for that – which can be a little frustrating. To compensate, the gallery has increased the level of interactivity in other areas. 'Family Fun Bags' containing quizzes and games relating to the displays are available from reception and child-orientated 'Spotlight Tours' are given several times a day. There's also a soft play area for under-5s in the new activity rooms where events and workshops are staged throughout the year. At these, children may be able to have a go at decorating their own T-shirts, constructing finger puppets or designing jewellery. In summer, the museum also stages its own theatrical productions.

Wandsworth Museum

11 Garratt Lane, SW18
t (020) 8871 7074
www.wandsworth.gov.uk
⊖ East Putney
⇌ Wandsworth Town
Bus 28, 37, 39, 44, 77a, 156, 170 220, 270, 337
Open Tues–Fri 10–5, Sat–Sun 2–5, closed bank hols
Free
Wheelchair accessible, with adapted toilets
Suitable for all ages
Allow at least 1hr

Organizes regular hands-on sessions for kids inspired by its permanent displays of local history.

Music

Listening to music

Pop is obviously a week-by-week phenomenon with no fixed calendar of events. For details of forthcoming pop concerts, consult the listing sections of the *Evening Standard* or the *Metro*, London's principal daily newspapers, or the weekly entertainment magazine, *Time Out*. Wembley Arena is a key venue for popular shows like *Disney on Ice*, as well as pop concerts, **t** 0870 060 0870, **www**.livenation.co.uk/wembley. The capital's biggest gigs (U2, The Rolling Stones, etc.) tend to take place at the revamped Wembley Stadium, **t** 0844 980 8001, **www**.wembleystadium.com or the new O2 Arena (formerly the Millennium Dome), **t** 0871 984 0002, **www**.theo2.co.uk. Classical music, on the other hand, does adhere to a calendar (admittedly a rather fluid one) and you might like to keep an eye out for the following:

London Coliseum

St Martin's Lane, WC2
t (020) 7632 8300
www.eno.org
⊖ Leicester Square, Charing Cross, Embankment
Bus 3, 6, 9, 11, 12, 13, 15, 19, 24, 29, 38, 176

The English National Opera, whose home this is, runs operatic workshops and short performances for ages 7 and over. Children and accompanying adults can take part in plot summaries and improvisation sessions, and listen to a sung excerpt from the opera in question. It's pretty good value – workshop prices start at just £3 and a free crèche is provided for toddlers.

London Symphony Orchestra Family Discovery Concerts

Barbican, Silk Street, EC2
t (020) 7638 8891
www.barbican.org.uk
⊖ Barbican, Moorgate, St Paul's
Bus 153
Adm Adult £6, child (under 16) £4
One or two a season, call in advance

A popular annual event designed to get children aged 7–12 interested in classical music. The programmes mainly comprise short pieces and there is lots of audience participation. Orchestra musicians mingle with the crowds during the interval and will give any child who brings along an instrument an impromptu music lesson.

Royal Opera House

Bow Street, WC2
t (020) 7304 4000
http://info.royaloperahouse.org
⊖ Covent Garden, Leicester Square
Bus 6, 9, 11, 13, 15, 23, 77A, 91, 176
Open Tours: Mon–Sat at 10.30am, 12.30pm and 2.30pm
Wheelchair accessible, with adapted toilets

As well as the free classical 'taster' concerts staged in its foyer, there is an education programme, which sees a number of special opera and ballet performances put on for schools and colleges each year. Information packs for teachers are available online ahead of concerts.

Wigmore Hall

36 Wigmore Street
t (020) 7528 8200
www.wigmore-hall.org.uk

⊖ Bond Street
Bus 6, 7, 10, 12, 13, 15, 23, 73, 94, 98, 113, 135, 137, 139, 159, 189
Adm Chamber Tots workshops £6 per child
   Organizes a jam-packed event programme for families made up of talks, lectures, concerts and workshops. The most popular are the 'Chamber Tots' sound workshops for under-5s.

Making Music

Whether it's pop, classical or 'world' music, your kids will always have much more fun making a racket than listening to one.

Guildhall School of Music
Silk Street, Barbican, EC2
t (020) 7638 2571
www.gsmd.ac.uk
⊖ Barbican, Moorgate, St Paul's
Bus 153
   This prestigious school runs weekly music courses for all abilities during term time. Children can learn an instrument or have vocal coaching and, if they reach a sufficient standard, join one of two youth orchestras.

Horniman Music Room Workshops
100 London Road, SE23
t (020) 8699 1872
www.horniman.ac.uk
⇌ Forest Hill
Bus 63, 122, 176, 185, 312, P4, P13
No fixed calender, call in advance
Free
   The Horniman Museum (*see* p.165) houses one of Britain's largest and most important collections of musical instruments. Children can explore their various sounds at one of the museum's regular workshops.

National Festival of Music for Youth
Royal Festival Hall, South Bank, SE1
t (020) 8870 9264
www.mfy.org.uk
⊖/⇌ Waterloo
Bus 1, 4, 26, 68, 76, 168, 171, 176, 188, 341, 501, 505, 521, X68
   In July, a vast collection of school orchestras and youth bands comprising some 12,000 musicians gather at the Royal Festival Hall for a huge musical jamboree (the biggest of its kind in the world), during which music workshops and classes for

both adults and children are held. In November, the festival's best musicians also play a 'Schools' Prom' concert at the Royal Albert Hall.

The Music House for Children
Bush Hall, 310 Uxbridge Road, London, W12
t (020) 8932 2652
www.musichouseforchildren.co.uk
⊖ Shepherd's Bush
Bus 207, 260, 283, 607
   Run from Bush Hall, there is an extensive music and arts education programme for children of all ages. Also group tuition throughout the week involving music, dance and drama.

Pottery cafés

Unleash the budding Wedgwood in your family with some ceramic painting. Many cafés prove great venues for parties and, as well as painting pots, you can sculpt, tie-dye or make jewellery.

Art 4 Fun
444 Chiswick High Road, W4, **t** (020) 8994 4100
www.chiswick.colourmemine.com
⊖ Chiswick Park
Adm £5.95; items from £3
Open daily
Suitable for all ages
   A magical place where children and parents can paint their own cups, plates, T-shirts or picture frames as well as trying clay T-shirt printing, tie-dye and face painting.

Ceramics Café
6 Argyle Road, West Ealing
t (020) 8810 4422
www.ceramicscafe.com
⊖ West Ealing
Open Tues–Sat 10–6, Sun 11–5
Adm £2 studio fee, £3–£15 for materials
Suitable for all ages
   Personalize plates, mugs and other tableware. Party packages available.

Theatre

On any given night, there will be well over 60 plays, shows and revues showing in the West End.

Obviously not everything that gets put on is suitable for children, but there are many theatres specializing in the type of big, all-singing, all-dancing shows that appeal to a family audience. For further details check the daily newspapers and weekly listings magazines such as *Time Out*.

Performances are typically at 7.30pm Monday to Saturday with additional matinée performances on Tuesday or Wednesday, and Saturday.

Grease

Piccadilly Theatre, Denman Street, W1
Box office **t** 0844 412 6666
www.greasethemusical.co.uk
⊖ Piccadilly Circus
Bus 88, 91, 139, 159, 453
Prices from £20

Constantly being revived, Sandy and Danny's high school romance is one of the most popular musicals of all time.

Les Misérables

Queen's Theatre, Shaftesbury Avenue, W1
Box office **t** 0870 890 1110
www.lesmis.com
⊖ Leicester Square, Piccadilly Circus
Bus 14, 19, 38
Prices from £12

This tale of the Parisian underworld is officially the world's most popular musical. It's been running in London since 1985, so they must be doing something right. The theatre runs a kids' club for 8–11-year-olds on the first and fourth Saturday of each month, and for 12–15-year-olds on the third, between 10.45 and 1.15 offering backstage tours, drama workshops and tickets for that afternoon's matinée performance.

The Lion King

Lyceum Theatre, Wellington Street, WC2
Box office **t** 0870 243 9000
www.lyceum-theatre.co.uk
⊖ Covent Garden, Charing Cross
Bus 1, 6, 9, 11, 13, 15, 23, 68, 77A, 91, 168, 171, 176, 188, 501, 505, 521, X68
Prices from £20

An extravaganza set in the heart of Africa, with a plot and songs that most of the audience will already know by heart. Book well in advance.

Lord of the Rings

Theatre Royal Drury Lane, Catherine Street, WC2
Box office **t** 0870 890 6002

www.lotr.com
⊖ Covent Garden
Bus 1, 4, 11, 13, 15, 23, 26, 59, 68, 76, 91, 139, 168, 171, 176, 188, 243, 341, 521
Prices from £15

Fabulously expensive musical version of the fabulously expensive film, this reportedly cost in excess of £25 million to stage and involves a cast of over 60 actors. Although the plot of the three great novels has necessarily been severely compressed, the stage show still clocks in at over three and a half hours, with two intermissions. Expect lots of special effects, and perhaps a little less in the way of character development.

Mary Poppins

Prince Edward Theatre, Old Compton Street, W1
Box office **t** 0870 950 9191
www.marypoppinsthemusical.co.uk
⊖ Leicester Square
Bus 3, 6, 9, 11, 12, 13, 15, 23, 24, 53, 88, 91, 109, 139, 156, 176, 184, 196
Prices from £20

Disney's sugary classic about the magical singing nanny and the adorable children in her charge (not to mention the chimney sweep with the bizarre cockney accent) has been given a slightly more sinister tone in this production, more in keeping with the original book. Nonetheless, it's still a guaranteed family favourite.

Mamma Mia!

Prince of Wales Theatre, Coventry Street, W1
Box office **t** 0870 850 0393
www.mamma-mia.com
⊖ Piccadilly Circus
Bus 3, 12, 14, 19, 22, 38
Prices from £25

Theatrical karaoke – all your favourite Abba songs shoehorned into a rather convoluted story.

The Mousetrap

St Martin's Theatre, West Street, WC2
Box office **t** 0870 145 1163
www.the-mousetrap.co.uk
⊖ Leicester Square
Bus 14, 19, 24, 29, 38, 176
Performances Mon–Sat 8, matinées Tues 2.45, Sat 5. Duration 2hrs 51mins
Prices from £12

The longest-running show in the world, having played continuously for the last 49 years. This gentle Agatha Christie mystery is a good way to introduce kids to the joys of the stage.

The Sound of Music

London Palladium, Argyll Street, W1
Box office **t** 0870 890 1108
www.london-palladium.co.uk
⊖ Oxford Circus
Bus 3, 6, 7, 8, 10, 12, 13, 15, 23, 25, 53, 55, 73, 88, 94, 98, 113, 137, 139, 159, 176, 189, C2
Prices from £25

The much-loved film has been revamped for the stage by Sir Andrew Lloyd Webber, following a TV search for the new Maria. Sing along to the Von Trapp family's greatest hits – 'My Favourite Things', 'Do-Re-Mi' et al – as they escape the Nazis into Switzerland, dancing all the way.

We Will Rock You

Dominion Theatre, Tottenham Court Road, W1
Box office **t** 0870 169 0116
www.queenonline.com/wewillrockyou
⊖ Leicester Square
Bus 3, 6, 9, 11, 12, 13, 15, 23, 24, 29, 53, 88, 91, 109, 139, 159, 176, 184, 196
Prices from £15

An absurd Ben Elton-penned plot links some of the flamboyant 70s and 80s rock band's greatest hits into a spectacular stage show.

Wicked

Apollo Victoria Theatre, Wilton Road SW1
Box office **t** 0870 400 0751
www.wickedthemusical.co.uk
⊖/ ≋ Victoria
Bus 2, 36, 185, 436
Prices from £20

A prequel musical telling tales of the witches of Oz before Dorothy arrived on the scene. The story centres on Elphaba, a misunderstood young girl who grows up to be the Wicked Witch of the West. Many of the characters, including Glinda the Good Witch of the North, will be familiar to anyone who has watched or read the Wizard of Oz.

Behind the scenes

London is, and has always been since the days before Shakespeare, a theatrical city, and there are plenty of opportunities to sample the smell of the greasepaint and the roar of the crowd. The following theatres offer backstage tours where you can explore dressing rooms, wardrobes and costume departments and find out about the

elaborate machinery used to get the scenery on and off the stage.

Globe Theatre

Bear Gardens, Bankside, New Globe Walk, Southwark, SE1
t (020) 7902 1500
www.shakespeares-globe.org
⊖/ ≋ London Bridge
Bus 11, 15, 17, 23, 26, 45, 63, 76, 100, 344, 381, RV1
Open 10–5 daily, for performance times call in advance
Adm Adult £9, child £6.50 (under-5s **free**), concs £7.50, family ticket (2+3) £20

Free tours for museum visitors begin every 15–30 minutes during opening hours. There is no need to book (for more details on the theatre, *see* p.119).

Royal National Theatre

South Bank, SE1
t (020) 7452 3400
www.nationaltheatre.org.uk
⊖/ ≋ Waterloo
Bus 1, 4, 26, 68, 76, 168, 171, 176, 188, 341, 501, 505, 521, X68
Tour Mon–Fri 6 times a day, Sat twice a day; tour lasts 1hr 15mins
Adm Backstage tours: £5, concs £4, family £13

Children's theatre

Going to see a big West End production is all very well, but it's liable to get kids hankering for a life on the stage. Thankfully, London is home to several theatre companies that not only put on their own child-friendly performances, but also offer training and advice (often for free) to aspiring young thespians. Here are some of the best.

Arts Depot

5 Nether Street, Tally Ho Corner, North Finchley, N12
t (020) 8369 5454
www.artsdepot.co.uk
⊖ West Finchley, Woodside Park
Bus 134, 263, 82, 125, 221, 460
Open Box office 10–8
Adm Shows from £8, children's workshops from £6

Just a few years old, this arts centre has two auditoriums (seating, respectively 150 and 400 people), offering a full range of theatre, music, comedy and dance (family shows usually take place at 3pm Sundays) as well as a variety of courses and activities for children – breakdance workshops, costume making, drama courses, etc.

Battersea Arts Centre

Old Town Hall, Lavender Hill, SW11
t (020) 7223 2223
www.bac.org.uk
⇌ Clapham Junction
Bus 77, 77A, 345
Open Mon 10–6, Tues–Sun 10–9
Adm drama workshops £4.50; children's theatre: adult £5.75, child £4.50; membership: child £10.75, family £16.50

Despite the local council having recently removed much of its funding, this hardy old centre continues (for now) to organize activity and theatre workshops for 3–16-year-olds, although be aware that they're hugely popular and places are limited. Performances of children's drama are staged every Saturday at 2.30pm.

Half Moon Young People's Theatre

43 White Horse Road, E1
t (020) 7709 8900
www.halfmoon.org.uk
⊖ Stepney Green
DLR Limehouse
Bus 25, 115, 309, 339, D3
Open 10–6 (performance times vary)
Adm £4.50 per person, regardless of age

This very serious-minded theatre group runs no less than seven youth theatre groups for all ages (up to 17) available to everyone with 'enthusiasm and commitment'. Performances are put on throughout the year and are very highly regarded.

Little Angel Theatre

14 Dagmar Passage, Cross Street, N1
t (020) 7226 1787
www.littleangeltheatre.com
⊖ Angel, Highbury & Islington
Bus 4, 19, 30, 38, 43, 56, 73, 341
Open Performances Sat at 11am and 3pm
Adm Adult £7.50, child £5; some performances have a 'pay-what-you-can' policy, for which the minimum charge is £1; puppet course £75

A wonderful puppet theatre that holds regular weekend performances and also runs 9-week puppet courses on Saturday mornings when kids can make and learn how to use puppets, before performing on the Angel stage. Children must be aged 3 or over.

London Bubble

t (020) 7237 4434
www.londonbubble.org.uk
Adm Adult £13, child £7.50

This popular roving theatre company moves its mobile show tents around the parks of London during the summer, staying on average one week in each. The plays are aimed squarely at 11-year-olds and under. It also holds workshops for ages 3–6.

Polka Theatre

240 The Broadway, SW19
t (020) 8543 4888
www.polkatheatre.com
⊖ /⇌ Wimbledon, ⊖ South Wimbledon
Bus 57, 93, 219, 493
Open Tues–Fri 9.30–4.30, Sat 10–5
Adm Tickets for performances range from £5–£10; workshops from £55 per term

The capital's only purpose-built children's theatre. Four shows a day are put on during the school holidays, two during term time. It also runs drama and puppetry workshops and after-school clubs for all ages. The shows are usually of a very high standard and a mixture of classics and new work.

Puppet Theatre Barge

Blomfield Road, Little Venice, W9
t 0783 620 2745
www.puppetbarge.com
Bus 6, 18, 46
Open Vary, phone ahead
Adm Adult £8.50, child £8

Moored on Regent's Canal, Little Venice, this old working barge is a delightful place to introduce your children to puppetry. The Moving Stage Marionettes Company, which operates the barge, puts on high-quality puppet shows for children and adults throughout the year. It's easy to find: look out for the bright red and yellow awnings. The barge is moored in winter, but in summer sails up and down the Thames, putting on shows.

Regent's Park Open Air Theatre

Regent's Park, NW1
t 0870 060 1811
www.openairtheatre.org
Adm Tickets for daytime performances start at £10, rising to £31; tickets for family shows are £12
⊖ Baker Street
Bus 2, 13, 18, 27, 30, 74, 82, 113, 139, 189, 205, 274

ADVENTURE PLAYGROUNDS | CINEMAS | INTERNET CAFÉS | MUSEUMS & GALLERIES | MUSIC | POTTERY CAFÉS | **THEATRE** | TV & RADIO

Wheelchair accessible, with adapted toilets, hearing loop and signed performances

This respected theatre company celebrated its 25th anniversary in 2007 and usually puts on some sort of child-friendly show during the summer holidays, as well as Shakespeare and a quality musical (for more details, *see* p.46).

Shakespeare's Globe

Bear Gardens, Bankside, New Globe Walk, Southwark, SE1
t (020) 7902 1400
www.shakespeares-globe.org
⊖ London Bridge
Bus 11, 15, 17, 23, 26, 45, 63, 76, 100, 344, 381, RV1
Open 10–5, daily, for performance times call in advance
Adm Museum: adult £8, child £5.50,under-5s **free** concs £6.50, family ticket (2+3) £24
Saturday 'Child's Play' Workshops **adm** £10
Limited wheelchair access, call disabled access information on **t** (020) 7902 1409

On select Saturdays, children aged 8–11 can take part in Saturday afternoon 'Child's Play' sessions at the Globe's education centre (*see* p.119).

Tricycle Theatre

269 Kilburn High Road, NW6
t (020) 7372 6611
www.tricycle.co.uk
⊖ Kilburn
Bus 16, 31, 32, 98, 189, 206, 316, 328
Open Performances Sat at 11.30am and 2pm
Adm Performances: £5 or £4 if booked before the day of the performance; workshops are £20 for a 9-week term

The theatre holds about 300 workshops a year for all ages offering nine-week courses in acting, singing, dancing, music, mime, puppetry and circus skills. Its own family theatre performances are both highly innovative and hugely popular, taking place every Saturday of the academic year (Sept–June) at 11.30am and 2pm. The theatre also shows Saturday matinée films for all the family at 1pm.

Unicorn Theatre

147 Tooley Street, SE1
t (020) 7645 0560
www.unicorntheatre.com
⊖/ ⮂ London Bridge
Bus 17, 381, RV1
Open Performance times vary, call in advance

Adm Adult £9.50, child £5
Wheelchair access, adapted toilets, café
An award-winning children's theatre (*see* p.120).

Pantomime season

The original interactive entertainment. Come December, ex-sportsmen, assorted soap stars and TV magicians join together for this most British of institutions. Throughout London you'll find versions of *Aladdin*, *Cinderella* and *Jack and the Beanstalk* in production. For details of performances in your area, check out the listings in the *Evening Standard*, *Metro* and *Time Out*.

TV & radio

Being a member of a studio audience for a TV or radio show can be quite a giggle for children. Most shows are free, but, please take note that tickets for the most popular ones are snapped up well in advance and many shows operate age restrictions.

BBC TV and Radio

t 0870 603 0304
www.bbc.co.uk/whatson/tickets
The BBC's dedicated children's channel, CBBC, now offers behind-the-scenes tours for children aged 7 and over to visit the studios and see how the programmes are made. They cost adult £9.50, child £7, family £27.

ITV, Channel 4 and Channel 5

Tickets for ITV, Channel 4 and Channel 5 shows can also be obtained through the following companies: **Applause Store**, **t** (020) 8324 2700, www.applausestore.com; **Be on Screen t** 0870 063 2932, www.beonscreen.com; **Clappers**, **t** (020) 8532 2770, www.clappers-tickets.co.uk; **Inspired PR**, **t** 0121 440 163; **Lost in TV**, **t** (020) 8530 8100, www.lostintv.com; **Powerhouse**, **t** (020) 7240 2828; **Standing Room Only**, **t** (020) 8684 3333, www.sroaudiences.com; **TV Recordings**, www.tvrecordings.com

Kids out

Plants and birds

There is lots of outdoor fun to be had in London. The city is dotted with parks – from great swathes of manicured greenery such as Hyde Park and Green Park to tiny patches of unspoilt wilderness. There are also urban farms where kids can get close to animals and take part in art activities.

Kew Gardens

Kew, Richmond, Surrey, TW9
Infoline **t** (020) 8332 5655
www.kew.org
⇌ Kew Bridge, Kew Gardens
⊖ Kew Gardens
Bus 65, 391, 237, 267
Open 9.30–dusk
Adm Adult £12.25, under-16s **free**, concs & wheelchair users £10.25, blind, partially sighted and carers **free**
Baby-changing facilities, 2 gift shops, 2 self-service restaurants, coffee bar, bakery, snack shop
Wheelchair accessible, with adapted toilets
Suitable for all ages

The Royal Botanic Gardens, to give Kew its proper name, is spread over a 300-acre site on the south bank of the Thames. It has grown, over the course of 200 years, into the largest and most comprehensive collection of living plants in the world, with more than one in eight of all flowering plants. In addition to great grassy lawns, flowerbeds and collections of rare trees, there are three enormous conservatories: the Palm House, full of tropical exotica; the late 19th-century Temperate House; and the Princess of Wales Conservatory, built in the 1980s and home to both the giant Amazonian water lily and Titan Arum, the largest, smelliest flower in the world. Children are well catered for with a dedicated botanical play zone, 'Climbers and Creepers'. There's an accompanying website for children aged 3–6 with online games and puzzles (**www**.kew.org/climbersandcreepers). The gardens have also started offering sleepovers for children where they can tour the grounds in the dead of night on the hunt for bats, owls and badgers (8–11 years, £40 per person).

WWT Wetlands Centre

Queen Elizabeth Walk, SW13
t (020) 8409 4400
www.wwt.org.uk

⇌ Barnes
Bus Train, then 33, 72, 209, 283
⊖ Hammersmith then bus 283
Bus 283
Open Winter 9.30–5, Summer 9.30–6 (last admission 1hr before closing), feeding times at 12 noon and 3.30pm daily
Adm Adult £8.75, child (4–16) £4.95, family ticket £21.95, under-4s **free**
Wheelchair accessible. Baby-changing facilities, shop, self-service restaurant. Suitable for all ages

This innovative 43-hectare site is split into 14 simulated habitats, including arctic tundra and tropical swamp. Picture boards help to identify what's what. Although best visited in good weather when you can join the free guided tours at 11am and 2pm, there are numerous hides from which you can see the wildlife (some are displayed on CCTV cameras). There's also a visitors' centre where you can pick up children's trails and hire binoculars. It also has a Discovery centre with water games for children and a ground-floor café with a kids' menu and outside seating. Upstairs, in the observatory, there's an interactive area where kids can discover life through the eyes of a duck, dragonfly or bird, follow migratory patterns across the globe, make bird sounds, build puzzles or just watch the wildlife through the window.

There's a cinema where visitors can learn about the centre and the work of the World Wildlife Trust, and seasonal wildlife-themed activities at weekends. In the holidays, kids can take part in bat walks, dragonfly hunts and the very popular pond safaris.

Open spaces

Alexandra Palace Park

Muswell Hill, N22
t (020) 8365 2121
www.alexandrapalace.com
⊖ Wood Green
⇌ Alexandra Palace
Bus 184, W3
Open 24hrs a day
Free

'Ally Pally', as it is affectionately known, has had a rather illustrious history. Built in 1862 for the second Great Exhibition, in 1936 it was the site of Britain's first television broadcast. Today, the park is one of the best equipped for sports in the capital. Among its many attractions are several football and cricket pitches, a pitch-and-putt golf course, a skateboard park, an ice rink, a boating lake and a couple of playgrounds with sandpits and swings. Both adults and children will enjoy the spectacular views that the park affords over London (for 20p you can take an even closer look through a set of fixed binoculars). Regular funfairs take place during the holidays and on bank holidays. The house also hosts a variety of craft and leisure activity shows, concerts and displays. Its proposed redevelopment is currently on hold following legal challenges by local residents who believe that its conversion into a 'leisure complex' will not be in keeping with its heritage and history.

Battersea Park

Prince of Wales Drive, SW11
t (020) 8871 7530
www.batterseapark.org
⊖ Sloane Square
⇌ Battersea Park, Queenstown Road
Bus 19, 44, 49, 137, 156, 319, 344, 345
Open Dawn till dusk daily, zoo 10–5 daily
Adm Park free; Zoo adult £5.95, child £4.50, family £18.50, under-2s free

One of London's best parks for children, Battersea has undergone a major revamp, which has seen the addition of a new running track and floodlit tennis courts (where children's tennis camps are held in August). There's also a small children's zoo, home to deer, lemurs, peacocks and wallabies (see p.176), a boating lake, a Victorian Pump House and, best of all, London's largest adventure playground. There's also a branch of the London Recumbents, t (020) 7498 6543, where you can hire bikes. The park organizes lots of summer events for children, including a teddy bears' picnic. In November there's usually an impressive firework display and bonfire.

Brockwell Park

Herne Hill, SE24
t (020) 7926 0105
www.brockwellpark.com
⇌ Herne Hill
Bus 2, 3, 37, 196
Open Dawn till dusk daily

Though its main draw is its famous lido (see Brockwell Lido p.187), especially in summer, the park has much to offer year-round. There are tennis courts, duck ponds, a bowling green, a basketball court, a football pitch, a miniature railway (£1 a ride) and a BMX track, as well as lots of open space. Take a break in the First Come First Served Café, at the top of the hill.

Coram's Fields

93 Guilford Street, WC1
t (020) 7837 6138
See p.58.

Crystal Palace Park

Anerley Road, Crystal Palace, SE20
t (020) 8778 9496
www.crystalpalacepark.net
⇌ Crystal Palace, Penge West
Bus 2, 3, 63, 122, 137a, 194, 202, 227, 249, 306, 322, 358
Open 7.30am till dusk daily, dinosaur area open from 9.30am till 1hr before park closes

This south London park once supported the great iron and glass bulk of the Crystal Palace itself, re-erected here following its starring role in the 1851 Great Exhibition in Hyde Park. Although the palace burned down in the 1930s, the park that bears its name is still well worth a visit with its grassy lawns, concert bowl and sports stadium. The highlight is the newly restored dinosaur park, a magnificent tableau of dinosaur models, which was first built way back in the 1850s – hence its claim to be the world's first theme park.

The site of the Crystal Palace itself is now occupied by an enormous TV transmitter, although the foundations and terraces remain, like some ghostly reminder of a lost city.

There is a 'one o'clock club' for under-5s open year-round, Mon–Fri 9.30–12.30 and 1–4, t (020) 8659 6554 and also children's events organized in the holidays for 6–12-year-olds, t (020) 8778 9496. However, the petting zoo, though rebuilt, is yet to be restocked with animals.

Discover

1 Bridge Terrace, E15
t (020) 8536 5555
www.discover.org.uk
⊖/⇌/DLR Stratford
Open Term Time Tues–Thurs, Sat & Sun 10–5, School Holidays 10–5 daily
Adm Over-2s £3.50, family £11, under-2s free
Wheelchair access, adapted toilets, snack shop, picnic area

This children's park is a good way out from the centre of town in Stratford, East London, but well worth the trip. Built at a cost of some £6 million, it bills itself as an 'interactive play centre', the idea being to try to teach children through play. So, in addition to a great collection of equipment – climbing frames, a giant model spaceship and a wet play area – the park also has a special 'Story Garden' where kids can dress up, make puppets and create their own stories. A host of events for children – storytellings, singalongs and arts and crafts days – is put on throughout the year.

Dulwich Park
College Road, SE21
t (020) 8693 5737
⇌ North Dulwich
Bus 12, 40, 176, 185, 321, P4
Open Summer 8am–9pm daily, winter 8–4.30 daily
Free

A great place to come after spending the morning at the Dulwich Picture Gallery (*see* p.161), this beautiful park has a well-equipped playground, a boating lake (boats £5.25 for 30mins), tennis courts, horse-riding tracks and a pleasant café (open 9–6, daily, children's menu available). The London Recumbents, **t** (020) 8299 6636, have their base here, where you can hire or buy bikes, trikes and tandem cycles. They also run cycle safety courses on a one-to-one basis. Resident rangers organize various activities from seed hunts to bat walks.

Epping Forest
Epping Forest Field Centre, High Beech Road, Loughton, Essex
t (020) 8502 8500
⊖ Loughton
Bus 20, 167, 210, 214, 215, 219, 220, 240, 250, 301, 531, 532, 549
Open Field Centre: Mon–Sat 10–5, Sun 11–5
Free

A piece of ancient Britain on the outskirts of modern London. Once part of a huge woodland that stretched from the River Lea to the sea, Epping Forest came into existence 8,000 years ago, just after the last Ice Age. Today, this 10-mile crescent is a wonderful mixture of dense woodland, grassland, heathland and ponds inhabited by a wide range of wildlife, including deer, woodpeckers, foxes and badgers. Close to the station is the excellent field centre, which provides maps of the forest and organizes various children's activities, including mini-safaris, nature trails and pond dippings. It can also supply details of walks. The forest also encompasses

two listed buildings – Queen Elizabeth's Hunting Lodge (**open** Wed–Sun 1–4 **free**, **t** (020) 8529 6681), and the temple, as well as the remains of two Iron-Age earthworks.

Green Park
Piccadilly, W1, and The Mall, SW1
t (020) 7930 1793
See p.92.

Greenwich Park
Charlton Way, SE3
t (020) 8858 2608
See p.153.

Hampstead Heath
Hampstead, NW3
t (020) 7482 7073
⊖ Belsize Park, Hampstead
⇌ Hampstead Heath, Gospel Oak
Bus 24, 46, 168, 214, C2, C11
Open 24hrs a day
Free

After the royal parks, this is London's most famous open space. It's also Central London's most countrified area, one of the few places that actually feels a little bit wild, a sense heightened by the lack of signposts – bring a map. Once the stamping ground of the poets Keats and Shelley, and of the highwayman Dick Turpin, these 800 acres provide a wonderful setting for a family walk. Kids will enjoy the well-equipped playground by Gospel Oak Station, complete with swings, slides and climbing frame, as well as the funfairs that are regularly set up in summer. Its open spaces are ideal for kite-flying, and there is a café nearby on the Parliament Hill side where you can recover. There are some wonderful views of the city, particularly from Parliament Hill (site of the famous lido, *see* p.187), and the park is also the loca-tion of the grand stately home, Kenwood House. The heath's information centre organizes family activities such as music workshops, bat walks and fishing lessons.

Highgate Wood
Muswell Hill Road, N6
t (020) 8444 6129
⊖ Highgate
Bus 144, W7
Open 7.30am till dusk daily
Free

This small patch of ancient woodland is inhabited by a staggering array of flora and fauna – over 70 species of birds, 12 species of butterfly, 180 species of bats, 80 species of spiders, plus foxes, squirrels and all manner of undergrowth-hugging beetles, slugs and worms. Pick up a nature trail from the woodland centre and head off into the trees. There's a playground (recently revamped, with a softer surface, aerial rope slides and a separate, supervised play area for under-5s), a sports ground and an excellent vegetarian restaurant (see p.233).

Holland Park
Kensington High Street, W8
t (020) 7361 3003
www.rbkc.gov.uk/ParksAndGardens/HollandPark/default.asp
⊖ Holland Park, High Street Kensington
Bus 9, 10, 27, 28, 49
Open Dawn till dusk daily
Free

Just off Kensington High Street, this is a lovely manicured park with an orangery, a Japanese Water Garden and free-roaming peacocks and pheasants. Your kids, of course, will ignore all of them, as they head to the park's groovy, multi-level adventure playground. There are eight children's play areas in all, including a special under-8s area. Sticky Fingers restaurant (which on weekends is very child-friendly) is just around the corner (see p.232). The ecology centre, **t** (020) 7471 9809, can provide maps and walks.

Hyde Park/Kensington Gardens
t (020) 7298 2100
See p.142.

Regent's Park
t (020) 7486 7905
See p.46.

Richmond Park
Richmond, Surrey
t (020) 8948 3209
www.royalparks.gov.uk/parks/richmond_park/
⊖/≋ Richmond
Bus 72, 74, 85, 371
Open Dawn till dusk daily
Free

This great swathe of west London parkland has long been closely associated with the monarchy. In the 15th century Henry VII had a viewing mound created in the park, allowing him to look out over his kingdom – the mound still stands today and the views remain magnificent, stretching from Windsor Castle in the west to St Paul's Cathedral in the east. The park is home to the Queen's own herds of red and fallow deer which roam the park pretty much as the fancy takes them. A huge variety of other species of wildlife, among them foxes, weasels and badgers, have also made the park their home. There's a playground at the Petersham gate, two public golf courses, a very good park café by the Roehampton Gate, snack bars in the Broomfield Hill and Pen Pond car parks, some great walking trails and you can hire bikes to explore the park's miles of roads from Richmond Park Cycle Hire, **t** 07050 209 249. Be aware that the park's roads are open to traffic. Cars are supposed to keep under the 20mph speed limit, but don't assume that they always will. Treat the park's paths as you would any other major road.

St James's Park
The Mall, SW1
t (020) 7930 1793
See p.93.

Syon Park
London Road, Brentford, Middlesex, TW3
t (020) 8560 0883
www.syonpark.co.uk & www.londonbutterflyhouse.com
⊖ Gunnersbury, then bus
≋ Kew Bridge, then bus
Bus 237, 267
Open Garden: 10.30–5 (or dusk if earlier) daily; Butterfly House: summer 10–5, winter 10–3; Syon House: Apr–Nov Wed–Thurs, Sun and bank hols 11–5; Aquatic Experience: summer 10–6, winter 10–5, daily
Adm Garden & conservatory: adult £4, child £2.50, family £9; house & garden: adult £8, child £4, family £18 ; Butterfly House: adult £5.25, child £3.95, family £16, under-3s **free**

Syon Park surrounds Syon House, a former abbey and residence of Henry VIII, which now provides a terribly grand London home for the Duke of Northumberland. It's sumptuous and elegant with a vast 19th-century conservatory but will in all likelihood hold little interest for children. They'll be much more enthralled by the other attractions, which include the London Butterfly House, where you'll find free-flying butterflies settling on your head and arms as you walk around, the huge indoor adventure playground, Snakes and Ladders (*see* p.156), the model railway (which tours the garden every Sunday) and a go-kart track.

Victoria Park

Old Ford Road, E3
t (020) 8533 2057
⊖ Mile End
⇌ Cambridge Heath, Hackney Wick
Bus 8, 26, 30, 55, 253, 277, S2
Open 6am till dusk, daily

Once upon a time, this 218-acre East End park's primary source of entertainment was provided by burning heretics at the stake. Today's leisure facilities include the ornamental gardens, an animal enclosure with goats and fallow deer, tennis courts, a bowling green, an adventure playground, plenty of green open spaces and two lakes, one housing a model boat club, the other a thriving fishing trade.

City farms & zoos

If children won't come to the countryside, then the countryside must come to the children, or so it was thought in the early 1970s when it was felt that kids were becoming 'nature deprived' and had little concept of what the countryside was like. So the idea of the city farm was born – the aim being to bring a little bit of country life back into the inner city. Here's a selection of some of the best.

Battersea Park Children's Zoo

Albert Bridge Road, SW11
t (020) 7924 5826
www.batterseaparkzoo.co.uk
⊖ Sloane Square
⇌ Battersea Park, Queenstown Road
Bus 19, 44, 49, 137, 319, 344, 345
Open 10–5, daily
Adm Adult £5.95, child £4.50, family £18

One of London's best small zoos, Battersea Park Children's Zoo is run by the same people who operate the Otter, Owl and Wildlife Park in the New Forest. It's home to a wide range of animals, including meerkats, lemurs, otters and wallabies. Children can stroke the goats and sheep at the petting paddock, join the keepers on their feeding rounds (the otters and meerkats are fed daily at 11am and 2pm, the monkeys on weekends at 3pm) and take part in animal-themed art sessions.

Coram's Fields

93 Guilford Street, WC1
t (020) 7837 6138
www.coramsfields.org
⊖ Russell Square
Bus 17, 45, 46, 168
Open Summer 9–8 daily, winter 9–dusk
Free

This lovely park has had a long association with children. It was here that the eponymous Thomas Coram established a foundling hospital in 1747 which, following the building's demolition in 1920, was turned into London's first dedicated children's park. Today, adults can only visit Coram's Fields in the company of a child. As well as being permanently staffed, it's also well equipped – in addition to lawns, sandpits, a paddling pool, sports pitches, a helter-skelter and a playground, you'll find the park's highlight, a small farm home to goats, sheep, pigs, geese, chickens, rabbits and guinea pigs. There are year-round kids' events, both to participate in (dance competitions, football matches, flower plantings) and watch (circus performances). There's also a small youth centre offering free IT resources for 13–19-year-olds and a good vegetarian café.

Deen City Farm & Riding School

39 Windsor Avenue, Merton Abbey, SW19
t (020) 8543 5300
www.deencityfarm.net
⇌ Mitcham
Bus 200
Open Tues–Sun 10–4.30
Adm Farm: **free**; Riding School: Prices start from £21 per hour for private lessons, £14 per hour for group lessons

A hands-on experience where kids can help muck out goats, pigs, rabbits and ponies, meet chickens, guinea fowl and geese (as well as snakes, ferrets, chinchillas and terrapins) and go for pony and horse rides under the auspices of its riding school. In summer, the farm holds special 'Young Farmer Days' with tractor rides and barn dances.

Freightliners City Farm

Paradise Park, Sheringham Road, off Liverpool Road, N7
t (020) 7609 0467
www.freightlinersfarm.org.uk
⊖ Holloway, Highbury & Islington
Bus 43, 153, 271, 279

Open Tues–Sun 10–5
Free

Summer playschemes introduce children to the various breeds of sheep, pigs, goats, cattle and poultry. You can buy free-range eggs and seasonal vegetables at the farm shop.

Hackney City Farm

1a Goldsmiths Row, E2
t (020) 7729 6381
www.hackneycityfarm.co.uk
⊖ Bethnal Green
≈ Cambridge Heath
Bus 26, 48, 55
Open Tues–Sun 10–4.30
Free

In the east end of London, this converted brewery houses farm animals and runs some popular craft workshops and activity days. Kids can try pottery, sculpture and weaving and learn the correct way to feed animals and shear sheep. There's a popular cafe and deli, offering Mediterranean fare.

Kentish Town City Farm

1 Cressfield Close, NW5
t (020) 7916 5421
www.ktcityfarm.co.uk
⊖ Kentish Town, Chalk Farm
Bus 24, 27, 31, 46, 134, 168, 214, C1, C2, C11
Open Tues–Sun 9.30–5.30
Free

Established in 1973, this was one of the first genuine city farms. Children can interact with cows, pigs and goats, and there's a garden. Pony rides are available for £1 at weekends (the horse riding club is only available to Camden residents).

Mudchute Park & Farm

Pier Street, Isle of Dogs, E14
t (020) 7515 5901
www.mudchute.org
DLR Mudchute, Crossharbour Station
Bus D6, D7, D8
Open 9–4, daily
Free
Café, shop, garden centre

London's largest inner-city farm was founded as a working farm at the end of the 19th century. It has riding stables (lessons for 7–16-year-olds are £21 per hour as part of a group), an education centre which organizes family days and summer play schemes, a wildlife area and lots of open space.

Surrey Docks Farm

Rotherhithe Street, SE16
t (020) 7231 1010
www.surreydocksfarm.org
DLR Surrey Quays, Canada Water
Bus 225
Open 9–1 and 2–5, daily, closed Mon and Fri during school hols
Free

A tiny farm overlooking the River Thames where you'll find goats, sheep and ducks, as well as a working forge. In summer the farm hosts various craft demonstrations, including metalwork and felt-making, and runs play schemes for youngsters.

Vauxhall City Farm

Tyers Street, SE11
t (020) 7582 4204
⊖ Vauxhall
Bus 2, 36, 77a, 88, 185
Open Tues–Thurs and Sat–Sun 10–5
Free

Next to the MI6 building, Vauxhall City Farm is home to all the usual suspects including pigs, rabbits, sheep, ducks and hens, as well as donkeys and ponies that give rides in summer.

Curious caves

Chislehurst Caves

Old Hill, Chislehurst
t (020) 8467 3264
www.chislehurstcaves.co.uk
Getting there It's off the A222 on the B264 near Chislehurst railway station
Open Daily during school hols, otherwise Wed–Sun, tours hourly 10–4
Adm Adult £5, child £4
Café, gift shop, on-site parking. 1hr from London

This 2,000-year-old tunnel network cut into the side of the Old Hill, Chislehurst, is some way outside central London, but is worth a visit. The first excavations were made by Druids fleeing the invading Romans, in the 1st century AD. In more recent times, it was used an ammunition dump in the First World War and, in the Second World War, became Britain's largest bomb shelter. Though stretching for over 22 miles, the caves are well lit and more spooky than scary. They are also available for private parties.

Sports and activities

14

Whether you want to take part or just watch, you'll find London a hive of sporting activity with everything from athletics to windsurfing catered for. And with the Olympics due to be staged in London in 2012 for the first time since 1948, the capital will see a whole new set of sporting facilities erected over the next few years, particularly in East London where the majority of the events will be held.

The capital's major clubs and sports centres are listed below, along with details of any specific children's schemes or courses that they run. Remember, you can find facilities for tennis, football, basketball and softball in many of London's parks (see p.172).

Athletics

Crystal Palace
National Sports Centre, Ledrington Road, Crystal Palace, SE19
t (020) 8778 0131
www.gll.org/centre/crystal-palace-national-sports-centre.asp
⇌ Crystal Palace
Bus 2, 3, 63, 122, 137a, 157, 202, 227, 249, 342, 358, 361, 450

For so long the spiritual home of British athletics, Crystal Palace will, come 2012, be superseded by the new Olympic stadium in east London. Until then, it will continue to host at least one star-studded athletics Grand Prix per year. Would-be athletes can apply to attend one of their yearly summer sports camps. Alternatively, for details of athletics provision in your area, contact England Athletics on **t** (0121) 452 1500, **www**.england athletics.org or the South of England Athletics Association on **t** (020) 7021 0988, **www**.seaa.org.uk

Badminton & squash

Both of these sports are great for promoting dexterity and hand-eye coordination. For details of child-friendly clubs contact Badminton England, **t** (01908) 268 400, **www**.badmintonengland.co.uk or England Squash on **t** (0161) 231 4499, **www**.englandsquash.co.uk.

Baseball & softball

Due to an increase in popularity, these two American sports have clubbed together to form the BaseballSoftballUK agency, **t** (020) 7453 7055, **www**.baseballsoftballuk.com.

Basketball

The English Basketball Association can help you find anything from a local court to have a knock-about in to a junior level club to join. Call **t** 0870 774 4225 for details, or visit **www**.englandbasket ball.co.uk. Wembley Arena, **t** 0870 060 0870 and Crystal Palace National Sports Centre, **t** (020) 8778 0131, both play host to regular basketball matches during the season, Oct–Apr.

Cricket

London's two premier grounds for watching this most tactical of sports, and England's most popular summer game, are Lord's, home of Middlesex Country Cricket Club, and the Oval, home of Surrey County Cricket club. The county championship season runs from April to September, with four-day matches usually taking place between Thursday and Monday, often with a one-day match sandwiched in between on the Sunday. Both grounds also host at least one one-day international match and a five-day international Test Match between England and one of the other nine major cricket-playing nations each year – the other nations being Australia, Bangladesh, New Zealand, India, Pakistan, Sri Lanka, South Africa, Zimbabwe and the West Indies. Tickets are in the region of £10–£25 – slightly more expensive for international matches. Both Lord's and the Oval run cricket courses for children aged 8 and over, and are enthusiastic supporters of 'Kwik Cricket', an easier, quicker version of the game for younger children.

Marylebone Cricket Club (MCC) and Middlesex County Cricket Club

Lord's Cricket Ground, St John's Wood Road, NW8
t (020) 7616 8500
www.lords.org
⊖ St John's Wood
Bus 3, 82, 113, 139, 189

Surrey County Cricket Club

The Oval, Kennington, SW8
t (020) 7582 6660
www.surreycricket.com
⊖ Oval, Vauxhall
Bus 36, 185

Fishing

A bit of string and a bent nail may be all your kids need to get the angling habit. Alternatively, you could invest in some equipment from one of the capital's many tackle shops (try Swifty's Bait & Tackle, 44 Wilcox Road, SW8, **t** (020) 7627 5907, www.swiftys-fishing-tackle.co.uk). Either way you will need a licence. Contact the **Environment Agency** (formerly the National Rivers Authority) on **t** (01734) 535 000, www.environment-agency.gov.uk/fish (licences can be bought online). They will also provide a list of fishing sites including some spots along the Thames (home to over 100 types of fish). Coarse and trout fishing licences cost: full Adult £24.50, child £12.25; 8-day £8.75, 1-day £3.25.

London Anglers Association

Izaak Walton Road, 2a Hervey Park Road, E17
t (020) 8520 7477
www.londonanglers.net

Football

It has always been the nation's favourite sport, but over the past decade and a half football has reached unprecedented levels of popularity. It now pervades all aspects of popular culture – millions of books, magazines, videos and even records are sold on the back of the game. The most successful players command seven-figure salaries, while the top clubs are now stockmarket-listed businesses with massive annual turnovers. Nonetheless, for all this growth, the game itself has remained as simple as ever. It requires the minimum amount of equipment (a ball, basically; goalposts can be fashioned with whatever comes to hand) and can be played practically anywhere. No wonder more British children play football than any other sport.

London is home to over a dozen professional football clubs, the biggest of which – Arsenal, Chelsea, Fulham, Tottenham and West Ham – play in the Premier League, the nation's most prestigious competition. League matches are played at weekends (usually kicking off at 3pm on Saturday), while cup and European matches are played midweek with the big clubs regularly attracting crowds of over 30,000. The games can be passionately exciting and the removal of the hooligan element in the late 1980s has led to more families coming to matches. Most grounds have family enclosures and the facilities, especially at Premier League grounds, are usually excellent. Tickets should be booked as far in advance as possible. Despite the high prices, they quickly sell out for top matches. A match ticket can cost anything from from £25–90 for an adult (usually around half that for children) depending on the quality of the seat and the opposition. Most clubs operate a two-tier pricing policy with the highest 'A' prices charged for matches between the top clubs (Arsenal, Chelsea, Liverpool and Manchester United, plus any particular local rivals) and cheaper 'B' prices for other matches.

England's international matches are played at the rebuilt 90,000-seat Wembley Stadium.

One note of warning – if you've never been to a football match before, your children will hear some pretty fruity language. Chanting, singing (often obscene songs about the opposition) and swearing are all an essential part of the experience.

At their best, football clubs can be a unifying point for the local community. Most London clubs now belong to the **Football in the Community** scheme whereby trained coaches organize holiday schools and after-school training for local children (both boys and girls) of all abilities.

Wembley Stadium
Wembley, HA9
t 0845 676 2006
www.wembleystadium.co.uk
⊖ Wembley Park, Wembley Central
⇌ Wembley Stadium
Bus 18, 83, 92, 182
310 spaces for wheelchair users

Arsenal Football Club
Emirates Stadium, Ashburton Grove, N5
t (020) 7704 4040
www.arsenal.com
⊖ Arsenal
Bus 4, 19, 29, 43, 153, 236, 253, 271, 393
Tickets Adult £30–90, child £13–15

Chelsea Football Club
Stamford Bridge, Fulham Road, SW10
t 0870 300 1212
www.chelseafc.co.uk
⊖ Fulham Broadway, Sloane Square
Bus 14, 211
Tickets Adult £30–90, child £15–30
Club shop, match day crèche for up to 20 children aged 1–5, from 2hrs before kick off

Fulham Football Club
Craven Cottage, Stevenage Road, SW6
t 0870 442 1234
www.fulhamfc.com
⊖ Putney Bridge
Bus 14, 22, 220, 270
Tickets Adult £30–50, child £15–20

Tottenham Hotspur Football Club
White Hart Lane, Bill Nicholson Way, 748 High Road, Tottenham, N17
t 0870 420 5000
www.tottenhamhotspur.com
⊖ Tottenham Hale, Seven Sisters
Bus 149, 259, 279, W3
Tickets Adult £27–71, child £14–21
Club shop

West Ham United
Boleyn Ground, Green Street, Upton Park, E13
t 0870 112 2700
www.whufc.co.uk
⊖ Upton Park
Bus 14, 74, 220
Tickets Adult £20–61, child £1–33
119 spaces for wheelchair users

Go-karting

Kids love to pull on their overalls, gloves and helmets, put their foot to the floor and race around a tyre-lined circuit. Apart from the raw thrill of speed (the karts reach a top speed of 30mph), they enjoy the idea of doing something 'grown-up', like driving, in a decidedly 'non-grown-up, go-as-fast-as-you-can' sort of way. London's indoor circuits offer training and racing for mini racing drivers aged 8–16. Everything is done with total care and attention to safety. The centres provide helmets and overalls and rigorous safety advice. Children should go along wearing long sleeves and trousers.

Expect to pay about £30 for an hour-long session.

Docklands F1 City
Gate 119, Connaught Bridge, Royal Victoria Dock, E16
t (020) 7476 5678
www.f1city.co.uk
DLR Royal Albert

Streatham Playscape Kart Raceway
390 Streatham High Road, SW16
t (020) 8677 8677
www.playscape.co.uk
⇌ Streatham
Bus 57, 109, 118, 133, 201, 250, 255

Ice-skating

London has half a dozen ice-skating rinks, many of which have popular disco nights. Most will not let children aged under three on the ice. Boots can usually be hired at the door. The average price, including skate hire, is adult: £6–8, child £4–6.

Alexandra Palace Ice Rink
Alexandra Palace Way, N22
t (020) 8365 4386

www.alexandrapalace.com/icerink.html
≋ Alexandra Palace
Bus 184, W3

Broadgate Ice Rink

Eldon Street, EC2
t (020) 7505 4068
www.broadgateice.co.uk
⊖/≋ Liverpool Street
Bus 133, 141, 172, 214, 271

One of London's few outdoor rinks. It's flooded and frozen between November and March.

Lee Valley Ice Centre

Lea Bridge Road, E10
t (020) 8533 3154
www.leevalleypark.org.uk
⊖ Walthamstow Central
Bus 158

Don't let the distance put you off. This large (184ft x 85ft) centre has public sessions seven days a week and 'learn to skate' programmes six days a week.

Sobell Ice Rink

Hornsey Road, Holloway, N7
t (020) 7609 2166
www.aquaterra.org/islington/skating/
⊖ Finsbury Park, Holloway Road
Bus 91

Offers parent and toddler sessions every Monday and Friday, during term time, at 1pm.

Streatham Ice Arena

386 Streatham High Road
t (020) 8769 7771
www.streathamicearena.co.uk
≋ Streatham Common
Bus 36, 50, 57, 109, 118, 133, 201, 250, 255

Somerset House

The Strand, WC2
t 0870 166 0423
www.somerset-house.org.uk
⊖ Temple, Charing Cross, Embankment, Covent Garden
Bus 6, 9, 11, 13, 15, 23, 77a, 91, 176

A New York-style open-air ice rink is set up in this grand mansion's courtyard for a few weeks during Christmas and New Year. Book ahead as it gets very busy and if you go and queue, it'll be a long wait.

Play gyms & gymnastics

Play gyms are a great way to get kids moving and develop coordination and motor skills. Gymnastics is also fun for kids to watch and/or participate in. For more details, contact the **British Amateur Gymnastics Association** on **t** 0845 1297 129, **www**.british-gymnastics.org

Crèchendo

Various locations across London
t (020) 8772 8120
www.crechendo.com

Using toys and soft climbing equipment, little kids are encouraged to fling themselves around in the name of social development at Crèchendo's six London play gyms. There are five age groups from 4 months to 4 years. Kids must be accompanied by an adult.

Tumbletots, Gymbabes & Gymbobs

Various venues across London
t (0121) 585 7003
www.tumbletots.com

Kids from crawling to pre-school can climb, jump and hang on specially designed equipment to improve their balance, coordination and general physical ability. Children aged 5–7 can explore equipment designed for adults in a supervised and safe environment at 13 locations across London.

Riding

There are dozens of stables and horseriding schools in London, some offering lessons to children as young as two and a half (who presumably have only just got the hang of walking).

Ealing Riding School

Gunnersbury Avenue, W5
t (020) 8992 3808
www.ealingridingschool.biz
⊖ Ealing Common
Bus 207, 607
Adm Private lesson per 30mins, adult £27, child £20
Age limit Five and over

Hyde Park Riding Stables

63 Bathurst Mews, W2
t (020) 7723 2813
www.hydeparkstables.com
⊖ Lancaster Gate
Bus 7, 15, 23, 27, 36
Adm Private lesson £69 per hour, group lesson £49 per hour
Age limit 5 and over

Lee Valley Riding Centre

71 Lea Bridge Road, Leyton, E10
t (020) 8556 2629
www.leevalleypark.org.uk
⇌ Clapton
Bus 48, 55, 56
Adm from £20 per hour
Age limit 5 and over

London Equestrian Centre

Lullington Garth, Finchley, N12
t (020) 8349 1345
www.londonridingschool.com

⊖ Mill Hill East
Bus 13, 82, 112, 143, 260
Adm from £25 per lesson
Age limit 4 and over

Ross Nye's Riding Stables

8 Bathurst Mews, W2
t (020) 7262 3791
⊖ Paddington
Bus 7, 15, 23, 27, 36
Adm Private lesson £60 per hour, group lesson £50 per hour
Age limit 7 and over

Trent Park Equestrian Centre

Bramley Road, Oakwood, N14
t (020) 8363 8630
www.trentpark.com
⊖ Oakwood
Adm from £20 per hour for group lessons
Age limit discretionary

Wimbledon Village Stables

24a High Street, Wimbledon, SW19

Sporting bodies

All England Netball Association
t (01462) 442 344
www.england-netball.co.uk
Amateur Rowing Association
t (020) 8237 6700
www.ara-rowing.org
Badminton England
t (01908) 286 400
www.badmintonengland.co.uk
British Baseball Federation
t (020) 7453 7055
www.baseballsoftballuk.com
British Canoe Union
t 0845 370 9500
www.bcu.org.uk
British Snow Sports
t (0131) 445 7687
www.snowsportgb.com
British Sub-Aqua Club
t (0151) 350 6200
www.bsac.com
British Swimming
t 0871 200 0929
www.britishswimming.org
British Tennis
t (020) 8487 7000

www.lta.org.uk
Croquet Association
t (01242) 242 318
www.croquet.org.uk
England Athletics
t 0870 998 6700
www.englandathletics.org
England Basketball
t (0114) 223 5695
www.englandbasketball.co.uk
English Ice Hockey Association
www.eiha.co.uk
Golf Foundation
www.golf-foundation.org
London Anglers Association
t (020) 8520 7477
www.londonanglers.net
London Gymnastics Federation
t (020) 8529 1142
www.longym.freeserve.co.uk
UK National Cyclists' Organization
t 0870 873 0060
www.ctc.org.uk
Volleyball England
t (01509) 631 699
www.volleyballengland.org

t (020) 8946 8579
www.wvstables.com
⊖ /≥ Wimbledon
Bus 93, 200, 493
Adm from £45 per hr weekdays, £50 weekends
Age limit 3 and over

Rugby

All of London's professional clubs provide coaching for both boys and girls throughout the season (roughly autumn to late spring), and several run summer camps. Professional club matches, in the Guinness Premierships and National League, are usually played on Saturday afternoons. For more information, contact the **Rugby Football Union** on **t** 0870 405 2000, **www.**rfu.com.

Harlequins

Stoop Memorial Ground, Langhorn Drive, Twickenham, Middlesex
t (020) 8410 6000
www.quins.co.uk
≥ Twickenham
Bus 267, 281
Tickets £15–30, wheelchair users **free**
Specific entrance for wheelchair users, adapted toilets

London Wasps

Adams Park, HIllbottom Road, Sands, High Wycombe
t (020) 8993 8298
www.wasps.co.uk
≥ High Wycombe, then match day shuttle bus
Tickets adult from £20.50, under-16s from £12.50

Saracens RFC

Vicarage Road Stadium, Watford
t (01923) 475 222
www.saracens.com
⊖ Watford
≥ Watford High Street, Watford Junction
Bus 298, 299, 307
Tickets Adult £15–50, child £5–10
Has an entrance for wheelchair users and a reserved section for disabled spectators.

London Irish RFC

Madejski Stadium, Junction 11, M4, Reading, RG2
t (01932) 783 034

www.london-irish.com
≥ Reading, then match day shuttle bus
Tickets adult £22–30, child £7–14
Wheelchair access, adapted toilets
Welcomes kids; girls can play up to the age of 12.

Skateboarding

Of course, for most kids, the whole point of skateboarding is not to do it in an organized way at clubs or centres, but rather as you please out on the streets (or at shopping centres or in front of the Queen Elizabeth Hall on the South Bank). But those skaters really wanting to test their skills might like to sample the half-pipes, bowls, tombstones, hips, fun boxes and grind boxes (your kids will know what they are) at the following skate parks.

Ally Pally Skatepark

Alexandra Palace, Muswell Hill, N22
⊖ Wood Green
≥ Alexandra Palace
Bus 184, W3
Open 24hrs daily
Free
The skatepark is between the ice rink and the children's playground.

Harrow Skatepark

behind Harrow Leisure Centre, Christchurch Avenue, Wealdstone, Harrow, HA3
≥/⊖ Harrow and Wealdstone
Bus H10
Open 9am till dusk daily
Free
There is an outdoor skatepark next door to Harrow Leisure Centre.

Meanwhile

Meanwhile Gardens, Great Western Road, W9
⊖ Westbourne Park
Open dawn till dusk daily
Free
Consisting of three interlinked bowls built on the site of London's very first skatepark (which opened way back in 1976).

Stockwell Bowl Skatepark

behind Brixton Academy
Stockwell Road, SW9
www.stockwellskatepark.com

Brixton
Open 24hrs daily
Free

South London's most popular skatepark, tucked behind the Brixton Academy, was first laid out in the late 70s. It is currently being redesigned and resurfaced following a poor renovation job a couple of years ago.

Skiing & snowboarding

You don't expect to come to London and go skiing, but you can if you want to. There are a surprising number of dry ski slopes in London. All have nursery slopes for beginners. Prices work out at somewhere in the region of £10–£15 for adults (for a one-hour session) and £5–£10 for children. For more information, contact the **Ski Club of Great Britain** on t (020) 8410 2000, **www**.skiclub.co.uk.

Bromley Ski Centre
Sandy Lane, St Paul's Cray, Orpington, Kent
t (01689) 876 812
www.c-v-s.co.uk/bromleyski
St Mary Kray
Bus 61, 208, R7
Open Mon–Thurs 12 noon–10pm, Fri 10am–10pm, Sat 9am–7pm, Sun 9am–8pm, closed Mon in winter

Sandown Sports Club
More Lane, Esher, Surrey
t (01372) 467 132
www.sandownsports.co.uk
Esher
Open Mon–Fri & Sun 10–10, Sat 1–8

Xscape
602 Marlborough Gate, Milton Keynes
t 0871 200 3220
www.xscape.co.uk
Milton Keynes
Open From 9am, closing times vary

Retail and leisure centre with shops, a cinema, a bowling alley, indoor climbing walls and a fitness club. The real treat here, however, is the Snozone, the country's largest 'real' snow slope. You'll find none of that funny dry netting stuff here; Snozone uses snow-cannons and keeps the temperature at a constantly chilly -2°C, making it suitable for proper skiing and snowboarding. Lessons are offered. All equipment can be hired on site.

Sports centres

There are nigh on 200 sports centres in London, offering a huge range of activities from badminton to martial arts. Many have swimming pools and most have special facilities for young children. Some of the best are listed below.

Britannia Leisure Centre
40 Hyde Road, Islington, N1
t (020) 7729 4485
www.gll.org/centre/britannia-leisure-centre.asp
Old Street
Bus 67, 76, 141, 149, 242, 243, 243A, 271

Offers football, tennis, a well-equipped gym, a climbing wall, basketball, swimming (including lessons), snorkelling and water polo.

Brixton Recreation Centre
27 Brixton Station Road, SW9
t (020) 7926 9779
www.gll.org/centre/brixton-recreation-centre.asp
Brixton
Bus 118, 196, 250, P4

Activities catered for at this revamped centre include badminton, basketball, gymnastics, swimming, tennis, trampolining. It also organizes holiday play schemes for 5–15-year-olds involving sports sessions in football, gymnastics and basketball, as well as arts and crafts workshops.

Crystal Palace
National Sports Centre, Ledrington Road, Upper Norwood, SE19
t (020) 8778 0131
www.gll.org/centre/crystal-palace-national-sports-centre.asp
Crystal Palace
Bus 2, 3, 63, 122, 137a, 157, 202, 227, 249, 342, 358, 361, 450

The home of British athletics (until the new Olympic Stadium opens in 2012, at least), this internationally renowned sports centre has an athletics stadium, an Olympic-sized pool and high-diving board as well as excellent facilities for badminton, basketball, gymnastics, hockey and martial arts. It stages numerous international sporting competitions and offers teaching and coaching to a high standard. Would-be athletes can apply to attend one of the centre's annual summer camps.

Michael Sobell Leisure Centre

Hornsey Road, Holloway, N7
t (020) 7609 2166
www.aquaterra.org/islington/Sobell/
⇌ Finsbury Park, Holloway Road
Bus 91

A multi-purpose centre offering badminton, basketball, cricket, football, martial arts, squash, table tennis, trampolining and ice-skating.

Oasis Sports Centre

32 Endell Street, WC2
t (020) 7831 1804
www.gll.org/centre/oasis-sports-centre.asp
⊖ Holborn, Covent Garden
Bus 1, 14, 19, 24, 29, 38, 176

Offering facilities for badminton, football, martial arts, swimming, table tennis and trampolining, Oasis also boasts London's only heated outdoor pool as well as a paddling pool for toddlers.

Queen Mother's Sports Centre

223 Vauxhall Bridge Road, SW1
t (020) 7630 5522
www.westminster.gov.uk/leisureandculture/
sports/queenmother.cfm
⊖ /⇌ Victoria, ⊖ Pimlico
Bus 2, 36, 185

Badminton, football, martial arts, netball, rounders, swimming.

Swimming

Children just love messing about in water. Whether it's tropically heated pools for the under-5s or all-weather lidos, there's something deeply appealing about a good splish-splash. Most indoor pools run mother-and-toddler sessions. Expect to pay around £3–5 for an adult, £2–3 for a child.

Indoor pools

Britannia Leisure Centre

40 Hyde Road, N1
t (020) 7729 4485

www.gll.org/centre/britannia-leisure-centre.asp
⊖ Old Street
Bus 67, 76, 141, 149, 242, 243, 243A, 271
Open Mon–Fri 9–9, Sat & Sun 9–6

Water slides, wave machine, pool inflatables and lessons for kids.

Crystal Palace Pool

National Sports Centre, Ledrington Road, Norwood, SE19
t (020) 8778 0131
www.gll.org/centre/crystal-palace-national-sports-centre.asp
⇌ Crystal Palace
Bus 2, 3, 63, 122, 137a, 157, 202, 227, 249, 342, 358, 361, 450
Open Mon–Fri 9am–9pm, Sat–Sun 9–6

Huge pool complex with an Olympic-size (50-m) pool, a 25-m training pool, a 20m diving pool (with high-diving boards) and an 18-m teaching pool.

Fulham Pools

Normand Park, Lillie Road, SW6
t (020) 7471 0450
⊖ West Brompton
Bus 74, 190
Open Mon–Thurs 6.30am–10.30pm, Fri 6.30am–9.30pm, Sat–Sun 8am–9pm

Recently refurbished, this now offers three pools, a water slide, water toys, a wave machine and a swimming 'fun club' for kids.

Kingfisher Leisure Centre

Fairfield Road, Kingston, Surrey KT1
t (020) 8546 1042
www.gll.org/centre/crystal-palace-national-sports-centre.asp
⇌ Kingston
Bus 57, 71, 111, 131, 285
Open Mon–Thur 6.15am–10pm, Fri 6.15pm–9pm, Sat–Sun 7am–8pm

Very family-friendly with a separate teaching pool and a wave machine.

Latchmere Leisure Centre

Burns Road, SW11
t (020) 7207 8004
www.kinetika.org
⊖ Clapham Junction, Battersea Park
Bus 44, 49, 319, 344, 345
Open Mon–Thurs 7am–9.30pm, Fri–Sat 7am–7pm, Sun 7–6

Child-friendly indoor pool which includes a seashore slope, wave machine and toddler's pool.

Outdoor pools

On bright summer days, and even late into the evenings, London's outdoor pools can be delightful. Parents can escape the bustle, lazing by the poolside as their children go berserk in the water while the sun beats down overhead. Prices are roughly the same as for indoor pools.

Brockwell Lido
Brockwell Park, Dulwich Road, SE24
t (020) 7274 3088
www.brockwelllido.com
⊖ Brixton
⇌ Herne Hill
Bus 3, 37, 196
Open May–Sept Mon–Fri 6.45am–8pm, Sat–Sun 10–6

Finchley Lido
Great North Leisure Park, High Road, N12
t (020) 8343 9830
⊖ Finchley Central
Bus 263
Open May–Sept 10–7 daily

Oasis Sports Centre
Endell Street, WC2
t (020) 7931 1804
⊖ Covent Garden, Holborn
Bus 1, 14, 19, 24, 29, 38, 176
Open Mon–Fri 7.30am–8pm, Sat–Sun 9.30–5pm

Parliament Hill Lido
Parliament Hill, Hampstead Heath (off Gordon House Road), NW5
t (020) 7485 4491
⊖ ⇌ Gospel Oak
Bus 214, C2, C11
Open May–Sept daily 7–9am, 10–6, 6.45–9 (Mon & Thurs only); Oct–April 7am–12 noon

Tooting Bec Lido
Tooting Bec Road, SW16
t (020) 8871 7198
⊖ Tooting Bec
Bus 249, 319
Open May–Sept 10–8, daily

Tennis

If you and your children don't fancy overcoming the obstacles inherent to the Wimbledon experience (see box, p.188), but just want to see some grass court tennis and spot a few famous players (so long as they're male), you might like to visit the Queen's Club's 'Stella Artois' Tournament which takes place a couple of weeks before. The atmosphere is more relaxed and tickets more available (and cheaper, £15–20). If your family fancies a game, many public parks have a couple of concrete courts and there are a few tennis clubs in London offering training for children aged 7 and over. Expect to pay about £5–6 an hour for an outdoor court, £12–£15 inside.

Wimbledon (All England Lawn Tennis and Croquet Club)
Church Road, Wimbledon, SW19
t (020) 8944 1066
www.wimbledon.org
⊖ Southfields, Wimbledon
⇌ Wimbledon
Bus 39, 93 or shuttle bus from Southfields or Wimbledon stations

Queen's Club
Palliser Road, W14
t (020) 7385 3421
www.queensclub.co.uk
⊖ Barons Court
Bus 28, 74, 190, 211, 220, 295, 391

Islington Indoor Tennis Centre
Market Road, N7
t (020) 7700 1370
www.aquaterra.org/islington/ITC
⊖ Caledonian Road
Bus 73, 274

Regent's Park Tennis Centre
York Bridge Road, NW1
t (020) 7262 3474
www.tennisintheparks.co.uk
⊖ Regent's Park
Bus 274

Westway Indoor Tennis Centre
1 Crowthorne Road, W10
t (020) 8969 0992
www.westway.totaltennis.net
⊖ Latimer Road
Bus 295

New balls please

Despite playing host to Wimbledon, the game's premier tournament, Britain's attitude towards tennis is, in truth, rather ambivalent. It has significantly fewer public courts than most other countries and, as a result, significantly fewer top-class players. The last home-grown winner of Wimbledon was Fred Perry (he of the sports shirts) in the late 1930s. Following the retirement of Tim Henman (who managed to reach the Wimbledon semi finals on four occasions), Britain has only one player, Andy Murray, ranked in the top 100 in the world. But then, for most of the year, the British public couldn't care less about tennis. During the last two weeks of June, however, it suddenly becomes everyone's favourite sport. Demand for Wimbledon tickets is huge, to put it mildly. In order to buy Centre Court or No.1 Court tickets, where all the big-name matches take place, you have to enter a ballot the previous September, and even then your chances of success are pretty remote. Alternatively, you could try turning up on a match day and queueing. The queue usually starts several days prior to the championship and can stretch for over a mile. Getting tickets for Wimbledon is not impossible, but it is very difficult – and even if you do get lucky, they're not cheap. Centre Court tickets start at £38 for the first Monday rising to £91 for the final Sunday. Outside court tickets are much better value, starting at £20 for the first Monday (£14 after 5pm) and dropping to £8 for the final weekend (£5 after 5pm), when fewer matches are scheduled. They also give you the chance to buy resale tickets for the show courts which go on sale daily at 2pm.

Watersports

Most of the centres listed run courses in sailing, windsurfing, canoeing and rowing – children must be able to swim, usually 50 metres, and there are generally age restrictions. For sailing activities on the Thames try the **Thames Sailing Barge Trust** on **t** (020) 8948 0428, **www**.bargetrust.org; the **Thames Sailing Club** on **t** (020) 8399 2164, **www**.thamessailingclub.org.uk; or the **Amateur Rowing Association**, **t** (020) 8237 6700 **www**.ara-rowing.org

Docklands Sailing and Watersports Centre

Millwall Dock, West Ferry Road, E14
t (020) 7537 2626
www.dswc.org
DLR Cross Harbour
Bus 77, D3

Canoeing, windsurfing and sailing sessions are available for ages 8 and over. Kids can also try dragon-boat racing and imagine being Vikings.

Islington Boat Club

16–34 Graham Street, N1
t (020) 7253 0778
www.islington-boatclub.org.uk
✪ Angel
Bus 43, 214
Children must be 9 or over

London Corinthian Sailing Club

Linden House, Upper Mall, W6
t (020) 8748 3280
www.lcsc.org.uk
✪ Hammersmith
Bus 9, 10, 27

Royal Victoria Dock Watersports Centre

Gate 5, Tidal Basin Road, off Silvertown Way, E16
t (020) 7511 2342
www.royaldockstrust.org.uk
DLR Royal Victoria

Surrey Docks Watersports Centre

Greenland Dock, Rope Street, SE16
t (020) 7237 4009
✪ Surrey Quays

Westminster Boating Base

Dinorvic Wharf, 136 Grosvenor Road, SW1
t (020) 7821 7389
www.westminsterboatingbase.co.uk
✪ Pimlico
Bus 24, C10

Days out

15

Brighton

Getting there By road: The A23 links Brighton directly with London. Alternatively, take the M23 part of the way, rejoin the A23, then follow the signs. The journey should take a little over an hour.
By rail: A regular train service runs from London Victoria (over 30 departures a day), the journey takes about 50mins. Trains also run from London Bridge, Clapham Junction and King's Cross.
By coach: National Express coaches and Southdown bus services arrive at Pool Valley bus station on Old Steine, not far from the seafront.
If your kids are aged 5 or over, it's a good idea to go by train. The seafront is an easy 10-minute down-hill walk from the station, giving your kids plenty of time to get excited about seeing the sea.
Tourist office 10 Bartholomew Square, **t** 09067 112255, **t** 09061 401506 (for children's events and activities). For a free accommodation brochure and a pocket-sized guide to Brighton and Hove, **email** brighton-tourism@brighton-hove.gov.uk or visit **www**.visitbrighton.com

Britain's seaside resorts tend to have similar characteristics. They are cheery and cosy and a bit old-fashioned. But Brighton is different. It's loud and determinedly modern, and remains so all year. It manages to be both fashionable, with its clubs and designer stores, and yet very family-orientated, with lots of child-friendly attractions. There's the pier with its funfair, arcades and endless supply of giant teddy bears; the Marina, with its arcades and bowling alleys; and, last but not least, the beach itself. Brighton boasts a mighty eight miles of seafront, made up of pebbles rather than sand, so bring your sturdiest sandals. There are good play facilities along the beachfront, which are accessed via decking walkways, including an invitingly sandy volleyball pitch, a basketball court and, further up near the ruined West Pier, an excellent children's play area, complete with children's toilets and baby-changing facilities. Here you'll find a large play pool, brightly coloured lookout posts with turrets and binoculars, a sand and water table and lots of space for picnicking families.

Brighton Museum

Royal Pavilion Gardens, **t** (01273) 292 820
www.brighton.virtualmuseum.info
Open Tues 10–7, Wed–Sat 10–5, Sun 2–5, Mon open on bank holidays only

Free
Gift shop, café, wheelchair accessible, monthly events for toddlers, families and ages 8 and over

Accessed via the Pavilion Gardens, this is a fun little museum with a spacious, light interior. The archaeology galleries and local studies centre complement the displays of art, photography and interior design, although families will mostly enjoy the masks and the costume galleries, where children can gawp at the PVC-clad Goths, gasp at the vast girth of George IV's trousers or try on an Edwardian costume. Downstairs there's an art room where kids can experience different colours in the spectrum through reading, drawing, colouring and making structures, as well as writing their impressions of the works of art they have seen.

Booth Museum of Natural History

194 Dyke Road, **t** (01273) 292 777
www.booth.virtualmuseum.info
Open Mon–Wed and Fri–Sat 10–5, Sun 2–5
Free
Gift shop, mother-and-baby room, guided tours, wheelchair accessible

Based on the collection of the Victorian naturalist and Brighton resident, Edward Thomas Booth, this holds a fascinating display of insects, butterflies, fossils and animal skeletons. Kids can get up close to all manner of specimens in the new hands-on Discovery Lab and special events are organized during the school holidays.

Brighton Palace Pier

Off Madeira Drive **t** (01273) 609 361
www.brightonpier.co.uk
Open Mon–Fri 10am–8pm, Sat–Sun 10am–10pm
Adm Free (rides are individually charged)
Three bars, various fast-food outlets, wheelchair access, disabled toilets

After the beach, this should probably be your first port of call. Vaguely reminiscent of an ocean liner on stilts, this beautiful snow-white pier stretches a mighty 1,722 feet out to sea and is lined with snack bars, stalls and child-friendly attractions. About halfway down, you'll find an amusement arcade full of all the latest video machines, plus all those strange games you only seem to get at seasides, offering you the chance to win a soft toy by manouevering a mechanical claw, or to add to a collection of 10ps perched on the edge of a moving ledge (which never seem to fall off despite the apparent precariousness of their position). The real action, however, is at the end of the pier where there are several gentle carousel-type rides, a couple of rather more intense rollercoasters, including the 'Crazy Mouse', and for those who really don't scare easily, the 'Super Booster', which look a bit like a long metal pole attached to a giant bread tin (this is the bit you sit in) which lifts you 125ft over the sea before spinning you round and round at speeds of up to 60mph.

Brighton Toy and Model Musuem
52/55 Trafalgar Street (under the railway station), **t** (01273) 749494
www.brightontoymuseum.co.uk
Open Tue–Fri 10am–5pm, Sat 11am–5pm(last admission 4pm) **Adm** Adults £3.50, children (4–14)£2.50, family (2+2) £10
Gift shop, wheelchair access
Located in the arches of the Brighton Railway Station is this superb collection of over 10,000 exhibits made up of doll's houses, puppets, toy theatres, tin cars and rare model trains (including a model railway featuring the surrounding Sussex countryside). The attached shop has a nice range of souvenirs, vintage toys and games.

Royal Pavilion
North Street, **t** (01273) 290900
www.royalpavilion.org.uk
Open Oct–Mar 10–5.15; Apr–Sept 9.30–5.45
Adm Adults £7.50, children (under 16) £5, family £19 (2+4), £11.50 (1+2)
Wheelchair access, adapted toilets. Queen Adelaide Tearoom, gift shop, children's quiz sheets, mother and baby room, guided tours (at extra cost), free audio guides available
The Pavilion is, without a doubt, Britain's most over-the-top Royal Palace. Designed by John Nash in the 1810s for the Prince Regent, it's a mishmash of Indian-style exterior and Chinese-style interior. Kids usually respond favourably to its fairytale-like exuberance.

Brighton Marina
t 01273 818 504
www.brightonmarina.co.uk
Open 10–6, daily
Quite a way east of the town centre, the Marina is still well worth a visit. It's a nice place to eat, shop and even stay at the stylish Alias Hotel Seattle,

t (01273) 679 799, **www**.aliashotels.com. There's also a leisure centre and a large entertainment complex with a cinema, an arcade, 10-pin bowling and pool. Boat cruises around the harbour, to the pier and out to sea are also offered. You can reach the Marina on the Volk's Railway, Britain's oldest electric railway, built in 1883.

Where to Eat
Alfresco
The Milkmaid Pavilion, King's Road Arches
t (01273) 206 523
www.alfresco-brighton.co.uk
Open 12 noon–10.30, daily
Pleasant, friendly Italian restaurant overlooking the seafront and the kids' playground with an outdoor seating area. Although it doesn't have a children's menu, it is popular with families, especially in summer when it can get very full. Highchairs available.
Brown's
3–4 Duke Street, **t** (01273) 323501
www.browns-restaurants.com
Open Mon–Sat 11am–11.30pm, Sun 12 noon–11pm
High-quality family restaurant near the Lanes. There's a separate children's menu (which includes free ice cream) and highchairs are provided.
English's
29–31 East Street, **t** (01273) 327 980
www.englishs.co.uk
Open Mon–Sat 12 noon–10.30, Sun 12.30–9.30
Seafood restaurant and oyster bar offering lots of choice for kids with adventurous culinary tastes, something other than cod and chips. There are six dining rooms and outdoor seating is available in summer overlooking the busy square frequented by shoppers, buskers and itinerant hair-braiders.
Harry Ramsden's
1–4 Marine Parade, **t** (01273) 690 691
www.harryramsdens.co.uk
Open Mon–Thurs 12 noon–9.30, Fri–Sat 12 noon–10, Sun 12 noon–9
This branch of the famous northern fish-and-chip chain is situated opposite the entrance to the pier and Sea Life Centre and can seat over a hundred people. The children's menu, featuring the cartoon characters 'The Diddlys', which includes soft drink and dessert. Highchairs available. Eat in or takeaway.

Momma Cherri's Soul Food Shack

11 Little East Street, **t** (01273) 774 545; also at 2–3
Little East Street, **t** (01273) 325 305
www.mommacherri.co.uk
Open Mon 5pm–10pm, Tues–Thur 12–2 and 5–11, Fri
12–2 and 5–12, Sat 11am–12 midnight, Sun 11–9

If you find yourself absolutely ravenous after
trekking around Brighton's attractions then you
could do a lot worse than a heaped plate of
momma's 'soul food'. Burgers, buffalo hot wings,
jerk chicken, gumbo, jambalaya and breakfasts
(complete with grits) are all on offer in this
friendly and popular restaurant. Children's
menus available.

The Regency Restaurant

131 King's Road, **t** (01273) 325 014
www.theregencyrestaurant.co.uk
Open 8am–11pm, daily

Traditional seafront fish restaurant with tables
on the pavement shaded by coloured umbrellas
and a range of locally caught fresh fish and
seafood dishes on the menu, plus some tempting
puds. Children's menu and highchairs available.

Cambridge

Getting there By air: Stansted airport is about
30 miles south of Cambridge and is linked to the
city by a regular bus service (and the M11).
By road: Cambridge is 55 miles north of London
and can be reached by the M11 from the south and
A14 from the north. Driving into Cambridge city
centre, which is largely pedestrianized, isn't really
an option. Thankfully there's an excellent 'park and
ride' scheme in operation. There are five such car
parks on the outskirts of Cambridge: Cowley
Road/A1309 to the north, Newmarket Road/A1303
to the east, Madingley Road/A1303 to the west,
and both Babraham Road/A1307 and Trumpington
Road/A1134 to the south of the city. Parking is free,
buses leave for the centre every 10 minutes
(7am–8pm). An Adult Day Return is £1.80, with up
to three children under 16 travelling free per paying
adult. For details contact Cambridgeshire County
Council, **t** (01223) 718 167.
By train: there are frequent services to London King's
Cross (50mins) and London Liverpool Street (1hr
10mins). Cambridge station is a mile and a half south

of the centre, but served by a regular bus service.
By coach: there is an hourly National Express
coach service from London Victoria coach station.
Tourist office The Old Library, Wheeler Street,
t 0870 856 2526. Extensive tourist information,
including accommodation and other bookings
available at **www.**visitcambridge.org
The centre has a souvenir shop and has details of
guided walking tours led from here by Blue Badge
Guides throughout the year (dramatic tours with
costumed characters take place in summer)

Cambridge, like its rival Oxford, is principally famous
for its university, one of the oldest and most respected
in the world. Like Oxford, it is a very beautiful
city with some of the country's most impressive
architecture, several delightful parks and the River
Cam, which flows to the north and west of the city.

Being smaller and more concentrated than Oxford,
it's a great place for pottering, be it on foot, by bike
or on the river. The centre of town, where you'll find
most of the colleges and university buildings, is
largely pedestrianized. The two main thoroughfares, Bridge Street (which turns into Sidney Street,
St Andrew's Street and Regent Street) and St John's
Street (which becomes Trinity Street, King's Parade
and Trumpington Street) are lined with shops,
tearooms and bookstores – look out for Galloway
and Porter booksellers, 30 Sidney Street, **t** (01223)
367 876, **www.**gallowayandporter. co.uk, who hold
a monthly warehouse book sale, with a wide range
of quality children's titles at bargain prices.

Cambridge and County Folk Museum

2–3 Castle Street, **t** (01223) 355 159
Open Apr–Sep Mon–Sat 10.30–5, Sun 2–5, Oct–Mar
Tues–Sat 10.30–5, Sun 2–5
Adm Adults £3, child £1 (one free child with every
full paying adult), under-5s **free.**
Gift shop, guided tours

Housed in a 16th-century, half-timbered farm-
house, this looks at the non-academic side of life in
Cambridge, with displays on the people who have
lived and worked in this area for the last 400 years.
Activity days for children aged 6–10 are organized
on some Saturday afternoons, and workshops for
7–11-year-olds are held during the school holidays.

Cambridge Museum of Technology

The Old Pumping Station, Cheddars Lane,
t (01223) 368650
www.museumoftechnology.com

Open Easter–Oct Sun 2–5; Nov–Easter first Sun of every month 2–5
Adm Steaming Days £5, otherwise £3, under-7s **free**
Shop, wheelchair accessible, call the museum for dates of 'Steaming Days' and other special events

Housed in a preserved Victorian pumping station, this is filled with the noisy contraptions of the industrial age: boilers, engines and several 'hands-on' pumps, a printing room (where you can print your own souvenirs), a collection of early Cambridge wireless instruments and other local artefacts.

Fitzwilliam Museum

Trumpington Street, **t** (01223) 332 900
www.fitzmuseum.cam.ac.uk
Open Tues–Sat 10–5, Sun 12 noon–5
Free
Café, gift shop, guided tours, mother-and-baby facilities, limited wheelchair access. Not suitable for pushchairs, although baby slings/harnesses available

The city's most respected museum will certainly be of interest, although you may want to skip the cases of European porcelain, Chinese vases and Korean ceramics and head straight to the mummies in the revamped Virtual Egypt Gallery, the painted coffins in the Antiquities Gallery, or the armour and weapons in the Applied Arts section. Family activity sheets are available.

Museum of Archaeology and Anthropology

Downing Street, **t** (01223) 333 516
http://museum.archanth.cam.ac.uk/
Open Tues–Sat 10.30–4.30
Free

The ground-floor 'Rise of Civilization' Gallery, full of ancient pots and bits of flint, is only worth a cursory inspection. Instead, make a beeline for the ethnographic collection on the first floor, a wonderful array of treasures brought back by 18th- and 19th-century explorers: native American feathered headdresses, Eskimo canoes and parkas (made from dried walrus hide), scary African tribal masks and suits of Japanese ceremonial armour, all arranged around a 50-ft-high totem pole. Drop-in arts-and-crafts workshops are arranged for families throughout the year.

Sedgwick Museum of Earth Sciences

Downing Street, **t** (01223) 333 456

www.sedgwickmuseum.org
Open Mon–Fri 9–1 and 2–5, Sat 10–4
Free (Discretionary donation encouraged)
Shop, some wheelchair access/assistance available

Houses the oldest geological collection in the world (although, in geological terms, this is a pretty slight claim) with various multi-million-year-old rocks and minerals displayed in antique walnut cases. It also has a large collection of fossil dinosaurs.

University Botanic Garden

Cory Lodge, Bateman Street
t (01223) 336 265, www.botanic.cam.ac.uk
Open Jan, Nov, Dec 10–4; Feb, Mar, Oct 10–5; Apr–Sept 10–6
Adm Adult £3, child (up to 17) **free**.
Café-restaurant (summer only), picnic areas, gift shop, mother-and-baby facilities, guided tours by arrangement, disabled access

The 40-acre University Botanic Garden, just south of Cambridge's centre, founded in 1762, is the city's most beautiful open space. If you're after a spot where kids can enjoy more uninhibited play, try Jesus Green, to the north of the city centre near the river, a large, open grassy space with a children's play area and an open-air swimming pool in summer. Otherwise, just to the west, you'll find Midsummer Common, a huge riverside meadow that plays host to fairs and circuses in summer and a large firework display on 5 November.

Scott Polar Research Institute Museum

Lensfield Road, **t** (01223) 336 555
www.spri.cam.ac.uk/museum
Open Tues–Sat 2.30–4 (except public hols)
Free
Shop, selling relevant children's books on exploration and polar wildlife

This museum of polar life and exploration features original artefacts from Scott's expedition.

Punting

The archetypal Cambridge pursuit can be enjoyed every day between Easter and October. Punts can be hired from Magdalene Bridge, Mill Lane, Garret Hostel Lane, the Granta Pub on Newnham Road and the Rat and Parrot pub near Magdalene Bridge. A deposit of around £25 is usually required, while the punts themselves will cost something in the region of £6–£8 per hour. Chauffeured punt trips are also available.

You'll be shown how to use the pole before you set off, but do be aware that it can be a pretty wet and soggy experience, especially during the learning process. However, the Backs do provide an idyllic space in which to dry off and have a picnic while you refine your technique – just remember to stick to the left.

Where to Eat

Cambridge Tea Room

1 Wheeler Street, **t** (01223) 357 503
Open 10–6, daily

Opposite the tourist information centre, this tearoom serves good cream teas and sandwiches.

Copper Kettle

King's Parade, **t** (01223) 365 068
Open Mon–Sat 8.30–5.30, Sun 9–5.30

Rather more welcoming following a recent revamp, this Cambridge institution overlooking the glorious vista of King's College has played host to generations of undergraduates who come to discuss the meaning of life over coffee and a Chelsea bun. No credit cards.

Don Pasquale

12 Market Hill, **t** (01223) 367 063
www.donpasquale.co.uk
Open Mon–Thurs 8–6, Fri–Sat 8am–9.30pm, Sun 9–6

With seating on the market square and a plentiful supply of highchairs, this is a fun place to eat pizza and watch the world go by.

Rainbow Café

9a Kings Parade **t** (01223) 321 551
www.rainbowcafe.co.uk
Open Tues–Sat 10–9.30

Popular and cheerful vegetaran restaurant with a large menu including several vegan, nut-free and gluten-free dishes. All meals are available as half portions for children under 12. Jars of organic baby food are provided free for very young diners.

Orchard Tea Garden and Restaurant

Mill Way, Grantchester, **t** (01223) 845 788
Getting there By road or by punt on the River Cam

Lounge in deckchairs under the trees and enjoy a delicious cream tea. You may even spot someone famous; in the 100 years since Rupert Brooke stayed at the orchard, some of the greatest poets, writers, philosophers and scientists have sipped tea here.

Oxford

Getting there By road: Oxford is about 48 miles from London and can be reached via the M40. Oxford's efficient 'park and ride' scheme operates daily (Mon–Sat 5.30am–11.30pm, restricted service on Suns and from Water Eaton) from five sites: Pear Tree and Water Eaton to the north, A44/A40/M40/M6/M1 and A4260; Thornhill to the east, M40/M25; Seacourt to the west/A420 and Redbridge to the south/A34. Journey times are between 8 and 20mins. **By train**: Services arrive frequently from London Paddington. **By bus/coach**: the Oxford Tube (**www.**oxfordtube.com) and Oxford Express (**www.**oxfordbus.co.uk/express1.shtml) both run every 12–15 mins to and from London Victoria (with stops and pick-ups along the way). The National Express coach (**www.** nationalexpress.com) takes longer and is not so frequent. The Airline (**t** 01865 785 400, **www.** theairline.info) operates coach services between Heathrow (every 20mins) and Gatwick (hourly) to Oxford, day and night.
Tourist information 15–16 Broad Street, **t** (01865) 726 871, **www.**oxford.gov.uk/tourism

Oxford, of course, is more than just a pretty town for tourists; it's a world-famous centre of culture and learning. Home to one of the country's two most prestigious universities, Oxford has, ever since its foundation in the 13th century, been preparing the great and the good for roles in public life. Tony Blair, Bill Clinton, Margaret Thatcher and even Henry VIII all studied at the university, although the term 'university' is slightly misleading – Oxford actually contains several independently operated colleges which together form the university and define the shape of the city. Most of the colleges are open to the public although, to preserve the academic ambience, many operate restricted opening times and charge hefty admission fees. Best for family visits is Christ Church college with its grand dining hall, where Charles I held his parliament, Lewis Carroll ate 8,000 meals and Harry Potter sat beneath the sorting hat awaiting his fate.

If you plan your itinerary carefully, you'll find lots to occupy your days. Oxford boasts a good many child-friendly attractions including parks, interactive museums, punts and lots of good spots providing panoramic views of the 'dreaming spires' and surrounding countryside.

Christ Church

St Aldate's, **t** (01865) 276 150
www.chch.ox.ac.uk
Open Mon–Sat 9–5, Sun 1–5
Adm Adult £4.50, child £3.50
The visitor entrance is at Meadow Gate

A great place for Harry Potter fans; tell the kids that the steps up into the dining hall were where Professor McGonagal greeted the new pupils in *Harry Potter and the Philospher's Stone*. The dining hall is also Hogwarts Hall, though somewhat modified by the CGI wizards at Warner Bros in order to seat all four of the school's houses.

Hands On

Science Oxford, 1–5 London Place, **t** (01865) 728 953
www.oxtrust.org.uk/handson
Open Sat, Sun and school hols 10–4
Adm Adult £5, child £2.20, family £8.80

Hands-on science gallery for children full of interactive games and experiments.

Museum of the History of Science

Old Ashmolean Building, Broad Street
t (01865) 277 280, **www.mhs.ox.ac.uk**
Open Tues–Sat 12 noon–4, Sun 2–5
Free

The museum contains displays of scientific instruments, such as sundials, quadrants, microscopes, telescopes and cameras, dating back to the 16th century (look out for Einstein's blackboard). There's an education room and library.

Pitt Rivers Museum

Parks Road, **t** (01865) 270 927
www.prm.ox.ac.uk
Open Tues–Sat 10–4.30, Sun 12 noon–4.30
Free

This elegant Victorian building houses a large ethnographic collection featuring numerous artefacts brought back by Captain Cook from his 18th-century journeys of discovery – a witch in a bottle, a puffer-fish lantern, shrunken heads, samurai swords and totem poles are just some of the gruesome horrors bound to attract the children.

Kids can take part in informal Family Friendly Fun sessions every Sunday from 2–4, using backpacks, sorting boxes, quizzes and activity trolleys. Pitt Stops are activity sessions that take place on the first Saturday of every month from 1–4. Sessions begin with a short talk and previous topics include body decoration, puppetry and weapons and

armour. Kids can also follow family trails in search of dragons, hats, masks, witches and more. A new extension to the museum, housing exhibition galleries, seminar rooms and lecture halls is due to open in late 2007.

Museum of Oxford

St Aldates, **t** (01865) 252 761
www.museumofoxford.org.uk
Open Tues–Fri 10–5, Sat–Sun 12 noon–5
Adm Adults £2, children 50p, family £4
Gift shop, toilets in the town hall, no disabled access, children's trails and school holiday activities

Exhibits range from a mammoth's tooth to Roman and medieval artefacts and a series of evocative room settings, which include an Elizabethan Inn, an 18th-century college room, a Victorian kitchen on washday and a 1930s living room. Activities for children are laid on throughout the year, focusing on all aspects of the city's history, from handling sessions of Anglo Saxon relics to talks about life in World War II.

The Oxford Story

6 Broad Street, **t** (01865) 728 822
www.oxfordstory.co.uk
Open Jan–Jun and Sept–Dec Mon–Sat 10–4.30, Sun 11–4; Jul–Aug daily 9.30–5
Adm Adults £7.25, children £5.25
Gift shop, disabled access

A bizarre and not wholly comfortable experience, as an electric cart winches you up a steep incline past three floors of tableaux depicting scenes from the city's long history – student riots, scientific breakthroughs, etc. – with accompanying sound and lighting effects. It stresses the academic side of things quite strongly, so may not suit very young children, but it's done in an entertaining way. There's a children's commentary and special events are held during the school holidays.

University Museum of Natural History

Parks Road, **t** (01865) 272 950
www.oum.ox.ac.uk
Open 12 noon–5, daily (not Easter and Christmas)
Free
Picnic area, some disabled access, children's page on website

Check out the dinosaur galleries, gemstones, extinct species, including the Dodo, and the working beehive (summer only).

The Botanic Gardens

Rose Lane, **t** (01865) 286 690
www.botanic-garden.ox.ac.uk
Open Mar–Apr & Sep–Oct 9–5, May–Aug 9–6,
Nov–Feb 9–4
Adm Adult £2, under-12s **free** (**free** to all in winter)
Created in 1621, this is the oldest botanic garden
in Britain. You can wander through nine small
glasshouses, filled with tropical and subtropical
plants. From the gardens you can follow the course
of the river, though the turnstiles at either end may
prove challenging with a pushchair. About halfway
along the route and to the left, there's a wooden
bridge that leads to the college boathouses – if
you're lucky you might encounter a training
session or even a race.

Port Meadow

Access via Walton Well Road and Thames Towpath
Open Any reasonable time, it is common land
Free
This huge water meadow is the largest green
space in Oxford. You can see horses, cows and
geese roaming freely.

University Parks

South Parks Road
Open 8am–dusk, daily
Free
Seventy acres of parkland on the west bank of
the River Cherwell with gardens, trees, riverside
walks and a duck pond.

River trips

Punting, the practice of pushing yourself along
the river in a flat-bottomed boat using a long
wooden pole, is particularly associated with
England's two great university towns. The image
of young men in flannels and straw hats mucking
about in boats on hot summer days is, for some,
as typically English as tea shops and cricket on
the village green. It's great fun, if a little tricky
(young children probably won't be able to handle
the heavy pole), but, once mastered, provides a
good way of seeing the local countryside. Punts
and rowing boats, for trips on the River Cherwell
down past the Botanic Gardens and Christchurch
Meadow, are available for hire from Magdalen
Bridge, Folly Bridge and the Cherwell Boathouse.
Sightseeing trips to Iffley, Sandford Lock and
Abingdon are also offered from Folly Bridge by
Salter Brothers, **t** (01865) 243 421,
www.salterbros.co.uk.

Where to Eat

Bangkok House

42a Hythe Bridge Stree, **t** (01865) 200 705
Open 12–3 and 6–11, daily, booking advised
The best prawn soup in town and the most
beautiful tables to eat it at. Kids will love gazing at
the intricate wooden carvings and trying out
milder dishes while their parents feast on delicious
Thai food. Close to the station; high chairs
available.

Donnington Doorstep Family Centre

Townsend Square, **t** (01865) 727 721
Open Mon–Fri 10–4
Good for a snack or a simple lunch, this drop-in
centre has nappy-changing facilities, highchairs
and activities and toys for children.

Gee's Restaurant

61a Banbury Road, **t** (01865) 553 540
www.gees-restaurant.co.uk
Open 12–2.30 (3.30 Sun), 6–10.30, daily
This bright Victorian conservatory offers plenty
of space for families to spread out over lunch. Kids
can choose from simple dishes such as spaghetti
or chicken and chips. Highchairs available.

The Isis Tavern

On the towpath between Donnington Bridge and
Iffley Lock
t (01865) 247 006
Open 11–11 (children till 7), daily
Good pub food and a garden with swings.

Windsor

Getting there By road: Windsor is 20 miles west of
London, off the M4 exit 6 and 50 miles northeast
of Southampton, off the M3 exit 3. A 'park and ride'
service runs between Windsor town centre and
Legoland operating at least every 30mins daily
from 10.15–6.45 (8.30 during peak season)
Additional 'park and ride' is available from Home
Park car park on the Datchet Road (B470) to
Windsor town centre Mon–Fri 7am–7pm.
By train: there are regular services to Windsor
and Eton Riverside from Waterloo.
By bus/coach: Services leave the Greenline coach
stop on Buckingham Palace Road at regular
intervals throughout the day, **t** 0870 608 7261

Tourist office Royal Windsor Information Centre, 24 High Street, **t** (01753) 743 900 **www**.windsor.gov.uk Above the centre itself is a small exhibition on the history of the town.

Dominated by the glorious 900-year-old castle, Windsor is a picturesque town with narrow cobbled streets. Visit on a fine summer weekend and it can be overwhelming, but on a midweek morning things are less frenetic. Windsor is really a three-site town: the castle (the official residence of the Queen); Eton, the public school (where princes William and Harry went to school); and finally (and no doubt your kids will remind you, the *real* reason you came) Legoland (*see* p. 202), one of the country's best theme parks, full of rides, games, models, activity centres, roller coasters and, no matter when you visit, hordes of fun-seeking kids.

Eton is open to visitors all year round. You can tour the grounds and see the oldest classroom in the world, its ancient desks scored with generations of schoolboy graffiti. If you come in termtime you can see the boys in their distinctive top hats and tailcoats. Nearby are lots of grassy meadows for picnicking.

Windsor Castle

Windsor, **t** (020) 7766 7304
www.royal.gov.uk
Open Mar–Oct 9.45–5.15 (last adm 4); Nov–Feb 9.45–4.15 (last adm 3)
Adm Adult £13.50, child £7.50, family £34.50, under-5s **free**
Souvenir shop, wheelchair accessible for most areas of castle; car parking in town

This splendid concoction of towers, ramparts and pinnacles is, today, the official residence of the Queen and the largest inhabited castle in the world – and it is *big*, almost the size of a small town. Although the State Apartments were ravaged by fire in 1992, you would be hard pressed to tell, following £37 million worth of restoration work. They are today as opulent as they ever were, decorated with hundreds of priceless paintings from the royal collection, including Van Eycks and Rembrandts, as well as porcelain, armour and fine furniture. Children may find them a little dry, however, in which case you should make a beeline for the Queen Mary dolls' house which never fails to illicit a gasp of envy (particularly from the girls). The tombs of knights and kings in St George's Chapel are also worth a look and kids might like to try and guess where the Queen and Prince Charles sit when attending a service (they sit on either side at the back of the choir in two curtained booths). If you've got the energy, climb to the top of the 12th-century Round Tower where, on a clear day, you can see no fewer than 12 counties. Changing of the Guard takes place outside the Palace on alternate days Mon–Sat at 11am, *see* website for dates.

Windsor Great Park

For something a little more sedate, head to Windsor Great Park, a vast 4,800-acre tree-filled green space stretching out to the south of the town. It contains a 35-acre formal botanic garden, the Swiss Garden, and a huge lake, Virginia Water, with a 100-ft totem pole standing on its banks. The paths are well marked, so it is pushchair-friendly.

According to legend, the ghost of Herne the Hunter haunts the park on moonlit nights. Wearing an antler headdress and riding a black stallion, he appears at the head of a pack of black hounds, which he leads in a midnight chase across the park.

Where to Eat

Crooked House Tea Rooms

51 High Street, **t** (01753) 857 534
www.crooked-house.com
Open 9.30–6, daily

Tearoom housed in the oldest freestanding building in Windsor. The cream teas are a must.

Don Beni

28 Thames Street, **t** (01753) 622 042
www.donbeni.co.uk
Open 12 noon–11, daily

Bright and clean Italian restaurant serving up pizzas and pasta, plus mouthwatering seafood, meat and fish dishes. Children are welcome and highchairs are available. Takeaway service.

Puccino's

31 Windsor Royal Station, **t** (01753) 859 380

Pop in for a quick coffee or pizza and pasta lunch; children's menu and highchairs available. There are other coffee bars in the station, but the friendly service here is a definite bonus.

Royal Oak

Datchet Road (*opposite Windsor and Eton Riverside Station*) **t** (01753) 865 179
Open 11am–11pm, daily

This attractive pub has a patio area, children's menu and highchairs.

Bricks & mortar

Hampton Court

East Molesey, Surrey, **t** 0870 752 7777
www.hrp.org.uk
Getting there Hampton Court is just southwest of
London near Kingston-upon-Thames, off the A3
and A309 (J12 from the M25)
By train: Trains run regularly from London
(Waterloo) to Hampton Court Station
By boat: You can take a cruise up the Thames
with the Westminster Passenger Service from
Westminster Pier
Open daily Nov–Feb 10–4.30, Mar–Oct 10–6
Adm Adult £13, child £6.50, family £36 (2+3),
under-5s **free**
*Café, restaurant, souvenir shops (look out for the
Tudor Kitchen shop which sells a range of Tudor
cooking implements and medieval herbs), guided
tours, wheelchair access, on-site parking
Suitable for all ages*

Hampton Court provides a fabulous day out for
children. This grand old building is full of treasures
including Henry VIII's state apartments, a series of
Georgian rooms and a real tennis court. Children
will love the huge Tudor kitchens where every day
a Tudor banquet is prepared by cooks in full period
dress. It's like stepping into a time warp where you
can see, hear, smell and even taste the days gone
by. Pick up a copy of the events programme on
arrival and collect your invitation cards to ensure
your place on one of the guided tours, which
enchant with tales of marriage and murder.

Henry spent a staggering £62,000 on Hampton
Court (that's around £18 million in today's money),
turning it into the most sophisticated palace in
England. Only part of the structure we see today,
however, dates from this time. Sir Christopher
Wren undertook further rebuilding work in the late
17th century, the most important element of which
was the planting of new landscaped gardens.
These have always been as big a draw as the palace
itself. The main attraction, of course, is the maze,
the most famous in the world. It was planted in
1690 for William III and lures in around 300,000
people a year. There are family trails and audio
guides, plus seasonal events including an ice rink at
Christmas and carol singing. Young children can
make use of the soft play area in the family room.

Bodiam Castle

Bodiam, Robertsbridge, **t** (01580) 830 436
www.nationaltrust.org.uk
Getting there Bodiam is 10 miles north of Hastings
off the B2244. The Kent and East Sussex Steam
Railway also makes trips from Bodiam to the
nearby town of Tenterden
By train: There are regular trains to Hastings from
Charing Cross
Open Mid-Feb–Oct 10–6, daily; Nov–mid-Feb
Sat–Sun 10–4
Adm Adult £4.60, child £2.50, family £11.50, under-
5s **free**
*Café-restaurant with children's menus, gift shop,
picnic areas, mother-and-baby facilities, wheelchair
accessible, on-site parking, children's trail, guide and
activity backpacks*

Bodiam is a proper fairytale castle with round
turrets on each corner, crinkly battlements, arrow-
slit windows and a portcullis; it is even surrounded
by a deep moat. The ground inside the castle walls,
most of which is covered in grass, makes a perfect
spot for a picnic and there are family events
throughout the year, including treasure hunts, arts-
and-crafts acitivities and theatre performances.

Hever Castle

Hever, near Edenbridge, **t** (01732) 865 224,
www.hever-castle.co.uk
Getting there Hever is about 8 miles west of
Tonbridge off the B2027; J6 off the M25
By train: There are regular trains to Tonbridge from
Charing Cross
Open Mar–Nov 11–6 daily
Adm Adult £9.80, child £5.30, family £24.90,
under-5s **free**
*Café with children's meals, gift shop, guided tours,
mother-and-baby facilities, wheelchair accessible,
on-site parking, adventure playground*

Hever is very much the antithesis of Bodiam,
with its antiques, fine tapestries and suits of
armour, as well as costumed waxworks of Henry
VIII and his six wives (this was where Anne Boleyn,
his second wife, lived as a child), and a display of
dolls' houses. The castle's grounds contain a yew
maze, a lake and an Italian garden with a lakeside
theatre. Here, a renowned season of plays, opera
and musicals takes place each summer. There's also
a water maze (April–October), with water jets that
spray visitors every time they take a wrong turning.

Leeds Castle

Maidstone, **t** (01622) 765 400
www.leeds-castle.com
Getting there Leeds Castle is 40 miles southeast of
London near Maidstone off the M20 and B2163
By train: There are direct services from London
Victoria to Bearsted, the nearest train station, from
where there's a regular shuttle bus to the castle.
Eurostar services from London Waterloo stop at
Ashford International, 20mins away
Open Castle: April–Sep 10.30–5, Oct–Mar 10.30–3
daily; park & gardens: April–Sep 10–5, Oct–Mar
10–3 daily
Adm Adult £13.50, child £8, under-5s **free**
Gift shops, restaurant, guided tours, some wheel-
chair access

Leeds Castle looks like a castle should look; dramatic,
romantic and mysterious. Set on two islands in
the middle of a lake in 500 acres of beautifully
sculpted Kent countryside, this was the famously
hard-to-please Henry VIII's favourite castle. The
interior is stuffed full of precious paintings and
furniture, but the 'don't touch' atmosphere means
that kids can't really interact with the space. It's a
different story, however, in the castle grounds, where
a maze, an underground grotto, an aviary and lots
of wide grassy spaces to run around on enable kids
to let off steam. What's more, family entertainments
are put on in the grounds throughout the year,
including a special Family Fun Weekend, plus
classical concerts with firework finales, treasure
trails, craft workshops, animal encounters and a
famous Balloon Festival in September.

Hatfield House

Hatfield, **t** (01707) 262 823
www.hatfield-house.co.uk
Getting there Hatfield is 21 miles north of London,
7 miles from the M25 (J23), 2 miles from the A1 (J4)
and is signposted from the A414 and A1000.
Hatfield train station is immediately opposite
By train: There are regular services from King's
Cross, which take approximately 25mins
Open House: April–Sept Wed–Sun 12 noon–5pm
(Thurs by pre-booked guided tours only); Park and
West Gardens 11–5.30, daily
Adm House, park and gardens: adult £8, child £4,
family £22; Park and gardens: adult £4.50, child
£3.50; Park: adult £2, child £1

Restaurant, picnic areas, shop, mother-and-baby
room, guided tours, wheelchair accessible, on-site
parking, children's play area, nature trails

Come to Hatfield to see how a real princess lived.
This grand, red-brick Jacobean mansion was built
in the early 17th century on the site of the Tudor
palace where Queen Elizabeth I spent her childhood days. The vast 4,000-acre grounds will
probably be of most interest to children, with their
formal gardens full of hedges, paths, ponds and
fountains and wilderness areas to explore. On your
travels, see if you can spot the oak tree under
which the young Princess Elizabeth supposedly
learned of her succession following the death of
her sister Mary in 1558.

The house itself is very grand inside, with its
imposing rows of paintings (look for the portrait of
Elizabeth) and vast oak staircase (appropriately
named the Grand Staircase) decorated with carved
figures. Kids will like the National Collection of
Model Soldiers, which has over 3,000 miniature
figures arranged in battle positions. Craft fairs and
theatre productions in the park are among the
programmed events that families can enjoy
throughout the year.

Knebworth House

Knebworth, **t** 01438 812661
www.knebworthhouse.com
Getting there Knebworth House is 2 miles from
Stevenage; the entrance is directly off J7 of the A1
Open April–Sep Sat & Sun, plus school hols, House:
12noon–5pm, park & gardens: 11–5
Adm House and grounds: adult £9, child £8.50,
family £31 (2+2), under-4s **free**; grounds only: adult
& child £7, family £24
On-site parking, café-restaurant, garden terrace
tearoom, picnic areas, gift shop, guided tours

Built in the 16th century, Knebworth was originally
a simple Tudor mansion, but was covered in Gothic
adornments in the 1800s. The interior may be of
limited interest (though quiz sheets are available
to make things more engaging for kids), but it's the
grounds that are the real draw. As you head south
away from the house you'll encounter a sunken
garden surrounded by trees, followed by an exquisite rose garden, a wildflower meadow and a
small maze. Beyond this is a wilderness area with a
'Dino Trail' – 72 life-size fibreglass dinosaurs lurking
menacingly in the foliage. There's also a huge 250-
acre park where herds of red deer roam freely.

The biggest attraction for children, however, will inevitably be the Fort Knebworth adventure playground, one of the biggest and best around with lots of derring-do climbing equipment and a great selection of slides, including a suspension slide (you travel down clutching on to a rope), the four-lane Astroglide, where you travel on a helter-skelter-type rush mat down a bumpy plastic chute, a twisting corkscrew slide and a vertical-drop slide. There is also a bouncy castle and a miniature railway, which provides looping 15-minute tours of the grounds. The website gives details of Tudor and Victorian trails for school groups, and has printable pictures of costumed figures and shields for children to add their own designs to and colour in.

Buckets & spades

Eastbourne

Getting there Eastbourne is on the south coast, 21 miles east of Brighton and 18 miles west of Hastings on the A259, just south of the A27
By train: There are regular train services from London (Victoria) and Brighton
Tourist information 3 Cornfield Road, Eastbourne, **t** (01323) 411 400, **www**.eastbourne.org

Eastbourne has a dignified air to it and a distinct lack of souvenirs and candyfloss. This haven of south coast tranquillity has become a popular retirement destination for older people. However, despite its polished veneer, Eastbourne has a good deal of family entertainment to offer. There's the pier, one of the best and most visited in the country; indoor and outdoor adventure playgrounds; The Sovereign Centre leisure complex with four pools and kids' activities; the Museum of Shops; facilities for go-karting, bowling, boating and mini-golf and, of course, the beach – a long stretch of sand and shingle with numerous rock pools (lifeguards patrol in summer). The seafront is framed by two towers: the Redoubt Fortress, where classical concerts and firework displays are held in summer, and the Wish Tower, with its collection of puppets and props.

Southend-on-Sea

Getting there Southend lies at the southernmost tip of East Anglia, at the mouth of the Thames estuary, 40 miles east of London (reached by the A127).

By train: Trains depart from London Fenchurch Street to Southend Central station regularly (1hr) and Liverpool Street to Southend Victoria (45mins)
By coach: National Express run a frequent service from London Victoria (2.5hrs)
Tourist office Southend Pier, **t** (01702) 215 620
www.southend.gov.uk

Situated on the north bank of the River Thames estuary, Southend offers families Kids Kingdom, an inflatable cavern flanked by ball pools, with a soft play haven for under-5s, and Sealife Adventure for some fishy tales in the rockpool demonstration area. Visit **www**.sealifeadventure.co.uk.

There's a sandy beach with facilities for sailing, water-skiing and windsurfing. The Adventure Island fun park on Marine Parade boasts over 40 attractions, some specifically designed for toddlers, while jutting out from the front is the town's famous pier, which at over 1.3 miles is the longest pier in the world. Walk to the end for some stunning coastal scenes.

Nature lovers

Ashdown Forest

Getting there It's just to the southeast of East Grinstead off the A22
Tourist information East Grinstead Tourism Initiative, West Street, East Grinstead, **t** (01342) 410 121, **www**.ashdownforest.co.uk

This great swathe of West Sussex forest and heathland provided the inspiration for A. A. Milne's tales of the famous bear, Winnie-the-Pooh. The village of Hartfield is the centre of Pooh country, from where you can visit 'Hundred-Acre Wood' where most of the Pooh stories were set. Other places which have became familiar through A.A. Milne's stories, such as the Enchanted Place, North Pole and Roo's Sandypit, are all within easy reach of Gill's Lap car park, which can be found just off the B2026. The Ashdown Forest Information Centre, **t** (01342) 823 583, lies one mile east of Wych Cross on the Hartfield road. Here children can learn more about local flora and fauna in its Exhibition Barn, and there are guidebooks and leaflets detailing walks in the area. There's also a garden with picnic tables and the only public toilets for miles around. Much of the rest of Ashdown is serious walkers' territory, with lots of nature trails and sandy tracks.

Drusilla's Park

Alfriston, **t** (01323) 874 100
www.drusillas.co.uk
Getting there 7 miles northeast of Eastbourne off the A27
Open April–Sept 10–5; Oct–Mar 10–4
Adm Adults £11.50, children £10.50, under 3s **free**, family £21–£56.25
'Explorers' restaurant, gift shop, mother-and-baby facilities, disabled access, on-site parking

At Drusilla's the watchword is small. As one of the country's most child-orientated zoos, it understands that the best way to get kids to appreciate animals is by providing them with as much access as possible to the animals' own world – not a feasible option with a tiger. Here, animals are displayed in different ways and from imaginative viewpoints. Children can watch frolicking meerkats from a plastic dome within the meerkat enclosure; they can walk through a bat house as the bats fly around their heads and see penguins cavorting underwater from a special viewing area. The zoo encourages lots of participation and organizes activities and games to help kids understand the zoo's inhabitants better – they can hang upside down like a monkey or a bat on a climbing frame, try to run as fast as a llama on a treadmill or get up close and personal with an owl, a snake or a monkey at one of the 'animal encounters' sessions. There are art competitions, talks by the keepers and numerous themed weekends (Reptile Weekend, Primate Weekend, etc.) – everything, in fact, for a perfect day at the zoo. Should the animals lose their appeal, you can climb aboard one of two miniature trains, which give tours of the park in summer, or head to the park's play area, where you'll find swings, slides, a paddling pool and a soft play area for toddlers.

Whipsnade Wild Animal Park

Whipsnade, Dunstable, **t** (01582) 872 171
www.zsl.org/whipsnade
Getting there It's signposted from the M25 (J21) and the M1 (J9 and J12)
By train: The nearest stations are Luton (served by King's Cross Thameslink) and Hemel Hempstead (served by Euston)
By coach: Green Line buses run from London Victoria, **t** (020) 8668 7261
Open Mar–Sept 10–6, Oct–Feb 10–4
Adm Adult £14.50, child £11.50, family £46 (2+2 or 1+3), under-3s **free**, car entry £11
Café, picnic areas, shop, wheelchair accessible, mother-and-baby room, on-site parking £3.50 fee

There are four ways to tour Whipsnade: on foot, where you will get to wander among free-roaming wallabies, peacocks and deer; in the safety of your car, for which you have to pay extra; aboard the Whipsnade narrow-gauge steam railway, which takes you on a tour through herds of elephants and rhinos; or, perhaps the best option, aboard the free open-top sightseeing bus, which not only offers elevated views of the animals, but can also deposit you at all the best walking spots.

There's a vast range of animals to see: Asian elephants, who enjoy Europe's largest elephant paddock (Whipsnade, at the last count, boasted no fewer than 6,000 acres of paddock for its 2,500 animals to roam around in); white rhinos; hippos, permanently submerged in muddy water; tigers (come at feeding time to see them on the prowl); giraffes, iguanas, flamingoes, penguins, wolves and many species of birds – including two delightful newcomers, hornbills named Horatio and Zazu.

The World of Wings flying displays and the Sealion Splash Zone guarantee some up-close-and-personal encounters. Remember to pack a raincoat!

Theme parks

Chessington World of Adventure

Chessington, **t** 0870 444 7777
www.chessington.co.uk
Getting there Chessington is a couple of miles north of Epsom, just off the A243, 2 miles from the A3 and M25 (J9 from the north, J10 from the south). There are regular train services to Chessington South station from London Waterloo
Open Apr–Oct 10–5, open on selected dates in Dec and Jan
Adm Adult £27–£31, child £17.50–£22.50 (4–11), family £28–£111.50(1+1–2+4), under-4s **free**
Fast-food outlets, baby-changing, on-site parking, some wheelchair access (safety restrictions apply on some rides – call for detailed leaflet – a limited number of wheelchairs available on request)

Note Height restriction: varies, but is usually 1.2m–1.4m

Chessington has rides for all ages, from top-of-the-range roller coasters to gentle carousels and roundabouts. Younger children are well catered for at Toytown, the Dragon River log flume, Professor Burp's Bubble Works and Beanoland, where you can enjoy a range of rides themed on Beano characters and watch costumed comic characters behaving badly.

It's easy to forget that, in amongst all the hi-tech gadgetry, there is also a zoo, known as 'Animal Land'. You can take a look at the resident tigers, leopards, lions, gorillas and meerkats aboard the Safari Skyrail, and even enter the squirrel and monkey enclosure to get a closer look at the animals. There are daily displays by sea lions, penguins and hawks and, at the 'Creepy Cave', you can all grimace at spiders, insects and other crawling horrors.

Legoland

Winkfield Road, Windsor
t 08705 040404
www.legoland.co.uk
Getting there Legoland is 2 miles from Windsor on the Windsor to Ascot Road, signposted from J6 of the M4. **By train:** There are regular services to Windsor and Eton Riverside from Waterloo
By coach: The bus service from Windsor town centre to Legoland departs from Thames Street every 15mins during opening times
Open 10–6, daily, park closes later in summer
Adm Adult £30, child £23; 2-day ticket adult £57, child £45
Several restaurants/cafés and catering stalls, picnic areas, mother-and-baby facilities, wheelchair accessible, wheelchair hire available, adapted toilets, on-site parking, first-aid and lost-parent facilities

A cross between a theme park and an activity centre, Legoland one of the country's top attractions. As such, it is a busy place and you should expect long queues. To make the most of your trip, it's best to arrive early or stay late (the park stays open until at least 7pm in summer),

The park has some good rides but the most popular attractions are the interactive zones, such as Lego Traffic, where children can operate electrically powered Lego cars, boats and balloons. In the Imagination Centre, kids are encouraged to make their own futuristic designs. Older children can create robotic models or take on the Extreme Team Challenge water slide, whilst their younger siblings splash around in Explore Land's Waterworks fountains, dash about in the indoor and outdoor play zones and enjoy some gentle boat rides.

After all this activity you can head for Miniland and marvel at the model buildings, complete with mini Tube trains and pleasure boats, or stop off for a picnic and watch the Wave Surfers in action. There are summer shows in the Lego Imagination Theatre, where you can watch a 3D medievel adventure film. Young kids may prefer a puppet show in the Explore Theatre, while all the family will enjoy the acrobatic thrills and spills in the Johnny Thunder Show.

Thorpe Park

Staines Road, Chertsey
t 0870 444 4466
www.thorpepark.com
Getting there Thorpe Park is on the A320 between Chertsey and Staines (J11 or 13 from the M25)
By train: There's a regular train service from Reading, Guildford and London (Waterloo) to Staines, from where you can catch a bus
Open April–Nov, times vary, but it usually opens at 10 and closes between 5 and 7.30
Adm Prices are cheaper if booked online. Adult £28.50, child £20 (4–11 inclusive), family ticket £78 (2+2), under 1m tall **free**
Fast-food outlets, gift shop, baby-changing facilities, first-aid centre, some wheelchair access, adapted toilets, on-site parking. Annual pass available

Thorpe's impressive range of water rides and slides make it the perfect option for a hot day, but do pack waterproofs, swimwear and a spare T-shirt.

Serious white knucklers are given plenty of heart-pounding options. Top of the pile has to be the deceptively named 'Stealth'. Europe's fastest roller coaster, this accelerates its victims from 0 to 80mph in just under two seconds – and there's nothing particularly stealthy about that.

There are also plenty of gentler attractions aimed at the whole family. Young children are well provided for, with various themed areas such as Mrs Hippo's Jungle Safari, Mr Monkey's Banana Ride, and Model World, which features miniature versions of the Eiffel Tower, the Pyramids and Stonehenge. They can also take a boat ride to Thorpe Farm to see goats, sheep and rabbits.

NEED TO KNOW

Being away from home can have its frustrations. Principal among them is you don't necessarily know where everything is, like where to go in an emergency or who to call for advice. London is a big city, it's true, but the following list of essentials should help to put parents' minds at rest and make families feel much more at home.

24-hour chemist

Zafash Chemist
233–235 Old Brompton Road, SW5
t (020) 7373 3506

24-hour dentist

Baker Street Dental Clinic
t (020) 8748 9365
www.24hour-emergencydentist.co.uk

Accident and Emergency

University College, London, Hospital,
Gower Street, WC1
t 0845 155 5000
www.uclh.nhs.uk

Babysitting

Sitters
t 0800 389 0038

Emergency

Police, Fire Brigade, Ambulance
t 999 or 112

Getting around

Transport for London
t (020) 7222 1234
www.tfl.gov.uk

Lost property

London Transport Lost Property Office
(including Black Cab Lost Property Office)
200 Baker Street, NW1
t 0845 330 9882

Taxi

Dial-A-Cab
t (020) 7426 3420
www.dialacab.co.uk

Useful websites

NHS Direct

www.nhsdirect.nhs.uk
Either log on or call 0845 4647 to obtain advice from trained hospital staff. This is a vital and reliable service that helps to cut down on unnecessary doctors' appointments and hospital visits, not to mention dragging unwell children out of their beds in the dead of night. Please use it.

A new, and welcome, innovation, particularly useful for visitors, are the NHS pay-on-demand walk-in centres. There are over a dozen in the capital (*see* p.211), all open to anyone on a drop-in basis. They provide minor treatments, information and advice. The centres are open daily from 7am to 10pm.

Boots the Chemists

www.boots.com
Boots' own website offers an online delivery service for toiletries, baby food, nappies, etc., plus advice and details of local Boots stores and other practitioners.

Maps

www.upmystreet.com
If you're staying in one area for a while you can key in your postcode and find out about all kinds of local services, from dry cleaners to estate agents.
www.multimap.com
Map service that allows you to home in on a particular area and find out about local restaurants, hotels and services.

Practicalities A–Z

Climate

If you've never been to Britain before, you're probably expecting to be consumed in clouds of fog and drizzle the moment you step off the plane. Britain has a reputation for dismal weather – it's the home of the legendary 'peasouper', after all (long since gone, following strict pollution laws) – and the state of the skies has long been the nation's favourite topic of conversation. The summers are rarely too hot, the winters seldom too cold. However, you may get a brief heatwave in July/August or the occasional week of snow cover in January (plus a small hurricane every 70 years or so) and this does tend to throw the transport system into confusion, so beware.

In London, the average temperature is 22°C (75°F) in July and August, dropping to 7°C (44°F) in December and January. Rainfall is generally at its heaviest in November. The best time to visit is probably late spring or early autumn, when you can look forward to mild temperatures, not too much rain, the odd sunny day and slightly shorter queues at the capital's major tourist attractions.

Electricity

Britain's electrical supply is 240 volts AC. When bringing an electrical appliance from abroad fitted with a two-prong plug, you'll need to purchase an adaptor and probably a transformer as well. British appliances use a type of three-prong, square-pin plug that will be unfamiliar to visitors from Europe and North America. All UK plugs have fuses of three, five or 13 amps.

Embassies & consulates

US Embassy
24 Grosvenor Square, W1
t (020) 7499 9000
www.usembassy.org.uk
Open Mon–Fri 8.30–5.30

Australian High Commission
Australia House, The Strand, WC2
t (020) 7379 4334
www.australia.org.uk
Open Mon–Fri 9–5

Canadian High Commission
38 Grosvenor St, W1
t (020) 7258 6600
www.canada.org.uk
Open Mon–Fri 8am–11am

Dutch Embassy
38 Hyde Park Gate, SW7
t (020) 7590 3200
www.netherlands-embassy.org.uk
Open Mon–Fri 9–5.30

High Commission of India
India House, Aldwych, WC2
t (020) 7632 3035
www.hcilondon.org
Open Mon–Fri 9.30–5.30

Irish Embassy
17 Grosvenor Place, SW1
t (020) 7235 2171
http://ireland.embassyhomepage.com
Open Mon–Fri 9.30–5

New Zealand High Commission
New Zealand House, 80 The Haymarket, SW1
t (020) 7930 8422
http://nzembassy.com
Open Mon–Fri 10–12 noon and 2–4

South African Embassy
South Africa House, Trafalgar Square, WC2
t (020) 7451 7299
www.southafricahouse.com
Open Mon–Fri 9.30–5

Families with special needs

Wheelchair access to London's public places – its theatres, cinemas, sports grounds, etc. – is relatively good. The London Tourist Board's website provides access details for all London's principal attractions, t (020) 7932 2000, www.visitlondon.com/city_guide/disabled/index.html. It also provides a list of wheelchair-accessible accommodation, as well as hotels which accept guide dogs.

Public transport is also improving, now that all new buses have to be 'low floor' and provide space for wheelchair users (who travel free). All DLR stations have lift and ramp access and are wheelchair accessible – which just leaves the tube. The situation here is still something of a nightmare for disabled travellers with few stations offering lift or ramp access and most trains having an 8in or so vertical gap between the platform and the carriage floor. You can find out all the latest details at: www.tfl.gov.uk/gettingaround/transport accessibility/1167.aspx. You can also write to the London Access and Mobility Unit, Windsor House, 42–50 Victoria Street, SW1, t (020) 7222 1234, which can provide leaflets detailing 'low-floor' routes and mobility buses, as well as large print materials, braille maps and audio tapes.

All black taxis are wheelchair accessible and many have additional aids for disabled travellers including ramps, swivel seats and induction loops. Wheelchair users and blind and partially sighted people are entitled to a 30–50 per cent discount on rail fares and can apply for a Disabled Person's Railcard (£18 a year) at major rail stations, www.disabledpersons-railcard.co.uk. A booklet, in PDF format, providing advice on rail travel for disabled passengers can be downloaded from www.nationalrail.co.uk/passenger_services/ disabled_passengers/index.html.

Britain has a growing number of specialist tour operators which specifically cater for the needs of physically disabled travellers, such as Can Be Done, t (020) 8907 2400, www.canbedone.co.uk. The Association of Independent Tour Operators, t (020) 8744 9280, www.aito.co.uk, can provide a list, as can RADAR (the Royal Association for Disability and Rehabilitation, see below) which also publishes its own guides to holidays and travel. The following organizations will provide information and advice.

Artsline
54 Charlton Street, NW1
t (020) 7388 2227
www.artsline.org.uk & www.theatreaccess.co.uk.
Free information on access to over 1000 arts venues around the capital.

Council for Disabled Children
National Children's Bureau, 8 Wakley Street, EC1
t (020) 7843 1900

www.ncb.org.uk/cdc
Part of the National Children's Bureau, this is a good source of information on travel health and provides links to a whole host of other resources.

Disability Now
6 Market Road, N7
t (020) 7619 7323
www.disabilitynow.org.uk
Produces a monthly disability newspaper 'DN', often containing holiday ideas and travel tips written by people with disabilities.

Holiday Care Service
2nd Floor, Imperial Buildings, Victoria Road, Horley, Surrey RH6 9HW
t (0845) 124 9971
www.holidaycare.org.uk
Provides information for disabled travellers about a whole range of holiday matters – transport, accommodation, attractions etc – for both the UK and abroad.

Magic Deaf
t (020) 7323 8551
c/o Tate Modern, Bankside, SE1 9TG
www.magicdeaf.org.uk
Provides details about museums and galleries in the capital who provide facilities or organize events for the hearing impaired.

RADAR (Royal Association for Disability and Rehabilitation)
12 City Forum, 250 City Road, EC1
t (020) 7250 3222
www.radar.org.uk
Produces guid books and information packs for disabled travellers, including its annual 'Holidays in Britain and Ireland for Disabled People' (£13.50).

Royal National Institute of Blind People
205 Judd Street, London WC1
t 08457 669 999 (UK helpline)
t (020) 7388 1266 (for callers from outside the UK)
www.rnib.org.uk
Advises blind people on travel matters.

In the US
American Foundation for the Blind
11 Penn Plaza, Suite 300, New York, NY 10011
t 212 502 7600; toll free t 1 800 232 5463
www.afb.org

Mobility International
132 E Broadway, Eugene, Oregon 97401
t 541 343 1284
www.miusa.org

SATH (Society for Accessible Travel and Hospitality)
347 Fifth Avenue, Suite 605, New York 10016
t 212 447 7284
www.sath.org

In Australia
National Disability Service
33 Thesiger Court, Deakin Act, 2600
t 02 6283 3200
www.nds.org.au

Infant matters

Babysitters
Finding a reliable and trustworthy childminder in a strange city can be a worrying task. Large hotels usually offer a babysitting service. Small ones may be able to arrange something on request. London also has several reputable agencies offering a network of qualified babysitters, nurses and infant teachers.

Sitters
6 Nottingham St, W1
t 0800 389 0038
www.sitters.co.uk

Hopes and Dreams
339–341 City Road, EC1
t (020) 7833 9388
Babysitting from 3 months–5 years. Hotel for over-2s to 11 years old.

Pippa Pop-Ins
430 Fulham Rd, SW6
t (020) 7731 1445
Award-winning hotel for 2–12 year olds; provides a crèche, nursery school and babysitting services.

Universal Aunts
t (020) 7738 8937
www.universalaunts.co.uk

Provides babysitters, entertainers, people to meet children off trains, and even guides to take children round London.

Breastfeeding
Public breastfeeding is not exactly taboo in London, but you are best off enquiring at individual restaurants as to where you might sit and feed in relative comfort. London's principal airports and train stations, and some of its department stores have mother-and-baby rooms. If in doubt, head for the nearest branch of Boots, though be aware that you may well have to feed your baby while other people change theirs. The main branch of Gap on Oxford Street, close to Bond Street station, has a dedicated nursing mothers' room.

Nappies
You can pick up bumper packs of disposable nappies, such as Pampers or Huggies or an own-name brand, at any London supermarket or major chemist. Some supermarket chains stock Nature Boy & Girl nappies from Sweden, which are 70% biodegradable. If you are worried about the cost (which can be formidable) or damage to the environment, London has plenty of sources of traditional re-usable nappies. Remember that there are nappy laundry services available (*see* below).

Green Baby
Leroy House, 436 Essex Rd, N13
t 0870 241 7661
www.greenbabyco.com
Washable nappies and disposables, plus toiletries, buggies and organic clothing available in-store or by mail order.

The National Association of Nappy Services (NANS)
t (0121) 693 4949
www.changeanappy.co.uk
Visit the website to find a service in your area. It couldn't be easier.

UK Nappy Helpline
t (01983) 401 959
Provices details of local cloth nappy contacts.

Sam-I-Am
t (01369) 830 040
www.nappies.net
Mail-order cotton nappies.

Snuggle Naps
t (0115) 2277 8440
www.snugglenaps.co.uk
Mail-order washable, designer nappies.

Insurance

It's vital that you take out travel insurance before your trip. This should cover, at a bare minimum, cancellation due to illness, travel delays, accidents, lost luggage, lost passports, lost or stolen belongings, personal liability, legal expenses, emergency flights and medical cover. The majority of insurance companies offer free insurance to children under the age of two as part of the parent's policy. Also bear in mind annual insurance policies, which can be especially cost effective for families with two or more older children. Always keep the company's 24-hour emergency number close to hand – if you have a mobile, store it in the memory.

The most important aspect of any travel insurance policy is its medical cover. You should look for cover of around £5 million. If you're a resident of the European Union, Iceland, Liechtenstein, Norway or Switzerland, you are entitled to free or reduced-cost medical treatment as long as you carry a European Health Insurance Card (EHIC). UK residents can apply on line at **www**.ehic.org.uk, or **t** 0845 606 2030 or by post using an application form available from the post office – you should receive your card within 21 days. This covers families with dependent children. Even so, you may have to pay for your medical treatment and then claim your expenses back at a later date, so hang on to your receipts.

In the US and Canada, you may find that your existing insurance policies give sufficient medical cover and you should always check them thoroughly before taking out a new one. Canadians, in particular, are usually covered by their provincial health plans. Few American or Canadian insurance companies will issue on-the-spot payments following a reported theft or loss. You will usually have to wait several weeks before any money is forthcoming. Here is a list of useful insurance contacts.

In the UK
Association of British Insurers
t (020) 7600 3333
www.abi.org.uk

The Financial Ombudsman Service
t 0845 080 1800
www.financial-ombudsman.org.uk
The government-appointed regulator of the insurance industry.

Churchill Insurance
t 0800 032 7140
www.churchill.com

Columbus Travel Insurance
t 0870 033 9988
www.columbusdirect.com

Directline
t 0845 246 8704
www.directline.com

Endsleigh Insurance
t 0800 028 3571
www.endsleigh.co.uk

Medicover
t 0870 735 3600
www.medi-cover.co.uk

In the US
Access America
t US/Canada 1-800-284-8300
www.accessamerica.com

Carefree Travel Insurance
t US/Canada 1-800-454-7107
www.carefreetravel.com

Travel Assistance International
t US/Canada 800 821 2828
www.travelassistance.com

MEDEX Assistance Corporation
t US 1-800-732-5309
www.medexassist.com

Lost property

If you lose anything while out and about in London, the chances are it's gone for good. However, you never can tell, and it is always worth checking to see whether some honest citizen has handed your valuable lost item in. If you lose something while on the plane, go to the nearest information desk in the airport and fill out the relevant form as soon as possible.

London Transport Lost Property Office (incorporating the Black Cab Lost Property Office)
200 Baker Street, NW1
t 0845 330 9882
Open Weekday mornings

Maps

There's little rhyme or reason to the layout of London's streets. Minimal urban planning is a great British tradition – to a Londoner's eyes, nicely arranged grids and blocks are foreign affectations to be resisted at all costs. Your first purchase upon arriving in London should, therefore, be a good street map – you can pick one up in most newsagents. Stanfords, London's premier map shop has, as you might expect, a wide selection.

If you (or more likely your kids) are computer literate, you can visit **www**.streetmap.co.uk and print out the map of the area you need. If you're hoping to stick around for some time, or have plans to visit attractions on the outskirts of town, you should consider getting hold of a copy of the London A–Z Street Atlas, a must for all disorientated Londoners – almost every household in the capital owns one. It contains street maps of every area in Greater London and is available in a range of formats from a huge, glossy, colour, hardback version to pocket-sized paperback edition (£22.50 and £5.50 respectively), **www**.a-zmaps.co.uk. You will find them stocked at bookstores, newsagents and petrol stations across London.

If you are brave enough to drive in London, you might like to pick up a 'London Parking Map', published by the Clever Map Company or, for out of London, one of the Ordinance Survey's excellent series of annually updated road atlases.

Train, Tube and bus maps are available from main underground and train stations. The most useful is the hybrid Journey Planner which shows both Tube and rail links. You'll find all your cartographic requirements catered for at:

Stanfords
12–14 Long Acre, WC2
t (020) 7836 1321
www.stanfords.co.uk
London's largest map shop.

The Travel Bookshop
13 Blenheim Crescent, W11
t (020) 7229 5260
www.thetravelbookshop.co.uk

Medical matters

Visitors from the EU, Iceland, Liechtenstein and Norway can claim free or reduced cost medical treatment under Britain's National Health Service, so long as they carry with them the appropriate form. In the EU, this is the EHIC card, which covers families with dependent children. The only things you will be expected to pay for are medical prescriptions (currently £6.85) and visits to the optician or dentist (these are free to children and senior citizens). Visitors from other countries should take out medical insurance.

In an emergency

If you require urgent medical treatment, you should call an ambulance by dialling **t** 999 or 112, or drive to the nearest hospital with an Accident and Emergency Department.

Chelsea & Westminster Hospital
369 Fulham Road, SW10
t (020) 8746 8000
www.chelwest.nhs.uk
⊖ Fulham Broadway
Dedicated A&E department for children

Central Middlesex Hospital
Acton Lane, Park Royal, NW10
t (020) 8965 5733
www.nwwlh.nhs.uk
⊖/ ⇌ Harlesden

Ealing Hospital
Uxbridge Road, Middlesex, UB1
t (020) 8967 5613
www.ealinghospital.org.uk
⊖ Ealing Broadway

Royal London Hospital
Whitechapel Road, E1
t (020) 7377 7000
www.bartsandthelondon.org
⊖ Whitechapel
Dedicated A&E department for children

St Mary's Hospital
Praed Street, W2
t (020) 7886 6666
www.st-marys.nhs.uk
ᚋ Paddington
Dedicated A&E department for children

St Thomas' Hospital
Lambeth Palace Road, SE1
t (020) 7188 7188
www.guysandstthomas.nhs.uk
ᚋ London Bridge
London's largest A&E department

University College London Hospital
Gower Street, WC1
t 0845 155 5000
www.uclh.nhs.uk
ᚋ Euston Square, Warren Street, Goodge Street

Whittington Hospital
Highgate Hill, N19
t (020) 7272 3070
www.whittington.nhs.uk
ᚋ Archway

Minor ailments
In 2000 the NHS set up walk-in centres to cater for people with minor ailments. You can use them to avoid hours of waiting at a hospital A&E department, although they will usually charge for their services. There are over a dozen centres in the capital (*see* below). They are open to anyone on a drop-in basis. The centres are open from 7am to 10pm. There are also some private walk-in centres dotted about, so check first about charges. For more information, contact NHS Direct, **t** 0845 4647 or www.nhs.co.uk.

Charing Cross NHS Walk In Centre
Charing Cross Hospital, Fulham Palace Road, W6
t (020) 8383 0904
ᚋ Hammersmith

Liverpool Street NHS Walk In Centre
Exchange Arcade, Bishopsgate, EC2
t 0845 880 1242
ᚋ/ ⇌ Liverpool Street

Soho NHS Walk In Centre
1 Frith Street, W1
t (020) 7534 6500
ᚋ Tottenham Court Road, Leicester Square

Useful numbers
Emergency (Police, Fire Brigade, Ambulance)
t 999 or 112
Operator **t** 100
Directory Enquiries **t** 118 500 or 118 800 or 118 118
International Operator **t** 155
International Directory Enquiries **t** 153

There are also centres in Parsons Green, SW6; Tooting, SW1; Edgware, HA8; Whitechapel, E1; Newham, E13; and Croydon, CRO1.

Chemists/Pharmacies
In Britain, only a limited range of drugs can be dispensed without a doctor's prescription. Chemists will also often stock a selection of basic medical and cosmetic products such as cough mixture, plasters (band-aids), bandages, nappies, vitamins and hairspray. Your local police station can provide a list of late-opening chemists.

Superstores often have chemists which are open late and on Sundays. **Boots**, www.boots.com, is the UK's largest chemist chain. Its branches also usually contain a photographic service. There are branches at 4 James Street, Covent Garden, WC2, **t** (020) 7379 8442; 73 Piccadilly, W1, **t** (020) 7409 2982; 44–46 Regent Street, W1, **t** (020) 7734 6126; 105–109 Strand, WC2 **t** (020) 7240 5963. Also try the following:

Bliss Chemist
5 Marble Arch, W1
t (020) 7723 6116
Open Until 12 midnight daily

Zafash Chemist
233–235 Old Brompton Road, SW5
t (020) 7373 2798
Open 24hrs a day, 365 days a year

Other useful contacts
Action for Sick Children
t 0800 074 4519
www.actionforsickchildren.org
Provides advice to help parents get the best possible health care for their children.

Action Against Allergies
PO Box 278, Twickenham, TW1
t (020) 8892 2711
Provides a wealth of leaflets and pamphlets on allergy issues.

Dental Emergency Care Service
t (020) 7955 2186
www.bda-findadentist.org.uk

Eye Care Trust
t 0845 129 5001
www.eye-care.org.uk

Medical Advisory Service for Travellers Abroad
t (0113) 238 7575
www.masta-travel-health.com
Provides deatils of travel health clinics throughout the UK.

NHS Direct
t (0845) 4647
www.nhsdirect.nhs.uk
Nurse-led, 24hr helpline offering confidential health advice. You can also get information and advice online.

St John Ambulance Supplies
t (020) 7324 4000
www.stjohnsupplies.co.uk

Money and banks

The currency in Britain is the pound sterling (written £) which is divided into 100 pence (written p). There are eight coin denominations: 1p, 2p, 5p, 10p, 20p, 50p, £1 and £2 (all issued by the Royal Mint) and four note denominations: £5, £10, £20 and £50 – the last is the most often forged and you'll find that a number of shops and restaurants refuse to accept £50 notes in any circumstances. All notes are printed by the Bank of England (apart from the forgeries, that is – or Scottish banknotes).

Most shops and restaurants accept the big name credit and debit cards: Visa, Delta, Mastercard, American Express, Barclaycard, Diners Club, Switch.

The biggest high street banks in London are Barclays, NatWest, HSBC and Lloyds TSB. Most have ATMs (also known as 'cash machines' or 'holes in the wall'), which can be used 24 hours a day and will often dispense money on foreign bank cards. Your bank's international banking department should advise you on this. All banks are open 9.30–3.30, although many are open later (until around 5pm). Some also open on Saturday

mornings. The easiest and safest way to carry large sums of money is by using travellers' cheques. These can be changed, for a small commission, at any bank or bureau de change. Try:

Thomas Cook
www.thomascook.com
Victoria Place, SW1, **t** (020) 7302 8660; 1 Marble Arch, W1, **t** 0845 308 9442; 30 St James's Street, SW1, **t** 0845 308 9570; 108 Fleet Street, EC4, **t** 0845 308 9399

Carrying money around

Use a money belt fastened around your waist under a tucked-in shirt or T-shirt. Pickpocketing is rife in certain parts of London, especially busy shopping areas such as Oxford Street. The most recent scams to watch out for are people copying your pin number at cashpoints and then stealing your credit card, and gangs of youths jostling you or swiping something from out of your back pocket. In short, do not put your purse or any other valuables in a back pocket or the rear zipper pocket of your backpack if you wish to see them again. Always keep wallets in your front trouser pockets and for best protection, carry shoulder bags over your chest with the opener flap on the inside. Otherwise, keep a close hold of your bag.

National holidays

Britain's national holidays are always arranged to fall on a Monday – Christmas, New Year's Day and Good Friday excepted. This not only allows people to enjoy a 'long weekend', but stops the nation from being cheated out of a holiday that would otherwise fall on a Saturday or Sunday. Shops and services tend to operate according to their Sunday hours and banks are always closed – which is why Britain's national holidays are usually referred to as bank holidays. *see* p.33 for a list of national holidays.

School holidays
State schools
Half-term Autumn, end of October, usually 1 week
Christmas two weeks
Half-term mid-February, usually 1 week
Easter two weeks

Half-term Spring Bank Holiday, late May/June, usually 1 week
Summer six weeks July/August

Private schools
Same half-terms
Christmas 3–4 weeks
Easter 3–4 weeks
Summer 8–9 weeks

Necessities

Wherever you're travelling with kids, it is always worth taking wet wipes, a full change of clothing, toys to fiddle with, drinks and snacks, plus some empty, disposable bags for unforeseen eventualities. Other items you might like to consider which could be picked up in London include:

- ▶ a torch/flashlight
- ▶ matches/lighter
- ▶ a night light
- ▶ safety pins
- ▶ an extension cord
- ▶ needle and thread
- ▶ a roll of sticky tape
- ▶ a net shopping bag
- ▶ moisturizing cream
- ▶ travel socket converters
- ▶ mild soap and baby shampoo
- ▶ playing cards, paper & crayons
- ▶ a forehead thermometer

One-parent families

There are various organizations in London offering advice and support for single parents travelling with children.

One Parent Families
255 Kentish Town Road, NW5
t 0800 018 5026
www.oneparentfamilies.org.uk
Runs a lone parent helpline.

Gingerbread
16–17 Clerkenwell Close, EC1
t 0800 018 4318
www.gingerbread.org.uk

Useful parenting websites
www.allkids.co.uk
www.babyandkids.co.uk
www.babycentre.co.uk
www.babydirectory.com
www.babyworld.com
www.eparenting.co.uk
www.familiesonline.co.uk
www.familycorner.com
www.forparentsbyparents.co.uk
www.kidsinmind.co.uk
www.kinderstart.com
www.mumsnet.com
www.parents-news.co.uk
www.practicalparent.org.uk
www.storknet.com
www.ukchildrensdirectory.com
www.ukparentslounge.com

One-Parent Family Holidays
t (01361) 810 710
http://.members.aol.com/opfholiday/

Opening hours

The traditional opening times for shops and offices in London are 9am until 5.30pm, although many shops are now open from 10am until 7pm. Most shops have one nominated day, usually Wednesday or Thursday, on which they stay open late, until 8 or 9pm. Sunday opening, most commonly between 11am and 5pm, has become the norm in recent years. Some of the capital's corner shops and supermarkets stay open 24 hours a day. Restaurants tend to open from 12noon–3pm and 6pm–11pm, although some stay open all day and later on weekends.

Post offices

You can buy stamps, post parcels and pay bills in London's post offices Mon–Fri 9–5.50 and Sat 9–12 noon, although if you want to send a postcard, most of the capital's newsagents sell stamps. The cost of sending a letter (up to 100g) to anywhere in the UK is 34p, while a postcard costs 48p to Europe and 54p to anywhere else. Post boxes, painted the same distinctive red as the capital's buses and older phone boxes, are common. You'll find post offices at 105 Abbey Street, SE1, **t** (020) 7237 8629; 43–44 Albemarle Street, W1, **t** (020) 7493 5620; 81–89 Farringdon Road, EC1, **t** (020) 7242 7262; 54–56 Great Portland Street, W1, **t** (020) 7636 2205; 24–28 William IV Street, Trafalgar Square, WC2, **t** (020) 7930 9580.

For more about Royal Mail services, visit **www**.royalmail.com. For complaints, call **t** 0845 740 740.

Safety

London is still a relatively law-abiding place, but in an emergency you can call the police, fire brigade or ambulance services on **t** 999 or 112. As a tourist, the crimes you are most likely to fall victim to are pickpocketing and petty thieving. London's busiest shopping districts – Oxford Street, Covent Garden, King's Road, Kensington High Street – are often targeted by organized gangs of pickpockets, but as long as you remain vigilant and take sensible precautions with your valuables, you should be able to enjoy a trouble-free holiday.

Of course, when travelling with children, you need to be extra vigilant. When on the streets or in a crowded place, make sure you never let them out of your sight. Always keep your children in front of you and continually take a head count. Under-2s can be kept safe on a wrist-rein. In the event that you do get separated, encourage your children to remain in one place and wait for you to find them. It is a good idea to give youngsters a whistle to blow in case they lose sight of you in busy areas. A bright cap or jacket makes them much easier to spot. If you have more than one child, colour match their clothes so that you only have one thing to watch out for. Older children may be trusted enough to explore by themselves within bounds. Even so, establish a central, easy-to-find meeting place. Ensure your children carry identification at all times and ensure you have an up-to-date photograph of them, too. Your children should also be made aware that they should never go anywhere with someone whom they don't know.

The golden rules

► Don't leave valuables in your hotel room.
► Keep most of your money in travellers' cheques.
► Keep all your valuables in a money belt fastened around your waist under a tucked shirt or T-shirt.
► Keep only small amounts of money in your wallet or purse. Keep your wallet in your trouser pocket and hold purses and bags close to your body with the flap facing inwards and the strap over your shoulder.
► Steer clear of unfamiliar areas of the city late at night.
► Try to avoid travelling alone on the Underground late at night.
► Do not leave bags hanging over chairs.
► Take care on busy shopping streets.

Telephones

There are still some red phone boxes left in London, although not nearly as many as the postcard industry would have you believe. British Telecom began removing these cast-iron monoliths in the early 90s, with the intention of replacing them with lighter, cheaper, plastic booths. The public raised such a fuss, however, that BT was forced to leave a significant number standing. They are still quite common in parts of the West End, but have almost completely disappeared from the suburbs, apart from in sleepy hamlets and villages.

All London's main Tube and train stations have ranks of public phones. You can buy excellent prepaid phonecards, such as Global or Tele2, which can be used from any phone using a pin number on the back of the cards. Ask at local newsagents.

Most payphones accept coins (any denomination from 10p up, the minimum call charge is 30p) and phonecards (available in denominations of £1, £2, £5, £10 and £20 from newsagents or post offices), although some only accept one or the other. Some booths let you pay by swiping a credit card. If possible, avoid using the phone in your hotel room as it is quite normal for the hotel to treble or even quadruple the call rate.

With ownership of mobile (cell) phones now nigh on ubiquitous, there are significantly fewer public phone boxes out on the streets than used to be the case. These days more and more travellers are choosing to take their mobile phones with them when abroad. To do this, your phone must be compatible with the GSM ('Global System for Mobile Communication'). Your network provider should be able to tell you if this is the case. Do also check your telephone company's pricing policy for making calls abroad. It is possible to rent mobile phones once abroad – try Rent-a-mobile, **t** 0790 593 3113, **www**.rent-a-mobile.co.uk – or, if your stay is to be an extended one, even buy one. Prices start at around £50 for a basic model.

Britain's domestic phones employ an unusual wide type of phone jack, and if you need to plug in a phone brought from abroad or a modem, you may have to buy an adaptor.

International calls are cheapest in the evening after 6pm and on weekends. The international dialling code is 00 followed by the country code:

France **33**
Germany **49**
Ireland **353**
Italy **39**
Australia **61**
New Zealand **64**
United States and Canada **1**

The telephone code for London itself is 020 (which you needn't dial for calls made within the city) followed by eight-digit number starting with either a 7 (for central London) or an 8 (for outer London). If dialling from outside the UK, remember to omit the initial 0.

The phone numbers of businesses and shops are listed in the Yellow Pages, available for £5 from BT. Also, check out their website at **www**.yell.co.uk.

Time

London is the official home of time. The prime meridian, the line of 0° longitude, runs through the quiet, southeast London borough of Greenwich and, since 1884, Greenwich Mean Time (GMT) has been the standard against which all other times are set. GMT is generally one hour behind western Europe. In summer, however, Britain switches to British Summer Time (BST) which is one hour ahead of GMT. Britain is five hours ahead of New York, eight hours ahead of San Francisco and 10 hours behind Tokyo and Sydney. In everyday conversation, the majority of Londoners will use the 12-hour clock – 9am, 3pm, etc. – but timetables are more often given using the 24-hour clock.

Tipping

Ten to 15 per cent is the usual rate in restaurants, taxis, hairdressers, etc. You are not obliged to tip, however, especially if the service was unsatisfactory. You would not normally tip a bartender in a pub. Restaurants sometimes add a service charge of 10–15 per cent, which should be shown on the menu. Tipping staff such as chambermaids and porters is discretionary, but much appreciated.

Toilets

The whereabouts of the nearest toilet is perhaps the single most important piece of information a parent can have. Most mainline stations have public toilets (20p per visit!) as do London's principal department stores and some fast-food outlets (notably McDonald's and Burger King). Pubs and restaurants, however, will sometimes only let you use their facilities (even in an emergency) if you're going to buy something. Public toilets on the streets of London are few and far between. The old-fashioned underground toilets have largely been phased out (there is still one in Leicester Square), but have yet to be replaced with an adequate number of street-level loos. You will come across the odd, free-standing automatic toilet known as a 'super loo' but, be warned, your 20p entitles you to a maximum 15 minutes' use of the facilities, after which the door will swoosh open revealing you (in whatever stage of undress) to the street. If in Covent Garden, check out the loos in St Paul's Churchyard, which have won awards for cleanliness and 'ambience'.

Tourist information

www.visitlondon.com
t 0870 566 366

The tourist office recently launched a child-friendly website dedicated to the capital with online games, offers and information about family attractions, www.kidslovelondon.com.

London Tourist Offices

Britain and London Visitor Centre
1 Regent Street, Piccadilly Circus, SW1
Open Mon–Fri 9–6.30, Sat–Sun 10–4

Heathrow Terminals 1,2,3 Underground concourse
Open daily 8am–6pm

Waterloo International Terminal
Open daily 8.30am–10.30pm

Greenwich Tourist Information Centre
Pepys House, 2 Cutty Sark Gardens, SE10
t 0870 608 2000
Open 10–5, daily

Liverpool Street Station
Liverpool Street Underground station, EC2
Open Mon–Fri 8am–6pm, Sat–Sun 8.45am–5.30pm

St Paul's Tourist Information Centre
St Paul's Cathedral, St Paul's Churchyard, EC4
t (020) 7332 1456
Open 10–5, daily

Victoria Station
Station Forecourt, SW1
Open Mon–Sat 8am–7pm, Sun 8am–6pm

Further Information

The most up-to-date information on the city's attractions and cultural life is provided by the main daily newspapers – the *Daily Telegraph*, *The Times*, the *Daily Mail*, the *Independent* et al – and, in particular, by the London daily *Evening Standard*, which produces a listings magazine *Metro Life* on Thursdays (with a special Kids' Section), and the *Guardian*, whose own listings magazine *The Guide* accompanies its Saturday edition. Also check out *Time Out*, the capital's best-selling weekly listings magazine, available in all major newsagents.

Tube safety and manners

When travelling on the Tube, keep your children close to you and in an orderly queue on the escalators. It is London practice to stand on the right so that people who wish to walk up or down can do so on the left. Once on the platform, move down so that other people have room to come and go. When you are on the train, it's best to sit down if there is a seat as this keeps the aisles free or allows people more space if they are standing. Don't stand by the doors if there is room to move down the carriage. During peak morning and evening hours, Tubes will be full of commuters and can get rather hot, so avoid these times if you can, especially if you have a pushchair. Carry water in case you or your children feel dehydrated. If you see any unattended luggage, don't touch it; ask other passengers if it is theirs and if it is suspicious, inform staff at the next Tube stop. If you pull the emergency cord, the train will stop at the next station. There are fines for misuse.

The London Tube Map

The first London Tube maps were done to scale but very hard to read. In the 1930s, a draughtsman called Harry Beck created a new map based on an electrical circuit diagram, making the distances between the stations in central London longer and those between outer London stations shorter. The result is one of the clearest and most copied diagrams in the world.

Sleep

The perfect family-friendly hotel should have all the facilities parents expect (large, well-equipped bedrooms; comfortable public rooms where they can relax in peace and quiet, sometimes away from the children; a baby-sitting/baby-listening or crèche service and a decent restaurant (with a menu that extends beyond pizza and chips) as well as all the things kids need (cots, highchairs, reasonable meal times, a supervised activity area, a swimming pool or garden). However, it should, above all, display a welcoming attitude to all members of the family.

The London Tourist Board runs an accommodation booking service dealing with everything from hotels and B&Bs to hostels, www.visitlondon.com/accommodation.

Hotels

If money is no object, you could, of course, go the five-star route: The Ritz, the Savoy, Claridges, the Dorchester – these are some of the most famous names. They're all centrally located with family suites and excellent facilities and all offer a guaranteed supply of petting and pampering – and all will charge £400 plus a night for a family of four; and even then there's no guarantee that your boisterous kids will be welcome in the restaurants and public rooms. At the other end of the scale are the budget hotels. A good one in the centre of town should set you back around £100 a night, for which you should get a TV, shower or bath, phone and breakfast. It can be even cheaper if you're willing to share a bathroom with other guests.

The big chains

The well-known international hotel chains are virtually guaranteed to be a safe bet. True, this type of hotel can be rather impersonal – their principal clients are businessmen, not families – but you can be sure the rooms will be clean and well equipped and the service reliable. Furthermore, many hotels offer a range of competitive packages and deals for families, as well as activity programmes and children's menus and some provide babysitting, baby-listening, cots and highchairs as standard. **Novotel**, the French-owned chain, offer Summer Fun Breaks which include family entry to a nearby attraction, while the Forte Group (who own the **Travelodge** chain among others) have, in the past, offered discounts of up to

50 per cent on some London hotels, a deal that includes reduced entry for kids to a West End show.

Best Western
t 0845 773 7373
www.bestwestern.co.uk
Doubles from £75 (prices do vary enormously, depending on the size and facilities of the hotel; this is by no means the minimum in all Best Western hotels)

Best Western operate 18 three- and four-star hotels in Greater London, including nine in Central London.

Choice Hotels
t 0800 444 444
www.choicehotelseurope.com
Doubles from around £80

The Choice Hotels group, which also includes Comfort Inns, Quality Inns, Sleep Inns and Clarion Hotels, offers a range of family deals, whereby kids get to stay for free in their parents room and receive free breakfast.

Holiday Inn
t 0870 400 9670
www.ichotelsgroup.com
Doubles from £60

Now part of the Intercontinental hotel group, there are 40 Holiday Inns and Holiday Express Inns in gGreater London. Most operate a 'kids eat free' restaurant policy and offer a range of family deals.

Novotel
t 0870 609 0962
www.novotel.com
Doubles from £49

Novotel, who operate hotels across the capital, are one of the most child-friendly chains around. Kids stay for free in their parents' room (and also get breakfast for free), are given a 'gift' when they arrive and also have a special indoor play area. Most hotels also have an outdoor play area and some have a pool. All Novotel restaurants offer a children's menu and activity sheets for kids to do while their parents are eating.

Premier Travel Inn
t 0870 242 8000
www.premiertravelinn.co.uk
Rooms From £48

The country's largest hotel chain, Premier Travel Inn offers basic, comfortable, and above all affordable accomodation. Their London hotels operate a 'Great Days out' scheme whereby up to two adults and two children get a room, breakfast and reduced entry to some of the capital's selected attractions (including Madame Tussaud's, the London Dungeon and the Tower of London).

Thistle

t 0870 414 1516
www.thistlehotels.com
Doubles from £150
    16 London hotels in locations including Bloomsbury, Kensington, Piccadilly and Trafalgar Square.

Travelodge

t 0870 085 0950
www.travelodge.co.uk
Rooms from £46
    Eight comfortable lodges in central London (including Covent Garden). The best rates are offered on the web.

Recommended hotels

The following are hotels which go out of their way to welcome and provide facilities for families.

22 Jermyn Street

22 Jermyn Street, SW1
t (020) 7734 2353
www.22jermyn.com
⊖ Piccadilly Circus
Doubles from £220, suites from £310
    Small luxury hotel behind Piccadilly Circus that welcomes children with their own newsletter, 'Kids' Talk', games, children's videos, a list of local child-friendly restaurants and teddy bear dressing-gowns. 24-hour room service; extra beds and cots available.

Ashley Hotel

15–17 Norfolk Square, W2
t (020) 7723 3375/9966
www.ashleyhotels.com
⊖/⇌ Paddington
Doubles from £50, family rooms from £95
    Cheap and cheerful family-run B&B (53 rooms) in three warren-like houses on a quiet square near Paddington Station. Family rooms are quite cramped (with tiny en-suite shower rooms), but from £80 per night for a family room, they are relatively good value. There are special rates for children sharing with parents and no charge for babies.

The Athenaum

116 Piccadilly, W1
t (020) 7499 3464
www.athenaeumhotel.com
⊖ Green Park
Doubles from £185, apartments from £380
    The Athenaeum is an upmarket hotel-apartment complex set in a row of elegant Piccadilly houses that prides itself on its family-friendliness. All the rooms are sumptuously appointed and each family apartment comes complete with sofas, plasma screen TVs, video games, hi-fi, washing machine and kitchen, allowing you to live a totally self-contained existence (but with the hotel's facilities – including a babysitting service – on call 24 hours a day). Guests are entitled to free use of the Athenaeum spa, gym and CD and video library.

Base2Stay

25 Courtfield Gardens
t (020) 7244 2255
www.base2stay.com
⊖ Earl's Court
Doubles from £99
    Adopting a sort of 'no frills' approach to hotel accommodation, Base2Stay offer simply decorated, comfortable, well-equipped rooms – all with flat screen TVs, free internet access and mini kitchens – at very decent rates.

Charlotte Street Hotel

15–17 Charlotte Street, W1
t (020) 7806 2000
www.firmdale.com
⊖ Tottenham Court Road
Doubles from £210, suites from £350
    At first glance, this swish boutique hotel just off Oxford Street would seem the very antithesis of family-friendly – somewhere for media types rather than children. And, while it does cater to its fair share of urban socialites, it's also very welcoming to younger visitors. Its loft suites, in particular, provide the perfect base for a travelling domestic brood with separate areas for children to play in, while their parents enjoy the hotel's luxurious modern conveniences.

County Hall Travel Inn Capital

Belvedere Road, SE1
t 0870 238 3300
www.premiertravelinn.co.uk
⊖/⇌ Waterloo

All rooms £99

Centrally located, excellent-value hotel above the London Aquarium, next to the new London Eye and just across the Thames from the Houses of Parliament. Part of the Travel Inn chain, this hotel provides reliable, no-frills accommodation with extra cots and children's menu available.

Crescent
49–50 Cartwright Gardens, WC1
t (020) 7387 1515
www.crescenthoteloflondon.com
⊖/⇌ Euston
Doubles from £97, family from £120
One of several B&B hotels on this Bloomsbury Crescent just north of the British Museum, this is perhaps the pick of the bunch. The rooms are fairly basically equipped, but cheap for the location. Ground-floor rooms available (but no lift to upper floors). No charge for under-2s; cots and highchairs available and babysitting by arrangement. You can hire rackets for use in the tennis courts in the square outside.

Draycott
26 Cadogan Gardens, SW3
t (020) 7730 6466
www.draycotthotel.com
⊖ Sloane Square
Doubles from £200, family from £500
A terribly grand B&B (or 'boutique suite hotel' as it prefers to refer to itself) overlooking Cadogan Gardens, the Draycott offers pretty much every facility you could wish for (minus a restaurant, of course): grandly furnished bedrooms, wi-fi, CD and DVD players, satellite TV and, for the kids, Playstations and gift packages.

Durrants Hotel
George Street, W1
t (020) 7935 8131
www.durrantshotel.co.uk
⊖ Bond Street
Doubles from £95, family from £210
Smart, very traditional family-run hotel (92 rooms), housed in an 18th-century building behind the Wallace Collection and within easy reach of Bond Street. It has a comfortable lounge – lots of pine and mahogany panelling – a good restaurant (dinner from 6pm) and can arrange a babysitting service. Extra cots and highchairs available.

Edward Lear
28–30 Seymour Street, W1
t (020) 7402 5401
www.edlear.com
⊖ Marble Arch
Doubles from £59.50, family from £89.50 (prices go down the longer you stay)
Extremely friendly hotel, just 50 yards from Oxford Street, housed in two 18th-century houses that were once the home of the famous nonsense-verse writer (and composer of *The Owl and the Pussycat*) Edward Lear. His illustrated limericks adorn the public rooms. The bedrooms are quite spacious but not necessarily en-suite, and there's no charge for under-2s, or for under-13s sharing their parents' room at weekends. Extra cots available.

Goring
Beeston Place, Grosvenor Gardens, SW1
t (020) 7396 9000
www.goringhotel.co.uk
⊖/⇌ Victoria
Doubles from £199, family from £335
Right in the heart of Royal London, a stone's throw from Buckingham Palace and the great parks, this is a very grand, upright, traditionally British sort of establishment that nonetheless does its best to accommodate the needs of families. The public rooms are furnished in country house-style with open fires in winter, the bedrooms are sumptuous with all mod cons and there's a large private garden. Guests are entitled to free use of the local health club and there's a babysitting service available.

Hart House Hotel
51 Gloucester Place, W1
t (020) 7935 2288
www.harthouse.co.uk
⊖ Baker Street, ⊖/⇌ Marylebone
Doubles from £125, family from £145
Very smart B&B housed in a West End Georgian mansion. The rooms vary in size – those near the top tend to be larger and brighter – and are decorated in a variety of styles, from antique to modern. Toys are provided for the kids, there are extra cots and a babysitting service is available.

Hilton Metropole

225 Edgware Road, W2
t (020) 7402 4141
www.hilton.co.uk/londonmet
⊖ Marble Arch
Doubles from £150, although prices do rise considerably in the high season

This huge hotel just outside the centre makes a good family choice. Kids stay for free in their parents' room and there's a swimming pool, a children's menu available in the restaurants and a babysitting service (not to mention great views out over London from the 23rd floor). Highchairs and video games also available. It's a 10-minute walk (or a two-minute bus ride) to Oxford Street.

Parkwood

4 Stanhope Place, W2
t (020) 7402 2241
www.parkwoodhotel.com
⊖ Marble Arch
Doubles from £79, family from £99 (prices go down the longer you stay)

Owned by the same people as the Edward Lear, this small hotel is just a few yards from Hyde Park. It boasts several large, bright family rooms as well as a gallery of pictures by children who have visited the hotel. Extra beds, cots and highchairs available plus babysitting by arrangement.

Hotel La Place

17 Nottingham Place, W1
t (020) 7486 2323
www.hotellaplace.com
⊖ Baker Street
Doubles from £127, family from £139

Small, family-owned hotel on a quiet street near Madame Tussaud's, with a good restaurant (supper served 6–8.30, highchairs available), pleasantly furnished rooms and a welcoming atmosphere. Babysitting can be arranged.

Rushmore

11 Trebovir Road, SW5
t (020) 7370 3839
www.rushmore-hotel.co.uk
⊖ Earl's Court
Doubles from £69, family from £99

Just around the corner from Earl's Court tube station, the Rushmore is a welcoming, family-friendly B&B with 22 decently priced, decently decorated rooms. The ones on the third floor have private patios. Breakfast is served in a light-filled atrium. Free cots available.

Apart'hotels

A relatively new concept for the UK, these self-catering apartments have all the facilities you'd expect at home, plus hotel services on call 24 hours a day. There are two room sizes: a studio (sleeps four) or apartment (sleeps six) and prices start at around £160 a night, though some are cheaper if you stay for over a month. The French company **Citadines, t** 0800 376 3898, **www**.citadines.com, has complexes in Covent Garden, South Kensington, Trafalgar Square and the Barbican.

Family-friendly hotel checklist

Here is a list of things to look out for when hotel-hunting.

▶ special family packages or discounts. Do remember that British hotels tend to charge per person rather than a room rate, so cramming everyone into the same room doesn't always make sound economic sense. However, many hotels do allow children sharing their parents' room to stay free of charge.

▶ a choice of family rooms with three or more beds

▶ rooms with interconnecting doors

▶ a constantly monitored baby-listening service

▶ access to whatever leisure facilities there might be. Nothing is guaranteed to put a damper on a child's spirits more than being told they can't use the swimming pool

▶ cots and highchairs

▶ children's meals. Are they healthy, served at a conveniently early time, in a family-friendly location, and if not, are children welcome in the restaurant?

▶ designated play areas for children. If there's an outdoor play area, is it safe and supervised?

▶ supplies of toys, books and, even better, computer games

▶ a babysitting service

▶ a crèche

▶ organized activities for children

▶ qualified child-care staff

Bed & breakfast

A British institution, these are small guest houses or private houses (usually located in residential areas outside the city centre) which hire out rooms at a reasonable price. Although you may have to share a bathroom, it is possible to get accommodation for as little as £15–30 per person per night. To find out how welcoming a potential B&B is to families, try asking the following questions.

▶ Are there cots and high chairs available?
▶ Is it possible to have separate children's meals at a time that suits them?
▶ Are the children expected to eat with the adults or at separate tables?
▶ Is there running-around space for children?
▶ Is there a comfortable lounge for the adults to relax in once the children have gone to bed?

The following agencies all have extensive lists of B&Bs throughout London.

Host and Guest Service

103 Dawes Road, SW6
t (020) 7385 9922
www.host-guest.co.uk

Throughout London. From £30 per person per night. You can download a brochure from the website.

London Bed and Breakfast Agency

71 Fellows Road, NW3
t (020) 7586 2768
www.londonbb.com

Throughout London. Double rooms from £25 per person per night, though they also offer much more expensive accommodation.

Uptown Reservations

50 Christchurch Street, SW3
t (020) 7351 3445
www.uptownres.co.uk

Upmarket B&B and self-catering apartments in Kensington, Knightsbridge and Chelsea. Family rooms from £125; double rooms from £95.

Renting a flat

For a stay of several weeks, or even months, it is probably worth thinking about renting a flat. Not only does this make sound economic sense, it will also give you the chance to become familiar with the local community – meeting the neighbours, shopping in the local grocery stores, etc. Self-catering also allows you to do what you like when you like. You can get up when it suits you, nurse your colicky newborn at 3am and scramble eggs whenever your toddler gets peckish. Again, there are some important questions that are worth asking.

▶ How far is your accommodation from the nearest shops, supermarket, launderette, restaurants, transport and park?
▶ How many bedrooms does the flat have? The phrase 'sleeps 6' does not necessarily mean that there will be three bedrooms; often a sofa in the living room converts into a bed, and you may even need to rearrange the room in order to create enough sleeping space.
▶ Are cots supplied and, if so, is there an additional charge for them?
▶ Are the children's rooms fitted with bunk beds and, if so, do these have safety rails?
▶ Is the garden or pool fenced off and are there any nearby ponds, streams or other potential hazards?
▶ Is it safe for children to play unsupervised in the garden?
▶ Can babysitting be arranged locally?

Holiday Serviced Apartments

273 Old Brompton Road, SW5
t (0845) 060 4477
www.holidayapartments.co.uk

Can supply serviced and unserviced apartments all over London; two-bed flats from £900 per week.

AAE Shortlets

1 Princess Mews, Belsize Crescent, NW3
t (020) 7794 1186
www.aaeshortlets.co.uk

Apartments in northwest London; two-bed flats from £700 per week.

Euracom

Stanmore Towers, 8–14 Church Street, Stanmore, HA7

t (020) 8420 7666
www.euracom.co.uk
   Two-bed flats from £400 per week plus booking
fee. You can download a PDF brochure from the
website.

Globe Apartments
36 James Street, W1
t (020) 7935 9512
www.globeapt.com
   Serviced apartments throughout central London
from £400 per week.

Home exchange

The principle could not be easier: you hand your
home over to another family, while they take on
yours. You need to supply details of your home
and family to an agency which lists you in their
directory. References may be checked and a holiday
agreement exchanged for added security.
   The advantages of home exchange are obvious.
You automatically have someone to care for your
home, and even your pets, while you are away.
Most importantly, exchanging homes with a family
with children the same age as yours means their
home is certain to be child-proofed and stocked
with all the baby equipment you need to make
your holiday fun and hassle-free. The savings can
also be huge. Your only real expenses are signing
up with an agency, transport to your destination
and the usual holiday expenses.
   Before you take the plunge, be specific about
what you require from a visiting family and the
sort of upkeep you expect, such as feeding pets,
watering plants, tidying and taking messages.
   To organize a home exchange contact one of the
following:

In the UK
NCT House-Swap Register
t (01626) 360 689
www.nct.org.uk/involve/spend/houseswap
   Membership fee £29.99
   Run by the National Childbirth Trust, its register
only lists families with at least one child under 12.

Intervac Home Exchange
t 0845 260 5776
www.intervac-online.com

Homelink International
t (01962) 886 882
www.homelink.org.uk
   Membership fee £115

Home Base Holidays
t (020) 8886 8752
www.homebase-hols.com

In the US
Homelink International
t 800 638 3841
www.home-exchange-us.homelink.org

Trading Homes International
t 310 798 3864
www.trading-homes.com

International Home Exchange
t (0800) 877 8723
www.homeexchange.com

Youth Hostels

Forget the dowdy image of cheesecloth, mung
beans and compulsory acoustic guitar sessions;
youth hostels have smartened up their act and
offer family rooms with no chore rotas attached.
Apart from being cheap and easy-going, youth
hostels can also more easily accommodate larger
family groups. Most hostels allow under-3s to stay
for free and can provide cots and highchairs. The
hostels at Hampstead and Rotherhithe also offer
a children's menu. The best YHA hostels in London
are listed below, for reservations call **t** 0870 770
8868, **www**.yha.org.uk.

London St Paul's Youth Hostel
36 Carter Lane, EC4, **t** 0870 770 5764
↔ St Paul's
Beds Adult £18.95, child £14.50

London Oxford Street Youth Hostel
14 Noel Street, W1, **t** 0870 770 5984
↔ Oxford Street
Beds Adult £23, child £19

London Thameside Youth Hostel
20 Salter Road, SE16, **t** 0870 770 6010
↔ Rotherhithe, Canada Water
Beds Adult £24, under-18s £19.50

Eat

Happily, the number of restaurants prepared to cater for the often fickle fancy of children is growing all the time. Sunday lunchtime, in particular, is often designated 'family time' in many eateries, with some even laying on entertainment in the form of magic shows and face painting.

How much?

Unless otherwise indicated you should be able to get a meal for one adult and one child, at whatever time, for less than £25–£30.

When?

London restaurants tend to serve lunch between 12.30 and 3pm and dinner between 7 and 10pm.

Cheap Eats

Café in the Crypt

St Martin-in-the-Fields, WC2, **t** (020) 7839 4342
⊖ Charing Cross
Open Mon–Wed 8–8, Thurs–Sat 8am–10pm, Sun 12 noon–6.30

Atmospheric subterranean café whose semi-dungeonesque appearance should appeal to youngsters. With a wide selection of hot dishes, and snacks as well as a decent children's menu, this is a good place to come after a hard morning's sightseeing. Half portions are (rather logically) half price. High chairs available.

Chelsea Kitchen

98 King's Road, SW3, **t** (020) 7589 1330
⊖ Sloane Square
Open Mon–Sat 8am–11.30pm, Sun 9am–11.30pm

Sells a wide range of (very cheap) sandwiches, salads and pasta dishes.

Ed's Easy Diner

15 Great Newport Street, WC2, **t** (020) 7836 0271
⊖ Covent Garden
12 Moor Street W1, **t** (020) 7434 4439
⊖ Tottenham Court Road
Trocadero, 19 Rupert Street, W1, **t** (020) 7287 1951,
⊖ Piccadilly Circus
www.edseasydiner.co.uk
Branches open Mon–Thurs and Sun 11.30am–12 midnight, Fri and Sat 11.30am–1am

It's a bit noisy, but the burgers and chips in this mock-1950s 'rock 'n' roll' diner (complete with jukebox) are good and they have a very reasonably priced 'Junior Bites' kids' menu, made up of burgers, hot dogs and chicken fillets (all £4.25). Highchairs available.

Frizzante

1a Goldsmiths Row, E2, **t** (020) 7739 2266
⊖ Bethnal Green, ≥ Cambridge Heath

Open summer Tues–Sun 10–5.30, winter Tues–Sun 10–4.30
Unicorn Theatre, 147 Tooley Street, SE1, **t** (020) 7645 0560, ⊖/≥ London Bridge
Open Tues–Fri 9.30–4, Sat 11–5, Sun 12 noon–5
www.frizzanteltd.co.uk

There are two branches of this great (and great value) Italian café and deli, both of which occupy child-friendly locations: in the Unicorn Theatre near London Bridge, and in amongst the fields and paddocks of Hackney City Farm (see p.177)

Giraffe

46 Rosslyn Hill, NW3, **t** (020) 7435 0343
⊖ Hampstead
29–31 Essex Road, N1, **t** (020) 7359 5999
⊖ Old Street, ≥ Essex Road
7 Kensington High Street, W8, **t** (020) 7938 1221
⊖ High Street Kensington
Units 1 & 2, Riverside Level 1, Royal Festival Hall,
t (020) 7928 2004, ⊖/≥ Waterloo
21 High Street, Wimbledon, SW19, **t** (020) 8946 0544, ⊖/≥ Wimbledon
For details of other branches, visit **www**.giraffe.net
Branches open daily 8am–11.30pm

With its bright, colourful décor and piped world music, Giraffe has a rather groovy, youthful ambience. Both adults and children are well catered for with a selection of menus. Children can choose between the 'Kids' Brunch', 'Kids' Grill' and 'Veggie Kids' options. Highchairs available.

Manze's

87 Tower Bridge Road, SE1, **t** (020) 2407 2985
www.manze.co.uk, ⊖ London Bridge, Tower Hill
Open Mon 11–2, Tues–Thurs 10.30–2, Fri–Sat 10–2.45

Manze's is the oldest pie and mash shop in London (it first opened in 1862) and, despite the many competing eateries, still one of the most popular with queues that regularly stretch right down the street at lunchtime (when it's open). The food is traditional and determinedly unglamorous

– minced beef pies, jellied eels and big dollops of mash all topped with liquor (parsley sauce) – not to mention very cheap. Where else can you feed a family of 4 for under £15?

American

Big Easy

332–4 Kings Road, SW3, **t** (020) 7352 4071
www.bigeasy.uk.com, ⊖ Sloane Square
Open Mon–Thurs and Sun 12 noon–11, Fri & Sat 12–12

If your kids like seafood, then you've come to the right place. This excellent, Louisiana-style diner specializes in huge plates of prawns, crabs and lobster (they also do burgers and ribs). Children get their own 'Little Urchins' menu made up of burgers and ribs (all child mains £5), along with paper and crayons.

Bodeans

10 Poland Street, W1, **t** (020) 7287 7575
www.bodeansbbq.com, ⊖ Oxford Circus
Open Mon–Fri 12 noon–3 and 6–11, Sat–Sun 12 noon–11

This American-style smokehouse has a takeaway service and deli upstairs and a restaurant downstairs, with TV screens showing American sports for adults and (on weekends only) a chic, black pad for the kids to lounge in, with TVs showing the latest cartoons and films. Kids eat free between 12 noon and 3pm Mon–Fri and from 12 noon–5pm on weekends (one child per adult).

Gourmet Burger Kitchen

13 Maiden Lane, WC2, **t** (020) 7240 9617
⊖ Covent Garden
Open Mon–Sat 12–11, Sun 12–10
15 Frith Street, W1, **t** (020) 7494 9533
⊖ Tottenham Court Road
Open Mon–Thurs 12 noon–11, Fri and Sat 11.30–12 midnight, Sun 11.30–10
45 Greenwich Church Street, SE10
t (020) 8858 3920, ⇌ Greenwich, **DLR** Greenwich, Cutty Sark
Open Mon–Fri 12 noon–11, Sat 11-11, Sun 11–10

One of the best of the 'upmarket burger' chains to have opened in recent years, the GBK offers a variety of unusual burger choices, including

chicken, avocado and bacon; aubergine and goat's cheese, and even venison. Kids get junior versions of the more traditional beef and chicken burgers. Adult burgers are served medium, junior burgers are served well done.

The High Chaparral

35 Greenwich Church Street, SE10, **t** (020) 8293 9143
⇌ Greenwich, **DLR** Greenwich, Cutty Sark
Open Mon–Sat 12 noon–11, Sun 12 noon–10

Fun little Tex-Mex diner where you can load up on fajitas, enchiladas and nachos.

Maxwell's

8/9 James Street, WC2, **t** (020) 7836 0303
⊖ Covent Garden, Embankment, Leicester Square
76 Heath Street, Hampstead, NW3
t (020) 7794 5450, ⊖ Hampstead
Branches open Mon–Sat 10am–12 midnight, Sun 10am–11.30pm

The children's menu at this diner-style eatery is full of games and puzzles; there are join-the-dots, pictures to colour in and word searches. It features lots of favourites, including chicken nuggets, fish 'stix', burgers and hot dogs, as well as a few surprises of its own – Mega Chocolate Madness Cake and deep-fried ice cream. At the James Street branch, the outside seating provides good views of the musicians and 'robot' men who busk this patch. Do be aware that the restaurant is rather less family-friendly during the evening, when it fills up with groups of young revellers.

Texas Embassy Cantina

1 Cockspur Street, SW1, **t** (020) 7925 0077
www.texasembassy.com, ⊖ Charing Cross
Open Mon–Thurs 12 noon–11, Fri–Sat 12 noon–12 midnight, Sun 12 noon–10.30

Popular Tex-Mex diner just a stone's throw from Trafalgar Square, housed in the former headquarters of the White Star Shipping Line (which owned the ill-fated Titanic). Its name is a reference to the brief period between 1836–45 when Texas was an independent country and opened an embassy in London near this spot. Children are catered for with a dedicated menu (which entitles them to unlimited drinks refills) of Tex-Mex-lite cuisine (filled tacos, cheese nachos and hot dogs) plus games, puzzles and balloons. Outside tables and highchairs available.

Fish & Chips

Rock and Sole Plaice

47 Endell Street, WC2, **t** (020) 7836 3785
⊖ Covent Garden
Open daily 11.30–10.30

The oldest fish-and-chip shop in the capital (it opened in 1871) and still one of the best, serving large portions of battered fish and big fat chunky chips. Outside seating and highchairs available.

Seashell

49–51 Lisson Grove, NW1, **t** (020) 7224 9000
www.seashellrestaurant.co.uk
⊖ Marylebone
Open Mon–Fri 12 noon–2.30 and 5–10.30,
Sat 12 noon–10.30

Albeit not quite as venerable as the Rock and Soul Plaice, this two-floor establishment has still been in business for over forty years. As well as the standard cod and plaice, some more upmarket choices are offered, including Dover sole and sea bass.

Hot & Spicy

Blue Elephant

3–6 Fulham Broadway, SW6, **t** (020) 7385 6595
www.blueelephant.com, ⊖ Fulham Broadway
Bus 11, 14., 28, 211, 295, C4
Open Mon–Thurs 12 noon–2.30 and 7–11.30,
Fri and Sat 12 noon–2.30 and 6.30–11.30, Sun
12 noon–3 and 7–10.30

Famous Thai restaurant offering great value, super-spicy Sunday lunchtime meals for £22 per head, with entertainment laid on for children (face painting etc). Kids will love the restaurant's jungle-like décor. The set lunchtime menu in the week is just £10 per head (although there's no entertainment).

Chutney Mary

535 King's Road, SW10, **t** (020) 7351 3113
www.chutneymary.com, ⊖ Fulham Broadway
Open Mon–Sat 12.30–2.30 and 5.30–11.30,
Sun 12.30–3 and 7–10.30

This pleasant, modern Indian restaurant is very popular with families, particularly on Sundays when they offer a children's menu for £10 consisting of a mixture of mild curry dishes and reliable stand-bys for fussy eaters – fish fingers, burgers, etc. There is a very pleasant conservatory. Highchairs available.

Masala Zone

9 Marshall Street, W1, **t** (020) 7287 9966
www.realindianfood.com, ⊖ Oxford Circus
Open Mon–Sat 12 noon–2.30 and 5.30–11.30,
Sun 12.30–3

This brightly-coloured, subtly-lit diner is the latest venture by the excellent Chutney Mary Group and offers a menu mainly comprised of inexpensive street-food dishes, which are piquant and sweet rather than overly spicy. There's also a Children's Thali available on request. The chicken burger comes highly recommended. Weekday lunchtimes are pretty busy and there's no booking, but the roomy upstairs level is a plus point for those with pushchairs in tow.

Mediterranean

Carluccio's

Garrick Street, WC2, **t** (020) 7836 0990
⊖ Covent Garden
8 Market Place, W1, **t** (020) 7636 2228
⊖ Oxford Circus
St Christopher's Place, W1, **t** (020) 7935 5927
⊖ Bond Street
Fenwick, New Bond Street, W1, **t** (020) 7629 0699
⊖ Bond Street
Reuters Plaza, Canary Wharf, E14, **t** (020) 7719 1749
⊖ Canary Wharf
12 West Smithfield, EC1, **t** (020) 7329 5904
⊖ Farringdon
www.carluccios.com
Branches open Mon–Fri 8am–11pm, Sat 9am–11pm,
Sun 9am–10.30pm

Though the branches of this small chain of restaurant-delicatessens can get crowded in the evenings, they make an excellent spot for lunch when families are treated to a real Mediterranean welcome. There are plenty of simple ravioli and spaghetti dishes for children and (if they're good) ice cream bombes for pudding. And once you've finished eating, you can always browse the delicatessen for supplies. Highchairs available.

Daphne

83 Bayham Street, NW1, **t** (020) 7267 7322

⊖ Camden Town

Open Mon–Sat 12 noon–2.30 and 6–11.30

Warm, welcoming and very popular Greek restaurant with a lovely sunny roof terrace. Children's portions and highchairs available.

La Lanterna

6–8 Mill Street, SE1, **t** (020) 7252 2420

www.pizzerialalanterna.co.uk

⊖ Tower Hill

Open Mon–Fri 12–3 and 6–11, Sat 6pm–11pm, Sun 1pm–10.30pm

Small, homely, traditional Italian restaurant serving good reasonably priced fare. Half portions and highchairs available. It can get quite crowded, especially in the evenings when live music is staged at the next-door café.

Monza

6 Yeoman's Row, SW3, **t** (020) 7591 0210

⊖ South Kensington, Knightsbridge

Open Tues–Sun 12 noon–2.30 and 7–11.30, Mon 7–11.30 only

A small, quaint Italian restaurant offering a range of pizza, pasta and risotto dishes to suit all tastes. Family-orientated with excellent service, its walls are decorated with motor-racing memorabilia (Monza hosts the Italian Formula 1 Grand Prix).

Tamesa@Oxo

2nd Floor, Oxo Tower, Barge House Street, SE1

t (020) 7633 0008

www.oxotower.co.uk/tamesa

⊖/≋ Waterloo

Open Mon–Sat 12 noon–3.30 & 5.30–11.30, Sun 12noon–4

If your budget isn't quite up to the grand prices of the Oxo Tower restaurant on the 8th floor, you can make do instead with the less inflated prices (and less elevated views) of this second floor establishment. It is a colourful affair, all bright purples and blues, with a menu encompassing all parts of the globe. The children's menu costs £5.50 and offers a choice of steak, fish and chips, and pasta and tomato sauce.

Oriental

Benihana

37–43 Sackville Street, W1, **t** (020) 7494 2525

⊖ Piccadilly Circus, Green Park

77 King's Road, SW3, **t** (020) 7376 7799

⊖ Sloane Square

100 Avenue Road, NW3, **t** (020) 7586 9508

⊖ Swiss Cottage

www.benihana.co.uk

Branches open Mon–Sat 12 noon–3 and 5.30–10.30, Sun 5–10

Fun Japanese noodle chain for families looking to experiment. Several dishes are specifically designed for children's tastes and kids, for their part, enjoy watching the skilful chefs preparing the food at their tables – Ninja style.

Chuen Cheng Ku

17 Wardour Street, W1, **t** (020) 7437 1398

www.chuenchengku.co.uk

⊖ Leicester Square

Open Mon–Sat 11am–11.45pm, Sun 11am–11.15pm

Has the longest menu in Chinatown, which can prove a little daunting – just ask for the day's specials, you're unlikely to be disappointed. If you're hoping to impress the waiters with your grasp of Cantonese, try asking for the following: Tsun Guen (mini spring rolls), Pai Gwat (steamed tiny spare ribs) or Har Gau (rice dumplings stuffed with shrimps). It's extremely child-friendly, with booster seats, highchairs and baskets of goodies for good little kiddies.

New World

1 Gerrard Place, W1, **t** (020) 7734 0396

⊖ Leicester Square

One of the best places to introduce your children to the joys of Chinese food. On Sundays it's packed with families tucking into bowls of dim sum (Chinese dumplings, the restaurant's speciality). Try the special child-size mini dim sum.

Royal China

40 Baker Street, W1, **t** (020) 7487 4688

⊖ Baker Street

Open Mon–Thurs 12 noon–11pm, Fri & Sat 12 noon–11.30pm, Sun 11–10

This terribly grand affair is one of the capital's best Chinese restaurants outside of Chinatown itself. Nonetheless, it welcomes (well-behaved) children and the dim sum is superb. Highchairs available.

Royal Dragon
30 Gerrard Street, W1, t (020) 7734 1388
⊖ Leicester Square

Excellent dim sum and a family-friendly atmosphere, particularly on Sundays.

Pizzas

Gourmet Pizza Company
Gabriel's Wharf, 56 Upper Ground, SE1
t (020) 7928 3188
www.gourmetpizzacompany.co.uk
⊖ Waterloo
Open 12 noon–10.30

This small, rather upmarket pizza restaurant has recently been subsumed into the Pizza Express empire, although it's still trying to retain its own identity. Even if its menu is not quite as original as it once was, it still enjoys a great riverside location and serves a decent pizza. Highchairs available.

Pizza on the Park
11 Knightsbridge, SW3, t (020) 7235 7825
www.pizzaonthepark.co.uk
⊖ Hyde Park Corner, Knightsbridge
Open Mon–Fri 8.15am–12 midnight, Sat–Sun 9.30am–12 midnight

This bright, cheery pizza restaurant is the perfect place to fill up after a morning spent in the park or nearby museums. Colouring books, crayons and balloons are handed out at weekends. Children's portions and highchairs available.

Pizza Organic
20 Old Brompton Road, SW7
t (020) 7589 9613, ⊖ South Kensington
75 Gloucester Road, SW7, t (020) 7370 6575
⊖ Gloucester Road
www.pizzapiazza.co.uk
Open daily 11.30am–12 midnight

An avowedly environmentally conscious restaurant, Pizza Organic, which is run by the same people as Pizza Piazza, offers stone-baked pizzas and a children's menu featuring the 'O-People'; six cartoon characters designed to teach children all about the exciting world of organic produce (good) and GM foods (bad).

Posh Nosh

Browns
47 Maddox Street, W1, t (020) 7491 4565
⊖ Bond Street
8 Old Jewry, EC2, t (020) 7606 6677
⊖ Bank
82–84 St Martin's Lane, WC2, t (020) 7497 5050,
⊖ Leicester Square, Covent Garden
Butler's Wharf, Shad Thames, SE1, t (020) 7378 1700
⊖ London Bridge, Tower Hill
www.browns-restaurants.com
Branches open Mon–Wed 9am–11pm, Thurs and Fri 9am–11.30pm, Sat 10–11.30, Sun 10–10.30

Well-to-do but ever family-friendly brasserie chain. Children get their own menu and crayons can be requested. The restaurants occasionally run deals whereby under-12s get to eat for free if accompanied by an adult. Be warned, it can be a bit pricey.

Locanda Locatelli
8 Seymour Street, W1
t (020) 7935 9088
www.locandalocatelli.com
⊖ Marble Arch
Open daily 12 noon–3 & 7–11

"If my children are not welcome (in a restaurant), then neither am I", so says Giorgio Locatelli, the proprietor of this very upmarket, yet also very family-friendly restaurant. But, then, Signor Locatelli is from Italy where the family meal is an entrenched part of the national way of life. The restaurant's kitchen is happy to adapt its more fancy dishes to children's tastes, while also encouraging older children to be more adventurous. And, who knows, when you visit you may find yourself sitting next to Madonna or Nigella Lawson or one of its other famous patrons.

National Dining Rooms
Level 1, Sainsbury Wing, National Gallery, Trafalgar Square, WC2
t (020) 7747 2525
www.nationalgallery.org.uk
⊖ Charing Cross, Leicester Square, Embankment
Open Thurs–Tues 10–5, Wed 10–8.30

A rather fancy lunchtime or afternoon option (it's only open during gallery hours) the National Gallery's new flagship restaurant is both reassuringly English and admirably family friendly. While adults tuck into the hearty fare of the main menu (beef, trout, rabbit etc.), kids can raid the junior menu for boiled eggs and soldiers (£2.50), macaroni cheese (£5.50) and fish and chips (£6.50).

Oxo Tower Restaurant

Oxo Tower, Barge House Street, South Bank, SE1
t (020) 7803 3888, **www**.harveynichols.com
⊖/⇌ Waterloo, Blackfriars
Open Mon–Sat 12 noon–2.30 & 6–11, Sun 12 noon–3 and 6.30–10

Serves great food and can offer some of the most stunning river views to be found in London (especially magical at night). They offer a brasserie kids' menu at weekends.

Searcy's

Level I, Barbican Centre, EC2
t (020) 7588 3008, ⊖ Barbican
Open Mon–Fri 12 noon–2.30 and 6–10.30, Sat–Sun 12 noon–3 and 5–6.30

This bright, airy modern-looking diner overlooks the Barbican's central courtyard and fountains. It's a bit hi falutin' (not to say a touch pricey), but does its best to accommodate families.

Pubs

Cutty Sark

Ballast Quay, off Lassell Street, SE10
t (020) 8858 3146
⇌ Greenwich, **DLR** Greenwich, Cutty Sark
Open Mon–Sat 11am–11pm, Sun 12 noon–10.30

A little further downriver from the Trafalgar Tavern, the Cutty Sark is another lovely riverside pub with great views of the Millennium Dome and Canary Wharf. Decorated in a nautical style with bits of old ships adorning the walls, it offers a children's menu made up of the usual fare – sausages, chicken nuggets, etc.

Dickens Inn

St Katharine's Way, E1, **t** (020) 7488 2208
www.dickensinn.co.uk, ⊖ Tower Hill, Tower Gateway, **DLR** London Bridge

The best of both worlds, this Tower stalwart (one of the oldest buildings on this stretch of the river) houses a pizzeria (upstairs) to keep the kids happy and a pub (downstairs) where adults can enjoy a pint (or two). In summer, it's a great spot for dining

alfresco with its balconies overlooking the dock. It stands next to the 'Grand Turk', a full-size replica of an 18th-century 'man-of-war'. Children's portions, high chairs and baby-changing available.

Dirty Dick's

202 Bishopsgate, EC2, **t** (020) 7283 5888
⊖ Liverpool Street
Open Food served daily 12 noon–2.30

Once upon a time, this East London boozer had on display a very strange collection of artefacts. They originally belonged to one Nathaniel Bentley, a local ironmonger who, in the 18th century, had a shop on nearby Leadenhall Street. He led a largely uneventful life up until the night before his wedding when his wife-to-be tragically died, after which Nathaniel refused to wash or change his clothes or alter any of the contents of his house for the rest of his life. His only company during this time were his cats who, when they died, where simply left where they fell to rot. Upon his death, the contents of his house (including the cats) were bought up by the owner of this pub and, strange as it may seem, put on display.

Now that the artefacts have been removed, this is today a rather a clean and spruce pub that rather belies its name, serving decent family meals in its vaulted cellar.

The Engineer

65 Gloucester Avenue, NW1, **t** (020) 7722 0950
⊖ Chalk Farm
Open Mon–Fri 12 noon–3 and 7–11, Sat–Sun 12.30–3.30 and 7–11 (kids' menu daily 12 noon–3)

Gastropubs are all the rage with the parenting set, mainly because of their more relaxed café-bar atmosphere, where it's okay to linger over a coke and a newspaper as well as enjoy the quality of the food. The Primrose Hill area is very popular with families, so several of its pubs are family-friendly. This one offers a special children's menu (available daily from 12 noon–3pm), crayons and colouring books, highchairs and nappy-changing facilities. Oh, and the food is pretty good too.

The Grenadier

Wilton Row, SW1
t (020) 7235 3074
⊖ Hyde Park Corner
Open Food served Mon–Sat 12 noon–1.30, Sun 12 noon–3

It's hard to beat a Sunday afternoon roast at this atmospheric pub. Kids can tuck into their meals while you revive yourself with one of the bar's famous Bloody Marys.

The Trafalgar Tavern
Park Row, SE10, **t** (020) 8858 2437
⊜ Greenwich, **DLR** Greenwich, Cutty Sark
Open Mon–Sat 11.30am–11pm, Sun 12 noon–10.30

Just east of the Royal Naval College, this friendly pub has been welcoming visitors since 1837. In the mid-19th century, Liberal cabinet ministers gathered here on the Sunday after Whitsun to feast on whitebait caught from the Thames. Unfortunately, the pollution of the river put an end to their revelries in 1868. Today, the refurbished pub provides an elegant setting for a riverside meal and whitebait is even back on the menu, although it's no longer caught in the Thames. Children's menu available.

Tea-Time Treats

Fortnum & Mason Fountain Room
181 Piccadilly, W1, **t** (020) 7734 8040
www.fortnumandmason.co.uk, ⊖ Piccadilly Circus
Open Mon–Sat 7.30am–11pm

A wonderfully elegant tea room set in the basement of the Queen's grocers. They offer a children's menu, but the highlight here is definitely their wide and delicious range of specially made ice creams, sorbets, sundaes and sodas. It's a haven of old-fashioned style and charm, suitable for older children. Once you've finished your ice cream, pop outside to watch the workings of the famous Fortnum & Mason clock.

Gloriette Patisserie
128 Brompton Road, SW3, **t** (020) 7589 4750
⊖ Knightsbridge
Open Mon–Sat 7am–7pm, Sun 9–6

This is a great place for anyone with a sweet tooth. Boasting a fantastic selection of tempting cakes, from creamy chocolate gateaux to glazed fruit tarts, it also sells a wide variety of snacks, ranging from salads to assorted tasty sandwiches.

Patisserie Valerie
Gelaterie Valerie, Duke of York Square, SW3
t (020) 7730 7978, ⊖ Sloane Square
Open Mon–Sat 8am–7pm, Sun 10–7
105 Marylebone High Street, W1, **t** (020) 7935 6240,
⊖ Baker Street, Bond Street
Open Mon–Fri 7.30am–8.30pm, Sat 8am–8.30pm,
Sun 9–6.30
43 Old Compton Street, W1, **t** (020) 7437 3466,
⊖ Leicester Square
Open Mon–Fri 7.30–7, Sat 8–7, Sun 9–6
162 Piccadilly, W1, **t** (020) 7491 1717
⊖ Green Park
Open Mon–Fri 7.30–7.30, Sat 8–8, Sun 9–7
27 Kensington Church Street, W8, **t** (020) 793 79574,
⊖ High Street Kensington
Open Mon–Fri 7.30–7pm, Sat–Sun 8–7
www.patisserie-valerie.co.uk

First established in the 1920s by Belgian-born baker Madame Valerie, each branch of this pâtisserie-cum-café chain has a pleasant continental ambience and stocks a wonderful array of sticky treats as well as savoury snacks and salads. The chain also recently opened a replica Italian *gelateria* on Duke of York Square, selling all manner of delicious ice creams.

Ritz Hotel
150 Piccadilly, W1, **t** (020) 7493 8181
www.theritzhotel.co.uk, ⊖ Green Park
Tea daily 1.30pm, 3.30pm and 5.30pm

Afternoon tea at the Ritz is rather steep at £36 a head, but the setting and the sight of the cakes, sandwiches and scones piled high on silver platters make it an experience few children are likely to forget. Book well in advance (at least three months for a weekend) and dress smartly (no jeans).

Treat Eats

Hard Rock Café
150 Old Park Lane, W1, **t** (020) 7514 1700
www.hardrock.com, ⊖ Hyde Park Corner
Open Sun–Thurs 11.30am–12.30am, Fri–Sat
11am–1am

Younger kids can enjoy the colour-in menu (£4.25, featuring macaroni cheese or fried chicken, as well as the staple burger and chips) and the collection of toys. Their older siblings will love the videos and spotting the jackets of surprisingly diminutive rock stars. Cross the road to the shop afterwards and be sure to go downstairs to the Vault for a tour of the curious bits and bobs left behind on the road to eternal stardom. Bo Diddley's home-made guitar, John Lennon's military jacket and Buddy Holly's trademark specs are among the highlights.

Planet Harrods

Fourth Floor, Harrods, 87–135 Brompton Road, SW1
t (020) 7730 1234, ✚ Knightsbridge
Open Mon–Sat 10–7, Sun 12 noon–6

An American-style restaurant where cartoons play constantly on big screens.

Planet Hollywood

13 Coventry Street, W1, **t** (020) 7734 6220
www.planethollywoodlondon.com
✚ Leicester Square, Piccadilly Circus
Open daily 11.30am–1am

Somewhat beleaguered, this once mighty chain is still hanging in there. Always filled with tourists and noisy beyond measure, it's nonetheless worth a look if you're in the area. Kids like the garish posters and cabinets full of movie memorabilia. The food is expensive (the under-12s kid's menu is £7.95) but perfectly reasonable (burgers, ribs, etc.).

Rainforest Café

20 Shaftesbury Avenue, W1, **t** (020) 7434 3111
www.therainforestcafe.co.uk
✚ Leicester Square, Piccadilly Circus
Bus 3, 12, 14, 19, 22, 38
Open Sun–Thurs 12 noon–11, Fri–Sat 12 noon– 12 midnight
Suitable for all ages

A wonderful theme restaurant, particularly popular with young children. As the name suggests, the tables and chairs have been placed in among the trees and foliage of an artificial rainforest. Inhabiting the dense under-growth are various mechanical animals, including chimps, monkeys, alligators, birds and snakes, who come alive every 15 minutes to whoop and chatter following a rather loud artificial thunderstorm. Games and face painting are laid on at weekends. The grill-style menu is tasty, albeit rather expensive. The kids' menu alone is a rather hefty £10.25, for which you get a choice of main (burgers, chilli and rice, pasta and tomato sauce etc.), drink and dessert.

Smollensky's

105 The Strand, WC2, **t** (020) 7497 2101
✚ Embankment, Charing Cross

Open Mon–Wed 12 noon–12 midnight, Thurs–Sat 12 noon–12.30am, Sun 12 noon–5.30 and 6.30–11
Bradmore House, Queen Caroline Street, Hammersmith, W6, **t** (020) 8741 8124
✚ Hammersmith
Open Mon–Sat 12 noon–2.30 and 5.30–11
Hermitage Wharf, 22 Wapping High Street,
t (020) 7680 1818
✚ Tower Hill
Open Mon–Fri 12–3 and 6–10.30, Sat 6–10.30, Sun 12 noon–6
For details of other branches, visit www.smollenskys.co.uk

This is the restaurant that started the whole craze for putting on children's entertainment at weekends – kids can have their faces painted, watch a Punch and Judy show, take part in magic tricks and eat something from the American-style kids' menu. Parents will appreciate the tinkling piano music and succulent grill steaks and fish specials. Children's entertainment on Saturday and Sunday afternoons, book in advance.

Sticky Fingers

1a Phillimore Gardens, W8, **t** (020) 7938 5338
www.stickyfingers.co.uk
✚ High Street Kensington, Holland Park
Bus 9, 10, 27, 28, 31, 49, 94
Open daily 12 noon–12 midnight

The owner, Bill Wyman, used to play bass guitar for the Rolling Stones and the restaurant is filled with rock-and-roll memorabilia – all of which will probably be lost on the restaurant's younger visitors. Nonetheless, they will enjoy the burgers, and the magic shows, activities and face painting on Sunday afternoons. Highchairs available.

TGI Friday's

6 Bedford Street, WC2, **t** (020) 7379 0585
✚ Covent Garden, Leicester Square
Open daily 12 noon–11.30
29 Coventry Street, W1, **t** (020) 7379 6262
✚ Piccadilly Circus, Leicester Square
Open daily 12 noon–11
www.tgifridays.co.uk

An ever-popular choice, this lively Tex-Mex diner is something of a bargain for families offering very reasonably priced children's meals. All the mains, comprising the usual hamburger, chicken in a bun, and fish finger options, are £2.95. They also offer free organic baby food for children aged 4–15 months. High chairs, booster seats and colouring books available.

Vegetarian

Food For Thought
31 Neal Street, WC2, **t** (020) 7836 0239
◉ Covent Garden
Open Mon–Sat 12 noon–8.30, Sun 12 noon–5
 Cheap and friendly, serving quiches, salads, soups, etc. It can get a little crowded, so turn up for an early lunch to be sure of a seat.

Manna
4 Erskine Road, NW1, **t** (020) 7722 8028
www.manna-veg.com, ◉ Chalk Farm
Open Mon–Sat 6pm–11pm, Sun 12.30–3 and 6–11
Spacious, popular and highly regarded veggie restaurant.

Oshobasho
Highgate Wood, Muswell Hill, N10
t (020) 8444 1505, ◉ Highgate
Open daily 8.30–7.30, the park gates close at 8.30pm
 Extremely popular vegetarian restaurant in the idyllic setting of Highgate Wood. Familes flock to its large outdoor seating area at the weekends. There's also a children's play area. If you're feeling adventurous after your meal, pick up a nature trail from the next-door woodland centre and head off into the trees. *See* p.174.

Food Chains

Ask Pizza
197 Baker Street, NW1, **t** (020) 7486 6027
◉ Baker Street
48 Grafton Way, W1, **t** (020) 7388 8108
◉ Warren Street
121 Park Street, W1, **t** (020) 7945 7760
◉ Marble Arch
103 St John Street, EC1, **t** (020) 7253 0323
◉ Farringdon
56 Wigmore Street, W1, **t** (020) 7224 3484
◉ Bond Street
74 Southampton Row, WC1, **t** (020) 7405 2876
◉ Holborn, Russell Square

Spice Quay, 34 Shad Thames, Butlers Wharf, SE1,
t (020) 7403 4545
◉ London Bridge, Tower Hill
145 Notting Hill Gate, W11, **t** (020) 7792 9942
◉ Notting Hill
222 Kensington High Street, W8, **t** (020) 7937 5540
◉ High Street Kensington
300 Kings Road, SW3, **t** (020) 7349 9123
◉ Sloane Square
160–162 Victoria Street, SW1, **t** (020) 7630 8228
◉ Victoria
www.askcentral.co.uk
Branches open 11.30am–11.30pm
 Pizza Express's main rival for the title of 'best pizza chain', Ask also specializes in thin-crust, Italian-style pizzas and has a similar continental ambience. There's no special children's menu, but families are made to feel very welcome with children's portions and highchairs readily available.

Belgo
Belgo Centraal, 50 Earlham Street, WC2,
t (020) 7813 2233, ◉ Covent Garden
Open Mon–Thurs 12 noon–11, Fri–Sat 12 noon–11.30, Sun 12 noon–10.30
Belgo Noord, 72 Chalk Farm Road, NW1,
t (020) 7267 0718, ◉ Chalk Farm
Open Mon–Fri 12 noon–3 and 5.30–11, Sat 12 noon–11.30, Sun 12 noon–10.30
Also *see* branches of **Bierodrome,** their gastropub counterparts, **open**: daily 12 noon–12 midnight
173–4 Upper Street, N1, **t** (020) 7226 5835, ◉ Angel
44–48 Clapham High Street, SW4, **t** (020) 7720 1118,
◉ Clapham Common or Clapham North
67 Kingsway, Holborn, WC2, **t** (020) 7242 7469;
◉ Holborn
www.belgo-restaurants.com
 Belgo Centraal and Belgo Noord make up the two branches of this very fashionable restaurant. All welcome children with open arms and free food (under-12s eat free, 2 kids per 1 adult, so long as the adult orders at least one main course from the à la carte menu). While adults try some Belgian specialities such as Moules Marinière (mussels with celery and onion) or chilled asparagus with Ardennes ham, children can tuck into the restaurant's more child-friendly (albeit still Belgian-centric) fare – wild boar sausages and mash, followed by waffles with fruit and white chocolate sauce – from the colour-in 'Mini-Belgo' menu. Be warned, the restau-

rant is very trendy and, as a result can get pretty busy, especially at weekends.

Café Pasta

2 Garrick Street, WC2, **t** (020) 7497 2779
◉ Leicester Square, Covent Garden
229 Kensington High Street, **t** (020) 7937 6314
◉ High Street Kensington
184 Shaftesbury Avenue, **t** (020) 7379 0198
◉ Leicester Square
www.cafepasta.co.uk
Branches open Mon–Sat 11.30am–12 midnight,
Sun 11.30-11

Pizza Express's pasta-mad sibling, this chain displays many of the same qualities: attractive décor, good food and a genuinely family-friendly atmosphere, achieved without recourse to games or gimmicks. Highchairs available.

Café Rouge

27–31 Basil Street, SW3, **t** (020) 7584 2345,
◉ Knightsbridge
Open Mon–Sat 8.30am–11pm, Sun 9am–10.30pm
Victoria Place, 115 Buckingham Palace Road, SW1
t (020) 7931 9300, ◉ Victoria
Open Mon–Fri 8am–11pm, Sat 9am–11pm, Sun 11–10.30
46 James Street, W1, **t** (020) 7487 4847
◉ Bond Street
Open Mon–Sat 10am–11pm, Sun 10am–10.30pm
Unit 5, Condor House, St Paul's Churchyard, EC4,
t (020) 7489 7812
◉ St Paul's
Open Mon–Sat 8.30am–11pm, Sun 9am–10.30pm
34 Wellington Street, WC2, **t** (020) 7836 0998
◉ Covent Garden
Open Mon–Sat 9am–11pm, Sun 9am–10.30pm
Hay's Galleria, Tooley Street, SE1, **t** (020) 7378 0097
◉ London Bridge
Open Mon–Fri 8.30am–11pm, Sat 9am–11pm, Sun 9am–10.30pm
Hillgate House, Limeburner Lane, EC4,
t (020) 7329 1234
◉ Blackfriars
Open Mon–Sat 8.30am–11pm, Sun 9am–10.30pm
Ibis Hotel, Stockwell Street, SE3, **t** (020) 8293 6660
DLR Greenwich, Cutty Sark
Open daily 10.30–11pm
For details of other branches, visit
www.caferouge. co.uk

Child-conscious French café chain offering a child's menu for £4.25 (croque monsieur and fries, sausage and mash etc.), as well as an activity pack with word searches, pictures to colour in and quizzes.

Caffè Uno

28 Binney Street, W1, **t** (020) 7499 9312
◉ Charing Cross, Leicester Square
24 Charing Cross Road, WC2, **t** (020) 7240 2524
◉ Charing Cross, Leicester Square
9 Kensington High Street, W8, **t** (020) 7937 8961
◉ High Street Kensington
40–42 Parkway, NW1, **t** (020) 7428 9124
◉ Camden Town
64 Tottenham Court Road, W1, **t** (020) 7636 3587
◉ Goodge Street
11 Edgware Road, WC2, **t** (020) 7723 4898
◉ Marble Arch
www.caffeuno.co.uk
Branches open daily 11am–11pm

Good for a quick pizza or bowl of pasta, Caffè Uno is a reasonably priced Italian chain. The brightly coloured children's menu is sponsored by the Cartoon Network and offers a choice of simple pizza and pasta dishes (spaghetti bolognese, etc.) plus the odd Anglicized addition (fish and chips), ice cream and a free drink – all for £4.95. High chairs, activity sheets and crayons available.

Fish!

Cathedral Street, SE1, **t** (020) 7407 3803
www.fishdiner.co.uk
◉ London Bridge, Borough
Open Mon–Thurs 11.30am–11pm, Fri and Sat 11–11, Sun 12 noon–10.30

Fish! is about as far from the traditional British chippy as it's possible to get. Its greatest strength is the quality and choice it offers. Not only are there about 12 different varieties on offer every day, but you can also choose the way in which it is cooked. Although children may baulk at some of the choices, they're bound to find something they like on the children's menu – which entitles them to two courses (they can choose chicken and chips if fish doesn't take their fancy), a drink and dessert. They are also given a Kids' Pack of games and puzzles. Highchairs available.

Pizza Express

125 Alban Gate, London Wall, EC2, **t** (020) 7600 8880
◉ Barbican, St Paul's
Open daily 11.30am–12 midnight
133 Baker Street, W1, **t** (020) 7486 0888
◉ Baker Street

Open daily 11.30am–12 midnight
21–22 Barrett Street, St Christopher's Place, W1,
t (020) 7629 1001, ⊖ Bond Street
Open Mon–Sat 11.30–12 midnight, Sun 11.30–11.30
Benbon House, 24 New Globe Walk, SE1,
t (020) 7401 3977
⊖ London Bridge
Open Mon–Thurs 11.30–11.30, Fri & Sat 11.30–12
midnight
9 Bow Street, WC2, **t** (020) 7240 3443
⊖ Covent Garden
Open Mon–Sat 11.30–12 midnight, Sun 11.30–11.30
6–7 Beauchamp Place, Knightsbridge, SW3,
t (020) 7589 2355
⊖ Knightsbridge
Open Mon–Sat 11.30am–12 midnight,
Sun 11.30–11.30
Cardamom Building, 31 Shad Thames, SE1,
t (020) 7403 8484
⊖ Tower Hill, London Bridge
Open Mon–Thurs & Sun 11.30–11, Fri & Sat 11.30–
12 midnight
7 Charlotte Street, W1, **t** (020) 7580 1110
⊖ Goodge Street
Open daily 11.30–12 midnight
30 Coptic Street, Bloomsbury, WC1,
t (020) 4636 3232
⊖ Holborn, Tottenham Court Road
Open daily 11.30am–12 midnight
26 Cowcross Street, EC1, **t** (020) 7490 8025
⊖ Farringdon
Open daily 11.30–11
49 Curtain Road, EC2, **t** (020) 7613 5426
⊖ Liverpool Street, Old Street
Open daily 11.30am–12 midnight
10 Dean Street, W1, **t** (020) 7439 8722
⊖ Tottenham Court Road,
Open daily 12 noon–11.30
20 Greek Street, W1, **t** (020) 7734 7430
⊖Leicester Square
Open daily 11.30am–12 midnight
4 Greenwich Church Street, Greenwich, SE10,
t (020) 8853 2770, **DLR** Greenwich
Open Mon–Sat 11.30–11, Sun 11.30–10.30
85 Parkway, NW1, **t** (020) 7267 2600
⊖ Camden
Open Sun–Thurs 11.30am–11pm, Fri–Sat 11.30am–
12 midnight
The Pheasantry, 152 King's Road, SW3,
t (020) 7351 5031
⊖ Sloane Square

Open Mon–Sat 11.30–12 midnight, Sun 11.30–11.30
2 Salisbury House, London Wall, EC2,
t (020) 7588 7262
⊖ Barbican, St Paul's, Bank, Liverpool Street
Open Mon–Fri 11.30–10.30, Sat 12 noon–5
80–81 St Martin's Lane, WC2, **t** (020) 7836 8001
⊖ Covent Garden, Leicester Square
Open Mon–Sat 11.30am–12 midnight, Sun 11.30–11
13–14 Thayer Street, London, W1, **t** (020) 7935 2167
⊖ Oxford Circus
Open Mon–Sat 11.30am–11pm, Sun 12 noon–10pm
6 Upper St James Street, Golden Square, W1,
t (020) 7437 4550, ⊖ Piccadilly Cirucs
Open Mon–Sat 11.30–11.30, Sun 12 noon–9.30
The White House, 9c Belvedere Road, SE1,
t (020) 7928 4091
⊖ Waterloo
Open daily 11.30am–12 midnight
www.pizzaexpress.com

Serving tasty, thin-crust Italian-style pizzas
(plus a few pasta dishes such as lasagne and
canneloni), this is by far the best pizza chain in
London. Whichever one you choose, you won't go
far wrong. Some of the more popular branches
offer crayons and colouring books.

Tootsies

35 James Street, **t** (020) 7486 1611, ⊖ Bond Street
107 Old Brompton Road, SW7, **t** (020) 7581 8942
⊖ South Kensington
Open daily 10am–11pm
120 Holland Park Avenue, **t** (020) 7229 8567
⊖ Holland Park
Open Mon–Fri 9am–11pm, Sat & Sun 9am–11.30pm
198 Haverstock Hill, NW3, **t** (020) 7431 7609
⊖ Belsize Park
Open Mon–Sat 10am–11pm, Sun 10am–10.30pm
48 High Street, Wimbledon, SW19,
t (020) 8946 4135
⊖ Wimbledon
Open Mon–Thurs 11am–11.30, Fri 11–11, Sat
9am–11pm, Sun 9am–10.30pm
www.tootsiesrestaurants.co.uk

Upmarket, rather trendy burger chain serving
American-style food in generous portions. Children
are given colouring books and crayons. Main
courses from the childrens' menu include burgers
(£4.95), sticky ribs (£4.95) and spaghetti with
tomato sauce (£3.75) and are served with dessert
(around £2.50) and a milkshake £1.50. Highchairs
available.

Wagamama

11 Jamestown Road, NW1, **t** (020) 7428 0800
Θ Camden Town
26 Kensington High Street, W8, **t** (020) 7376 1717
Θ High Street Kensington
10a Lexington Street, W1, **t** (020) 7292 0990
Θ Oxford Circus
4a Streatham Street, WC1, **t** (020) 7323 9223
Θ Tottenham Court Road
101 Wigmore Street, W1, **t** (020) 7409 0111
Θ Oxford Circus
1 Tavistock Street, WC2, **t** (020) 7836 3330
Θ Covent Garden, Charing Cross
14a Irving Street, WC2, **t** (020) 7839 2323
Θ Leicester Square
8 Norris Street, Haymarket, SW1, **t** (020) 7321 2755
Θ Piccadilly Circus
22 Old Broad Street, EC2, **t** (020) 7256 9992
Θ Liverpool Street, Bank (closed Sat & Sun)
4 Great St Thomas Apostle, EC4, **t** (020) 7248 5766
Θ Mansion House (closed Sat & Sun)
2b Tower Place, Tower Hill, EC3, **t** (020) 7283 5897
Θ Tower Hill
Unit 7, Riverside Level 1, Royal Festival Hall, SE1,
t (020) 7021 0877
Θ Waterloo
1a Ropemaker Street, EC2, **t** (020) 7588 2688
Θ Moorgate (closed Sat & Sun)
www.wagamama.com
Branches open various; check 'See It, Do It' chapters
or phone individual branches for details

Though rather canteen-like with its long refectory tables, this fast-growing noodle house chain is surprisingly family friendly, although the (inevitable) hustle and bustle may appeal more to older children. They've recently introduced a number of dedicated children's meals, including 'mini chicken katsu', 'mini ramen' and 'kids' ebi rice'. Highchairs available.

Yo! Sushi

52 Poland Street, **t** (020) 7287 0443
Θ Oxford Circus, Tottenham Court Road
County Hall, Belvedere Road, SE1, **t** (020) 7928 8871
Θ Waterloo
95 Farringdon Road, Clerkenwell, EC1
t (020) 7841 0785
Θ Farringdon
St. Albans House, 57 Haymarket, SW1
t (020) 7930 7557
Θ Piccadilly Circus
www.yosushi.com
Branches open various; check 'See It, Do It' chapters
or phone individual branches for details

A dining experience unlike any other – you pick sushi dishes from an enormous conveyor belt whilst your drinks are prepared by a special drinks-mixing robot. Children get a games bag and their own menu, which offers such Japanese delicacies as salmon teriyaki, crunchy Chinese broccoli (every child's favourite) and tuna sandwiches, and comes with a pair of special child-friendly chopsticks. During the week under-12s eat for free. Highchairs and clip-on baby seats available.

Shop

As far as families are concerned, there are two types of shop: those that children visit under duress – clothes shops are a good example – and those that parents visit under duress – Hamleys, for instance. Inevitably, after a shopping trip, one half of the family will be left feeling pretty grumpy and upset, either because they've been made to try on a particularly nasty sweater, or because they've been dragged through a seething mass of teddy bears. We've done our best to cover both types from the most granny-friendly knitwear shops to the most overwhelming toy stores.

Arts, crafts & hobbies

The Bead Shop

24 Earlham Street, WC2
t (020) 7379 9214
www.londonbeadshop.co.uk
⊖ Covent Garden
Bus 6, 9, 11, 13, 15, 23, 77A, 91, 176
Open daily 10.30am–8pm

Getting kids to make their own jewellery is a great way of filling a spare afternoon. The Bead Shop, tucked away behind Cambridge Circus, near Covent Garden, provides thousands of coloured baubles, beads and fasteners.

British Museum Shops

22 Bloomsbury Street, WC1
t (020) 7637 9449
⊖ Tootenham Court Road, Russell Square, Holborn
Open Mon–Sat 9.30–6, Sun 12 noon–6

There are four outlets which, in total, make up the British Museum shopping experience: a souvenir and guide shop on the west side of the Great Court, selling souvenir mugs, books, T-shirts, etc (the place to pick up that all-important Rosetta Stone pencil sharpener or mummy T-shirt); the slightly more fancy Grenville shop, next to Room 3 by the entrance, which specializes in expensive reproductions of museum exhibits – replica sculptures, jewellery, clothes, etc.; a book shop on the north side of the Great Court; and last but not least, a specialist children's shop on the east side of the Great Court, filled with pocket-money-priced souvenirs for young visitors. You can also shop online at **www**.britishmuseum.co.uk.

Comet Miniatures

44–48 Lavender Hill, SW11
t (020) 7228 3702
www.comet-miniatures.co.uk
⇌ Clapham Junction **Bus** 77, 77A, 345
Open Mon–Sat 9.30–5.30

A haven of hobbydom, Comet sells all manner of collectibles – rare Japanese toys, film figures, comics etc. – as well as thousands of plastic aircraft assembly kits.

Kite Store

48 Neal Street, WC2
t (020) 7836 1666
⊖ Covent Garden
Bus 6, 9, 11, 13, 15, 23, 77A, 91, 176
Open Mon–Wed, Fri–Sat 10–6, Thurs 10–7

The Kite Store sells just about every size, shape and colour of kite imaginable. It also stocks a range of aerobatic toys including boomerangs, yo-yos and water-powered rockets. Pride of place, however, goes to the cutting-edge 'flexifoil' kites, which are capable of lifting a grown man clear off the ground.

St Martins Accessories

95 St Martin's Lane, WC2
t (020) 7836 9742
www.stmartinsmodelcars.co.uk
⊖ Covent Garden
Bus 6, 9, 11, 13, 15, 23, 77A, 91, 176
Open Mon–Fri 9.30–6, Sat 11–5

Everything the model-car enthusiast could want: racks and racks of model sporting classics – Ferraris, Porsches, Aston Martins and more – all rendered in perfect miniature detail.

Stanley Gibbons

399 The Strand, WC2
t (020) 7836 8444
www.stanleygibbons.com
⊖ Charing Cross
Bus 6, 9, 11, 13, 15, 23, 77A, 91, 176
Open Mon–Fri 9–5.30, Sat 9.30–5.30

The biggest name in the world of stamps, the Stanley Gibbons stamp emporium on the Strand has become a mecca for collectors from all over the world. As well as a vast collection, it also has a museum, a show room and even an auction house. It's very grand and attracts some seriously wealthy enthusiasts but, nonetheless, is still a great place for kids to come and start a collection by picking up a £1 bag of assorted stamps.

Baby & nursery

Dragons of Walton Street

23 Walton Street, SW3
t (020) 7589 3795
www.dragonsofwaltonstreet.com
⊖ South Kensington
Open Mon–Fri 9.30–5.30, Sat 10–5

This is where society mothers come to furnish their nurseries in the latest designer fittings. The handmade, hand-painted furniture is undeniably beautiful, but also exorbitantly expensive.

Nursery Window

83 Walton Street, SW3
t (020) 7581 3358
www.nurserywindow.co.uk
⊖ South Kensington
Open Mon–Sat 10–6

Not nearly as grand as the nearby Dragons, Nursery Window is still rather well to do. It sells a cheery range of fabrics, toys and accessories.

Green Baby

345 Upper Street, N1
t (020) 7359 7037
⊖ Angel
52 Greenwich Church Street, SE10
t (020) 8858 6690
DLR Cutty Sark
www.greenbaby.com
Branches open Mon–Sat 10–5, Sun 11–5

Baby goods for the environmentally conscious, such as washable nappies and organic toiletries. Also stocks pushchairs and Baby Trekkers and runs a mail-order service, **t** 0870 240 6894.

Mothercare

26 Kings Mall Shopping Centre, W6, **t** (020) 8600 2860, ⊖ Hammersmith
526 Oxford Street, W1, **t** 0845 365 0515
⊖ Bond Street
www.mothercare.com
Branches open Mon–Wed, Sat 10–7, Thurs–Fri 10–8, Sun 12 noon–6

This is perhaps the country's most famous and reliable children's chainstore. It's been around for

years and is still selling toys, nursery equipment, well-made, reliable clothes and maternity wear at reasonable prices. Also has a mother-and-baby room.

Books & comics

London's book scene is dominated by two giant multinationals: Waterstone's and Borders (incorporating Books Etc). Both operate a chain of huge bookstores throughout the capital (Waterstone's, Piccadilly, is the largest bookshop in Europe) with good, well-stocked children's sections and comfortable interiors. For something a little different, try Foyle's in Charing Cross Road. Although its famously sprawling layout has been rationalized in recent years, tracking a book down here is still a real adventure, and the children's section is fantastic. A second, smaller branch of Foyle's recently opened at the Southbank Centre.

Harrods, Selfridges and the dedicated kids' department store, Daisy and Tom, have also all got great children's book departments (see pp.244–5).

A network of smaller, specialist bookstores including several dedicated children's bookstores are mostly located on the outskirts of town. These include the Golden Treasury (Southfields and Fulham), the Children's Bookshop (Muswell Hill), The Bookworm (Finchley) and Word Play (Crouch End).

In a more teenage vein, if your kids are big Spider Man comic fans, try Gosh! on Great Russell Street where you can pick up *Marvel*, *DC* and *2000 AD* back copies (as well as compilations of newspaper strip cartoons such as Peanuts and The Far Side), or Comic Showcase at 63 Charing Cross Road. For science fiction, head to the new Forbidden Planet megastore on Shaftesbury Avenue, which has a huge collection of SF comics, books and models.

Chains & large bookshops

Borders & Books Etc

30 Broadgate Circle, EC2, **t** (020) 7628 8944, ⊖ Liverpool Street; 122 Charing Cross Road, WC2, **t** (020) 7379 8877, ⊖ Tottenham Court Road; 70 Cheapside, EC2, **t** (020) 7236 0398, ⊖ St Paul's; 9–13 Cowcross Street, EC1,

t (020) 7608 2426, ⊖ Farringdon; 176 Fleet Street, EC4, t (020) 7353 5939, ⊖ St Paul's; 263 High Holborn, WC1, t (020) 7404 0261, ⊖ Holborn; 54 London Wall, EC2, t (020) 7628 9708, ⊖ Moorgate; 421 Oxford Street, W1, t (020) 7495 5850, ⊖ Oxford Circus
www.bordersstores.co.uk
Branches open 9.30–8, Sunday 12 noon–6

Foyle's

113–19 Charing Cross Road, WC2, t (020) 7437 5660 ⊖ Tottenham Court Road, Bus 14, 19, 24, 29, 38, 176
Open Mon–Sat 9.30–9, Sun 12 noon–6pm
Riverside, Level 1, Royal Festival Hall, SE1, t (020) 7437 5660, ⊖ Waterloo
Open Mon–Sat 10am–10pm
www.foyles.co.uk

Waterstone's

128 Camden High Street, NW1, t (020) 7824 4948, ⊖ Camden Town; 150–152 Kings Road, SW3, t (020) 7351 2023, ⊖ Sloane Square; 87 Brompton Road, SW1, t (020) 7730 1234, ⊖ Knightsbridge, 203–206 Piccadilly, W1, t (020) 7851 2400, ⊖ Piccadilly Circus; 82 Gower Street, WC1, t (020) 7636 1577, ⊖ Goodge Street; 9/13 Garrick Street, WC2, t (020) 7836 6757, ⊖ Leicester Square; 11 Islington Green, N1, t (020) 7704 2280, ⊖ Angel; 19–23 Oxford Street, W1, t (020) 7434 9759, ⊖ Tottenham Court Road; The Grand Building, Trafalgar Square, WC2, t (020) 7839 4411,⊖ Charing Cross; 1–3 Whittington Avenue, Leadenhall Market, EC3, t (020) 7220 7882,⊖ Bank
www.waterstones.com
Branches open Mon–Sat 9.30–8, Sun 12 noon–6

Children's & specialist bookshops

The Bookworm

1177 Finchley Road
t (020) 8201 9811
⊖ Golders Green
Bus 7
www.thebookworm.uk.com
Open Mon–Sat 9.30–6

Children's Bookshop

29 Fortis Green Road, N10
t (020) 8444 5500
⊖ East Finchley

Bus 7
Open Mon–Sat 10–6

Forbidden Planet

179 Shaftesbury Avenue, WC2
t (020) 7420 3666
⊖ Tottenham Court Road, Covent Garden
Bus 14, 19, 24, 29, 38, 176
Open Mon–Fri 10–7 (Thurs till 8), Sat 12–6

The Golden Treasury

29 Replingham Road, SW18, t (020) 8333 0167, ⊖ Southfields; 95–97 Wandsworth Bridge Road, SW6, t (020) 7384 1821, ⇌ Clapham Junction
www.thegoldentreasury.co.uk
Branches open Mon–Fri 10–6, Sat 9.30–5.30

Gosh! Comics

39 Great Russell Street, WC1
t (020) 7636 1011
⊖ Tottenham Court Road
Bus 7
Open 10–6, Thurs–Fri 10–7

The Lion and the Unicorn

19 King Street, Richmond, TW9
t (020) 8940 0483
⊖/⇌ Richmond
Bus 72, 74, 85, 371
www.lionunicornbooks.co.uk
Open Mon–Sat 10–6

Tales on Moon Lane

9 Princess Road, NW1
t (020) 7722 1800
⊖ Camden Town
25 Half Moon Lane, SE24
t (020) 7274 5759
⇌ Herne Hill
www.talesonmoonlane.co.uk
Branches open Mon–Fri 9–5.30, Sat 9.30–6, Sun 11-4

Word Play

1 Broadway Parade, Crouch End, N8
t (020) 8347 6700
⊖ Archway, Highgate
⇌ Crouch Hill
Bus 43, 271
Open Mon–Sat 9–5.30, Sun 11–5

Clothes & shoes

Barney's
6 Church Road, Wimbledon, SW19
t (020) 8944 2915
⊖/≹ Wimbledon
Bus 93
Open Mon–Sat 10–6, Sun 12 noon–5

Just up the hill from the All England Tennis Club, this is the perfect place to pick up an outfit on your way to Centre Court. It stocks all the big names in children's design – Catimini, Roobarb & Custard, Paul Smith and Elle. *Expensive.*

Bon Point
38 Old Bond Street, W1, **t** (020) 7495 1680
⊖ Bond Street, Green Park
15 Sloane Street, SW1 **t** (020) 7235 1441
⊖ Sloane Square, Knightsbridge
www.bonpoint.com
Branches open Mon–Sat 10–6

The favourite shop of parents whose children live in a whirl of country house parties and coming-out balls, Bon Point can afford to charge pretty much whatever it likes (and it does). Nonetheless the clothes are adorable: lots of velvet and frills for the girls, sharp suits and sensible jumpers for the boys. *Expensive.*

Brora
344 Kings Road, SW3, **t** (020) 7352 3697, ⊖ Sloane Square; 66 Ledbury Road, W11, **t** (020) 7229 1515, ⊖ Notting Hill Gate; 81 Marylebone High Street, W1, **t** (020) 7224 5040, ⊖ Baker Street; 186 Upper Street, N1, **t** (020) 7354 4246, ⊖ Angel

Cashmere galore, all the way from a mill in Scotland. Makes for the most luxurious babygros and booties around. *Expensive.*
www.brora.co.uk
Branches open Mon–Sat 10–6

Catimini
52a South Molton Street, W1
t (020) 7629 8099
⊖ Bond Street
Bus 6, 7, 10, 12, 13, 15, 23, 73 94, 98, 113, 135, 137, 139, 159, 189
www.catimini.com
Open Mon–Sat 10–6, Thurs 10–7

Funky printed romper suits, dresses and coordinating accessories. Catamini is one of the top names in contemporary childrenswear. Mail order available. *Expensive.*

Clarks
260 Oxford Street, W1, **t** 0844 499 3257
⊖ Oxford Circus
203 Regent Street, **t** 0844 499 9021
⊖ Oxford Circus
www.clarks.co.uk
Branches open Mon–Wed & Sat 10–7, Thurs & Fri 10–8, Sun 12 noon–7

Having your feet measured here is one of the timeless rituals of British childhood. The shoes and the designs are classic, affordable, comfortable and utterly dependable (i.e. everything your children will hate). *Inexpensive.*

Frocks Away
79 Fortis Green Road, N10
t (020) 8444 9309
⊖ Highgate
www.frocksaway.co.uk
Open Mon–Sat 9.30–6.30

It's a 'lifestyle boutique' for 'Yummy Mummies' with staff they refer to as 'Frocksmiths'. All the terrible puns aside, however, this is a pretty decent one-stop shop offering a range of stylish clothing and shoes for both mothers and their fashion-conscious offspring. *Mid Range–Expensive.*

Gap Kids
145 Brompton Road, SW3, **t** (020) 7225 1112, ⊖ Knightsbridge; 208 Regent Street, W1, **t** (020) 7287 5095, ⊖ Oxford Circus; 121–123 Long Acre, WC2, **t** (020) 7836 0646, ⊖ Covent Garden; 122 King's Road, SW3, **t** (020) 7823 7272, ⊖ Sloane Square; 223–235 Oxford Circus, W1, **t** (020) 7734 3312, 376–384 Oxford Street, W1, **t** (020) 7408 4500, ⊖ Oxford Circus; 315 Oxford Street, W1, **t** (020) 7409 7517, ⊖ Bond Street
www.gapkids.com
Branches open Mon–Sat 10–8, Sun 12 noon–6

Sweatshirts, T-shirts, denims etc. renowned for durability. Some branches also contain a subsidiary, Baby Gap, which sells a colourful range of practical babywear and toddler clothes. *Mid-Range.*

Gymboree
198 Regent Street, W1
t (020) 7494 1110

Oxford Circus
Bus 3, 6, 12, 13, 15, 23, 53, 88, 94, 139, 159, X53
www.gymboree.com
Open Mon–Sat 10–7 (Thurs 10–8), Sun 11.30–5.30
Large store selling everything from swimsuits to winter woollen coats. *Mid-Range.*

H&M

174–6 Oxford Street, W1, **t** (020) 7612 1820,
Oxford Circus; 481–483 Oxford Street, W1,
t (020) 7493 4004, Marble Arch; 103–111
Kensington High Street, W8, **t** (020) 7368 3920,
High Street Kensington
www.hm.com
Branches open Mon–Wed & Fri–Sat 10–7, Thurs
10–8, Sun 12 noon–6
Inexpensive children's and baby clothes made from natural fibres in trendy but tasteful colours and designs. *Inexpensive–Mid-Range.*

Humla Children's Shop

23 St Christopher's Place, W1, **t** (020) 7224 1773
13 Flask Walk, NW3, **t** (020) 7794 7877
Branches open Mon–Sat 10.30–6.30
One of the best children's chains around, the Scandinavian-based Humla sells some wonderfully earthy original design clothes (knitwear is a particular speciality) as well as traditional wooden toys, mobiles and bunk beds. *Mid-Range–Expensive.*

Iana

186 Kings Road, SW3
t (020) 7352 0060
Sloane Square
www.iana.it
Open Mon-Sat 9–6 (till 9pm Wed), Sun 11–6
Parents can coo over the smart, brightly coloured Italian designs (for ages up to 14) while their charges escape to the play area (till summoned). *Mid-Range.*

Igloo

300 Upper Street, N1
t (020) 7354 7300
Angel
www.iglookids.co.uk
Open Mon–Fri 10.30–6, Sat 10–6.30
A sort of 'let's have the show right here' shop, set up by two mothers (with five children between them) who found the city's children's clothing stores not suitable to their needs and decided to do something about it. Rather than focus on any one designer

they've picked their stock from a wide range of sources, from high end labels, such as Catamini and Petit Bateau, to more affordable designers, and now offer clothes, shoes and accessories for both sexes aged 0–8. *Mid Range.*

Jigsaw Junior

126–127 New Bond Street, W1, **t** (020) 7491 4484,
Bond Street; No.6 Duke of York Square, Kings
Road, SW7, **t** (020) 7730 4404, Sloane Square;
83 Heath Street, NW3, **t** (020) 7431 0619,
Hampstead
www.jigsaw-junior.com
Branches open Mon–Sat 10.30–6
Stocks a good range of colourful children's clothes plus miniature versions of adult clothes for fashion-conscious teenagers. Prices are fairly reasonable. *Inexpensive–Mid-Range.*

The Little Trading Company

7 Bedford Corner, The Avenue, Chiswick, W4
t (020) 8742 3152
Turnham Green
Open Tue–Sat 9.30–6
Great little second-hand shop aimed at families on a budget. As well as a wide range of good-quality children's clothes, it also stocks books, games and toys. You get a discount if you have some of your own children's clothes to hand over (providing they're in good condition, of course). *Inexpensive.*

Marks & Spencer

458 Oxford Street, W1, **t** (020) 7935 7954
Marble Arch
173 Oxford Street, W1, **t** (020) 7437 7722
Oxford Circus
143 Camden High Street, NW1, **t** (020) 7267 6055
Camden Town
www.marksandspencer.co.uk
Branches open Mon–Sat 10–6.30 (Thurs 10–8),
Sun 12 noon–6
The high temple of British underwear, Marks sells an excellent range of sturdy, classic children's designs. Best of all, if you have second thoughts, you can take your purchases back for a full refund, no questions asked. *Inexpensive–Mid-Range.*

Mothercare

See p.239
Inexpensive–Mid-Range.

Next

325 Oxford Street, W1, **t** 0870 386 5217
⊖ Oxford Circus
54/60 Kensington High St, W8, **t** 0870 386 5477
⊖ High Street Kensington
15–17 Long Acre, WC2, **t** 0870 386 5325
⊖ Covent Garden
203 Oxford Street, W1, **t** 0870 386 5007
⊖ Oxford Circus
508–520 Oxford Street, W1, **t** 0870 386 5319
⊖ Marble Arch
160 Regent Street, W1, **t** 0870 386 5283
⊖ Piccadilly Circus
11 Strand, WC2, **t** 0870 386 5197
⊖ Charing Cross
www.next.co.uk
Branches open Mon–Sat 10–6.30 (Thurs 10–8),
Sun 12 noon–6

High-street staple selling good kidswear.
Inexpensive–Mid-Range.

Oilily

9 Sloane Street, SW 1
t (020) 7823 2505
⊖ Knightsbridge
Bus 19, 22, 137, C1
Open Mon–Sat 10–6 (till 7 Wed), Sun 12 noon–5

Oilily's trendy colourful adult designs tranlate
very well into children's sizes. They now cater for all
sizes from newborn to teens, offering a range of
clothes, scarves, hats, bags and nightwear.
Mid-Range.

O'Neill

7 Carnaby Street, W1, **t** (020) 7734 3778
⊖ Oxford Circus
9–15 Neal Street, WC2, **t** (020) 7836 7686
⊖ Covent Garden
www.oneilleurope.com
Branches open Mon–Sat 10–7 (Thurs 10–8),
Sun 12 noon–6

For the cool street-surfer look that older kids and
teens are after. *Mid-Range.*

One Small Step One Giant Leap

46 Cross Street, N1
t (020) 7354 4126
⊖ Angel
Open Mon–Sat 10–6, Sun 11–5

Groovy little shoe shop offering a wide range of
footwear from a host of sources, from no-nonsense
bargain labels, such as Ecco and Start-Rite, to

higher-end designers, including Birckenstock
and Timberland. *Mid-Range.*

Petit Bateau

62 South Molton Street, **t** (020) 7491 4498
⊖ Bond Street
106 Kings Road, SW3, **t** (020) 7388 0818
⊖ Sloane Square
171 Regent Street, W1, **t** (020) 7734 0878
⊖ Oxford Circus
www.petit-bateau.com
Branches open Mon–Sat 10.30–6.30, Sun
12 noon–6

If you've ever fancied dressing your kids like
the ever so elegant little monsieurs and mademoi-
selles you see being paraded around Parisian parks
by their parents, then this is the place to come. It
offers a full range of nursery equipment and baby
clothes as well as beautifully tailored toddler and
children's outfits. *Expensive.*

Rachel Riley

15 Pont Street, SW1, **t** (020) 7259 5659
⊖ Sloane Square
82 Marylebone High Street, W1, **t** (020) 7935 8345
⊖ Baker Street
Branches open Mon–Sat 10–6
www.rachelriley.com

What started out as a cottage (or rather
'maison') industry in the south of France where
the eponymous Ms Riley began making clothes for
her family and friends has grown into something
much bigger over the past decade. Despite
operating two outlets in London and one in the
States, everything here is still handmade, giving
the garments something of a rustic artisan
aesthetic (if not price). *Expensive.*

Slam City Skates

16 Neal's Yard, WC2
t (020) 7240 0928
⊖ Covent Garden
Bus 6, 9, 11, 13, 15, 23, 77A, 91, 176
www.slamcity.com
Open Mon–Sat 11–7, Sun 12–5

All you need for the baggy, laid-back skater look.
Decks and accessories are also available if you want
to do more than just look the part. *Mid-Range.*

Tartine et Chocolat

66 South Molton Street, W1
t (020) 7629 7233

⊖ Bond Street
Bus 7, 23, 27, 28, 31, 52, 70, 302
www.tartine-et-chocolat.fr
Open Mon–Sat 10–6
Adorable babywear from Paris. *Expensive.*

Trotters
127 Kensington High Street, W8, **t** (020) 7937 9373
⊖ High Street Kensington
34 Kings Road, SW3
t (020) 7259 9620
⊖ Sloane Square
www.trotters.co.uk
Branches open Mon–Sat 9–6.30 (Wed 9–7),
Sun 10–6
The clothes are good but designery – Paul Smith and Ralph Lauren are prominent labels – and there's a wide selection of toys and books to keep the kids amused while parents browse and make their purchases. *Mid-Range–Expensive.*

Young England
47 Elizabeth Street, SW1
t (020) 7259 9003
⊖ Sloane Square, Victoria
Bus C1
www.youngengland.com
Open Mon–Fri 9.30–5.30
A rather patriotic establishment. All the clothes are made in England using home-grown materials and are based on traditional designs.

Department stores

London is home to some of the shopping world's most famous department stores. There's Harrods, of course (*see* below and p.145) and Harvey Nichols in Knightsbridge, and Selfridges and John Lewis on Oxford Street. All have good children's clothes and/or toy departments. There's one department store in London, however, devoted solely to children. Daisy & Tom is a Harrods for the under-15s. Founded by bookshop mogul Tim Waterstone (and named after two of his children), it provides everything a child could want – books, toys, games, a play area, a carousel, an automated puppet show – as well as catering to the more mundane concerns of parents with its extensive range of clothes, baby equipment and pushchairs. It's even got a hairdressing salon where kids can pick up a First Haircut certificate.

Daisy & Tom
181–3 Kings Road, SW3
t (020) 7352 5000
⊖ Sloane Square
Bus 11, 19, 22, 211, 319
www.daisyandtom.com
Open Mon–Fri 9.30–6 (till 7 Wed), Sat 9.30–6.30,
Sun 11–5
Wheelchair and pushchair accessible, with adapted toilets, parent-and-baby room, childrenswear department, toy department, children's book department, play area, café

Harrods
87–135 Brompton Road, SW1
t (020) 7730 1234
⊖ Knightsbridge
Bus 10, 19, 52, 74, 137
www.harrods.com
Open Mon–Sat 10–9, Sun 12–6
Wheelchair and pushchair accessible, with adapted toilets, parent-and-baby room, childrenswear department, toy department, food department, café, car park
For further details *see* p.145.

Harvey Nichols
109–125 Knightsbridge, SW1
t (020) 7235 5000
⊖ Knightsbridge
Bus 10, 19, 52, 74, 137
www.harveynichols.com
Open Mon–Sat 10–8, Sun 12 noon–6
Wheelchair and buggy accessible, adapted toilets, parent-and-baby, car park, childrenswear department, food market, café

House of Fraser
318 Oxford Street, W1
t 0870 160 7258
⊖ Oxford Circus
Bus 6, 7, 10, 12, 13, 15, 23, 73 94, 98, 113, 135, 137, 139, 159, 189
www.houseoffraser.co.uk
Open Mon–Wed, Fri–Sat 10–8, Thurs 10–9
Sun 12 noon–6
Wheelchair and buggy access, adapted toilets, parent-and-baby, childrenswear department, café

John Lewis
278–306 Oxford Street, W1
t (020) 7629 7711
⊖ Oxford Circus

Bus 6, 7, 10, 12, 13, 15, 23, 73 94, 98, 113, 135, 137, 139, 159, 189
www.johnlewis.co.uk
Open Mon–Wed, Fri–Sat 9.30–7 (Thurs 9.30–8)
Wheelchair and pushchair accessible, with adapted toilets, parent-and-baby, childrenswear department, play area, café

Peter Jones
Sloane Square, SW1
t (020) 7730 3434
⊖ Sloane Square
www.peterjones.co.uk
Open Mon–Mon–Sat 9.30–7 (till 8 Wed), Sun 11–5
Wheelchair and pushchair accessible, accessible parking, adapted toilets, childrenswear department, café

Selfridges
400 Oxford Street
t (020) 7629 1234
⊖ Oxford Circus
Bus 6, 7, 10, 12, 13, 15, 23, 73 94, 98, 113, 135, 137, 139, 159, 189
www.selfridges.co.uk
Open Mon–Sat 10–8, Sun 12 noon–6
Wheelchair and pushchair accessible, with adapted toilets, parent-and-baby, car park, childrenswear department, toy department, café

Markets

For antique toys, head towards Notting Hill for Portobello (the world's largest antiques market) or Camden Passage in Islington. For bric-a-brac and the odd discovery, Brick Lane on Sunday mornings is well worth a visit – be sure to turn up early if you want to get the best bargains. Going to Brick Lane market also gives you a chance to see a fascinating part of London. For clothes and music, Camden is worth a trip, while Greenwich on weekends has a good range of market fodder, from CDs and clothes to antique furniture, bric-a-brac and toys.

Brick Lane
Brick Lane, E1 and surrounds
⊖ Aldgate East, Shoreditch, Bethnal Green, Liverpool Street
⇌ Liverpool Street
Open Sun 6am–1pm

Camden Lock
Camden Lock Place, off Chalk Farm Road, NW1
t (020) 7284 2084
www.camdenlock.net
⊖ Camden Town, Chalk Farm
⇌ Camden Road
Bus 24, 27, 29, 31, 134, 135, 168, 214, 253, 274, C2
Open Sat, Sun 10–6; some stalls stay open throughout the week

Camden Passage
Camden Passage, off Islington High Street, N1
⊖ Angel
Bus 4, 19, 30, 38, 43, X43, 56, 73, 171a, 214
Open Wed 7–2, Sat 8–4

Greenwich
Stockwell Street, SE10 and surrounds
⇌ Greenwich
Bus 53, X53, 177, 180, 188, 199, 286, 386
Open Sat–Sun 9–5

Portobello
Portobello Road, W11 and surrounds
⊖ Notting Hill Gate, Ladbroke Grove, Westbourne Park
Bus 7, 23, 27, 28, 31, 52, 70, 302
Open Sat–Sun 5.30am–3pm

Music & computer games

London is home to several vast record emporia, each with floors filled with copious amounts of CDs, tapes, videos, DVDs and computer games.

The Apple Store
235 Regent Street, W1
t (020) 7153 9000
⊖ Oxford Circus
www.apple.com/uk/retail/regentstreet
Open Mon–Sat 10–9, Sun 12 noon–6
The Macintosh Corporation's flagship London store is full of all the latest gadgets and gizmos – iPods, iMacs, iPhones, etc – as well as all the relevant accessories and paraphernalia. The store stages regular in-store events – including performances by musicians to promote its iTunes products – and offers tutorials on digital

photography, movie- and music-making. Visit the website or see in-store for details.

Chappell of Bond Street

152 Wardour Street, W1
t (020) 7432 4411
⊖ Oxford Circus, Tottenham Court Road
Bus 3, 6, 9, 12, 13, 14, 15, 19, 22, 23, 38, 53, 88, 94, 139, 159
www.chappellofbondstreet.co.uk
Open Mon–Sat 9.30–6, Sun 10–5.30

This famous music shop recently relocated, but has decided to keep its original name despite the potential for confusion this may cause. It's still a great place to pick up that first recorder or quarter size violin or other torture (sorry, musical) instrument. When you visit you'll probably hear skilled musicians taking the shop's banks of pianos, keyboards and guitars for test drives and there are racks full of sheet music and songbooks, stocking everything from Beethoven to the latest chart hits.

Computer Exchange (CEX)

32 Rathbone Place, W1
t 0845 345 1664
⊖ Tottenham Court Road
www.cex.co.uk
Open Mon–Wed & Sat 10–7.30, Thurs & Fri 10–8, Sun 10–7

Game

86 Cheapside, EC2, **t** (020) 7796 2543
⊖ St Paul's
100 Oxford Street, W1, **t** (020) 7637 7911
⊖ Oxford Circus, Tottenham Court Road
185 Kensington High Street, W8, **t** (020) 7938 4922
⊖ High Street Kensington
124 Camden High Street, NW1, **t** (020) 7428 5961
⊖ Camden
www.game.co.uk

HMV

150 Oxford Street, W1, **t** 0845 602 7800
⊖ Oxford Circus
40–42 King Street, WC2, **t** 0845 602 7803
⊖ Covent Garden
www.hmv.co.uk
Branches open Mon 9–8, Tues–Sat 10–8, Sun 12–6

Virgin Megastore

14–16 Oxford Street, W1, **t** (020) 7631 1234
⊖ Tottenham Court Road

1 Piccadilly W1, **t** (020) 7439 2500
⊖ Piccadilly Circus
Bus 3, 6, 9, 12, 13, 14, 15, 19, 22, 23, 38, 53, 88, 94, 139, 159
Open Mon–Sat 9am–10pm, Sun 12 noon–6
213–219 Camden High Street, NW1,
t (020) 7482 5307
⊖ Camden Town
Open Mon–Sat 10–7.30 (till 8 Thurs), Sun 12 noon–6
62–64 Kensington High Street, W8
t (020) 7938 3511
⊖ High Street Kensington
Open Mon–Sat 10–7, Sun 12 noon–6
Kings Walk Shopping Centre, Kings Road, SW3
t (020) 7591 0957
⊖ Sloane Square
Open Mon–Sat 10–7, Sun 12 noon–6
1 Piccadilly, W1
t (020) 7439 2500
⊖ Piccadilly Circus
Open Mon–sat 9am–11pm, Sun 12–6
www.virginmegastores.co.uk

Shopping centres

Lacking the charm or character of some of the central London shopping areas, shopping centres do at least offer the convenience of having shops, restaurants and leisure facilities all under one roof. They also have crèches, thereby allowing you a couple of hours' relaxing retail therapy without having to worry about your kids.

Bluewater

Greenhithe, Kent
t 0870 777 0252
⇝ Greenhithe
www.bluewater.co.uk
Open Mon–Fri 10–9, Sat 9–9, Sun 11am–5pm

Still the big daddy of shopping centres, massive Bluewater offers over 300 shops (including branches of House of Fraser, Baby Gap, Clark Kids, the Disney Store, H&M Kids, Mothercare, Petit Bateau and the Early Learning Centre), dozens of fast-food outlets and chain restaurants, a multiplex cinema and a Crèche (which takes ages 2–4 on weekdays and 2–8 at weekends and on bank holidays for £5.50 an hour). The centre also has facilities for a range of activities (including a lake where you can hire pedalos, a climbing wall with a and a 'Wild Explorer Trail') for when you begin to wither under the constant glare of the fluorescent shop lighting.

Brent Cross Shopping Centre

Brent Cross, NW4
t (020) 8202 8095
⊖ Brent Cross, Hendon Central
www.brentcross-london.com
Open Mon–Fri 10–8, Sat 9–7, Sun 12–6

Around 100 shops (including branches of Game, Marks & Spencer, John Lewis, Baby Gap and the Early Learning Centre), plenty of places for food, a children's play centre, and buggy hire.

Lakeside Thurrock

West Thurrock, Essex
t (01708) 869 933
⇌ Lakeside
www.lakeside.uk. com
Open Mon–Fri 10am–10pm, Sat 9–7.30, Sun 11–5

Over 300 shops (including branches of the Disney Store, Gap Kids, House of Fraser, the Early Learning Centre, the Games Workshop and Marks & Spencer) and food outlets, market stalls, cinema and the 'Sprogg' crèche for 2–7-year-olds.

Specialist shops

Not all of London's shops can be classified neatly and some even revel in their acute specialization on a single theme. Here are a couple of the best.

Cybercandy

3 Garrick Street, WC2
t 0845 838 0958
⊖ Covent Garden/Leicester Square
Bus 6, 9, 11, 13, 15, 23, 77A, 91, 176
www.cybercandy.co.uk
Open Mon–Sat 10–10, Sun 11–8

Appealing to both children and nostalgic adults in equal measure, this shop stocks sweets from all over the world, as well retro British classics such as Moondust and Spangles.

The Back Shop

14 New Cavendish Street, W1
t (020) 7935 9120
⊖ Bond Street
Bus 135, C2

www.thebackshop.co.uk
Open Mon–Fri 10–5.45, Sat 10–2

If your children suffer from bad posture, this is the place to come for chairs and desks designed to help them sit up straight.

Sports shops

Niketown

236 Oxford Street, W1
t (020) 7612 0800
⊖ Oxford Circus
Bus 6, 7, 8, 10, 12, 13, 15, 23, 25, 55, 73, 94, 98, 113, 135, 137, 139, 159, 176, 189
http://niketown.nike.com
Open Mon–Wed 10–7, Thurs–Sat 10–8, Sun 12 noon–6

The biggest sports name in town. The Nike swoosh didn't become one of the world's most recognizable logos without the powers that be treating their retail branding with all due seriousness. According to the marketing blurb, the giant Oxford Circus Niketown is more than just a sports shop. It's a theme store, a mini-museum, an 'experience'. It's certainly a fascinating place, the shop treating sport almost as a religion. Each dedicated section – football, golf, tennis, running, etc. – has a distinctly sacred feel, with video images and memorabilia taking the place of rituals and relics. In fact, it's sometimes difficult to remember that it is basically just somewhere to buy trainers – and not particularly cheap ones at that. Still, if your kids are insisting on the latest Air Zooms, then this is definitely the place to come.

Lillywhites

24–36 Regent Street, W1
t 0870 333 9602
⊖ Piccadilly Circus
Bus 3, 6, 12, 13, 15, 23, 53, 88, 94, 139, 159, X53
www.lillywhites.com
Open Mon–Sat 10–7 (Thurs 10–8), Sun 12–6

This is a well-established sports equipment store catering for everyone from footballers and cricketers to abseilers, skateboarders and canoeists.

Soccerscene

56–7 Carnaby Street, W1, **t** (020) 7439 0778
⊖ Oxford Circus
156 Oxford Street, W1, **t** (020) 7436 4399

⊖ Oxford Circus
49 Long Acre, W1, **t** (020) 7240 4070
⊖ Covent Garden
www.soccerscene.co.uk
Branches open Mon–Sat 9.30–7
   Easily the best football shop in London. You can pick up the kit of almost any team in the world here, as well as any amount of balls, boots and shin pads, not to mention books, magazines and videos galore.

Toys & games

Cheeky Monkeys

202 Kensington Park Road, W11
t (020) 7792 9022
⊖ Notting Hill Gate
Bus 7, 23, 27, 28, 31, 52, 70, 302
www.cheekymonkeys.com
Open Mon–Fri 9.30–5.30, Sat 10–5.30
   Nice selection of wooden toys and imaginative fancy-dress outfits. There are five other branches across town.

The Disney Store

360–66 Oxford Street, W1, **t** (020) 7491 9136
⊖ Oxford Circus
9 The Piazza, Covent Garden, WC2
t (020) 7836 5037
⊖ Covent Garden
www.disneystore.co.uk
Branches open Mon–Sat 10–8, Sun 10–7
   The store is full of lovable characters as familiar as friends, as well as a vast array of cartoon-related merchandise: videos, play figures, mugs and costumes, clothes and games. The video screen belting out classics never fails to attract children.

Early Learning Centre

36 Kings Road, SW3, **t** (020) 7581 5764
⊖ Sloane Square
174 Kensington High Street, W8, **t** (020) 7937 6238
⊖ High Street Kensington
www.elc.co.uk
Branches open Mon–Sat 9–6 (Wed 9–7), Sun 11–5
The Early Learning Centre is concerned about the impact toys can have on a child's development. Uncontroversial, wholesome fun is the name of the game, and the toys, aimed mainly at the pre-school

age group, are uniformly excellent. The shop has several special play areas where kids can try out the toys.

Hamleys

188–196 Regent Street, W1
t 0800 280 2444
⊖ Oxford Circus
Bus 3, 6, 12, 13, 15, 23, 53, 88, 94, 139, 159, X53
www.hamleys.com
Open Mon–Fri 10–8, Sat 9.30–8, Sun 12 noon–6
   London's premier toy store, Hamleys has six floors of the latest must-have playthings. *See* p.59 for more details. There's a much smaller branch of Hamleys at Covent Garden, 3 The Market, The Piazza, Covent Garden, WC2, **t** (020) 7240 4646, open Mon–Sat 10–7 (Thurs 10–8), Sun 12 noon–6.

Harrods

87–135 Brompton Road, SW1
t (020) 7730 1234
⊖ Knightsbridge
Bus 10, 19, 52, 74, 137
www.harrods.com
Open Mon–Sat 10–9, Sun 12–6
   Harrods has the best toy department of any department store. The Toy Kingdom on the fourth floor even rivals Hamleys for the sheer range of toys on offer. You can find everything, from limited edition Steiff Teddies and one third-size Ferraris with full leather interior to the latest video games. There's also a well-stocked children's book shop and, next door, Planet Harrods, an American-style restaurant where cartoons play constantly on big screens. Throughout the year the toy department organizes various events and activities for children, including such delights as Teddy Bear Days and Easter Egg hunts.

Traditional toys

   Parents who despair of modern trends in toy design will be pleased to know that there are several shops in London specializing in more traditional toys. These range from miniature theatre sets and hand-painted wooden puppets to carved wooden animals, kaleidoscopes and paper aeroplanes. Look out for the Hill Toy Company, Benjamin Pollock's Toy Shop (where miniature theatre sets are a particular speciality, *see* p.80), mail-order specialists Tridias and the self-explanatory Traditional Toys, which stocks old-fashioned toys from all round the world.

Benjamin Pollock's Toy Shop

44 Covent Garden Market, WC2
t (020) 7379 7866
⊖ Covent Garden, Leicester Square
Bus 6, 9, 11, 13, 15, 23, 77A, 91, 176
www.pollocks-coventgarden.co.uk
Open Mon–Sat 10.30–6, Sun 11–4

Compendia Traditional Games

11 The Market, Greenwich, SE10
t (020) 8293 6616
DLR Cutty Sark
Bus 53, 54, 177, 180, 188, 199, 202, 286, 380, 386
www.compendia.co.uk
Open 11–5.30 daily

Peter Rabbit & Friends

42 The Market, Covent Garden, WC2
t (020) 7497 1777
⊖ Covent Garden
Bus 6, 9, 11, 13, 15, 23, 77A, 91, 176
www.peterrabbit.com
Open Mon–Sun 10–6

Rainbow

253 Archway Road, N6
t (020) 8340 9700
⊖ Highgate
Bus 43, 134, 263
www.rainbow-toys.co.uk
Open Mon–Sat 10.30–5.30

Tridias

25 Bute Street, SW7
t 0870 420 8633
⊖ South Kensington
Bus 49, C1
www.tridias.co.uk
Open Mon–Fri 9.30–6, Sat 10–6

Traditional Toys

53 Godfrey Street, SW3
t (020) 7352 1718
⊖ South Kensington
Bus 11, 19, 22, 49, 211, 319, 345
www.traditionaltoy.com
Open Mon–Fri 10–5.30, Sat 10–6, Sun 11–4.30

Quiz answers

1

The Underground, or more commonly, the Tube, is the correct name for the London subterranean rail system.

2

Mercury, Venus, Earth, Mars, Jupiter, Saturn, Uranus, Neptune, Pluto.

3

The Ashes are the burnt remains of the stumps, which were presented to the English team by the ladies of Melbourne following an English tour of Australia. It's also the name given to the Test Match series that takes place between the two countries every two years. The winner receives a replica urn – the original can be seen in the museum at Lord's Cricket Ground.

4

West Ham.

5

6,000.

6

They make up the yellow set on the board of the London version of Monopoly.

7

The answer is c), a whopping 17,000, or roughly one for every 350 people living in the capital.

8

Decency Boards were wooden panels that ran along the top deck of old horse-drawn buses. They were designed to prevent unscrupulous gentlemen from getting a crafty look at ladies' ankles.

9

It is named after an aviary that James I had installed near this avenue.

10

Sir Henry Tate, of Tate & Lyle sugar fame, invented the sugar lump and so made his fortune.

11

They both have blue blood running through their veins. Of course, the Royal Family actually has red blood, like everyone else. 'Blue blood' is an expression used to denote that someone has aristocratic ancestry. Lobsters, on the other hand, do actually have blue blood.

12

A groundling was the name given in Elizabethan times to a member of the audience who watched a play standing in front of the stage.

13

Richard III. His evil scheme, if he was responsible, didn't do him much good, however. Within a couple of years he too was dead, slain at the Battle of Bosworth Field by the future Henry VII.

14

Parading through the streets of London as part of the Lord Mayor's Show (see London's Year for November, p.37).

15

The Royal Mint. The Bank of England is Britain's central bank and the only bank in England and Wales that can issue paper money. It's also the bank of all the High Street banks such as Natwest, Barclays and Lloyds TSB. Many, many billions of pounds are stored in its vaults.

16

a) Triceratops means 'three-horned face'.
b) Deinocheirus means 'terrible hand'.
c) Baronyx means 'big claw'.

17

It took 10 years to build the Victoria & Albert Museum's current home. On its completion in 1899 it was given its royal name, having previously been nicknamed the 'Brompton Boilers'.

18

It took Sir Francis Chichester nine months and one day to sail around the world.

Index

Main Page references are in **bold**.
Page references to maps are in *italics*.

Discover the very best of London with Cadogan's brand new mini guide. From world-class museums, eye-popping gallery spaces and historic buildings to sedate royal parks and 'village' life, Cadogan's expert author unveils the capital's many secrets. Whether you live and work in London or are just visiting for a few days, let Cadogan tempt you through the maze of streets and show you the very best of the city, whatever the weather!

ISBN: 978-186011-377-2
£8.99   USA$14.95

Markets are an essential part of London, popular with adults and children alike. Cadogan's fully revised guide provides an in-depth analysis of each market, as well as highlighting the best sightseeing attractions close by. Packed with listings for nearby restaurants for instant refuelling after all that shopping. and complemented by a dedicated section covering the boom in urban farmer's markets, this is the perfect accompaniment to an exciting day of foraging.

ISBN: 978-186011-306-2
£9.99   USA$13.95